NEW
JERUSALEMS

NEW JERUSALEMS

THE LABOUR PARTY AND THE ECONOMICS OF DEMOCRATIC SOCIALISM

ELIZABETH DURBIN

FOREWORD BY ROY HATTERSLEY

ROUTLEDGE & KEGAN PAUL
London, Boston, Melbourne and Henley

First published in 1985
by Routledge & Kegan Paul plc

14 Leicester Square, London WC2H 7PH, England

9 Park Street, Boston, Mass. 02108, USA

464 St Kilda Road, Melbourne,
Victoria 3004, Australia and

Broadway House, Newtown Road,
Henley-on-Thames, Oxon RG9 1EN, England

Phototypeset in Linotron Sabon
by Input Typesetting Ltd, London
and printed in Great Britain by
The Thetford Press Ltd, Thetford, Norfolk

Library of Congress Cataloging in Publication Data

Durbin, Elizabeth F.

New Jerusalems.
Bibliography: p.
Includes index.
1. Great Britain—Economic policy—1918–1945
2. Labour Party (Great Britain)—History—20th century.
3. Socialism—Great Britain—History—20th century.
I. Title.
HC256.3.D79 1984   338.941   84–13306

ISBN 0–7100–9650–X

I will not cease from Mental Fight,
Nor shall my Sword sleep in my hand
Till we have built Jerusalem
In England's green & pleasant Land.
                              William Blake

CONTENTS

FOREWORD

Socialism is far more than a theory of economic organisation. But the achievement of the superior moral society which socialists aim to create is dependent on radical change in the structures of the economies of both eastern and western Europe. It goes without saying that socialists – believing that liberty and equality are both indispensable parts of their creed – reject the centralised command economies of Comecon and the Warsaw Pact. But it has not always been equally obvious that the democratic socialists – who reject the State capitalism into which the theory of Marxism has often turned in practice – have a coherent and consistent economic theory of their own.

What has often been portrayed as a conceptual weakness in democratic socialism is, in fact, a conceptual strength. By their nature, radicals do not accept the intellectual tyranny of an all-embracing economic prescription which, if it is rigidly and rigorously applied, provides an automatic solution to all our economic and industrial problems. Advocates of the benevolent effect of market forces have to invent their own definitions of success to allow them even to advance the claim that free competition solves all our problems. Advocates of rigid control and centralised planning have very little historical evidence with which to justify their claim that they can meet the needs of more people with more success than is possible under rival forms of economic organisation. Democratic socialists insist on a more empirical approach to the achievement of their goals. It is possible, by collective action, to meet the conditions of the time in a way which increases equality and, in consequence, gives reality to the notion of liberty by providing the power which makes the generality of men and women capable of exercising the rights of free citizens.

Since socialism is a philosophy not a method of accounting, it would be wholly unreasonable to expect socialists to provide a simple and infallible economic remedy which works like a cure for the king's evil – one touch and the cure is certain. But in the brief sixty years since the Labour party first took office and began to wrestle with the real economic world, a general theory of democratic socialist economics has begun to evolve. It is a rejection of established free market orthodoxy.

> It is orthodox Treasury dogma, steadfastly held, that whatever might be the political or social advantage, very little additional employment can, in fact, and as a general rule, be created by State borrowing expenditure.

The Labour party was opposing that view when it was described by the Tory Chancellor of the Exchequer in 1929. It is opposing it today.

The essential ingredient of a socialist economic strategy is that the government is capable – given the will – of changing the economic condition of the country which it governs. Keynes offered the seminal advice about demand management and campaign for high employment. The Webbs and their ideological successors argued the virtues of 'planning' – insisting that, when the technique was properly applied it enhanced rather than restricted freedom. However,

> Those who agreed with Durbin and Gaitskell rejected both the Webbian vision of administrative control and guild socialist faith in workers' control. They shared the market economists' belief in the freedom of choice and the economic efficiency afforded by the market pricing system. But they were also convinced that without a strong central planning authority, sectional powers could subvert the public interest by creating inflationary pressures in a fully employed economy and by exploiting their monopoly power to allocate resources in their own interest.

Hugh Gaitskell died almost a quarter of a century ago, and Evan Durbin was drowned fifteen years earlier attempting to save the lives of a group of children who had swum into difficulty. Yet what their work demonstrated remains wholly relevant to the theory of socialist economic management. Indeed, had the Labour party understood and accepted what they had to say, it would have appealed to a far wider stratum of the electorate, enjoyed a great deal more popular success, and changed the nature of British society.

In the pages which follow Evan Durbin's daughter first traces the progress of democratic socialist economic thought – the theorists (the Webbs, the Coles and the Keynes) and the theorists who became practitioners, the Daltons, the Gaitskells and the Croslands. All of them were professional economists of one sort or another. But none of them thought of economic organisation as an aim in itself. Like Evan Durbin himself they were prepared to describe, in language which their opponents no doubt found overly sentimental, the sort of society (not the sort of economic organisation) which they hoped to see. Durbin wrote in *The Politics of Democratic Socialism* that

> It is, in our view, the supreme social duty, the one enduring achievement, so to think and so to act that men and women may sing at their work and children may laugh at their play.

But he insisted that 'there is no easy road to social salvation, no gate round the corner that we may simply unlatch and walk into a garden of peace. We can only deal with each social problem as it arises.'

It was the *practicality* of the Gaitskell/Durbin prescription which its critics sought to denigrate, pretending that philosophers who planned for the application of their philosophy were not really philosophers at all. But the distinction between a visionary and a dreamer is the difference between the determination to see dreams come true and the self-indulgent insistence that visions are an end in themselves. Elizabeth Durbin had written a book of impeccable academic authority, but her dedication is as much concerned with the objects of her father's analyses as with the techniques with which the analyses are made. The flyleaf carries lines from Blake, not Marshal, Pigou or Keynes, 'I will not cease from Mental Fight. . . .'

The glory of democratic socialism in Britain is the way in which its prophets have also been its practitioners, pursuing the ideal by perfecting the ways in which it can be achieved. But that glory has been sustained by the way in which the practitioners have never depended upon the sterile analysis of economic systems alone. The economy has to be managed for some purpose. The purpose of hard economic analyses is the creation of the means by which the New Jerusalem can be built out of dark satanic mills.

Roy Hattersley

ACKNOWLEDGMENTS

Since I set out to discover my father, Evan Durbin, almost ten years ago I have been encouraged, helped and sustained by a host of friends, colleagues, scholars and professional staff in many institutions and in many ways.

My first debt is to my father's friends and comrades. For many years they contributed generously to the Durbin Trust Fund, which was administered by Dr. John Bowlby, Lord Diamond and the late Hugh Gaitskell, and which paid for my education. As important, they have maintained a warm and active interest in my life, and particularly in this project. They have entertained me most kindly, they have shared their memories and their thoughts, they have listened, commented and criticized constructively. In recognition of their unique assistance, I have listed all those to whom I talked at the end of the book. In addition, I would like to give special thanks for the important intellectual contributions made by Dr. John Bowlby, Douglas Jay, the late Professor Tom Marshall, Professor James Meade and the late Sir Michael Postan.

My second debt is to Dick Netzer of the Graduate School of Public Administration at New York University. As Dean of the School he warmly encouraged me to spend my sabbatical leave on what might have been an academic wild goose chase, and he strongly supported my subsequent research efforts. I would also like to thank other NYU colleagues who helped me in significant ways at various stages: Anne-Marie Foltz, Kristina Ford, Herbert Klarman, Israel Kirzner, Oscar Ornati, Lanna Stiefel and S. Mike Miller, now at Boston University, and to the faculty members at GPA and in the economics department who came to my earliest presentations.

My third debt is to the various intellectual homes I have found in the course of my research. I would like to thank the Warden, Sir Norman Chester, and Fellows at Nuffield College, Oxford, for inviting me as an academic visitor, the students for their stimulating interest and the college staff for taking good care of me. I also enjoyed the rich intellectual hospitality at the London School of Economics, as an academic visitor in the government department. Further, I have appreciated the opportunity to present draft papers to the American Economic Association, to the History of Economics Society in the USA, to the History of Economic Thought Society in Britain and to the economics department at the University of Glasgow.

Among the many scholars and experts on both sides of the Atlantic, who have contributed valuable insights, commented on earlier versions and saved me from many errors, I am particularly grateful to: Margaret Bray, A. W. Coats, Bernard Corry, Michael Danes, José Harris, George Jones, David Marquand, Edward Nell, Laurence Moss, Ben Pimlott, Sergio Steve, Philip Williams and Donald Winch.

The work of poring through papers was greatly eased by the exceptional archival and library services provided by Stephen Bird and Irene Wagner for the Labour party, by Patricia Pugh for the Fabian Society, by Angela Raspin for the British Library of Political and Economic Science, London School of Economics, and by Christine Kennedy for Nuffield College library. I would like to thank the Labour party and the Fabian Society for permission to quote from unpublished documents commissioned and prepared for a number of their official committees.

For permission to rummage through the private papers of Colin Clark, Evan Durbin, Hugh Gaitskell, James Meade and John Strachey, I am indebted to Vernon Bogdanor, Marjorie Durbin, Baroness Gaitskell, Professor Meade and the late Celia Strachey. For permission to quote from unpublished materials I am grateful to the following: to the second Earl Attlee from Clem Attlee's correspondence in the Cole papers; to Miss Kirke and Mr Todd from Sir Vaughan Berry's materials on the XYZ Club; to H. J. D. Cole from G. D. H. Cole's letters in the Pethick-Lawrence papers; to the British Library of Political and Economic Science from the papers and diaries of Hugh Dalton; to Marjorie Durbin from Evan Durbin's papers; to Baroness Gaitskell, Julia McNeal and Cressida Wasserman from Hugh Gaitskell's papers; to Lady Harrod from a letter of Sir Roy Harrod; to Lord Kahn from correspondence with James Meade; to Professor Meade from many documents and letters in his papers; to Nuffield College library from a letter from Herbert Morrison to G. D. H. Cole; to the Master and Fellows of Trinity College, Cambridge, from letters from F. W. Pethick-Lawrence to Hugh Dalton.

In preparing for publication, I received invaluable and extensive editorial assistance from David Lipsey, and extremely useful suggestions from Nicholas Butler and Professor Donald Moggridge. They are largely responsible for the much improved final manuscript, although not of course for any remaining errors. Of the many typists who had a hand in successive drafts, I would especially like to thank Beverly Bergtorf and Doreen Szcupiel. For excellent support services, I am most grateful to the administrative staff of GPA, in particular Daniel Boffey and Beryl Pantaleo.

Finally, I would like to acknowledge the financial support of the history and philosophy of science program at the National Science Foundation, which enabled me to take a semester's leave at a critical juncture. I am deeply thankful for the emotional and practical support given by Marjorie Durbin, the late Dr Edward Sachar and Seymour Weissman.

INTRODUCTION

This study began as an exploration of my own intellectual roots; it has emerged as an historical analysis of the ideas which helped to provide rationales for the British Labour party's form of the 'mixed' economy. In the decade before the Second World War the Labour movement undertook an organized and deliberate search for a practical platform of specific proposals to bring socialism to Britain. These efforts culminated in the official adoption of *Labour's Immediate Programme* at the 1937 annual conference. Its resolutions formed the basis of the campaign platform which the Labour Party successfully took to the country in the 1945 election; most of its pledges were carried out by the 1945–51 Labour governments. This book focuses upon the economic aspects of that programme, and upon the contribution of a group of young economists led by Hugh Gaitskell and Evan Durbin, my father.

In 1976 I returned to England, where I was born and educated, and spent the year going through my father's papers, investigating his involvement in Labour party policy making, talking to his friends and colleagues, discussing ideas with scholars, friends and practising socialists, and roaming through the haunts of my childhood and his:

> the meadows of the Thames, the wooded downs of Sussex, the ancient stones of Purbeck, the grey, grass-crowned bastions of Cornwall, the oak-wooded valleys of Exmoor, the ascetic colour of the Wiltshire chalk, and the splendour of the Chiltern beeches curving over the little hills.[1]

Evan Durbin was a member of Parliament and the junior minister of works in the Labour government at the time of his death in 1948. The son of a Baptist minister, he was born in Bideford, Devon, in 1906, went to Taunton School in 1919 and up to Oxford as a scholar at New College in 1924. He took his first degree in zoology, and stayed on to study for a second degree in philosophy, politics and economics (PPE). His economics tutor, Lionel Robbins, helped him to obtain the Ricardo fellowship at University College, London, for a year, and then hired him as a lecturer at the London School of Economics in the autumn of 1930. There he stayed until entering the civil service as a wartime adviser, serving as Attlee's personal assistant for three years. In 1945 he was elected Labour MP for Edmonton, a constituency in north London. He is best remembered for his book, *The Politics of Democratic Socialism*, published at the outbreak of war; it has become an influential book for successive generations of 'revisionists', from Tony Crosland to Roy Hattersley.

Durbin and Gaitskell first met at New College, arriving in the same term. Hugh, who had been to Winchester, went straight into PPE, and so left Oxford two years before Evan. After a year as a Workers' Educational Association tutor in Nottingham, he moved to London to become an economics lecturer at University College (UC), where he also remained until the war broke out except for a year in Vienna on a Rockefeller fellowship. It was at UC that Evan and Hugh formed the close and affectionate friendship which was to remain the solid foundation of their professional collaboration and political alliance until Evan was drowned off a Cornish beach, after saving my sister and a friend from the undertow.

Hugh, whose father was an official of the Indian Civil Service in Burma, grew up in much more affluent circumstances than his friend. He came from a family with strong Tory principles and a tradition of imperial service; they were greatly shocked by his 'conversion' to socialism during the general strike.[2] Born in 1906, the youngest of three, Hugh spent most of his childhood staying with relatives in England, when he was not at boarding school. Despite frequent and prolonged separations from their parents, the Gaitskell children grew up in a warm, affectionate atmosphere. His mother was especially charming and lively, and his father was a selfless public servant and model of conscientious integrity, who died when Hugh was nine. Hugh later recalled that as a boy he was most attached to his older brother, Arthur. At Oxford he blossomed into the delightful companion, dedicated socialist, enthusiastic dancer and straightforward dispeller of humbug so vividly remembered by his friends. It was not until the late 1930s that he also began to reveal the leadership qualities widely admired in his public life. After he died in 1963, Roy Jenkins wrote that he left 'a memory which is a standing contradiction to those who wish to believe that only men with cold hearts and twisted tongues can succeed in politics'.[3]

Evan, too, was the cherished youngest child in an openly affectionate and jolly family. Although life on a Baptist minister's income was fairly spartan, and alcohol and the theatre strictly forbidden, his parents eschewed fire and brimstone, emphasizing the loving side of the Christian message. They were deeply disappointed when Evan gave up his early ambition to follow his father and grandfather into the Christian ministry. Socialism became his earthly mission, although he continued to preach as an undergraduate; his sister remembers attending services in remote villages, where she was required to sit at the back so that she might better comment on the delivery of the earnest nineteen-year-old. His mother, who was herself an active saver of souls, often joined her father, William Mottram, on the extended missions which he led as the temperance secretary of the Congregational Union of England and Wales; she never really recovered from her sorrow that her beloved child had renounced his belief in the Lord Jesus.

The Durbins were also ardent supporters of Gladstonian liberalism. Evan later recalled that 'as a child I was seriously confused about the distinction between God and Mr. Gladstone'.[4] Thus, both Evan and Hugh rebelled against their parents' values, Evan rejecting Liberal nonconformism, Hugh Tory Anglican imperialism. Interestingly, as an undergraduate at least, Evan felt that socialism or government by traditional aristocracy were the only alternatives. Sir Henry Phelps Brown, a school friend, received a mock-serious letter when he renounced socialism for liberalism in 1927; Evan wrote:

> I am very sorry you have turned rat – coward – traitor and renegade. Seriously, I think you are making a mistake. Apart from economic theory – and you can't really think any Government will last long enough to do much harm by the application of wrong theories – surely the Labour movement is a much more important thing to help control and influence than the little body of 'politicians for politics sake' that is the Liberal Party. If ever I find the political or economic premises on which Socialists build their faith – seem to me to be fallacious, I shall swap over to Conservatism . . . you can't support 45 millions in a Distributive State of England.[5]

Yet, despite their rebellious political and religious views, Evan and Hugh were strongly influenced by family traditions of community service and responsible leadership.

Both friends valued intelligence, dedication, tolerance, common sense and fun. Both set great store on 'personal relations' and among the reserved English they stood out as passionate men willing to share their emotions with others. I shall always remember Hugh weeping openly as he spoke at a ceremony dedicating Durbin House, a block of flats in Edmonton, some years after Evan's death. Both had friends who have never forgotten the attention devoted to their character development, 'a passion for improving the human race, beginning with me', as Hugh's friend, Jim Orrick, put it.[6] Durbin's diary was famous as a testament of his commitment to his friends; no one parted from him without a date set for their next meeting, even if it was three months hence. Both were born teachers, who inspired their students with the clarity of their lectures, as well as taking an active personal interest in their well-being. Of the two, Evan appeared to be the more serious-minded, although he was a great tease; the phrase often used to convey his strength of character is 'rocklike'. His outspoken appeals to conscience and deflation of pretension could even be a little intimidating; the Earl of Longford, who had first-year rooms on the same staircase in New College, has never forgotten being confronted during an early conversation, 'Have you ever been hungry, man?'[7] Hugh was more easy-going and socially graceful; but he was equally committed to the socialist cause, and no less ambitious to see his ideas put into practice.

As professional economists during the 1930s, Evan and Hugh were actively involved in the development of the theory of socialist planning, as well as the appropriate economic policy for the Labour party, while they struggled to sort out the deluge of new ideas and conflicting viewpoints which characterized economic theory at the time. As professional politicians, they ran as Labour party candidates, built their own strategy 'think tank', spoke at conferences, lectured on a variety of subjects to Labour groups throughout the country and earned, according to Evan, a reputation as 'identical twins' in the Labour movement.[8] The Countess of Longford, a close friend since Oxford, perhaps more aptly likened their role in the 1930s to Rosencrantz and Guildenstern.[9]

In their work for the New Fabian Research Bureau founded by G.D.H. Cole and for Hugh Dalton's Labour party policy subcommittees, Durbin, Gaitskell and their friend, Douglas Jay, have been credited with introducing Keynesian ideas to the Labour party.[10] But their influence was both broader and deeper, for they were concerned not simply with current policy debates, but with more general practical and theoretical issues. At the practical level they dealt with the problems of devising appropriate strategies and programmes to introduce socialism to Britain by democratic parliamentary methods. At the theoretical level they were challenged to outline the dimensions of the new state, which could feasibly replace existing capitalism. They believed passionately that it was possible to achieve a 'New Jerusalem', a society which was to be both more efficient and more just. They made major contributions to the Labour party's official and unofficial policy efforts in this period. But they also opened up new questions and laid the intellectual foundations for the continuing debates about the nature of the socialist vision in Britain, its relation to existing institutions and the criteria for evaluating its performance.

Much of the evidence of their work has been buried in committee memoranda and unpublished manuscripts. I have found that study of the controversies in which Evan and Hugh participated reveals in part the intellectual origins of current schisms within the Labour party. Thus, I believe that careful consideration of the problems which they faced and of the conclusions which they drew can assist this generation to build its own version of the 'New Jerusalem' for England's green and pleasant land.

Outline of the book

The book combines chronological history with analytic discussions of the important theoretical and policy issues, as they appeared to the chief participants at the time. Thus, in Part I, I set the stage by providing a framework for discussion in Chapter 1; a review of the relevant economic thought in Chapter 2; and in Chapter 3 an account of Britain's economic problems, the Labour party's policy debates in the 1920s and its internal political conflicts, which climaxed in the dramatic split of August 1931.

Part II introduces the 1930s with an overview of the struggles within the Labour party, the development of its new programme, its leaders and the influential members of the new generation who were engaged in the policy-making process. I then discuss the search for a new theory of socialist economics and a new economic programme up to 1935, against the background of developments in economic theory. In Chapters 6, 7 and 8, I describe the work on economics at the New Fabian Research Bureau, founded by G.D.H. Cole in 1931. Chapter 6 presents their attack on the party's traditional policies towards nationalization and redistribution; Chapter 7 traces their attempt to devise a socialist policy to cope with unemployment; Chapter 8 explores the beginnings of the work on a theory of democratic socialist planning. In Chapter 9 the informal discussions organized by Durbin and Gaitskell on the appropriate strategy for the Labour party are detailed. Finally, in

Chapter 10 I trace the work of Hugh Dalton's finance and trade subcommittee of the Labour party's policy committee and its contributions to the party's official and unofficial programme.

In Part III I present three perspectives on the contemporary conception of how to achieve 'socialism in our time', as they developed before the war. Chapter 11 examines the new socialist economics, which emerged from the economic revolutions and controversies of the decade. Chapter 12 describes the final stages of hammering out the Labour party's official and unofficial economic policy positions. In Chapter 13 I assess the new economic revisionism, which provided its intellectual justification. I argue that the economic rationale for a mixed economy, which the British democratic socialists developed in the process, was a crucial component of their belief in the socialist alternative to capitalism. Yet, they used economics for this purpose quite differently among themselves. I distinguish three approaches, each of which ultimately rests upon a different vision of the new society. In a concluding chapter I summarize my views of the contributions made by Evan Durbin and Hugh Gaitskell and their comrades in the 1930s, and of their relevance today.

Parts II and III constitute the main contribution to original research on the 1930s. Besides my father's papers, I had access to the private papers of Hugh Gaitskell, Colin Clark and James Meade, the economists of the younger generation who contributed important memoranda to the Labour party's policy committees. I went through the minutes and papers of the New Fabian Research Bureau among the Fabian papers deposited in Nuffield College, Oxford, and I checked through the minutes of the Labour party's national executive committee at Transport House. I also looked through parts of the Cole papers at Nuffield, the Dalton papers at the London School of Economics, the Keynes papers in the Marshall Library, Cambridge, and the Pethick-Lawrence papers in Trinity College, Cambridge. I have been given all kinds of materials, photographs, files, many letters, out-of-print books, and even Evan's much-annotated copy of Hayek's *Road to Serfdom*. Most gratifyingly, I rediscovered the extensive handwritten notes for his proposed 'Economics of Democratic Socialism', among Gaitskell's papers; they had been missing for twenty years and have been returned to Marjorie Durbin.

This book naturally contains a great deal of economic argument, which the general reader may not always follow. I have provided simple accounts of the major economic issues to enable the non-economist to understand what they were arguing about. I have also organized the material into clearly defined topics, with an introductory overview at the beginning and a summary conclusion at the end of each chapter. The book is biased in the sense that I have concentrated on a small group of people and have given fuller treatment to their work, particularly unpublished manuscripts, where I thought it was interesting and revealing. I have tried to present an objective picture of the strengths and weaknesses of the various arguments, but I cannot pretend that I was a dispassionate observer. I set out to find out about my father, his friends and their contributions. I have discovered much that does not appear to be public knowledge. I hope that, by sharing their concerns with a wider audience, I may help to redirect current attempts to restrict the government's economic role, and to reanimate the search for appropriate ways to reform capitalism and to reduce social injustice in this generation.

PART I
THE HERITAGE

CHAPTER 1
ECONOMICS, POLICY MAKING AND THE LABOUR PARTY

This book examines in detail the intellectual process of economic policy making within the British Labour party during the 1930s. There are two central issues which all democratic political parties face in designing an economic policy: how they should respond to the demands of the electorate, and how they propose to intervene in the economic system. Parties committed to major social reform must also deal with a third issue – how to introduce those changes. Opinions about economic policy are thus influenced by the political and social views of the policy makers and by the nature of the economic, political and social problems which the society faces.

The interactions between economic thinking and policy making are complicated, yet they receive little systematic attention from economists and remain something of a mystery to non-economists. Economic theories shape the causal explanations which economists bring to analyse the economic problems, while political, social and moral values determine their goals and thus influence their policy recommendations. However, the focus on particular problems, the choice between different economic means, and even the use of one economic model rather than another, may also be affected by the values of the economic adviser and by the policy process itself. A second objective of this book is therefore to clarify these complexities and to understand the limitations of economics in policy formation. It is hoped that by using this period as a kind of case study more general conclusions can be drawn about the problems of finding consistent economic policies which may reduce economic and social injustice and help bring about change in advanced industrialized democracies.

Both political and economic analysis are necessary to understand the nature of the Labour party's achievements in their historical context and to assess the intellectual controversies and contributions to the economic policy-making process. In this chapter the political and economic problems faced by the party in the 1930s are summarized. The role of economic thinking in policy formation is explored in some detail, because it provides the analytic framework for later discussion. In particular, the economist's usual dichotomy between political goals and economic theory, between normative ends and scientific means, is examined critically to suggest that economists' views are often influenced by their political values in confusing ways. Finally, the Labour party's origins and its main ideological strands are briefly reviewed, in order to give some sense of the different policy perspectives which exist within the party.

Democracy, socialism and government intervention in the market system

Two major economic policy issues faced Britain in 1930, the high unemployment associated with the world depression and the overvaluation of the pound following the return to the gold standard in 1925. The Labour party had the further problem of finding a way to introduce socialism to Britain as an alternative to the capitalist system, by the democratic and parliamentary methods to which it was committed. In August 1931 the Labour government, which had been in power since 1929, split over the question of cutting government expenditure, in particular unemployment assistance, in an effort to stem a disastrous run on the pound. As a result, the Labour prime minister, James Ramsay MacDonald, formed a National government with only a handful of Labour followers and won a landslide election in October. The Labour party remained out of power until Churchill formed the wartime coalition government.

The Labour party achieved a broad consensus within its own ranks for the programme reflected in the document *For Socialism and Peace*, adopted at its 1934 conference, and for the shortened version, *Labour's Immediate Programme*, which represented the party's aims in the first stage of the transition to socialism. Nevertheless, there was considerable disagreement among the democratic socialist economists, both about specific policy issues and about their theoretical justification. As it turned out, the electorate also rejected this programme in the 1935 election, even though the party had consciously struggled to moderate its socialist aims in order to broaden its electoral appeal. It was only after the massive upheaval of war and its effect on social expectations that the party's commitment to fundamental social reform struck a responsive chord.

A belief in democratic methods means that any political party has to develop policies which will get its candidates elected before any other goals can be accomplished. In the 1930s the Labour party was committed to introducing socialism as the alternative to capitalism. This meant that for election purposes policies had to be designed which would appeal to some of the middle class, for the party could not achieve power by relying on the working-class vote. Furthermore, socialism would have to be introduced in stages because no government could realistically expect to pass in five years all the legislation which would effect such fundamental changes; hence, the 'Immediate Programme', or first priorities. Consequently, it was also necessary to work out what economic steps should be taken first, what political reforms were required to accomplish those immediate goals and what programmes would ensure re-election for the second stage. This political strategy of evolutionary reform was reflected in an economic strategy of partial socialization of the existing market system rather than an immediate take-over by the state; hence, the 'mixed economy'. Throughout this period the party and its policy committees were much preoccupied with the problem of how to accomplish the transition from the current order, which required little explicit government intervention, to one with substantial public control.

For socialist and non-socialist alike, the pressing economic problems faced by Britain raised basic questions about the appropriate role for government in the market system. Since socialists wanted to restructure the market system, the role of government in planning and managing economic affairs was central to their alternative. During the 1920s the British Labour party adopted as its official policy the control of the economy through the nationalization of the means of production, distribution and exchange. It became the task of the 1930s to articulate a practical strategy for accomplishing this goal by democratic means.

At the same time, governments of all political persuasions were trying to tackle the enormous economic and social problems of unemployment resulting from the great depression. Keynes and other economists are credited with developing the theoretical and practical tools which could solve the unemployment problem, and for convincing governments of their responsibility to maintain employment and growth by fiscal and monetary policies. Socialists did not need convincing that the government should manage the economy. Their problem was to define the limits of government intervention. In particular, they struggled over the appropriate means to control the monetary system, the amount of investment and the level of employment, over what industries to nationalize and over what principles to adopt for their management.

The Keynesian revolution during the 1930s appeared to provide answers to the problem of economic management. Some socialist economists recognized that the new analysis could also be used to maintain employment and investment levels as one part of their own overall planning strategy. However, an explicit commitment to Keynesian policies for full employment did not come until 1944–5. Not all socialist economists accepted Keynes's ideas; some were suspicious of his Liberal connection and of theories which sought to make the capitalist system more workable.

At the policy-making level, the issue of control over the economy was decided implicitly in the party's debates over the nationalization of the commercial joint stock banks in addition to the Bank of England. At a more academic level, there was a continuing colloquy among socialist economists on the nature and principles of democratic socialist planning. The major difference of opinion lay between those who wanted to use the market pricing system to allocate resources and those who wanted to use government controls to determine output goals and to plan the physical distribution of resources. Other non-socialist groups had also become convinced of the need for planning to avoid the breakdown of the capitalist system.

Economics and policy making

Economic policy, in so far as it is conscious and rational, is formed in a process which includes defining policy goals, identifying the economic problems to be faced and finding the appropriate programmes and strategies for their solution. This process requires two kinds of abstraction; one is the articulation of goals and policy perspectives, the other is the understanding of how the economic system functions. In order to understand what economists have to say about economic policy, their role as theorists needs to be distinguished from their role in policy making. As theorists, they build abstract models to explain the workings of the economic system, that is, how the system is defined, how it fits together and how it functions. As participants in policy making, economists use their understanding of the economic system to identify economic problems, to explain cause and effect in the area of policy concern and from their knowledge of the important quantitative and qualitative relationships to make estimates of the probable impact of alternative strategies. Economists usually ascribe the responsibility for articulating policy goals to all the other participants in the policy-making process – to political leaders, to party strategists, to administrative and executive officials and to all other interested and influential pressure groups – rather than to themselves.

On the whole economists trained in the Anglo-American tradition are not much given to serious study of their own ways of thinking. This may account for the persistent illusion that economics is a practical science, despite growing evidence to the contrary. Broadly speaking, there are two schools of thought about the proper mode for economic analysis. What might be called the 'pure science' school sees the task of the economist as follows: first, to build theories which explain the workings of the economic system, much as physics builds theories to explain, for example, the working of the solar system; second, to develop hypotheses about behaviour from these models; finally, to test the validity of the theories by empirical verification of the hypotheses. To do this requires the analyst to differentiate those variables explained by or explaining the economic system from those other factors which may affect behaviour but which economics does not explain. In short, it is believed that economic explanations are only concerned with 'market' variables, such as prices, quantities and incomes. Important 'non-market' variables, such as consumers' preferences, technology and institutional structure, must be assumed 'constant' for economic models to be used for predictive purposes.

This purist view, that economics can be conducted as it were in a social and political vacuum, has continuously been challenged by economists of more eclectic viewpoint, particularly those most concerned about policy problems. They find the development of ever more abstract models and complicated techniques less and less relevant to real-world situations. Such economists view their science as one among many other moral and social sciences; they can, therefore, be said to subscribe to the 'blended science' school. Their analysis will explicitly include non-economic factors such as political and social institutions and personal characteristics, in an effort to provide a broader, if less rigorous, understanding of human behaviour.

The usual approach of economists to the role of theory in policy formation is to distinguish between a theoretical explanation and a policy goal. Policy goals describe the normative ends which are sought; economic theory analyses the scientific means to achieve those ends. Thus, it is argued, economic models explain the workings of the economic system, but policy is determined by views of how the world ought to be, that is, by moral laws and belief systems which economic theory is not expected to explain. For example, while economic theory can be used to make judgments about efficiency (because economics spells out the conditions for maximizing output with the minimum use of resource inputs), it cannot be used to evaluate the justice of the income distribution generated by that system. However, this distinction becomes confusing when economists do not express their policy advice in these terms, but include their own moral values in their recommendations, sometimes quite unconsciously.

This superficially plausible distinction between positive means and normative ends frequently breaks down in practice for a number of reasons. First, the political process rarely yields precise policy goals. Second, political values are not necessarily independent of economic decisions. Often policy objectives and priorities are formulated as a result of economic choices already made. Third, the decisions to be made are sometimes very complex, requiring considerable technical expertise, so that economists are inevitably drawn into defining objectives as well as means. Fourth, disputes between economists, while apparently about theory and its uses, may conceal their hidden policy agendas. Finally, it should be recognized that non-economists do not always share the economists' views of the relation between economic theory and policy goals. Politicians, for example, are less concerned with the niceties of theoretical models or estimating procedures and are more concerned to find further justification, the stronger the better, for policies they may want to pursue on political, social or moral grounds. Certainly, it is obvious that the non-economists involved in the policy process use economic analysis and advice for their own purposes, and that these may be very different from the original intent of the economic analyst.

All these problems arise in trying to sort out the reasoning behind economic arguments in the 1930s. Even where there was apparent agreement about political goals, there were disputes about the use of economics or political strategy. For example, while democratic socialist economists agreed about the use of parliamentary methods to bring about socialism, they spent considerable effort specifying their political goals and the strategy to be employed in replacing capitalism. They also disagreed at various times about the wisdom of pursuing expansionary policies, about the necessity of nationalizing the joint stock banks and about the appropriate pricing policy for nationalized industries, as well as the relevant economic models for analysing these policy problems. At the same time, there were major breakthroughs in economic theory, not only in the new Keynesian models, but also in value theory. There were also significant shifts in policy prescription; one of the most dramatic was Keynes's abandonment of the Liberal party creed of free trade, when he publicly proposed a revenue tariff in 1931.

There are three main sources for differences in opinions about economic policy, those which raise theoretical questions, those related to empirical judgments and, finally, those which reflect different policy goals. The most obvious theoretical differences arise when there are disagreements about how the economic system is seen to operate in the abstract. However, such differences are not always obvious. For instance, in the early 1930s there were violent controversies about increasing or decreasing public expenditure, yet neither side could really articulate their theoretical disagreement for the simple reason that the model relating deficit spending to increases in employment during a depression had not yet been built. Even now there is considerable debate over the exact nature of the theoretical revolution embodied in Keynes's *The General Theory*, although most analysts accept that its model of income determination was a major breakthrough in the understanding of how the economy works at the aggregate level.

Theoretical revolutions of this magnitude, which require major shifts in ways of thinking, are accompanied by widespread changes in definitions and assumptions, as well as in causal explanations. Some of these apparently terminological battles can disguise another kind of theoretical difference; there can be agreement about the model but disagreement about its application to reality. In order to use abstract models to make prognostications about real-world events, two steps are required. First, the problem must be defined, that is, the focus of concern must be identified. Second, the manner in which the model is to be applied must be specified, that is, which factors are expected to vary and in what way, and which are to be held constant. The assumptions made in building a model describe both the focus and the use of the model, which explains why it is so important to make them explicit. When there are serious controversies about basic explanations of the system, it is often difficult to distinguish differences between theories from differences in their application. For example, during the 1930s one source of disagreement was the importance of longer-run considerations in dealing with unemployment. It was not until late in the decade that economists recognized that one way to describe the problem was to say that a focus on unemployment assumed a short-run model with capital stock held constant, while a trade cycle focus assumed a long-run situation in which capital stock could also be varied.

Empirical differences arise in the assessment of the impact of changes in explanatory factors on the matters of concern. Thus, even where economists are agreed upon the relevant model and the appropriate assumptions, they may differ considerably in their view of important quantitative relationships, such as the multiplier effect or the elasticity of demand. This accounts for a great deal of the technical disputes between economists about the quality of data and estimating procedures. It is obvious that the choice of policy alternatives may be very sensitive to even apparently small variations in the estimates of crucial relationships. Given the imperfections of data, the wide use of proxy variables, and often serious estimating problems, it is difficult to judge the relative merits of conflicting policy advice based on differences in empirical estimates.

Finally, there are the policy differences which reflect the values and attitudes of their protagonists. Given the complexities of theoretical modelling and the vagaries of empirical verification described above, economists who engage in policy analysis have a special responsibility to be explicit about their personal beliefs in their communications with others, particularly those not familiar with the peculiarities of economic thinking. These beliefs will affect both the policy goals of individual economists and their view of the appropriate strategy, that is, the order and degree of changes needed to accomplish those goals. More subtle are the individual assessments of the feasibility and effectiveness of different policy instruments. For example, many argue that Keynes switched to recommending a general revenue tariff because he put a higher priority on reducing unemployment than on free trade. A revenue tariff, which would automatically increase the cost of all imports relative to the price of exports, would encourage domestic expansion without threatening the value of the pound.

In the early 1930s politicians and economists alike of all philosophical persuasions were agreed that reduction of unemployment was a primary goal. Yet the various forms of advice offered were often diametrically opposed, a major reason being that there was no agreed theoretical model to explain the phenomenon; there was not even agreement about whether it was a cyclical problem, a monetary problem or a structural problem. Historians and political scientists who do not understand the nature of the economic arguments and the role of economic theory are liable to make serious errors in their interpretation of events and motivations. For example, some historians seem to imply that if someone agreed with Keynes's policy recommendations for expansionary policies before *The General Theory* appeared, the person had actually understood Keynesian macroeconomic models as economists now understand them.[1] This is to misunderstand the nature of Keynes's theoretical work in the period. It is true that, as Keynes refined his theoretical position, his justification of the case for expansionary policies grew stronger. It is also true that the outline of the theory of income determination was known to some economists before the publication of *The General Theory*. However, the final links between monetary and market-price systems were not forged until then, when Keynes spelled out the role of business expectations and liquidity preference in determining the rate of interest, and hence the level of investment. Therefore, it is simply not true to say that 'by the end of 1932 at the latest, all the bricks which went to make the Keynesian employment theory were available and could have been used by the unions, had they been minded to assemble them'.[2] If Keynes had not yet done it, it is absurd to suggest that others not even trained in economics could have.

The Labour party and socialism

The Labour party sprang from the amalgamation of two working-class movements which were gathering momentum in the late nineteenth century, the industrial organization of workers in trade unions and their political organization by the Independent Labour party (ILP).[3] In February 1900 a conference was held with delegates from the ILP, the Trades Union Congress (TUC) and various socialist societies, of which the Fabian Society was to prove the most enduring and the most influential. The conference inaugurated the Labour Representation Committee (LRC), which was charged with promoting the election to Parliament of members who would represent the interests of working men and women. After a shaky start the LRC succeeded in sending twenty-nine of its fifty candidates to Westminster in the 1906 election, whereupon it changed its name to the Labour party. The newly elected MPs chose Keir Hardie as the first chairman of the parliamentary delegation.

Before the First World War the Labour party remained a small pressure group within the House of Commons. The Liberal party still dominated British politics as the major force for progressive reform. Although the party was laissez-faire and free trade in its origins, a 'new liberalism' calling for extensive social legislation to mitigate the effects of the untrammelled market system swept it to power in the first decade of the twentieth century. With David Lloyd George and Winston Churchill as its brilliant new stars, these Liberal governments introduced national insurance schemes for old age, sickness and unemployment, laid the foundations for a universal system of public education and increased the progressive income tax. But the successful battle with the House of Lords over Lloyd George's 1909 budget was destined to become one from which the Liberals never recovered.[4] Although Lloyd George as the triumphant wartime coalition leader won by a landslide in the 1918 election, the party was further split and lost at the polls in successive elections thereafter. First elected as a minority government in 1923, the Labour party was the main political beneficiary of Liberal decline.

From its foundation the British Labour party has encompassed a wide range of political views. In the early days the main division in aspiration was between the socialism of the political societies and the labourism of the trade unions. Socialists sought to change society as a whole, while the trade unions wanted to improve conditions for workers in general and for their members in particular. Many unions and individual unionists were also committed socialists, but their main organizational thrust was around the immediate issues of employment, wages and working conditions. The failure of the Liberals to help achieve union political goals had finally convinced the TUC to support the LRC in 1900.

The trade union leadership remained predominantly non-socialist in the Labour party's early years. The rank and file of the unions and the party were well aware of their position in Britain's hierarchical class system; they sought the opportunity to rise within it, not to overthrow it. There were periods when it seemed possible that the union movement might become revolutionized, particularly during the prewar industrial unrest and during the events leading up to the general strike in 1926. But each time the forces in favour of working within the system reasserted themselves. Thus, in the first half of this century, union influence moderated the tone and pace of socialist goals within the Labour party. An important result, at least until recently, has been the peripheral effect of Marxist thought on the Labour party. The Social Democratic Federation, the founding organization most closely identified with Marxian analysis and revolutionary tactics, withdrew almost immediately after failing to get the LRC to commit itself to thoroughgoing socialist objectives. Thereafter, throughout the 1920s and 1930s, the Labour party fought to keep Communists out of its membership and Marxism out of its philosophy.

It was the ILP which voiced the socialist trumpet call for exploited workers in the early days. Its brand of socialism expressed the moral outrage and the passionate yearnings of the British working class; its leaders provided the inspiration and the dedication to work against all odds for the new heaven and the new earth. Founded in 1893, its leaders included Keir Hardie, James Ramsay MacDonald and Philip Snowden. MacDonald served as the first secretary of the LRC, and in 1911 he took over the chairmanship of the parliamentary Labour party. When the Labour party won the largest number of seats in 1923, the King invited MacDonald to form the first Labour cabinet;

MacDonald chose Snowden as the first Labour chancellor of the exchequer.

The Fabian Society, which began as a small discussion group in 1884, has provided the intellectual forum for thrashing out a philosophic viewpoint and an appropriate policy programme for successive generations of educated, middle-class British socialists. Sidney Webb, George Bernard Shaw and Graham Wallas were among its early leaders; together they worked out an anti-Marxian non-revolutionary basis for their faith in the gradual permeation of socialist ideas. Although they were committed to 'the transfer to the community of the administration of such industrial Capital as can conveniently be managed socially', they were firm believers in parliamentary democracy.[5]

The Fabians also set great store on being practical. The Webbs in particular stressed organizational efficiency and the importance of expertise; indeed, they devoted themselves to mastering a wide array of social, political and historical subjects as part of their contribution to the socialist movement. They were impatient with intense, philosophical discussions, which they regarded as 'unprofitable talk'. In general they saw collectivism as 'a businesslike way of transacting the business of society'.[6] The collection of facts became one of the most important characteristics of the Fabian style. It was felt that 'no reasonable person *who knows the facts* can fail to become a Socialist, or, at the very least, to be converted to the Socialist policy on any subject or problem presently under discussion – that out of their own mouths, or rather out of their published material, the defenders of capitalism can be made to prove that it is inefficient, brutal and idiotic.'[7] Finally, if Fabianism is what Fabians do (Sidney Webb's view), through their tireless involvement in legislative reform at all levels of government, their participation on commissions and committees of all kinds, their constant lectures, conferences and meetings, and their prodigious output of books and tracts, they also showed that something could be done to help the poor, to right ancient wrongs and to transform society by slowly changing its institutions. In short, they were 'both optimists and enthusiasts'.[8]

To this tolerant British blend of messianic utopianism, collectivist management ethic and practical bread-and-butter issues which the Labour party inherited at its foundation, a fourth ingredient must be added from the heyday of guild socialism; it was the belief in a socialist democracy built upon workers' participation in economic decision making. Guild socialism swept through the British trade union movement in the decade of the National Guilds League from 1915 to 1925. As a theory of socialism, it combined a syndicalist view of workers controlling their own industries with a collectivist approach to the public ownership of productive resources. It was to founder, along with ideas of direct political action by trade unions, in the failure of the general strike. But it left its political heritage in the periodic demands for workers' control in the socialist state. Among its intellectual leaders G.D.H. Cole and R.H. Tawney were to become important advisers to the Labour party and intellectual mentors for the next generation of British socialists.

To summarize, the trade unions provided the Labour party with its organizational base, the ILP its emotional inspiration and driving force, and successive generations of Fabians the intellectual arguments to articulate and defend the party's socialist goals. Although there were important differences in the exact nature of their socialist vision amongst the party's organizers, they all shared two basic characteristics. First, they believed in the British parliamentary system; secondly, they rejected both capitalism and Marxism. Between these extremes they also agreed on three general principles of socialism, the commitment to a society based on co-operation rather than competition, a high degree of economic and social equality and the stress on collective needs over private ends. However, throughout its history, party members have disagreed on their definition of the eventual socialist state, on the general strategy for its achievement and on the specific tactics appropriate for the Labour party at any particular moment.

Before the First World War the differences within the party reflected the social visions of the main founding groups. The trade unions sought to redistribute economic goods and services to workers and to mitigate the effects of the capitalist industrial system by whatever means possible. If they could improve the living standards of their own workers through direct negotiation with employers, they would. If the Liberal party had represented workers' interests more effectively, the LRC might never have been formed. The unions therefore tended to support socialist principles only when they served their own immediate and practical concerns.

The intellectual and middle-class Fabians also emphasized economic power. However, they were opposed to the advancement of special-interest groups, because they were concerned with the good of society as a whole. Thus, their view of socialism entailed the collective ownership of the means of production to replace private capitalists. They believed that socialism would enable the economic system to be administered efficiently by eliminating the waste and muddle of the market. In contrast to the unions and the Fabians, the ILP responded to the social and idealistic aspirations of the downtrodden. They viewed socialism as an evolutionary escape from the injustices of the capitalist system. Their commitment was emotionally powerful, based on faith in the transformation of present sufferings into a harmonious and altruistic future. The guild socialists shared an emotional faith in the redeeming qualities of a new society based on co-operative fellowship. But they also sought to redistribute political power systematically, both in the workplace and in society at large.

So long as the party was little more than a pressure group for the working class, it was enough to enunciate its aspirations and remain vague on specific ends. But once the party gained power, these differences within it became more evident and more serious. They were to affect both political events and the attempt to work out appropriate economic policies for the Labour party in the 1920s.

CHAPTER 2
MARKET THEORY AND
SOCIALIST
ECONOMICS

The history of economic theory in Britain has closely followed the development of market economics. Market economics represents the economic system as an interrelated set of markets for goods and factors connected by the prices and quantities determined in each market. It has evolved from the classical theories of Smith, Ricardo and Mill through the marginal revolution expressed in the work of Jevons, Marshall and Pigou to the Keynesian revolution of the 1930s, but has remained the dominant orthodoxy. From the point of view of this study the most significant changes lie in the expansion of the theoretical grounds for government intervention in the market system, since the heyday of laissez-faire in the mid-nineteenth century.

Historically, one of the basic aims of British socialists has been to replace the individual capitalist system of private property rights over the means of production by their public ownership for the collective good of all. Because they have sought the overthrow of the capitalist system, it might be thought that socialists would reject market economics. However, in Britain there has been a tradition, beginning with the early Fabians, of adapting orthodox market analysis to justify socialist goals. Nevertheless, the recurring downswings of the trade cycle, culminating in the severe world depression of the early 1930s, revived arguments that the capitalist system was finally collapsing. It was assumed by many socialists that simply introducing socialism would be sufficient to end the blight of unemployment. But among the professional economists who were socialists, there was considerable doubt that the problem could be solved that easily, and wide disagreement about the appropriate explanations and solutions. Some subscribed to very orthodox theories and policies, indistinguishable from the most conservative bourgeois economics; others developed their own unorthodox explanations of the causes and cures for unemployment. The development of Keynesian theories in the 1930s provided a new rationale for government intervention, which had important repercussions on socialist thinking about the operation of the capitalist system and plans for a socialist economy.

Economic theory and the rationale for government intervention

Modern economists for most purposes separate economic theory into two branches, microeconomics and macroeconomics. The theory of microeconomics describes an economic system based on the behaviour of individual consumers, producers and owners of factors of production and through equilibrium analysis shows how individually motivated decisions interact to explain behaviour in the market for each good and for each factor. The theory of macroeconomics analyses the aggregate behaviour of all markets in the final determination of total output and total income for the whole economy. The focus of microeconomics is upon the allocation of resources between goods, the distribution of income between factors and the structure of production. The focus of macroeconomics is directed to the level and growth of the whole output, or the national product, and the aggregate levels of employment, wages, profits and income. Prices in the first case refer only to real prices, in other words they measure the actual use of resources in production. In contrast, the aggregate price level is affected by monetary factors, as well as by the aggregate employment levels of labour and capital; changes in the price level, inflation or deflation, will help to determine the rate of real growth.

Classical economists were concerned with the factors determining real growth, that is, with macroeconomic theory. Based on three factors – land, labour and capital – classical theory derived the prices of goods from the payments to these factors. The payments themselves were explained by separate theories for each factor: the wages paid to labour were determined by the long-run cost of subsistence; the rent paid to each piece of land was determined by the difference between the cost of production at the margin (or least productive land) and the actual cost of production; the profit paid to capital was simply whatever was left over after land and labour had been paid. In this theory, it was assumed that land was fixed, that labour could be varied and that capital was the residual. These assumptions resulted in three important characteristics. First, the law of diminishing returns, which described the declining marginal productivity of variable factors, only applied to labour. Second, since only labour varied, changes in the quantity of labour became the major factor determining the rate and direction of growth in real output at the macroeconomic level. Third, the fixed factor, land, received a 'surplus' payment, which meant its value could be altered without affecting the amount supplied. The last characteristic implied, among other things, that the surplus, or rent, could be taxed without reducing the supply of the factor for production by its owner, the basis, for example, of Henry George's single tax.

The marginal revolution recognized that the law of diminishing returns could be applied to any variable factor relative to some other fixed factor. The generalization of this rule is basic to the analysis of the economic system still incorporated in the theory of microeconomics practised to this day. However, the long-run assumptions necessary for the law to operate with respect to all factors shifted the emphasis from the macro conditions for growth to the micro considerations of allocation within given resource constraints. Without the resource constraints it was not possible to provide a determinate equilibrium solution, that is, the system could not logically yield a unique and stable set of prices and quantities in each and every market. With the publication of Keynes's *The General Theory of Employment, Interest and Money*, the factors explaining the aggregate level of activity were again incorporated into models of the system. Only in the late 1930s was the full significance of these distinctions between macro- and microeconomics appreciated.

The prevailing orthodox microeconomic explanation for unemployment was that wages in the labour market were too high and that only a decrease could restore 'equilibrium'. It was assumed that in the long run prices would adjust through market competition to reduce any temporary unemployment. Long-run equilibrium thus implied full employment of all resources, and unemployment was theoretically possible only in the short run. One crucial aspect of the Keynesian revolution was to show how equilibrium could be reached theoretically at less than full employment levels.

While classical theory was used to oppose intervention in the market system, both the marginal and Keynesian revolutions provided grounds for government intervention, albeit for very different reasons.

The marginal revolution and market intervention

Before the marginal revolution of the 1870s, the model of perfect competition developed by the classical school had strongly supported laissez-faire doctrines opposed to government intervention in the self-regulating mechanisms of the evolving capitalist market system. In a public lecture in 1870 J.E. Cairnes complained that political economy had become 'known to the general public as a scientific development of laissez-faire'.[1] Indeed, the classical theory inherited from Ricardo and Mill was used to prove conclusively that nothing could be done to raise wages or to redistribute income. The natural wages theory demonstrated that even if wages could be raised for a short period, the resulting increase in the population would bring them back to subsistence levels. This theory, combined with the wages fund theory, was used to show that the share of aggregate output going to workers could not be increased either. When Jevons attacked the classical theory in his *Theory of Political Economy* published in 1871, he was able to demonstrate that the wages fund and natural wage theories failed to link wages with productivity, and that the labour theory of value applied only in the special case where labour was the sole variable factor of production. Furthermore, he argued that the logical and conceptual links between the Ricardo–Mill theories of distribution and of value meant that an attack on one implied an attack on the other.[2]

Jevons's book was the initial British statement of what became known as the 'neo-classical' system elaborated by Marshall and his followers. In an obituary essay on Marshall's life and contributions, Keynes compared the two:

> In truth, Jevons' *Theory of Political Economy* is a brilliant but hasty, inaccurate, and incomplete brochure, as far removed as possible from the painstaking, complete, ultra-conscientious, ultra-unsensational methods of Marshall ... it lives merely in the tenuous world of bright ideas when we compare it with the great working machine evolved by the patient, persistent toil and scientific genius of Marshall. Jevons saw the kettle boil and cried out with the delighted voice of a child; Marshall too had seen the kettle boil and sat down silently to build an engine.

Keynes listed the seven major contributions of Marshall's engine outlined in the *Principles of Economics* (1890) as: (1) the theory of value determined simultaneously by supply and demand; (2) the general theory of economic equilibrium based on the elaboration of the concepts of marginal analysis and substitutability; (3) the explicit introduction of time as a factor in economic analysis; (4) the conception of consumers' rent, in particular its application to show 'that *laissez-faire* breaks down in certain conditions theoretically'; (5) the analysis of monopoly and increasing returns; (6) the introduction of the idea of 'elasticity'; (7) the importance attached to historical background, 'as a corrective to the idea that the axioms of today are permanent'.[3]

It was Pigou (Marshall's favourite pupil and successor, according to

Keynes) who took Marshall's arguments on consumers' surplus and developed them into a more sophisticated engine for understanding the economics of welfare, the branch of microeconomics concerned with the conditions for optimal allocation. In his books, *Wealth and Welfare* (1912) and *Economics of Welfare* (1920), he built a system based on the idea of aggregate welfare and the size and distribution of national income. Pigou developed the concepts of marginal private and marginal social net product, and showed that where these diverge the free-market system cannot result in a socially optimal distribution of resources.

In Britain the ideas of the neoclassical economists were enormously influential in providing the intellectual underpinnings of the arguments for government intervention embodied in the 'new liberalism' of the late nineteenth century.[4] The idea of social freedom had been developed by the idealist philosopher, T. H. Green, from John Stuart Mill's central idea of individual liberty. Liberal philosophers, of whom L. T. Hobhouse was the leading exponent, argued that it was the government's responsibility to intervene to ensure that social freedom was translated into social justice, thus reversing almost a century of liberal faith in non-intervention. Political pressure for intervention came from the increasing electoral and trade union power of the working class, which followed the second Reform Act of 1867 and the pro-union legislation of the 1870s, as well as from a growing uneasiness about the conditions of the urban poor. The abandonment of the Ricardian distributional and wage theories opened up questions about poverty and social reform, about redistribution and progressive taxation, and led eventually to the consideration of unemployment as an economic, not a personal, problem.

Two other contributions to discussions of economic policy were made by economists before 1900. One was to clarify the distinction between subjective 'normative' precepts and neutral 'positive' analysis. This meant that economic policy arguments were less confused with the politics of laissez-faire than classical political economy had been. The other was to re-examine the role of the state in economic life in a more objective and systematic fashion.

The justification for government intervention by neoclassicists was based upon the particular conditions in specific markets; it did *not* apply to the general level of economic activity. The theory of microeconomics in its current form, which has been derived from the marginal revolution, provides theoretical grounds for the government to intervene in industries which have been monopolized or which yield significant externalities, that is, where third parties (often society at large) can gain or lose by the unregulated operation of the market.

Similarly, policies to help the poor and to redistribute from the rich to the poor are justifiable in those cases where the transfer does not adversely affect the size of national income. The criteria for intervention are those of allocative efficiency, not those of maximum growth rates; they are still based upon models which assume the full employment of all resources.

The Keynesian revolution and economic management

In contrast to microeconomic theory, there was no generally accepted theory to explain aggregate levels of economic activity before the 1930s. Thus, while economists of many persuasions were agreed that unemployment was the overriding policy problem by the late 1920s, there was no clear understanding of its causes because there was no theory that related the level of economic activity to the functioning of the market. Although there are continuing disputes about the precise nature of the Keynesian revolution and in particular its relevance to today's problems, it is now accepted that *The General Theory* does provide these connections. The policy implications which flowed from the new model also ushered in a policy revolution, as governments first recognized and then undertook responsibility for the overall management of the economy.

Of course, this does not mean that economists prior to the 1930s (including Keynes) did not have theories to explain many important aspects of aggregate economic activity. Indeed, it is important for a proper appreciation of Keynes's theoretical contribution to understand the nature of macroeconomic theorizing before *The General Theory*. The main point is that, just as classical theory lacked a uniform theory to explain factor payments, there were different theories to explain different aspects of aggregate economic performance. For example, monetary theory was used to explain changes in interest rates and prices, while trade cycle theory analysed ups and downs in total output, price levels and employment. Otherwise, unemployment was usually considered to be a labour market problem – either wage rates were higher than productivity or there were structural problems of maladjustment to shifts in demand between industries and countries.[5] There was no unified theory of income determination to connect monetary policy with fluctuations in real output and employment. Recently, Sir Austin Robinson described what it was like to learn economics at Cambridge in 1920:

> I went to lectures by Pigou on value theory in the Arts School in Cambridge. I then got on a bicycle and bicycled right across

Cambridge to Hubert Henderson lecturing on monetary theory. I then got on a bicycle again and bicycled to Emmanuel College and listened to Lavington lecturing on industrial fluctuations. These were then three entirely different subjects which were in no way connected with each other and which, in Cambridge at any rate in those days, had not been in any proper sense integrated together.[6]

Robinson attributed the work of connecting monetary theory with price theory partly to Dennis Robertson in *Banking Policy and the Price Level* (1926), partly to Keynes in *A Treatise on Money* (1930), 'but more than ever' in *The General Theory* (1936).

During the 1920s Robertson and Keynes worked together closely; indeed they both felt it was impossible to say where the contribution of one began and the other ended in their own works. Robertson had always been concerned with the real factors which affected investment and, in particular, with the fluctuations in investment which led to fluctuations in prices. Unlike Keynes he was pessimistic about the ability of the monetary system to increase investment through low interest rates.[7] Therefore, he and Keynes were as one during the 1920s over the need for direct state action to expand the economy through public works. They only disagreed on theoretical matters after the publication of *A Treatise*, when Robertson continued to concern himself with the causes of fluctuations rather than with the level of unemployment. Robertson's book made two major contributions: it introduced the terminology of savings and investment to the British literature, carefully distinguishing between them, showing their separate functions in the economy and analysing the different factors which affected their determination; it also presented cases in which the decision to save without the proper banking policy would not increase output, but would lower prices. In short, Robertson discovered that it was possible for savings and investment to be equated at less than full employment, an important step towards demolishing faith in the self-regulating powers of the market.

Before *The General Theory* there were three different approaches to money: (1) the cash balance or liquidity approach, which was based on Marshallian microeconomic principles of individual maximization in the supply and demand for money as though it were any other good; (2) the aggregate approach associated with Irving Fisher, which separated the theory of value (the Marshallian system of real prices) from the theory of money (and money prices); (3) the income approach, which began to emerge in the 1920s out of dissatisfaction with the first two and was expounded by Keynes in his *Treatise on*

Money.[8] James Meade recently described the crucial contribution of *The General Theory* model in the following terms:

> Keynes's intellectual revolution was to shift economists from thinking normally in terms of a model of reality in which a dog called *savings* wagged his tail labelled *investment* to thinking in terms of a model in which a dog called *investment* wagged his tail labelled *savings*.[9]

The effect of this revolution was to direct the focus of concern away from the price level towards the levels of output and employment.

In *A Treatise*, Keynes had carried Robertson's analysis one step further to show that savings did not necessarily equal investment at all.[10] The central theoretical construct to be found in its 'fundamental equations' was that savings equal investment *only* at full employment equilibrium, when the real interest rate (that is the factor price) also equals the market interest rate (that is the money price). If savings were greater than investment, the market rate of interest would be higher than the real rate; to bring interest rates down, savings must be cut and investment increased before the system would return to equilibrium. The analysis was still focused upon price changes rather than output changes; but the use of the savings and investment framework, the attempt to combine real and monetary factors and the development of more sophisticated models of investment behaviour, which included 'bullish' and 'bearish' expectations, were major steps forward. Economists differ in their overall assessment of *A Treatise*: some prefer it to *The General Theory* because of its dynamic properties and its connection of the domestic to the international economy; others view it as technically brilliant, but largely conventional.[11]

During the 1920s Keynes considerably revised his views about the effect of monetary policy on employment. By 1930 he was theorizing that a fall in prices was a consequence as much as a cause of unemployment.[12] On the question of governmental responsibility for economic management, Donald Winch has concluded in his important study that by the end of the 1920s the first steps towards the new interpretation of the role of the state had been taken. However, he has cautioned against interpreting policy attempts to improve economic conditions in the 1920s as the conscious recognition of the need 'for economic management as we understand this term today'.[13]

Socialism and economic theory

The classical justification for laissez-faire was that free competition expanded the area of the market by bringing about an improved division of labour. In the early years of the revolution from agricultural to industrial production the argument seemed eminently plausible and, further, to provide a complete justification for the capitalist system of private ownership. Consequently, socialists who opposed capitalism were also the major critics of orthodox classical economics; to oppose capitalism was to reject market economics, as Karl Marx did in *Das Kapital* (1867). His own explanation of the economic system drew upon classical theory, except that Marx attributed the surplus payment for a fixed factor to capital and argued that it had been expropriated from labour, his basic unit of value. Marx combined this analysis of capitalism with his understanding of the social dynamics of the class system and of historical materialism. One of the most powerful 'blended science' models, it has outlasted its narrower economic theories and its failure in predicting the collapse of capitalism, at least so far.

British democratic socialists, who rejected Marx for political reasons, were unlikely to accept his unorthodox economics. Thus, they either had to adapt orthodox market economics for their own purposes or they had to devise their own unorthodox systems. The marginal revolution of the 1870s enabled two generations of British Fabians to adapt orthodox microeconomics to support their political goals. However, neoclassical economics only provided short-run explanations of unemployment because of its full-employment assumptions. Most socialists viewed periodic slumps as endemic to the capitalist system. Therefore, those socialist economists who rejected Marxism were obliged to find alternative explanations to challenge the prevailing orthodoxy. It was not until the Keynesian revolution of the 1930s that a generally acceptable model of macroeconomic activity was available, which enabled democratic socialist economists to rejoin the ranks of orthodoxy as part of the new consensus.

Microeconomics and the orthodox socialists
At their first meetings in 1884 the Fabians searched for the appropriate economic theory to explain the capitalist system, which would also justify their belief in the superiority of a socialist system based on collectivism rather than individualism. They studied Marx, but rejected his analysis; they then invited Philip Wicksteed and F. Y. Edgeworth to come and explain the new marginal revolution and to expound the mathematics of Jevons's theory. Thus, according to Graham Wallas, 'under Webb's leadership, we worked out the Jevonian anti-Marx value theory as the basis of our socialism'; he later wrote:

We therefore came into the Society ready-made Anti-Marxists, and at once began that insistence on the Ricardian Law of Rent as applied to Capital and ability, as well as to Land which made William Morris say, 'These Fabians call their noddles their Rents of Ability'.[14]

George Bernard Shaw also studied Marx, and he became an ardent advocate for a time. However, after much persuasion he was eventually converted to the Webbian view, although he still thought *Das Kapital* was a great book: 'It knocked the moral stuffing out of the bourgeoisie, and made an end for ever of the middle class self complacency and optimism.'[15]

In the original *Fabian Essays* Shaw wrote the chapter on the economic basis of socialism, which he concluded thus:

> What the achievement of Socialism involves economically is the transfer of rent from the class which now appropriates it to the whole people. Rent being that part of the product which is individually unearned, this is the only equitable method of disposing of it . . . .
>
> It is to economic science – once the Dismal, now the Hopeful – that we are indebted for the discovery that though the evil is enormously worse than we knew, yet is not eternal – not even very long lived, if we only bestir ourselves to make an end of it.

The advantage of this analysis was that it opened up the possibility of redistributing a much wider range of 'unearned' incomes (not just that from land as Henry George had suggested) without reducing the supply of the factors which received such 'rental' payments. The approach also stressed the importance of transferring to the state all those means of production which earned the 'surplus', so that it would benefit society as a whole, not just individual owners. The argument was used to justify various forms of institutional collectivism, from the municipalization programmes favoured by the Webbs ('gas and water' socialism) to the nationalization of whole industries.

There were, however, some problems with the analysis. First, it was not at all clear how the unearned 'rental' portion of any given factor payment was to be distinguished from its earned resource cost. Second, the plans for transferring rent to the whole community were quite vague. As Hugh Gaitskell pointed out seventy years later, the theoretical arguments confused three questions:

> First, whether not only rent but interest and profits too were 'surplus' incomes in the sense that if the payments in question were cut or abolished the supply of 'land', 'capital' and 'risk bearing' would decline; secondly, whether the payment and

receipt of rent, interest and profit as such were morally wrong, irrespective of the character and wealth of the recipient; and thirdly, whether the existing distribution of income and wealth among persons and classes was just.[16]

Gaitskell criticized the early Fabians for relying on such complicated arguments about economic abstractions; he preferred to state the case for socialism on 'straightforward ethical principles'. The early Fabian economic basis was considerably weakened by later, more sophisticated applications of marginal analysis, for example, by distinctions between agricultural land and urban rentals and by consideration of the supply effects of low interest rates on savings and of low profit rates on investment. Gaitskell concluded that, although there might well be important examples of fixed supply, there was a strong case 'against building an argument for Socialism on the theory that all "unearned" incomes were technically "surplus"'.

The main impact of the early Fabians was their insistence on gradual permeation and on finding practical ways to expand the role of government to counteract the effects of the capitalist system. Although Beatrice Webb deemed 'Abstract Economics as sheer waste of time', the use of orthodox economics to justify the socialist position had its convenient aspects.[17] On the one hand, it earned a certain intellectual respectability from the authorities whom the Webbs sought to influence; on the other hand, it prevented dissipating energy on the complex and possibly fruitless task of developing a more identifiably socialist economics. However, by avoiding further theoretical work they missed the opportunity to apply the broader spectrum of Marshallian analysis to the problem of monopoly and externalities in particular industries. A more thorough use of the available economic tools could have helped to develop specific policies and criteria for nationalization.

In fact, there was little to choose between Liberal economists, such as Marshall, and the Fabians on policy matters. Winch has pointed out that any differences between them were not so much conceptual as practical; they concerned the extent of current abuse and the cost of major social change:

> On questions involving the redistribution of income and wealth there were already several important links between the orthodox tradition in economics and the views of English radicals and socialists. Among the economists there seems to have been complete agreement that the gap between rich and poor was excessive, and that its existence could not be justified on economic grounds.[18]

As orthodox economics developed less value-laden explanations of the market system, economists also became more aware of the validity of many of the questions socialists raised about the workings of the capitalist system. Indeed, Edward Cannan, the professor of political economy at the London School of Economics, wrote in the 1917 edition of his book, *Theories of Production and Distribution*, 'The economist of today is far less hostile to socialism in general than his predecessors of the classical school'.

In the next generation of Fabians, Hugh Dalton, a student and assistant lecturer under Cannan, applied marginal analysis to the questions of income inequality and public finance, which were central to socialist economic policy. Dalton had studied economics as an undergraduate at King's College, Cambridge, from 1906 to 1910, where he attended lectures by Pigou and Keynes. He also joined the Fabian Society, through which he met most of the important socialist leaders. Pigou was one of his tutors; of his influence, Dalton later wrote:

> His *Wealth and Welfare*, published in 1912, had on me something of the same effect as Moore's *Principia Ethica*. It changed old confusions into new clarity. It laid down sharper criteria for economic policy then I had found before. It brought out new conclusions, significant for practical action, from old generalities. It was a book that helped me, more than any other, to formulate my own approach from ethics, through politics, to economics. He was splendidly free from party or class prejudice, but he believed, as Marshall did before him, that great inequalities of wealth and opportunity are both unjust and wasteful of welfare.

Dalton knew Keynes better; he found his lectures on money 'intellectually fascinating', with an air of knowledge of the real world:

> Keynes was a Man of the World, including the City, always on the move, with shining wings, from point to point, changing his opinions and prescriptions at short notice. Pigou was a Man of the Temple of Truth, fixed in Cambridge. His system never greatly changed . . . . Keynes was always inventing new machines and new ways of using old machines.[19]

According to Dalton's biographer, Ben Pimlott, Keynes was more personally interested in Dalton's close friend and companion, the poet Rupert Brooke; indeed, unlike Dalton, Brooke was elected to the elite society of 'Apostles' gathered around G. E. Moore, who nicknamed Dalton 'Daddy'.

Dalton's main contributions to academic economics were his two books, *Some Aspects of the Inequality of Incomes in Modern Communities* (1920) and *Principles of Public Finance* (1922). Both did well, particularly the textbook on public finance, which was still selling 4,000 copies a year in 1953. The first book was by far the more scholarly and 'ambitious', according to its author. In four parts the book discussed the relation of inequality to justice and to practical policy problems; it reviewed the history of economic thought on the subject, and outlined the theory and evidence on the distribution of income between factors of production. Finally, in the most important breakthrough for socialist economics, Dalton connected this theory and evidence to the problem of the distribution of personal incomes. His nbasic thrust was to criticize neoclassical theory for concentrating on factor distribution and for ignoring the problems of inheritance, which Dalton defined broadly to include opportunity, custom and public property. His policy recommendations included the expansion of transfer payments, 'the improvement of education, the extension of the field of employment of women, the modification of the laws of inherited wealth, various forms of taxation, and the regulation of the currency, in such a way as to secure a steady and gradual increase in the value of money' and 'the larger policy of a gradual reorganization of industry on a socialistic basis'.[20] Dalton's own assessment of the book was that it contributed most in its discussion of inherited wealth, of personal income distribution and of 'the borderland between law and economics'; in addition, 'I find it remarkable, looking back to this book, that I had then no apprehension of mass unemployment'.[21]

The economic analysis in both books drew heavily on Pigou and on Cannan, whose article on 'The Division of Income' published in 1905 Dalton identified as a major turning-point. Dalton concentrated on the microeconomic criteria of allocative efficiency for assessing redistribution and taxation. He argued that it was not necessary to decide how much inequality should be reduced, because the road to equality 'is far longer than this generation will have the power to cover'; however, he was concerned with the possible 'backslidings of productive power' (Pigou's negative transferences).[22] Dalton is best known by modern economists for his early discussion of the problems of measuring inequality and its reduction. He had intended to discuss this question fully in his first book, but the pressure of his timetable shrank it to an article published in the *Economic Journal* in September 1920. In his memoirs Dalton commented 'rather an ingenious piece of writing'; but it was based on hypotheses 'which were a bit unreal'. It seemed appropriate that, almost sixty years later, as respite from poring over Dalton's dusty and not very tidy papers in the library, the author was to hear Amatya Sen expound upon the assumptions behind the 'Dalton criteria' to a rapt audience of the latest generation of LSE students.

As a socialist economist Dalton is remembered best for his conclusions on the distribution of personal incomes and its dependence on the distribution of inherited wealth. Gaitskell has explained that Dalton's analysis 'immensely clarified Socialist thinking and directed it in the right direction – away from sterile, out-of-date, somewhat academic arguments of earlier writers, and towards the real problems confronting the practical democratic Socialist'.[23] Since Dalton had identified the two major causes of inequality as the inheritance of wealth and the educational system, he had pointed the way to reform. Thirty years later, Gaitskell saw no great advance on Dalton's pioneering work; he concluded, in the same article, 'His ideas were significant not only because of their direct relationship to the Socialist goal of greater equality, but because they broke away from the doctrine that the nationalisation of industry was the sole method of advance'. It was Gaitskell himself, together with his friend and colleague Evan Durbin, who initiated the next generation's efforts to apply the principles of microeconomics to the theory and practice of socialist planning.

Macroeconomics and the heretical socialists

The orthodox neoclassical explanation of unemployment was that wages in the labour market were too high and that only by cutting them could 'equilibrium' employment be restored. This prescription was disagreeable for Labour supporters and its justification was intuitively contradictory to all concerned about poverty and income inequality. Consequently, there were various attempts to circumvent this apparent reincarnation of the 'iron law of wages', particularly after the great depression of the 1890s. The simple-minded socialist view was that periodic unemployment was the fault of the capitalist system; once socialism was introduced, it would vanish. More sophisticated attempts were made to develop alternative theories, on the one hand, and ameliorative policies, on the other. The writings of J. A. Hobson were essential to the first of these approaches and the work of the Webbs to the second.

Hobson, a prolific economic writer and visiting lecturer who never made it into academia, has been identified by Peter Clarke as one of the more radical intellectuals behind the new Liberal thinking at the turn of the century. He joined the Labour party after the First World War and worked with G. D. H. Cole on its advisory committee in the 1920s. Later he confessed that 'he never felt quite at home in a body governed by trade union members and their finance, and intellectually led by full-blooded Socialists'.[24]

In his first book, *The Physiology of Industry*, co-authored with A. F. Mummery in 1889, Hobson set out to attack the classical school, in particular the assumption that savings always enriched the community. Hobson and Mummery argued that, since it was consumption levels which determined output levels, increased savings would reduce consumption and cause unemployment. They recognized that

> the basis on which all economic teaching since Adam Smith has stood, viz. that the quantity annually produced is determined by the aggregates of Natural Agents, Capital, and Labour available, is erroneous, and that, on the contrary, the quantity produced, while it can never exceed the limits imposed by these aggregates, may be, and actually is, reduced far below this maximum by the check that undue savings and the consequent accumulation of over-supply exerts on production.[25]

It was this recognition which prompted Keynes to give the book extensive coverage in the appendix to *The General Theory* as an important precursor of his own theory. He felt that their account represented an early understanding that overproduction was possible, and that individual self-interest as a determinant of saving did not always ensure the community's interest in sustaining full employment. He argued that it put one half of the matter 'with absolute precision', though it still overlooked the possible role of changes in the rate of interest and in the state of business confidence. Keynes concluded that it was 'the first explicit statement of the fact that capital is brought into existence not by the propensity to save but in response to the demand resulting from actual and prospective consumption'.[26]

Later, after Mummery had been killed while mountaineering, Hobson developed a more complete explanation of the underconsumption theories with which his name has since been associated. In correspondence with Roy Harrod, Keynes wrote:

> Thanks very much for taking so much trouble about the Mummery. Hobson never fully understood him and went off on a side-track after his death. But the book Hobson helped him to write, *The Physiology of Industry* is a wonderful work. I am giving a full account of it but old Hobson has had so much injustice done to him that I shan't say what I think about M's contribution to it being, probably, outstanding.[27]

One early injustice had been to exclude him from teaching in Britain, which Hobson felt was 'due to the intervention of an Economics Professor who read my book and considered it as equivalent in rationality to an attempt to prove the flatness of the earth'.[28] A later injustice was committed by Evan Durbin, whose first professional publication, *Purchasing Power and Trade Depression* (1933), was a critique of underconsumption theories. In this book, according to Clarke, 'the views of Hobson, rather to his chagrin, were lumped together by Durbin with the cruder fallacies of other heretics'.[29]

In Hobson's version of underconsumption, which was best expressed in *The Problem of the Unemployed* (1896), excessive savings arose from the maldistribution of income, because those with the power to consume (the rich) did not necessarily desire to do so. If the 'owners of capital and labour who take super-marginal payments may be held to get them in virtue of the higher personal effort and efficiency in putting their "savings", brains and labour-power to the best uses . . . we get a justification of the competitive laisser-faire economy.' If everyone had 'equal opportunities for employment', then the income disparities served an economic purpose; but as Hobson observed:

> Most remunerative uses are safeguarded for capitalists in control, or are only open to certain orders of investors. Human labour cannot, it is notorious, have full knowledge and free access to all sorts of work, from the work of research and invention, or of business control, to the various grades of mental and manual skilled and unskilled labour.

When Hobson examined the actual operations of supply and demand, he found that supply was often restricted and that certain buyers and sellers had access to a 'surplus' element, which corresponded to the rent for land. Since this surplus had no rational or equitable basis, he argued that 'an element of "unreason" permeates the bargaining process in all markets'. Later he associated this analysis of distribution with 'the definitely humanist and ethical trend of my Ruskinian thought'.[30]

Clarke has argued that Hobson was not in fact a precursor of Keynes. Although 'it is naturally tempting to jab Hobson's elbow', his hints and suggestions 'hardly amount to an anticipation of *The General Theory*, or even *The Treatise on Money*', because Hobson's concerns were very different from Keynes's.[31] Like the Fabians, Hobson was concerned with 'surplus' income, with 'the protean individualist fallacy', and with a 'broad assault upon laissez-faire', so that underconsumption was not in fact central to Hobson's economic thought. Because of Hobson's 'sheer lack of respect for academic standards', Clarke also believes it would be a mistake to think of him 'as an otherwise predestined Professor of Economics, cruelly martyred in the cause of underconsumption'. In addition to his heresy on matters of thrift and the sometimes virulent forms of his anti-capitalism, Hobson also tried to develop an 'organic' and humanistic view of society, which he argued was 'my most destructive heresy, and therefore the one for which I have least succeeded in gaining attention, even in the form of hostile criticism, from orthodox economists'.[32]

Hobson's economics were based on a mixture of moral outrage at the distributional implications of the market system and an intuitive sense that it was not operating at full capacity. The analysis entirely ignored the monetary system and its impact on investment and savings; it concentrated exclusively on consumption, rather than on the entire process of income determination. Hobson himself was actually sceptical about public works; his policy reliance on taxation arose from concern about the surplus, not about the macroeconomic use of fiscal management. Winch has pointed out that 'arguments derived from Hobson merely tended to strengthen the case for old-fashioned redistributive measures and the abolition of private ownership of the means of production'.[33] However, even the Fabians found his arguments difficult to swallow; an article on Hobson's underconsumption theory in the *Fabian News* of May 1895 concluded:

> We cannot pretend to sit in judgment on this explanation of the depressions of trade. It is unquestionably an attractive one, and we can see no flaw in the author's argument. But we cannot yet venture on the mental revolution which its acceptance would require.

William Beveridge, who worked closely with the Webbs, argued in his book *Unemployment: A Problem of Industry* (1909) that unemployment could not be ascribed to underconsumption because 'Mr Hobson's thesis really explains little or nothing that cannot be explained as mere misdirection of energy'. In a letter, he confessed that Hobson 'possesses a peculiar theory which I am unable to follow'.[34]

In pointed contrast to Hobson's theoretical endeavours, the Webbs concentrated upon detailed empirical research and practical reforms. While Beatrice was a commissioner on the Royal Commission on the Poor Laws from 1905 to 1909, they wrote a comprehensive set of proposals to deal with the unemployment problem, with Beveridge as their assistant. The Webbs' views on unemployment are important both for their influence on socialist thinking and as a milestone in the development of the modern approach to unemployment. In her minority report submitted in 1909, Beatrice Webb called for the breakup of the Poor Laws and governmental organization of the labour market. She recommended that a ministry of labour be set up to co-ordinate the development of unemployment policies along four main lines: (1) a network of labour exchanges to which the unemployed must report; (2) a ten-year programme of public works to be applied counteractively to the trade cycle; (3) a voluntary system of state-aided unemployment insurance; (4) a maintenance system for the hard-core unemployed who accepted remedial training.

In 1907 the Labour party drafted an unemployment bill, which was debated in the House of Commons. Drawing on the work of the Webbs, it was proposed to set up local committees where the unemployed could register. If there were no jobs at standard wages, a decent benefit must be paid. Thus, the revolutionary principle was asserted that every worker had the right to work or to maintenance. Although the bill did not pass, many of these ideas were subsequently adopted by the Liberal government, largely through the efforts of Lloyd George at the Treasury and Winston Churchill at the board of trade. However, the actual reforms were significantly different from the Webbs' plan; for example, attendance at the labour exchanges was made voluntary, but the insurance system compulsory, and the development commission for public works was weak and underfunded. Nevertheless, José Harris has concluded, in her fascinating and comprehensive study of unemployment policies in prewar Britain, that 'by 1914 fatalistic acceptance of the inevitability of the trade cycle and doctrinaire prejudice against the relief of unemployment had largely passed away'.[35]

Some subsequent analysts have interpreted the Webb approach, especially its recommendations for countercyclical public works, as a precursor to the expansionary policies later advocated by Keynes. For example, Robert Skidelsky has argued that the public works proposal was 'an early statement of the theory of "idle balances"', which was used by the Liberal party under Keynes's guidance to recommend government borrowing for this purpose in the 1920s.[36] Despite the Webbs, the Labour party itself remained officially cautious on public works and silent on government loans; their economic policies relied heavily on progressive taxation. Skidelsky has suggested that the latter was 'at least "socialistic" in intent and effort', while using idle balances seemed 'to be mere capitalistic tinkering'.

Winch and Harris have disagreed with Skidelsky for a number of reasons. Winch has argued that Beatrice's proposals were quite limited theoretically, which helped their early acceptance:

The great virtue of the scheme to contemporaries was that it called for no important change in the economic and social order, no new encroachment by the state in economic life; the timing of the *existing* expenditure plans was to be modified, that was all. Furthermore, it was basically a method of compensating for savings in private economic activity; it was not based on any new insight into the root causes of such savings.

Winch concluded that by the 1920s what was needed was a 'new theoretical explanation which would lay bare the causal mechanisms underlying cycles and general employment'.[37]

Harris, who analysed attitudes to the unemployment question in much broader terms, has added that, even though the Webbs came closer than any other contemporary reformers to devising an 'economic' remedy for unemployment, they were 'much more interested in creating an administrative science for the treatment of unemployed workmen analogous to the science of public health'.[38] She has also concluded that Beatrice was ambivalent throughout her life about whether the personal characteristics of the unemployed or the 'disease of industry' was the prime cause of unemployment. Although Beveridge and the Webbs believed in the crucial shift from moral and personal to industrial and environmental explanations of unemployment, they proved as judgmental as their predecessors in some respects. Despite their scientific analysis of unemployment, Harris feels that they were harsher and more pessimistic towards its victims. For example, their training schemes were explicitly designed to provide income maintenance only to those who behaved in socially acceptable ways.

Another of the attractions of countercyclical public works to the Webbs was that they were cheaper during a depression. In discussing Graham Wallas's reaction to the Webbs, Clarke has contrasted their analysis with his more Hobsonian approach: 'For the Webbs the Fabian theory of rent had led to an increasingly institutional approach to collectivism but for Wallas it pointed to fiscal solutions'.[39] In the 1880s Wallas believed that collectivism was the only alternative to the individualist conception of property, but later he was more aware of its defects as a comprehensive alternative. One of the defects which Wallas discerned in his Fabian colleagues was a certain impatience with democracy and an increasing reliance on the expert to introduce organizational efficiency as the basis for collectivist intervention. In the 1930s these contrasting perspectives were to be applied systematically to the question of planning, the administrative solution reflected in theories of physical controls and the fiscal solution in theories of economic management.

Conclusions

In their use of economics, socialist economists have disagreed about the appropriate theoretical models, about their application to explain the workings of the economic system, about their judgments of what is happening empirically and about the definition of their goals and strategy. This chapter has focused on the theoretical dilemma of using orthodox economics to analyse economic questions from a socialist perspective. With the emphasis of orthodox economics on the mechanisms of the individualistic market system, socialist economic theorists either have to adapt orthodox economics or develop their own theory of socialist economics to explain and justify government intervention to secure their collectivist goals.

British socialists took both routes prior to 1930. One early Fabian justification for socialism was based upon neoclassical economics, which was used to identify a surplus available for redistribution. Later, Dalton applied Pigovian social welfare economics, to analyse the problem of income inequality and to outline the principles of public finance necessary to correct it. In contrast, Hobson rejected market economics; he built his own system to take account of institutional and moral factors, believing that the maldistribution of income was the most fundamental explanation of capitalism's economic woes. There were limitations to both these approaches; it will be useful to discuss them in order to assess the contributions made by the next generation of British democratic socialists.

The mainstream Fabian approach lacked an understanding of macroeconomics, as Dalton later acknowledged. This gap, of course, was not peculiar to socialist economists, since it was a defect of the neoclassical system in general. What is perhaps surprising is that British socialists appear to have been ignorant of important theoretical work on the economics of socialism by Walras, Pareto, Barone and Weber and on the analysis of public goods by Mazzola and Wicksell.[40] Although Dalton referred to Pareto in his review of distribution theory, he only discussed his contributions to the problem of measuring inequality.

Unlike the Fabians, Hobson was concerned with macroeconomic problems. Although his theory of underconsumption has been interpreted as an early version of the Keynesian theory of effective demand, his explanations of excessive savings arose from microeconomic considerations of income distribution and his analysis lacked any understanding of monetary problems. Hobson was very suspicious of 'monetary palliatives' and by 1929 was actually opposed to the expansionary policies proposed by Keynes and others.[41] In short, although he was right about the possibilities of overproduction and of conflicts between the individual and community interest in saving, he was right for the wrong reasons.

In further contrast to the Fabians, Hobson, like Marx, rejected the whole system of orthodox economics. But unlike Marx, he focused upon the maldistribution of income rather than the class system, and used ethics and aesthetics rather than sociology and political science as his disciplines. In a chapter of his autobiography entitled 'An Economic Journey Towards Humanism', Hobson described his own system in the following terms:

> If one gets away from the economics of the market in which money is the measure of work and wealth into the economics of human values, one is inevitably drawn into what may appear to be 'the jumble' of politics, ethics, arts, religion which constitutes the setting of my thought. My main endeavour, however, has been to show that though the human treatment of economic activities links up with all these other activities, they do not form a 'jumble' but a moving harmony of relations, in which the several values, though capable of separate study, must finally be seen as contributory factors in the art of living. I cannot pretend that my development of this thesis has been an orderly continuous intellectual journey. Far from it. My earliest statement of the over-saving heresy was a quarrel with orthodoxy within the range of quantitative economic science. It was only later on that it led me to a closer analysis of the bargaining processes in the market for goods and services which disclosed the inequities of income that gave rise to 'over-saving' and the waste it brought about in periods of depression . . . . In most of my closer reasoning my prime concern has been to give a consistent intelligible account of the bargaining process . . . . This line of analysis led me to present economics in a distinctively qualitative way . . . . In other words, whether under monopoly or so-called competitive conditions, markets are intrinsically unfair modes of distribution.[42]

Although Hobson tried to build a system using a multidisciplinary approach, his emphasis on fairness and on harmony confused humanistic and scientific methodologies even more than usual in 'blended' models.

Such a system is certainly enough of a jumble to earn the scorn of economists who believe in the scientific merits of their discipline. Dalton, for example, made fun of Hobson's confessed attraction to Ruskin; he described Ruskin as a man who glorified war, hated democracy and opposed the education of women, and concluded:

The quality of Ruskin's thought on purely economic questions is exemplified by his petulant desire to 'destroy most of the railroads in England, and all the railroads in Wales', and by his proposal that all machinery should be legally prohibited in agriculture and in many branches of industry, because it 'throws a number of persons out of wholesome employment, who must henceforward either do nothing or mischief'. And yet Mr. Hobson finds in Ruskin a greater economic wisdom and deeper humanity than in Mill![43]

Yet it was Hobson rather than Dalton who struggled with some fundamental issues for socialist economic theorists. For while it is entirely appropriate to use orthodox economics for understanding how a predominantly private and capitalist system functions, and consequently for socialists to use it to diagnose what is wrong with that system, it is much less clear whether market theory is appropriate for understanding the economic operations of a socialist system based on public ownership and collective ends. Orthodox microeconomics provides some criteria for distinguishing between public and private goods (that is, between collective and individual consumption) and for isolating industries with significant monopoly elements. Both these applications can be used to provide rationales for government intervention in specific cases. Before 1930 British socialist economists did not pursue these theoretical arguments systematically themselves and appear to have ignored the European writers who did.

However, the use of orthodox economics by socialists raises much broader questions. First, is market economic analysis based upon individual preferences the appropriate model for evaluating the overall performance of a socialist system? Using the market criteria of efficiency, a collective system which successfully reproduces the conditions of perfect competition can in principle maximize output and minimize cost. But in what other ways should a socialist system be evaluated, and how are other criteria to be incorporated with those of economic efficiency? The Fabian approach was to use orthodox economics where the analysis helped to justify socialist goals, and not to bother with ultimate questions of methodology; Dalton begged the question by arguing that it belonged to the future. Hobson's approach was to try to describe a system which incorporated socialist ends as part of its functioning. Neither really dealt with the issue of how to apply the static analysis of orthodox microeconomics to the process of dynamic social change. It remained for the next generation to tackle these questions, with varying degrees of success.

CHAPTER 3
ECONOMIC POLICY AND THE LABOUR PARTY 1918–31

After the 1931 crisis the Labour party reacted violently against MacDonald and Snowden and their perceived betrayal of the socialist cause. Despite their lifelong leadership, they were expelled from the party, their motives were impugned, their policies derided and their contributions distorted, minimized and, eventually, forgotten. Recent biographies by David Marquand and Colin Cross have helped to set the record straight and to re-evaluate their roles in the Labour movement. This generation may find it easier to sympathize with their dilemma as leaders of a party which was committed to help the poor and to introduce major social reforms, in an era of economic decline and government retrenchment.

To appreciate both MacDonald's position and the reaction against him, one must distinguish between the national failure to regain Britain's prewar position or to find jobs for its returning heroes and the Labour party's failure to design an effective programme for socialist action. Throughout the 1920s unemployment was never below one million, and often higher. Yet successive governments resisted intervening in the domestic market on the advice of Treasury and Bank of England officials. Their goal was to return to the gold standard at the prewar exchange rate, but the ensuing overvaluation of the pound only compounded Britain's economic problems. In the late 1920s Keynes emerged as the leading critic of the deflationary effect of this strategy and began his campaign for expansionary policies to bolster domestic employment.

The Labour party had been strengthened by its wartime experiences. MacDonald gained credibility as a principled internationalist when he led the Independent Labour party (ILP) in its stand against the war. Meanwhile, Arthur Henderson, an MP from the Friendly Society of

Ironfounders and the secretary of the Labour party before the war, served for two years as minister of education in the coalition government and earned respect as a capable member of the government. Together with Sidney Webb, he was also responsible for a major reorganization of the party's structure. They opened it to individual membership in place of indirect membership through a union or socialist society; they doubled the number of constituency parties; and they drew up a written constitution.

At its 1918 conference the party finally adopted a formal policy statement for the first time; it was called *Labour and the New Social Order*. Drafted by Webb, this document explicitly committed the Labour party to socialism. It stated four principles, which 'formed the basis of Labour Party policy for over thirty years'.[1] They were: (1) the 'Universal Enforcement of the National Minimum', to include full employment with a minimum wage and minimum working conditions for a maximum forty-eight-hour week; (2) 'Democratic Control of Industry', which emphasized nationalization and worker participation; (3) the 'Revolution in National Finance', that is, highly progressive taxation plus a capital levy to pay off part of the war debt; (4) the 'Surplus for the Common Good', which meant the use of tax revenues to improve education and culture. The constitution included the famous 'Clause Four' which promised:

> To secure for the workers by hand and by brain the full limits of
> their industry, and the most equitable distribution thereof that
> may be possible, upon the basis of the common ownership of the
> means of production and the best obtainable system of popular
> administration and control of each industry and service.[2]

While this apparent commitment to take over private industry helped to distinguish the Labour party's goals from those of the Liberals, it offered nothing in the way of specific plans or legislative priorities.

Nevertheless, Labour won more seats at the polls than the Liberals in the 1923 election. Since together they outpolled the Tories, MacDonald was asked to form a government, a great triumph for a party not yet twenty-five years old. However, the fragile majority fell within nine months, and the Tories led by Stanley Baldwin swept into power for the next five years. In 1925 the new Tory chancellor of the exchequer, Winston Churchill, was persuaded to put Britain back on the gold standard. The following year, when the coal owners sought wage cuts as the price of maintaining the industry's international competitiveness, the miners rebelled; calling on the promised support of the Trades Union Congress (TUC), a general strike was declared. A watershed in the history of the Labour movement, the strike

collapsed in nine days. Once again trade unionists directed their attention to Parliament. Thus, economic policy and the fate of the Labour
party were inexorably enmeshed even before the catastrophic summer
of 1931.

Official economic policy and mounting controversy

The two central issues of economic policy during the 1920s revolved
around Britain's exchange rate and domestic unemployment. In an
insightful analysis of the period, Donald Winch has shown that by
1931 the two issues were inextricably intertwined.[3] The British government, the Treasury and the Bank of England did recognize their duty
to regulate and protect the currency. They did not acknowledge the
same sense of responsibility for controlling the level of unemployment,
which was still perceived as the inevitable result of natural market
forces. Following accepted economic analysis it was thought that
monetary policy could be conducted independently from industrial
policy, and that domestic policy could be separated from international
policy. The conventional economic wisdom broadly held was that, just
like any private business, the government should only intervene at the
macroeconomic level to maintain the currency and to balance the
budget.

The contemporary dictates of 'sound finance' also required that the
national debt be reduced on a regular basis, whatever the state of the
economy. Since the national debt had grown enormously during the
war, the falling prices and stagnating revenues of the 1920s greatly
increased the burden of interest payments and debt reduction on the
expenditure budget, even before interest rates were raised to support
the pound after 1925. It was also believed that the government should
not have 'too large' a budget. Therefore, immediately after the war
when the budget was abnormally large, there was a deliberate,
systematic and successful policy to slash government expenditure.[4]
Finally, it was also a generally accepted principle to *cut* government
expenditure when revenues fell, as they inevitably did in times of
economic distress. In short, to put it in modern terms, both exchange
policy and budget policy in this period actually depressed the economy
even further, while belief in the automatic forces of the market ruled
out positive government action to reverse the trend.

The main arguments in favour of the gold standard were that it
would restore London as the centre of international finance, that it
would revive world trade and reduce unemployment in the export
industries and that it would ensure a self-regulating price mechanism

to handle both the balance of payments and the domestic money supply. There was little discussion of whether to devalue and no discussion of alternative means to balance international payments. The decision to return was made on moral and political grounds, rather than economic, according to Donald Moggridge in his authoritative study of British monetary policy in the period. The reasons had their roots in banking and financial attitudes towards gold, debt repayment and maintaining bankers' confidence, and 'in a deep faith in the apparent mechanism of the prewar gold standard'.[5] But the war had shattered Britain's domination of world markets and the authorities discovered that the system was no longer self-regulating in Britain's favour. A considerable amount of discretionary management was necessary to maintain the pound's value after 1925.

Besides its deflationary effects, the overvalued pound also placed serious limitations on government policy making. With a priority put on exchange stability, the options available for dealing with unemployment were reduced, and governmental acceptance of its responsibility for maintaining domestic stability was postponed. This situation meant that de facto responsibility for macroeconomic policy rested with the Bank of England. The gold standard acted as a barrier to government intervention, not only in monetary policy narrowly defined, but more widely by restricting intervention in the market system to help industry expand. In the political balance, the return to the gold standard favoured the stability of the pound at the expense of employment stability, and favoured the City and financial interests over industrial and labour interests.

Although it was thought at first that unemployment was due to the dislocation of the war, even before 1925 it had become apparent that Britain's industrial problems were deep-rooted; they involved long-term structural shifts in the patterns of trade and the development of newer, more efficient competitors abroad. This realization spurred efforts to develop government policies to deal directly with the unemployment problem. These efforts were threefold: (1) the use of unemployment insurance to ameliorate the condition of the unemployed; (2) the development of countercyclical relief work through the unemployment grants committee; and later (3) the establishment of the industrial transference board to assist the unemployed in distressed areas to move to the more prosperous midlands and south-east England.

Despite prewar reforms in the government's unemployment programme, neither the income scheme nor relief works were functioning well. Contribution levels to the insurance system had been calculated on the basis of a seasonal and cyclical unemployment rate of 4 to 5 per cent, with the idea that the risks could be spread evenly. The slump of 1920–1, however, prevented any early build-up of the fund; subsequently, higher rates of unemployment meant that the insurance principle essentially broke down, because constant infusions from the general revenues were necessary to continue payments. The so-called 'anomalies', which developed in the 1920s, arose from the expedients to preserve the insurance facade. In the end even these failed to conceal that the state was no longer acting as an insurance broker but as a relief agency.[6] This system was rendered even more iniquitous by successful Treasury moves to shift the financial responsibility for unemployment relief from the national exchequer to local authorities. Such changes only exacerbated the situation, since obviously the worst-hit areas were the least likely sources of revenue.

The experience with countercyclical relief works was similar. Already seriously underfunded before the war, the unemployment grants committee distributed approximately £115 million between 1921 and 1929, which, together with £50 million for road construction, provided an average 44,000 jobs at any one time, employing approximately 1 per cent of the work force.[7] Here again the financing was shifted to local authorities. The development of arguments for and against public works expenditure provided the first systematic efforts to link monetary and fiscal policies and to trace their effects on aggregate output and employment.

The orthodox argument against public works expenditure became known as the 'Treasury view'. The classic statement of this official position was given by Churchill in his budget speech of 1929:

> It is orthodox Treasury dogma, steadfastly held, that whatever might be the political or social advantages, very little additional employment can, in fact, and as a general rule, be created by State borrowing and expenditure.[8]

It was implicitly assumed that only a certain amount of funding was available at any given time for borrowing by both private and public spenders. Consequently, the more the government borrowed and spent, the less was available for the private market. This fundamental belief combined the neoclassical economic argument that competition would force prices and wages to readjust at full-employment equilibrium with the political view that the government should not intervene in the market-place.

The seeds of Keynes's mounting attack upon orthodox economic policy were sown in his experiences at the Versailles conference and can be detected as early as his diatribe, *The Economic Consequences of the Peace* (1919).[9] At first Keynes supported a return to a modified form of the gold standard at prewar parity, if it could be done soon. By 1923, in his *Tract on Monetary Reform*, he favoured fixing the value of currencies at current values. He contended that British policy makers faced a choice of giving priority to stable domestic prices or to a stable pound, or, in his terms, between 'deflation' and 'devaluation'. Keynes himself recommended putting the goal of stable domestic prices first; he therefore supported a moderate inflation to encourage risk-taking businessmen and to help employment rather than rentiers. He argued against the gold standard in principle, because it was an arbitrary regulator of the domestic economy; in practice he argued against any value of the pound which he thought would be deflationary domestically. When his recommendations were rejected, he fulminated in the *Economic Consequences of Mr. Churchill* (1925) against the overvaluation of the pound (10 per cent by his estimate), the unjust wage cutting that would be necessary in the export industries and the general deflationary consequences for the economy as a whole.

Keynes's theoretical position was still entirely based on orthodox monetary theory. He focused upon controlling price levels rather than output levels. He disputed the official position both because he disagreed with their estimate of Britain's economic position relative to other countries and because he placed different values on the importance of employment income compared to investment income and of domestic stability compared to exchange stability. His unorthodoxy as a policy adviser lay in linking domestic policy to exchange policy. At this stage, his arguments were pragmatic, not theoretical.

The most organized criticism of orthodox policy came from the Liberal party. Keynes was the intellectual leader in developing the party's position and Lloyd George the political leader. Beginning in 1923 a group of Liberals, led by Walter Layton and including Reginald McKenna, chancellor of the exchequer under Asquith, conducted surveys and wrote reports on the nature and incidence of unemployment. At the same time, in a series of Liberal summer schools the entire outlook of the party was debated. An innovative, yet practical, philosophy of state intervention was worked out, which attempted to steer a course between laissez-faire individualism and collectivism.

In 1928 a series of industrial and economic proposals were published in a book called *Britain's Industrial Future*. Better known as the Liberal 'Yellow Book', it recommended vigorous reconstruction and development, increased public investment in roads, housing, electricity, waterways, telephones and agriculture, all to be financed by government loans from a national investment board. Lloyd George drew heavily on these proposals for his 1929 election manifesto, *We Can Conquer Unemployment*. For the first time a major political party was proposing 'to treat unemployment on a scale and in a manner comparable to war'.[10]

Keynes played a central role in all these debates. He wrote a series of articles in the *Nation* in the summer of 1924 outlining his economic perspective; later, in *The End of Laissez-Faire* he spelled out the political implications of his economic policies. These articles were an important watershed in Keynes's thinking because for the first time he argued for an increase in expenditure on public works, not simply to make up cyclical losses, but for the deliberate purpose of instigating an expansionary process. He also specifically questioned the ability of private market forces to maintain the appropriate level of aggregate savings and to allocate savings between foreign and domestic investment in the nation's best interest.

Although the policies recommended by the orthodox 'Treasury view' and the rebellious expansionists were in direct conflict, at this point their theoretical justifications were not in fact that far apart. Winch has concluded that 'the difference between expansionists and contractionists was ultimately one of political priorities rather than economic analysis'.[11] The orthodox view emphasized exchange rate stability and sound finance; the rebels were primarily concerned with domestic employment and were willing to experiment with finance. The former expressed the interests of the City, while the latter supported the interests of industry and labour. One relied on market forces as the regulator of economic activity, the other required an increase in government intervention and responsibility for dealing with unemployment. One worked on the traditional assumptions of full employment, the other was increasingly doubtful about the usefulness of applying such models to an economy suffering from chronic unemployment.

The Labour party and economic policy 1918–29

Since the Labour party was considerably to the left of the Liberal party, particularly after its official commitment to socialism in 1918, it would be natural to suppose that it was the chief critic of orthodox economic policy. In one sense it was for socialists believed that unemployment was one of the most iniquitous effects of the capitalist system, a constant reminder of the human waste of competition and of the helplessness felt by the millions who were paying for adherence to the belief in 'self-regulating' market forces. They further thought that unemployment could only be solved by doing away with capitalism, which they intended to accomplish through the common ownership of the means of production. Until this could be achieved, the immediate goal of socialists was to ameliorate the condition of the people who were unemployed by whatever means possible. In short, since they believed that only socialism would cure unemployment, the main policy concern of trade unionists and Labour supporters in the interim was concentrated upon short-run issues of unemployment insurance and relief systems, rather than upon a long-run strategy of job creation. Naturally, socialists were opposed to government plans which might prolong the capitalist system unnecessarily. They were cautious about the Liberal party as their rival for the progressive vote and were deeply suspicious of Lloyd George's devious Welsh wizardry.

Labour's lack of interest in job-creation strategies was combined with a curious but understandable mixture of almost complete ignorance of the banking and money systems and a touching faith in the old-fashioned virtues of personal thrift. Furthermore, one of the immediate political tasks of the Labour party in the 1920s was to establish its credibility as a responsible alternative government. Thus, orthodox economic policy was appealing to Labour's leaders, and most of the rank and file of the Labour movement were sympathetic to the need for sound finance and balanced budgets. Finally, in the person of Philip Snowden, the Labour party had a shadow chancellor of the exchequer who out-Gladstoned Gladstone in his passion for budgetary stringency.

In short, the Labour party's economic policy in the 1920s was caught between its long-term goal of overthrowing the system and its belief in the morality of sound finance, whatever the system. Despite various efforts to confront this dilemma, the party failed to work out practical plans either to establish socialism or to maintain the existing system. Its failure underscored the general difficulties of a political party committed to progressive reform in a depressed market economy. For a party seeking to replace that system, the fundamental question arose whether to use existing institutions to bolster capitalism and to mitigate its effects in the short run or to proceed with long-term plans to take over the instruments of control. Disputes over the appropriate economic policy revealed other divisions within the party, which presaged in significant ways the climactic end of the second Labour government and foreshadowed the continuing debates of the 1930s.

Official party policy

Before 1914 the Labour party had avoided specific policy commitments in order to avoid a confrontation between the socialists and the trade unionists. Growing trade union militancy and the cautious phrasing of early drafts helped to forestall major conflicts in the altered circumstances of 1918. Workers' control was a sensitive issue, particularly in the form expressed by guild socialists and some members of the ILP concerned with industrial democracy. However, Sidney Webb, who was hostile to 'syndicalist follies', drafted an evasive statement on the form of administration and control of industry. The subject was not included in the twenty-six resolutions based on *Labour and the New Social Order*, which were debated and adopted at the first annual party conference in 1918.[12] These resolutions became the official statement of the Labour party's intentions, if elected to power.

Only seven of the twenty-six resolutions dealt explicitly with economic policy. They covered: (1) the task of social reconstruction; (2) the need for increased production; (3) the maintenance and protection of the standard of life; (4) the prevention of unemployment; (5) unemployment insurance; (6) control of capitalist industry; (7) national finance. There were also resolutions on specific public services including education, housing and abolition of the Poor Law, and on certain industries – railways and canals, electricity supply, coal and iron mines, life assurance and agriculture – as well as political resolutions, such as the emancipation of women, reform of the House of Lords, home rule for Ireland, constitutional devolution and local government.

The resolutions as a whole committed the party to 'the gradual building up of a new social order based . . . on the deliberately planned cooperation in production and distribution, the sympathetic approach to a healthy equality, the widest possible participation in power, both economic and political, and the general consciousness achieved by the socialisation of industry in order to secure the elimination of every kind of inefficiency and waste, . . . more honest determination to produce the very best, . . . improvement in social, political and industrial organisation . . . and the indispensable marshalling of the nation's resources so that each need is met in the order to, and in proportion to, its real national importance'. The party called for the immediate nationalization of railways, mines and electricity; land, canals, harbours and steamships, industrial life assurance and 'the entire manufacture and retailing of alcoholic drink' were to follow less immediately. (The party considered that roads, posts and telegraphs were already publicly owned and they had previously committed themselves to the nationalization of armaments in the party's war aims.) The party proposed to maintain the system of war controls over capitalist industry to economize on 'centralised purchasing' and 'rationing . . . under collective control'. Finally, the party was committed to maintain and protect a minimum standard of life for all by maintaining wage standards, 'rigorous observance of the Fair Wages Clause in public contracts', and by amending existing legislation 'to secure to every worker by hand or brain at least the prescribed minimum of health, education, leisure and subsistence'. The party supported a legal minimum wage and threatened industrial action to maintain these standards.

On the specific problem of unemployment, the party's resolution followed closely the policies proposed by Beatrice Webb in the minority report to the Poor Law Commission. It outlined two obligations of the government: (1) 'to arrange the next ten years' programme of national and local government works and services – including housing, schools, roads, railways, canals, harbours, afforestation, reclamation, etc. – as to be able to put this programme in hand, at such a rate and in such districts, as any temporary congestion of the Labour market may require'; and (2) to ensure 'that the aggregate total demand for labour shall be maintained, year in and year out, at an approximately even level'. The resolution stated that the second duty could be secured 'by nothing more difficult or more revolutionary than a sensible distribution of the public orders for works and services'. The Labour party also proposed a reformed system of unemployment insurance organized by the trade unions 'duly supplemented by the government subvention guaranteed by Part II of the Insurance Act'. In two subsequent pamphlets, the party expressed the prevailing view that the current unemployment was due to the dislocation of world trade worsened by the terms of the Versailles treaty (*Unemployment, the Peace and the Indemnity*, 1921) and its own view that all unemployed persons had the right to receive a benefit as long as they remained unemployed, regardless of their previous contribution (*Unemployment: A Labour Policy*, 1921).

The party's resolution on national finance called for an overhaul of the taxation system. National revenue should come 'mainly from direct taxation alike of land and accumulated wealth, and of income and profits, together with suitable imposts upon luxuries, and that death duties and the taxation upon earned income should be substantially increased and equitably regraded'. The party proposed to revise the system of land taxation, to abolish taxes on co-operative societies and to develop the Post Office Savings Bank 'into a national banking system for the common service of the whole community'. The party also called for a capital levy to pay off the war debt, which would exempt those with fortunes below £1,000 and use progressive tax rates. The social services would be extended and would be financed from inheritance taxes and increased progressivity in direct tax rates.

The party continued the work of refining its position in the early 1920s. Arthur Greenwood, the party's research director, chaired committees on taxation and the cost of living between 1920 and 1921.

Hugh Dalton worked on a number of committee memoranda; he later summarized their views as follows:

> My mind and that of many of my colleagues, including economists both inside and outside the Labour party at this time was on the price-level. We wanted to bring it down. 'Labour unrest' before the war, and since, was due to rising prices more than to unemployment. . . . I wanted deflation, and was not afraid to call it by that name, and was quite prepared to use part of the proceeds of the Capital Levy to bring in and cancel currency notes. . . . Keynes' criticism of [this policy], when mass unemployment had struck us – and we had more than a million unemployed in 1921 – first shook my faith, till then almost absolute, in Pigou's economic judgment: of the banks I was never so confident.[13]

Dalton's main contribution to the party's discussion of economic policy was his work on the capital levy. He wrote the Labour party's pamphlet, *Labour and the War Debt* (1922) and a book, *The Capital Levy Explained* (1923). The levy was designed as a deliberately redistributive measure to tax wealth and to reduce the war debt. He lobbied for its adoption in the election manifesto all over the country, first becoming known in the Labour movement for these activities. Both Snowden and MacDonald expressed to him their fear that the issue had lost the party a number of seats in the elections of 1923 and 1924.

Besides the capital levy, a number of other resolutions were adopted at party conferences. The most significant was introduced by Sidney Webb in 1925; it called 'for the Public ownership and control of the Banking and Credit System and the encouragement and development of Co-operative and Municipal Banks'.[14] The resolution recognized the importance of controlling investment to ensure the success of the party's development plans, as well as its socialist intent to reduce bank charges and profits. In his speech Webb also expressed his belief that private banking contributed to the destabilizing trade cycle. Although this debate marked the first time that the party had addressed the question of banking and investment policy directly, as with the other resolutions, no specific and legislative proposals were put forward.

To summarize, the party's long-term goal of socialism was to be introduced by nationalization of industry, which would remove the inefficiencies of capitalism, increase the level of aggregate production and introduce industrial democracy. Overall planning and a centralized banking system would ensure the maintenance of high levels of demand by organizing public investment more rationally between areas and over time. Inequality would be further reduced through increased social services financed by heavier taxation of the rich. Until socialism was introduced, the Labour party was mainly concerned with the immediate problem of alleviating the distress of the unemployed. The trade unions in particular were doubly concerned; unemployment undermined their bargaining power and the dole undermined wage standards. On the whole they were sceptical about public works because of their connotations of relief work and the dreaded Poor Law, which had pervaded the reality of working-class life for a century. Thus, the party's commitment to public works was ambivalent; as a planning goal for the organization of the labour market over the trade cycle public works were part of a long-run scheme, but as the basis for an immediate programme they were less important than instituting a universal system of non-contributory unemployment benefits financed from general revenues.

Snowden's economic policy

During his apprenticeship in the Independent Labour party (ILP) and as the party's chief spokesman on finance, Snowden had developed his own opinions on economic policy and on the appropriate economic strategy for introducing socialism. His biographer, Colin Cross, has summarized these principles under five main headings. First, Snowden was a free-trader because he believed tariffs increased the cost of food for the poor, made profits for the capitalists and were inefficient. Second, he did not believe that socialism should mean government extravagance, particularly because taxes were taken from the earnings of the poor. Third, he held that the budget should always run a surplus so that the national debt could be paid off; he felt that the interest payments redistributed income away from the workers to the rentiers. Fourth, he wanted to concentrate taxation on a progressive income tax, to abolish indirect taxes on food and to increase death duties. Fifth, he expected to increase the total amount paid in taxes in order to finance new social services; he was opposed to Lloyd George's contributory insurance schemes for this reason. Indeed, he firmly believed that the rich could afford to pay for a wide array of services to the poor.

Snowden believed that taxation and budget policy should be used to remedy the injustices of capitalism, but that they should not be used to manipulate the economy. He was a gradualist of the evolutionary MacDonald kind, who felt that responsible finance would be run on the same principles under socialism as under capitalism. In addition, he agreed with most socialists that unemployment was an inevitable consequence of the capitalist system and would only disappear with the abolition of capitalism. Meanwhile, the idea of fiddling with the value of money filled him with horror; 'it was as much the elementary duty of civilised government to maintain the value of money as to run a police force to check theft'.[15] Snowden was a self-educated man, respected for his terse lucidity and diligent research. Cross has suggested that by the time he became chancellor his clarity had 'hardened into prejudice'; he seemed to confuse 'the mechanical tools of economics with the moral principles of thrift and frugality on which from childhood he lived his own life'.[16]

Snowden defined his perception of his role as chancellor in a speech to the House of Commons in July 1924:

> It is no part of my job as Chancellor of the Exchequer to put before the House of Commons proposals for the expenditure of public money. The function of the Chancellor of the Exchequer, as I understand it, is to resist all demands for expenditure made by his colleagues and, when he can no longer resist, to limit the concession to the barest point of acceptance.[17]

In particular, he resisted the expenditure of public money on public works, unless they were sound investments in their own right. He believed that unemployment could not be cured quickly, and a cure could only happen if costs of production were reduced, particularly in the export industries. Snowden also supported the return to the gold standard, and thereafter accepted it as part of the fixed order of the economy.

Snowden's point of view was widely accepted in the Labour party and his policies were applauded by his colleagues. His financial secretary at the Treasury, William Graham (whom Cross describes as 'the nearest thing Snowden ever had to a son'), was in full agreement, calling in August 1924 for a 'sound and healthy deflation'.[18] Even Beatrice Webb commented in her diary after his budget speech, 'Philip has had a great triumph . . . he has turned out to be the best available Chancellor.'[19] The contrast between Snowden's conservative financial views and his fervent socialist faith dramatically reflects the tortuous path which the Labour party had to tread between political respectability in establishment terms and policies that would gain political support from the struggling masses, in order to become a viable alternative government.

Dissent and policy revisions

The main source of disagreement with economic orthodoxy came from the ILP. As a faction within the Labour party, it became increasingly radical with the election to Parliament of the militant 'Clydesiders' in 1923. Its leaders challenged the vague promises of *Labour and the*

New Social Order and tried to get the party to adopt a more radical set of concrete proposals to achieve 'Socialism in Our Time'. One of its study groups chaired by J. A. Hobson, who had also served under G. D. H. Cole on advisory committees for the Labour party, produced a detailed policy statement, *The Living Wage* (1926). This report proposed a system of family allowances financed through direct taxation, the nationalization of the Bank of England to control credit and monetary policy and the establishment of a national minimum wage. The basic rationale was the familiar underconsumption thesis that by increasing wages and consumption, production would rise and unemployment would fall. Income would be redistributed by raising working-class incomes directly, rather than indirectly through taxation and social expenditure policies.

Frank Wise, a former civil servant who was to become the chief left-wing spokesman on finance in the early 1930s, led the ILP attack on Snowden's policies and tried unsuccessfully to get the ILP measures adopted at successive conferences in the late 1920s. This rebellion against the party line was not so much directed against official policy, as against gradualism, and particularly a gradualism without strategy or purpose. It was a revolt against the utopian philosophy of leaders such as MacDonald and Snowden, who believed that socialism would evolve of its own course out of the natural decay of capitalism.

Far more serious in the long run were the disagreements over orthodox policies which were beginning to come from the moderate trade unionists, in particular Ernest Bevin. Always suspicious of financial interests, according to his biographer, Alan Bullock, Bevin was 'one of the first to grasp' the implications of the return to the gold standard in 1925 and to understand Keynes's polemic against it.[20] Bevin recognized that any attempt to be more competitive in world markets meant wage cuts and longer hours for British workers, and that such deflationary policies would only increase unemployment. Yet, in contrast to the ILP, Bevin only disagreed with the party leaders on economic grounds. Politically he supported MacDonald against the ILP at the crucial 1927 and 1928 conferences.

Other critics of the party's economic policies, such as Sir Oswald Mosley, were less powerful in the long run, but attracted more attention in the short run. In contrast to the stress on taxation policy in *The Living Wage*, Mosley's group concentrated on monetary policy, many of their ideas being similar to those expressed in the Liberal party's Yellow Book. A few other voices were heard in the wilderness. Cole spoke vehemently against the return to prewar parity, likening it somewhat dramatically to 'a Great God named Par who is worshipped daily at the Treasury. . . . Par likes unemployment; it is his form of human sacrifice'.[21] F. W. Pethick-Lawrence, who became Snowden's financial secretary in 1929 and an influential party adviser in the 1930s, also spoke against the gold standard.

Dalton, who entered the House of Commons in 1924, gained a reputation as a 'financial expert', which, he said, 'was not very difficult in those days. . . . I got quite a long way by rising, in the middle of some pundit's speech, and saying: "The right honourable gentleman means Treasury *Bonds*, I think, not Treasury *Bills*"'.[22] However, he also ran foul of Snowden on two scores: first, he spoke in favour of imperial preference to reduce tariffs on certain imports; and, second, he opposed the return to the gold standard at prewar parity. Persuaded by Keynes he argued that it was premature and deflationary. In 1926 Dalton was elected to the party's national executive committee (NEC), where he served as a leading policy maker for the next twenty-five years; 'a very good innings' he noted in his memoirs, when 'other people began to write memoranda for me!'[23]

The work of drafting a revised policy statement for the Labour party began at the end of 1927. Mosley, who was on the drafting committee, wrote to MacDonald 'urging the Labour party to carry out a revision of monetary policy, on the lines advocated by Keynes and McKenna'.[24] Although many of the proposals found their way into the final report, the wording was vague. In the end R. H. Tawney wrote the final draft, titled *Labour and the Nation*. It stated the moral case for gradual socialism under five main principles – an increased standard of living, 'step by step' nationalization of industry, the extension of social services, the adjustment of taxation and international peace and co-opera- tion. It was, if anything, less specific and forthright than the earlier *Labour and the New Social Order*. There was a heavy emphasis on social services of all kinds, including unemployment compensation, but only the vaguest commitment to industry nationalization, with the exception of coal. 'National finance' consisted of various tax measures, all guaranteed to be 'scientifically adjusted' to the ability to pay and 'the progressive reduction of expenditure on armaments'. There was no mention of overall budgetary policy, except under 'development of industry and trade', where it was proposed to introduce 'more stringent control of Banking and Credit, and their closer adaptation to the needs of industry'. The aim of the party was to obtain a 'Socialist Commonwealth' of all nations, to reduce conflict and promote co- operation which was 'the law of life'. The party made 'an unqualified pledge' to deal immediately and practically with unemployment, repu- diating as 'an outrage' the suggestion that unemployed workers were not anxious to obtain employment. The structural problems of casual employment and distressed areas arising from 'the surplus of labour in certain industries' were recognized, and 'permanent machinery for the prevention of unemployment' was promised.[25] The document was discussed at the 1928 party conference, where Philip Snowden also moved the adoption of a separate draft memorandum on banking and currency.[26]

This report called for the reorganization of the Bank of England as a public corporation, the creation of more municipal banks and a policy of stable domestic prices and foreign exchange values, but did not mention the party's earlier commitment to nationalize the joint stock banks. Snowden defended this position, stressing the importance of keeping the Bank of England 'free from political influences' and minimizing the role of the commercial banks. Speaking for the ILP, Frank Wise disputed both points. He argued that the City already had a Conservative bias, and that without control over capital formation and investment finance, 'we can say "good-bye" for a very long time to many of the items at present in our programme', in particular the development plans to reduce unemployment. Dalton and Pethick-Lawrence both spoke in favour of the report and against nationalizing the joint stock banks; Dalton in high-flown metaphor claimed they were 'little minnows by the side of the whale'. With a few minor amendments, *Labour and the Nation* and the banking memorandum were passed without a division.

The Liberal election manifesto, *We Can Conquer Unemployment*, contained much more detailed and specific plans for dealing with unemployment than Labour was offering. Cole composed a reply, *How to Conquer Unemployment: Labour's Reply to Lloyd George*, which criticized the Liberal plan as insufficient and based on 'madcap finance'. Dalton, who was in the thick of policy making as a member of the NEC, was frustrated by the failure to get a strong platform, commenting in his diary: 'We are letting L. G. and Mond-Turner and the rest simply march past us. We are led by timid, nerveless old men.'[27] He had been especially impressed with Keynes's 'lucid positive Employment Policy', but he did not join forces with Oswald Mosley, noting of him as early as 1927 that 'he often shows a surprising lack of judgment'.[28]

The electorate rejected the Tory programme of 'Safety First', based on orthodox arguments against public works, and voted in 287 Labour members, 59 Liberals and 261 Tories. Thus, the Labour party formed a minority government dependent upon Liberal support for the second time.

The second Labour government, 1931 and the aftermath

Early hopes that the Labour government would provide a fresh approach were quickly dissipated in the deep world depression which followed the American stock market crash of October 1929. However, it only gradually became apparent that the government had neither the will nor the ability to devise an effective policy to prevent the dramatic increase in unemployment. Even more disturbing from the perspective of its socialist supporters, it also became clear that the Labour government had neither immediate plans nor long-term strategies for introducing a significant degree of socialism. Thus, even before the financial and political crises of the summer of 1931, a sense of disillusion and frustration mounted within the Labour party.

With the onset of world depression the disputes of the 1920s erupted into major confrontations between economic conservatives and radical interventionists, between deflationists and expansionists, between free traders and protectionists, between the savers of capitalism and the defenders of class interests. These divisions followed no traditional party boundaries, particularly when Britain's national honour was called in question. Even staunch believers in the self-regulating market were forced to recognize that some form of government intervention was inevitable. Meanwhile, the expansionists, led by Keynes, were beginning to realize that tariff protection might be necessary to create jobs without sacrificing the pound. Whether intervention should continue to defend the pound or not, whether other forms of intervention to cope with unemployment could be devised – these became the burning economic policy questions of the second Labour government.

The government initiated two major thrusts to tackle the unemployment problem, a job-creation programme and a bill liberalizing some aspects of unemployment insurance. The second, which the trade unions sought, also attempted to put the whole scheme on a more secure financial footing. Both measures were doomed to failure after the onslaught of the depression. The failure of the first led to basic questioning of the practical and theoretical problems of an expansionary employment policy; the failure of the second helped to bring down the government.

The government made some headway on the general provision of social services, but nothing dramatic enough to mark a major step forward in the reduction of inequality. Arthur Greenwood, the minister of health, reactivated a housing subsidy scheme and pursued a vigorous slum-clearance programme. On other matters little progress was made. Charles Trevelyan at the board of education failed to get his bill raising the school-leaving age to fifteen past the House of Lords. More indicative of the government's weakness to its own supporters was the failure to undo the despised Trades Disputes Act put through by the Tories after the general strike. As these failures to initiate significant progress towards socialism mounted, the government was becoming increasingly preoccupied with the problems of propping up capitalism and preventing the worst effects of the depression from hitting the British working class.

The revised unemployment insurance scheme aimed to increase benefits and to place its fund on a 'sounder' financial basis. Its effect was to increase the annual payment from the exchequer even faster than unemployment. When cuts in government expenditure were demanded to maintain confidence in the pound in August 1931, these government expenditures seemed a natural place to start, because the fall in prices also meant that the standard of living of those receiving unemployment benefits had actually risen. But for Labour supporters the unemployment benefit had become the symbol of forcing the poorest to pay for the obvious failures of the monetary authorities and of the capitalist system as a whole.

The government also tried to promote public works by local authorities and to organize rationalization schemes for inefficient industries, but they discovered many practical obstacles to a more effective job-creation programme. First, they had little direct control over public works, because the Treasury had successfully shifted the responsibility for initiating, operating and financing public works to local authorities. Second, the time lags between authorizing projects and actually starting construction proved much longer than anticipated. However, the main block was Snowden, who concurred with his advisers in the Treasury and the Bank of England that public works were useless at best and inflationary at worst. While he was in power, he continued to resist to the best of his considerable ability all attempts to squeeze extra funds for such purposes out of the exchequer. Snowden's strict adherence to orthodox finance acted as another depressant on the economy, for he insisted on balancing the budget and on repaying the national debt. As a lifelong free trader he also vigorously opposed any attempts to expand domestic employment behind a protective barrier against foreign imports.

Although the Labour government was short on programmes and strategies for dealing with unemployment, it was long on economic advice. One of MacDonald's first acts was to set up an official inquiry into the relationship of finance to industry, chaired by Lord Macmillan. Keynes and T. E. Gregory were appointed as its economists, and Ernest Bevin as the union representative. This was followed in January 1930 by the organization of the Economic Advisory Council (EAC), the first time a British government was to receive official advice on economic policy on a regular basis. The prime minister chaired its deliberations, with Hubert Henderson as the permanent secretary in charge of four other officials. Among its fifteen appointed members were Bevin and Walter Citrine representing the trade unions, Cole, Keynes, Tawney and Sir Josiah Stamp as economists, two bankers, five industrialists and two scientists. Later, when it proved impossible to extract any consensus on unemployment policy from the larger group, Keynes persuaded MacDonald to set up a smaller committee of economists with himself in the chair, Henderson, Stamp, Professor Pigou from Cambridge and the recently appointed Professor Lionel Robbins from the London School of Economics. Colin Clark was hired as a junior assistant for the council and Richard Kahn for the committee of economists.

On the whole, the council has been judged a failure because it did not live up to the claims made on its behalf, nor did it exercise a major influence on the policies actually pursued by the government.[29] However, the EAC did have some important repercussions on the future development of the Labour party's policies. First, it provided the prime minister with his own economic staff and ready access to the advice of prestigious experts. In the case of Keynes, it also meant that the leading opponent of the orthodox policies of the Treasury and the Bank of England had the prime minister's ear. Second, other Labour members of the council, Bevin, Citrine and Cole in particular, were to benefit enormously from their education through its deliberations, as well as the Macmillan committee's, which enabled them to understand the political, as well as the economic, implications of the government's policy options in 1931.

The EAC failed to make any clear-cut recommendations because of the fundamental split between the economists and the businessmen on the central issue of expanding the domestic economy. While Snowden tried to prevent discussions of free trade, monetary policy or government's responsibility for unemployment, Keynes hurt MacDonald's feelings by describing himself as 'the only Socialist present'.[30] Matters were no better on the committee of economists. Although Keynes persuaded the majority to recommend a 10 per cent revenue tariff and an expansionary public works programme, he failed to win a consensus for the final report in October 1930. Even among those who signed with him – Henderson, Stamp and Pigou – there was a series of fights and endless redrafts. Robbins completely disassociated himself from Keynes's recommendations and wrote his own dissenting report, an emotional plea for free trade.[31]

By early 1931 it was becoming evident that rising unemployment was putting pressure on the budget through decreased revenues and increased unemployment benefits, while the international liquidity crisis was beginning to put pressure on the pound. In December 1930 Snowden had set up a royal commission to look into the problem of the large and rapidly growing debt of the unemployment insurance fund, and in February 1931 he appointed the May committee to inquire independently into ways to cut public expenditure. Yet, his April budget was very mild. It was not until May that the Credit-Anstalt collapsed and the shaky international monetary system began to unravel.

In June the royal commission on unemployment insurance reported that a solvent and self-supporting fund was not possible in the present conditions and recommended curtailed borrowing, a twenty-six-week limit to benefits and a means test for those whose benefits had run out. A group of one hundred trade union MPs rejected the commission's recommendations; the means test in particular enraged Labour supporters by resurrecting the hated dole and raising the spectre of the dreaded Poor Law, the very antithesis of all they stood for. Eventually the government had to back away from implementing the report. This vacillation, the actuarial chaos of the fund and the relatively 'high' benefits became the symbols of the Labour government's financial unsoundness.[32] At the same time the political message to Labour leaders was unambiguous; the unemployed must not be sacrificed to balance the budget by the Labour party.

In mid-July the Macmillan committee released its report, strongly recommending a policy of managed currency and price stability. In an addendum, written largely by Keynes, the case for expansionary policy was convincingly stated, but the argument was explicitly presented as a long-term view, not intended for dealing with the short-term liquidity crisis facing the government. Bevin fought a rearguard battle to recommend leaving the gold standard; in the end he signed the report but suggested that the Treasury and Bank should be looking for 'an alternative basis', if Britain could not expand without devaluation. In late July the May committee recommended a drastic £96 million cut to balance the budget including the £66 million from unemployment insurance. Unlike the judicious Macmillan report, this one was widely publicized, adding to the hysteria. Keynes attacked the majority report in private letters to the prime minister (to whom he said that the recommendations would result in a 'most gross perversion of justice') and in an article in the New Statesman.[33]

It was in this atmosphere that the cabinet was hastily summoned back to London in early August. They were told that the government must immediately meet a deficit of £78 million, in order to regain foreign confidence and secure loans from the United States and France. They agreed upon cuts amounting to £56 million, but they could not agree on a £22 million cut in unemployment benefits proposed by Snowden. At this point a crucial meeting was held between representatives of the general council of the TUC led by Bevin and the cabinet's economy committee. The TUC recommended suspension of the sinking fund, new taxation on all fixed-interest-bearing securities, a graduated levy to replace the unemployment insurance fund and a possible revenue tariff. There was a bitter fight between Bevin and Snowden; according to the TUC minutes, Bevin emphasized that 'the Government's proposals meant a continuance of the deflation policy, and to that the council was opposed'.[34] In the crucial vote on 24 August, Henderson, Clynes, Graham, Greenwood, Alexander, Lansbury, Johnston, Adamson and Addison voted against the unemployment cuts, and the cabinet was split. After the formation of the National government Snowden introduced an Economy Bill, which the House of Commons passed on 10 September. The government got its new foreign credits, but the run on the pound continued. On 21 September, Britain went off the gold standard, and the pound fell by more than a quarter.

The attribution of responsibility for the 1931 crisis and its political implications were feverishly debated at the time and are still matters of substantial controversy among historians and political commentators. Skidelsky, for example, has argued that the party's commitment to 'Utopian Socialism' prevented the government from understanding the relevance of the unorthodox economic radicalism propounded by Keynes and others, and 'doomed it to failure and sterility in this crucial period'.[35] Contradicting this view, McKibbin has concluded that the government's policy was actually highly unorthodox in comparison to other countries, because 'relatively generous social services were not only maintained but somewhat increased in scope' and 'no serious attempt was made to balance the budget'.[36] Winch and Marquand consider that the truth was far more complex, and that the cases for economic orthodoxy and unorthodoxy were not clear-cut. Marquand has concluded that the real tragedy of the second Labour government was not that its approach was too orthodox, but that 'after its first six months in office that approach ceased to be relevant'.[37]

It is hardly surprising that Labour party supporters at the time should have viewed the whole affair as a bankers' ramp, or as Dalton later called it, 'money-lenders' madness'.[38] The cabinet was obviously misled on some crucial issues, although it is not clear that it was deliberate. Sidney Webb was said to have remarked when Britain went off the gold standard, 'We were not told we could do that'. Marquand has verified that this option was never discussed in the cabinet. During the discussion of foreign loans, Addison later told Dalton that he had asked whether it would be better and cheaper to leave the gold standard right then. In reply, 'Snowden was more insulting to him than anyone had ever been in his life before'; but none of his colleagues backed him up, and the cabinet passed on. Snowden's last proposals to the Labour cabinet still contained the £50 million for debt repayment, which he reduced to £30 million in his September economy bill, enough to offset the previously proposed cut in unemployment benefits.

Consequently, it is also understandable that Labour party members felt utterly betrayed by MacDonald and Snowden, and hastened to expel them from the party. These feelings were intensified when MacDonald, contravening an earlier promise, dissolved Parliament in late September; they were confirmed when the new government won by a landslide in October. The electorate had been convinced that the Labour party was spendthrift and irresponsible, and that a coalition government was necessary to cope with a national financial emergency. Although many historians now agree that the prime minister did not deliberately plot to lead a national government, it still remains an extraordinary step for a lifelong socialist leader to collaborate with the Conservative party. Marquand has suggested that the rejection of Keynes's recommendation to devalue was 'the most tragic, as well as the most disastrous, mistake of MacDonald's life'.[39] However, MacDonald also rejected similar advice more consistently presented by his own supporters.

Keynes had first proposed the revenue tariff in confidential committee reports in 1930. However, in March 1931 he went public in an article for the *New Statesman*, which caused a huge furore.[40] Although he continued to press for the revenue tariff, he explicitly recommended *against* devaluation in the Macmillan committee report. In early August, Keynes proposed that the prime minister seek advice on the choice between deflation and devaluation, and fancifully suggested a 'Committee consisting of all living ex-chancellors of the exchequer'.[41] He assured MacDonald that 'many people, even in the City – very likely the governor of the Bank of England himself' were in favour of devaluation 'at the bottom of their hearts'. Next week Keynes published his article criticizing the May committee in which he recommended suspension of the sinking fund, continued borrowing for unemployment benefits and the revenue tariff; he did *not* mention devaluation. Needless to say, the governor of the Bank did not recommend devaluation, nor did Snowden, nor Hubert Henderson as the other economic adviser, nor the Treasury nor the City. Keynes's tariff strategy was doomed from the start, given Snowden's position and the government's dependence on Liberal free traders to stay in power. It also confused the situation by deflecting attention from the overvalued pound and by adding fuel to the clamour for protection by special-interest groups: definitely not Keynes's most constructive intervention.

If devaluation was the appropriate policy for August 1931, Bevin had been arguing for it longer and more consistently than Keynes. On the Macmillan committee he had stated his view that there was no solution to the unemployment problem until Britain went off the gold standard. At the April meeting of the EAC in 1931, he declared that the gold standard was not 'sacrosanct' and only stood to profit the rentier classes. Bevin did not believe in tariffs, but he preferred them to wage cuts. MacDonald was fully aware of the party's commitment to the unemployed; indeed, he had been one of the architects of the 'Work or Maintenance' policy, worked out by the fledgling Labour Representation Committee in 1907. Henderson had worked together with him at that time, as he had sternly reminded a group of ministers 'babbling about abuses and anomalies' as early as October 1930, according to Dalton's diary. The tragedy was that MacDonald did not listen to the voices of his own supporters.

At a fundamental level, the policy options before the Labour government were political rather than financial. There was no course of action, acceptable to opposition leaders, to foreign bankers and to Labour's rank and file, which the cabinet could also agree was socially just.[42] In the final analysis, MacDonald sided with the orthodox views of Snowden and his advisers against continued and consistent arguments for different options by important and influential Labour leaders. In the hysterical atmosphere of August 1931, MacDonald was seriously misled by all his advisers (except Keynes and Bevin), who wildly exaggerated the dangerous repercussions of devaluation. By deciding to negotiate for a government of national unity, MacDonald had been persuaded that the crisis raised issues of national survival, rather than questions of class interest and party loyalty. This diagnosis was soon demonstrated to be completely wrong; the financial crisis was resolved when Britain devalued, not when unemployment benefits were cut.

Conclusions

In the broad context Britain's second Labour government was one of the earlier political casualties of the world depression, which saw incumbent governments ditched by a frustrated electorate in many countries. In the United States and Sweden, for example, governments pursuing conservative economic policies were swept aside by more left-wing interventionists. In Germany, in contrast, the social democrats were defeated by the ominous rise of Hitler, who promised right-wing intervention by a fascist corporate state. In Britain, the National government remained in control throughout the decade, although when Baldwin replaced MacDonald in 1935 the coalition façade had disappeared for all practical purposes. The exchange problem was resolved by devaluation, and an era of protection was ushered in. Thus, the political and economic stage was set for the 1930s.

With the benefit of hindsight it is obvious that expansionary policies did not stand a chance under the second Labour government, given the orthodoxy of Snowden, the Treasury and the Bank of England. However, the strength of the argument for sound finance within the Labour movement should not be minimized either. MacDonald was after all returned with a large majority as prime minister, and most of the rebellious cabinet members were defeated. Apart from the appeal to the British to rally to defend the country from outside influences (Britain's Armada complex), many working-class socialists, such as Snowden, never doubted for a moment that the principles of sound finance would apply to the socialist state as well as to the capitalist. Their eyes were fixed on the redistribution of income through taxation, equal opportunity through social programmes and public control of industry through nationalization. They might vote for nationalizing the banks, but they did not question that the budget would have to be balanced and the national debt repaid on time. Nor should the commitment to free trade be underestimated. Even Dalton had supported Snowden and Robbins against Keynes, noting in his diary on 23 October 1930: 'I was taught to despise Protectionism at Cambridge. I do so still.'

Many of MacDonald's critics within the party rattled revolutionary sabres, but lacked any plans for the class war they seemed to advocate. Even middle-of-the-road efforts to promote expansionary policies as the cure for unemployment were similarly hamstrung. On the one hand, there were programmes such as Mosley's, which appeared to be duplications of Liberal tinkering to mend the capitalist system. On the other hand, serious efforts to develop distinct socialist solutions to the unemployment problem were based either upon extravagant expenditure on social services or upon demands to nationalize the entire banking system, or some combination of the two. All these proposals raised the spectre of a direct confrontation with the establishment and threatened the attempts to promote the party as a respectable alternative government.

The main effect of the 1931 crisis on the party's policy outlook was to reject the gradual evolutionary approach which MacDonald and Snowden symbolized. The generation of leaders who replaced them were determined to come up with a thoroughly worked-out practical programme and strategy to introduce socialism to Britain. They had also been alerted to the transitional problems raised by the impact of socializing measures on Britain's financial position, particularly on the foreign and domestic owners of capital. Party advisers began to ask fundamental questions about the nature of finance and credit policy in a socialist state, as their leaders demanded to know more about the role of finance and banking in the capitalist economy in order to avoid another 1931-type catastrophe. These questions led socialist economists to consider the modern problems of growth, investment, fiscal and monetary management and to move beyond a narrowly distributional approach based on neoclassical microeconomics.

At the same time, the continued and intensifying unemployment problem in Britain precipitated major policy controversies across a broad spectrum of political views. The contradictions between traditional market explanations of unemployment and daily reality were already spurring the exploration of new theoretical constructs to explain the apparent failure of the market system. Socialist economists were naturally drawn into these theoretical and practical debates, since they were anxious to find solid grounds for rejecting the principles of sound finance which had split the party. Thus both the intellectual ferment within the economics profession and the policy exigencies of the divided and defeated Labour party opened up the way for socialist economists to examine the problems of economic management and its role in the socialist state.

PART II
THE SEARCH

CHAPTER 4
NEW BROOMS, NEW POLICIES: THE LABOUR PARTY 1931–5

The combination of economic depression and political crisis had a profound effect on the Labour party in the early 1930s.[1] The experience stirred deep emotions among Labour supporters, which left no one unmarked. It also raised fundamental questions about the role of the Labour party, for it seemed as though the only choice was between capitulation to the market forces of capitalism or preparation for a drastic take-over of the economic system. While MacDonald and Snowden represented capitulation, extremists to the right and to the left were also abandoning the party to advocate different forms of intervention. Mosley opted for the fascist version of government intervention through the development of state corporatism at home and imperial markets abroad. John Strachey and others who saw no hope for market recovery became convinced Marxists, and some joined the Communist party. Of those who remained in the Labour party, many pushed for a policy of immediate nationalization of banks and basic industries and the assumption of emergency powers to circumvent the parliamentary process.

The remnants of the party's moderates led by Arthur Henderson, who had been elected chairman of the parliamentary Labour party (PLP) after the August crisis, hurriedly put together an election manifesto when Parliament was dissolved in early October. Titled 'Labour's Call to Action: The Nation's Opportunity', the document reaffirmed the party's 'faith in the considered principles of its programme of 1929 laid down in *Labour and the Nation*'. Yet in many ways this was misleading, for the programme, which was debated at the annual conference in Scarborough, contained many more specific proposals and an important shift in emphasis. For instance, the conference condemned the gold standard, tariffs, deflationary policies and 'curr-

ency inflation'; it resolved to bring 'the banking and credit system of
the country . . . under public ownership', to create 'a national investment board with statutory powers in relation to both home and foreign
investment' and 'to stabilise wholesale prices at a reasonable level'; it
also proposed to reorganize as public utilities 'the most important
basic industries, such as Power, Transport, Iron and Steel', as well as
coal. Understandably, the party rejected Snowden's method of
balancing the budget by means of cuts and pledged itself to maintain
and develop the social services and to restore 'the urgent claims of the
unemployed'.

The conference accepted most of the resolutions unanimously, but
there were some efforts to present a more radical tone. In the drafting
stage Attlee wrote a memorandum on 'industrial policy' in which he
stated:

> It is, I think, now beyond doubt that the position of London as
> the centre of world capitalism is incompatible with a socialist
> regime or even a 'moderate' Labour Government. 'The City' in the
> middle of a socialist state is as anomalous as would be the Pope
> in Moscow.[2]

He also called for 'more drastic and complete nationalisation of
important industries straight away'. At the conference Frank Wise, one
of the co-authors of *The Living Wage* and member of the Independent
Labour party (ILP), introduced an amendment to specify the nationalization of the Bank of England and the joint stock banks.

However, Bevin opposed the amendment in an eloquent speech. He
described his attempts to get the conference to abandon its hopes of
achieving socialism by progressive taxation and industry nationalization in the late 1920s; he told of his appeals to the party, to the
Macmillan committee and even to 'Mr. Keynes and other Professors',
'to tackle the very basis of finance – the gold standard'. He believed
himself that the control of money was the key to introducing socialism:
'You can talk about socialising your railways and other things;
socialise credit and the rest is comparatively easy'. Wise dropped his
amendment, and the Labour party went to the country on a platform
opposing the gold standard, tariffs, unemployment benefit cuts, and
offering nationalization and monetary control as the alternatives. Their
slogan was: 'We must plan or perish'.

The Tories in the National government had tried to persuade
MacDonald to include protection in their election promises. But
knowing he would lose Snowden and some Liberals on this issue,
MacDonald asked for 'a doctor's mandate'. It was a bitter campaign,
with Snowden hurling invective and scorn at his erstwhile comrades;

Runciman, the Liberal president of the board of trade in the National government, threatened that Labour would confiscate deposits in the Post Office Savings Bank to meet the budget deficit. This scare tactic had a lasting impact on Dalton and other moderates, convincing them that too much nationalization, particularly of financial institutions, could alienate thrifty working-class people and moderate middle-class voters.

The election was a disaster for the Labour party. It was reduced to fifty-two seats in the House of Commons, with its leadership decimated. The seventy-year-old George Lansbury was the sole surviving cabinet member; consequently, he was elected chairman of the PLP. Of the remaining MPs, only Attlee and Cripps had had ministerial experience. Henderson lost his seat and did not return to the House of Commons until 1933; he remained secretary and treasurer of the Labour party until his death in 1935. Hugh Dalton and Herbert Morrison, who became prominent members of the party's national executive committee (NEC), did not re-enter the House of Commons until 1935.

Although weak in its effect on national policies, the Labour party remained a vital and vocal part of the British political scene in the 1930s. In the public arena the party was much given to passionate controversies between left and right, between pacificism and rearmament, between Popular Fronts and United Fronts. But in less frantic settings, in the policy subcommittee of the NEC, in the economic committee of the Trades Union Congress (TUC), in Fabian pamphlets, committees and conferences and in a variety of unofficial research groups, an organized and deliberate effort was made to rethink the principles of democratic socialism and to articulate a coherent and electorally viable policy, which would deal with the problems faced by a future Labour government committed to reforming British society along socialist lines.

New organizations

The policy subcommittee of the NEC was the main vehicle within the party structure for generating research, discussion and formal policy recommendations. In addition, the TUC had organized its own forum for discussing policy questions and taking resolutions to its general council. Together these bodies must be credited with the main work of thrashing out the party's new programme in the early 1930s. These committees also made use of the research undertaken by a number of unofficial groups founded in reaction to the failure of the second

Labour government. The most important of these were the Society for Socialist Inquiry and Propaganda (SSIP, pronounced 'zip'), the New Fabian Research Bureau (NFRB) and the XYZ club.

The policy subcommittee of the Labour party

After the 1931 election the NEC reorganized its own policy subcommittee by setting up four standing committees with the power to co-opt members; it also appointed advisory panels for itself and the policy subcommittee, as well as a series of ad hoc committees on special topics. All of these operated throughout the 1930s. The four crucial policy committees were on finance and trade, on reorganization of industry, on local government and social services and on constitutional matters. They were responsible for drafting policy resolutions for the NEC to present to the annual conference for debate, amendment and formal acceptance (or rejection) as the party's official position.

The finance and trade committee (FTC) was chaired by Hugh Dalton; it developed the institutional reforms and the financial policy appropriate to introduce socialism. The reorganization of industry committee, chaired by George Latham, but with Herbert Morrison as a prime mover, produced detailed plans for the nationalization of specific industries. The local government and social services committee, chaired at first by Morrison but later by others, thrashed out some of the social programmes which were to form the basis of the postwar 'welfare state'. The constitutional committee, on which Sir Stafford Cripps and Harold Laski served, dealt with the legal powers necessary to implement Labour's policies. It was for these committees that literally hundreds of memoranda, some of monograph length, were written by a wide variety of socialist sympathizers throughout the 1930s.

Dalton and Morrison dominated the policy subcommittee of the NEC throughout the period. Although very different in temperament and background, they got along well together; they shared a common commitment to developing a practical programme for the party, which would broaden its electoral base. Dalton was passionately committed to Labour party politics, particularly after his adoption as the candidate for the depressed Durham mining constituency of Bishop Auckland in the 1920s. Once in Parliament he became an expert on finance and foreign affairs and very close to Arthur Henderson, whom he served as under-secretary in the Foreign Office during the second Labour government. An energetic writer, speaker and organizer, he was known as an inveterate schemer and a great cultivator of young talent. Like Cole and Tawney, he was also deeply attached to the English countryside and fond of taking long tramps, particularly over his beloved Wiltshire Downs.

In contrast to this Old Etonian and Cambridge economist of cosmopolitan tastes and experience, Herbert Morrison was a Londoner through and through. It was his unique role as the highly successful secretary of the London Labour party in the 1920s which first won him national recognition within the movement. Born in 1888, the son of a Brixton police constable with high Tory principles, Morrison was brought up in a stable lower-middle-class neighbourhood of clerks and public employees like his father, whose values he was later to represent in the Labour party. Morrison was educated at local schools before entering the movement as a part-time organizer and journalist. While still in his teens, he was active in his trade union, the National Union of Clerks, but it was as chairman of the Brixton ILP that he first discovered his natural flair and enthusiasm for party organization. Chosen as secretary of the London Labour party in 1915, he remained in the thick of London Labour politics for the next twenty-five years. In 1923 he won the Hackney South parliamentary seat for Labour for the first time; although he lost in 1924, he was back in the House of Commons again in 1929. Since he gained a great deal of experience and public notice for his campaigns to municipalize London's electricity and transport, he was a natural choice as minister of transport in the second Labour government. In March 1931 he entered the cabinet.

A reserved man personally, unlike the ebullient and outspoken Dalton, Morrison was none the less a genial companion and 'a master of cheeky banter'.[3] A workaholic with 'a powerful urge for political activity and for domination', many considered him restlessly ambitious. An excellent minister, he was admired by the civil servants for his administrative ability; he had great respect for professionals and was good at winning personal loyalty among his colleagues. His biographers describe him as an exceptionally honest politician with a deep concern for the practical and the efficient; he was to say later that his supreme purpose in public life was 'the achievement of tidiness'. The prototypical Webbian, Morrison also became the spokesman of his own class; he recognized its significance as a new force in politics of vital importance to broaden the Labour party's base.

The economic committee of the TUC

Ernest Bevin and Walter Citrine had reorganized the structure of the TUC after the débâcle of the general strike. They set up an economic committee as a forum for discussing economic policy questions, where Bevin could report on developments at the Economic Advisory Council and the Macmillan committee. By the end of 1932 the committee had become the TUC's most influential policy body; Bevin spent a great deal of time with its secretary, Milne Bailey, drafting reports for the general council and the annual congress. Bullock, Bevin's biographer, does not think their declarations had much effect on the party's policy: the 'real value of the committee's work was in educating its own members and . . . members of the General Council in the discussion of economic problems'.[4] The committee drew up a report on *Tariffs and World Trade* in 1932, which did little to convince unionists of Bevin's view that tariffs were not necessarily evil and could serve a useful purpose in protecting the economy from external shocks. The major influence of the committee on Labour party policy was in its work on the public control of industry and trade. In major show-downs with Morrison in the early 1930s, the TUC ensured worker representation on the boards of nationalized industries; its nationalization plan for the coal industry was also adopted by the party in 1936. These confrontations confirmed Bevin's deep distrust of Morrison, already roused by Morrison's handling of the negotiations to set up the London Passenger Transport Board under the second Labour government.

One of the lessons learnt from the traumatic events of August 1931 was the pressing need for regular communication between the TUC, the party's NEC and the PLP. Consequently, two members of the party's NEC were invited to join the TUC's economic committee; Hugh Dalton and Herbert Morrison were chosen; and sat on it throughout the 1930s. In addition, the National Joint Council was reconstituted in the winter 1931–2. The executive committees of both the Labour party and the PLP were asked to send their chairman and two members to meet at least once a month with the chairman and six members of the TUC's General Council. Bullock has concluded that the Joint Council became 'the most authoritative body in the Labour movement in formulating policy, especially foreign affairs'.[5]

However, it was the power of Bevin's personality which ensured that the voice of the union movement was heard, not only in the councils and committees of the Labour party, but in regular attendance at the annual party conference, in public speaking all over the country and in advising business and government bodies. Born in a Somerset village without the name of his father on his birth certificate, Bevin grew up in great poverty, while his mother struggled to find work to support her family; she died when he was only eight, and he was cared for by his brothers and sisters. With only a rudimentary education, he started work as a manual labourer, and later as the driver of a horse-drawn delivery cart in Bristol. A regular chapel-going Baptist, he also attended Workers' Educational Association classes, and in 1908 became the secretary of a local right-to-work committee. In 1910 he joined the Dockers Union in the Bristol dockyards, where he discovered his extraordinary talents as an organizer and negotiator. Bevin rapidly rose to the position of national organizer, and in 1921 he was chosen secretary of the newly federated Transport and General Workers Union. He was elected to the General Council of the TUC in 1925, where he remained the most prominent union leader, until he was invited to join Churchill's wartime coalition as the minister of labour.

Bevin and Walter Citrine, the secretary of the TUC, dominated the trade union movement in the 1930s as organizers on behalf of union interests at the national level, as well as within the Labour party. Ross Martin has described their roles as 'complementary and reinforcing', despite their temperamental incompatibility and mutual personal antipathy.[6] Deeply loyal to the union movement, Bevin could be ruthless to those he considered irresponsible, and was particularly suspicious of political manipulators and 'clever' intellectuals. Yet he was a passionately eloquent speaker, with an expansive imagination, a direct simplicity and a remarkable capacity for sorting out the essentials of any situation. Citrine, by contrast, was cool and methodical, 'relying on the persuasiveness of carefully assembled data and logical exposition'. Later he was to say, 'I cannot now recall a single issue of first-class importance on which we seriously differed. On tactics, yes, but not on basic policy.'

New Cole groups: SSIP and NFRB

Almost a year before its climactic end, Margaret Cole discussed disappointment in the Labour government's performance with H. L. Beales, a reader in economic history at the London School of Economics (LSE), and R. S. Lambert, editor of the *Listener*. She was chosen to sound out her husband on what could be done 'to recall to Ministers the programme and policies on which they had fought the election'.[7] With the trade union support of Ernest Bevin and Arthur Pugh, the Coles arranged the series of conferences which gave birth to SSIP and NFRB.

SSIP was organized first in early 1931 with Bevin in the chair and Cole as one of the vice-chairmen. Its main purpose was to propagandize practical socialist policies and to 'ginger up' thinking and activity within the Labour party. The enthusiastic response to its organizational debut reflected the 'sorely needed heart lift to Socialists who had been near to leaving the Labour movement in despair at its sterility', according to Margaret Cole, the group's unofficial historian. Some party stalwarts were dubious about the intentions of these 'loyal grousers' after their experience with the ILP and 'Socialism in Our

Time', but the presence of Bevin and the exodus of MacDonald miti-
gated these fears to some extent.

Meanwhile, the NFRB got off the ground in March 1931 with the
blessings of the Webbs, Hugh Dalton and Arthur Henderson from
party headquarters. Cole had already produced its first publication,
Memorandum on a Plan of Research into Economic Policy before the
collapse of the Credit-Anstalt in May. Attlee chaired the Bureau's
executive committee for the first two years, followed by the Right
Honourable Christopher Addison. Dick Mitchison was the honorary
treasurer, Cole the honorary secretary until his resignation in 1935,
and Durbin and Gaitskell, assistant honorary secretaries. The Bureau's
research work was divided among three sections, the economic section,
the international section and the political section. Cole chaired the
socialization and workers' control subcommittees of the economic
section, but it was Gaitskell and Durbin who organized the rest of the
economic committees. Leonard Woolf was the prime organizer of the
international section with help from Richard Greaves. W. A. Robson
ran the political section, taking over from the erratic Harold Laski,
who left the Bureau's executive committee in 1933 after he was co-
opted into the party's constitutional subcommittee. Laski, the
professor of political science at LSE and a powerful left-wing orator,
was later elected to the party's NEC as a constituency representative.
He was widely known as a passionate participant in Victor Gollancz's
highly successful Left Book Club. Dame Margaret Cole felt that the
NFRB was 'not spectacular enough for Harold', unlike Addison and
Attlee, who were conscientious and helpful members of the executive.

The NFRB was born of frustation with the Labour government, as
well as with the original Fabian Society, which by the 1930s was
conducting little research and fast becoming 'moribund', according to
Margaret Cole. Finally, in 1939 the New Fabians and the 'old' Fabians
amalgamated to form the Fabian Society as it still exists today. The
NFRB, although much smaller and less prestigious, flourished
throughout the decade; it produced an astonishing number of
important and influential books, such as *Parliamentary Reform* by
Ivor Jennings, *Public Enterprise* edited by W. A. Robson, *The Road
to War* by a 'Small Group of Experts', *The People's Army* by L. Clive,
and books on Russia and Sweden following official visits by groups
of New Fabians. Various collective studies were also published by
members of the economic section, which, together with the numerous
pamphlets and countless unpublished memoranda, constitute the intellectual contribution to economic policy formation of the New Fabian
economists. Pimlott has credited 'the industrious and prolific New

Fabians' with introducing Keynesian policies to Labour policy through the work of its committees.

In the very early days Dalton and Morrison harboured some misgivings about the role of these groups because of their suspicions about Cole's reliability. In the case of Dalton, the feelings were aggravated by diametrically opposed views on two specific policy issues, emergency powers and nationalization of the joint stock banks. As early as 1918, Morrison had criticized Cole, who 'might do a little less research and lecturing and a little more of the rough and tumble work of the Labour Movement'.[8] Morrison also disagreed with Cole's views on worker participation in nationalized industries. Even a sympathetic commentator, A. W. Wright, has attributed official Labour's doubts about Cole to his own stubborn integrity and radical mistrust of Parliament. 'Somehow he was not quite sound, prone to reckless irresponsibility, a "permanent undergraduate" in Attlee's telling phrase.'[9]

These reactions were reinforced in the highly charged atmosphere following the National government's sweeping victory in October 1931. The NFRB was constantly offering to help the party, only to receive polite acknowledgment of its efforts. The Bureau's minutes of 22 January 1932, for example, record that the 'General Secretary reported conversations with Dalton in which the latter doubted if the Taxation Committee could serve any useful purpose'. However, by mid-1933 the tone had changed considerably. In June the general secretary reported to the NFRB executive 'that he had received a letter from Dalton on behalf of the Labour Party Committee on National Planning asking for a memo from the Bureau'. Finally, in November 1933 Cole reported that the policy committee had decided to accept our 'offer of cooperation'. Thereafter, much of the economic section's research activities were in direct response to a series of such requests, largely from Dalton. Eventually Durbin and Gaitskell were co-opted onto the finance and trade subcommittee in 1936.

The XYZ club

The earliest of the unofficial groups to work directly for Dalton's finance and trade committee was the XYZ club, or 'City Group' as it was identified in the NEC minutes. The club was founded in January 1932 by a few Labour sympathizers in the City, the centre of London's financial market, who felt that the Labour government had taken the blame for the City's unwise support of Austrian and German banks. Dalton recorded that he first met Nicholas Davenport, 'Toreador' of the *New Statesman*, at a lunch with Cripps in early September 1931, because 'we of the Policy Committee are trying to meet as many City blokes as possible these days'.[10] Later in the year Vaughan Berry organized a small group of City colleagues; he recalled on the thirtieth birthday of XYZ:

> In December 1931 I invited a few men to dinner to discuss the possibility of forming a small group which would meet regularly to discuss financial problems from a socialist point of view, and be ready to offer its help to the Labour Party. I was myself at that time an assistant manager of the Union Discount Company, in charge of their international business, in an excellent position during the gold-standard years to watch the development of the crisis. I had been horrified by the Labour Party's ignorance of the City machinery and their complete lack of contacts with the banking world. I felt that something must be done to break this apartheid and, as it would never be done by the director caste, it must be attempted by those lower down. Even on the managerial level, however, and in the course of business, I had met dozens of bank managers, I knew none who admitted to the mildest Labour sympathies, so I fell back on City editors as a start.[11]

Consequently, Berry invited Cecil Spriggs of the *Manchester Guardian* and Nicholas Davenport to the first meeting on 9 January 1932, together with Williamson, an accountant, and Quigley, a statistician with the Central Electricity Commission.

At this meeting they talked about 'the short-term position of the merchant banks'. They also discussed the club's policy and agreed that their object should be to 'provide the Labour leaders with advice on administrative financial problems'. They also decided to remain anonymous to protect their jobs ('those were really dark days for Labour sympathisers'). Berry later felt that it was also convenient for Dalton to refer grandly to 'my experts', conjuring up images of managing directors, rather than the reality of lowly middlemen and Fleet Street scribblers. In the early days the members were much in demand to instruct party members about the intricacies of money management in the City, in particular the handling of foreign loans in 1931 (Berry remembered a meeting at Rothschilds after the collapse of the Credit-Anstalt in May 1931 at which every bank was present and most surprised to see the others). Dalton introduced Berry to Bevin, and presumably to Colin Clark through whom Berry and Davenport were invited to speak at an NFRB/SSIP conference in late January 1932. The early members did not presume to be experts on economic policy and deplored postwar tendencies for economists to dominate the proceedings.

Berry later described the club's activities in the 1930s as follows:

> Meetings were held regularly until 1940 whenever we could secure

cheaply a private room – many at the Craven Hotel, Charing Cross, later at P.E.P., occasionally at members' houses, only rarely in the House of Commons. Early in 1932, through Middleton, [Assistant] General Secretary of the Labour Party, I offered our services to the Party, which accepted them at once. A meeting was held at Transport House with Greenwood, Pethick-Lawrence and Hugh Dalton to settle ways of co-operation. Hugh Dalton became our chief liaison and thereafter practically a member. . . . Labour leaders who came as guests included Attlee, Pethick, Cripps and, an interested and useful contributor, Lees-Smith. Other guests were infrequent as most papers were the work of members and the club generally was kept, not much more intimate, but much more private than it is now. I remained organizer (out of pocket!) till 1940.

In this manner, the XYZ club members helped Dalton to draft the resolution on currency, banking and finance submitted to the Leicester Labour party conference in 1932.

Later the club expanded to include Francis Williams, City editor of the *Daily Herald*, George Strauss of Strauss and Co. (metal merchants), C. F. Chance, a stockbroker, John Wilmot, elected to Parliament in 1933, Charles Latham, chairman of the finance committee of the LCC, George Wansbrough, director of Robert Benson and Co., and James Lawrie from Lloyds Bank. In 1934 they were joined by three young economists, Evan Durbin, Hugh Gaitskell and Douglas Jay, a staff writer on *The Economist* at the time. Francis Williams, in his autobiography, summarized XYZ's contributions in the 1930s as follows:

> It has indeed, I think, some claim to have exercised in a quiet sort of way more influence on future government policy than any other group of the time and to have done so in the most private manner without attracting publicity to itself.[12]

New leadership and new politics

The minuscule parliamentary Labour party struggled to provide an effective opposition. Lansbury was in some ways an appropriate leader for the circumstances; a principled Christian and strong pacifist, he had suffered great hardship as a young man and had grown up fighting for unpopular causes on street corners. His inspirational kind of leadership was important to maintain the morale of the Labour movement.

But his relations with the NEC and the TUC were not good. Henderson was preoccupied with the Geneva disarmament conference, and himself a sick man; Bevin and Citrine had no patience with Lansbury's woolly-minded emotionalism.[13]

Lansbury's chief lieutenants in the House of Commons were Attlee and Sir Stafford Cripps, who worked closely together in the early 1930s. Attlee's background was similar to other middle-class party leaders; his father was a solicitor and he went to public school and to Oxford. But his subsequent career was not typical, for, unlike the academic route taken by Dalton and others, Attlee worked his way up through the rank and file of party organization. As a young man he joined Toynbee Hall, the famous east London social work settlement, at the same time as Beveridge and Tawney. The experience was a revelation to the shy and reserved young man, who was soon converted to socialism through his contact with the Fabians and all the leading intellectuals of the progressive movement at the turn of the century. Attlee joined the Stepney branch of the ILP in 1908, and was elected MP for Limehouse in 1922. Chosen as MacDonald's parliamentary private secretary in 1923, he was appointed postmaster general in March 1931. 'Modest and unassuming to the point of self-effacement', Attlee did not impress many with his leadership qualities until the Second World War.[14] However, in an ideological party with many strong, passionate contenders for power and influence, he had unique qualities as an unflappable listener of absolute integrity with an immense capacity for orderly administrative work. Durbin, his personal assistant during the war, later commented: 'he may lose his hat, he never loses his head'.[15] Famed for his laconic speech, the stories of his shrewd perceptions about people and situations are legion.

In contrast, the aristocratic Cripps was an inspiring speaker 'with remarkable ability to communicate his idealism to others, especially the young'.[16] Educated at Winchester and in London, he was appointed a KC in 1926, the youngest at the time; he became very rich, although he donated most of his wealth to a wide variety of left-wing causes including SSIP and the NFRB. He was persuaded by Morrison and others to enter MacDonald's second Labour government as solicitor general in October 1930 to relieve the shortage of Labour legal experts. An immensely sincere and deeply religious man with boundless energy and enthusiasm, Cripps was an attractive leader in many respects. However, he could also be extremely arrogant, contemptuous of boring meetings and less brilliant colleagues, and insensitive to the needs of his more cautious, working-class comrades. Pimlott has described him as 'impervious to the advice of any but a handful of close associates', and concluded that he had 'absolutely no sense of the concepts of solidarity and loyalty to majority decisions upon which the Movement and the Party had been built'. Even Beatrice Webb, who was his mother's sister, noted that her favourite nephew lacked judgment, a fatal leadership flaw in British political terminology.

The antagonism between Attlee and Cripps in the House of Commons and Dalton and Morrison on the NEC was important for its immediate impact on party policy and for its long-run effect on the future leadership. Although their power in the party was undoubtedly enhanced by the weakness of the PLP, Dalton and Morrison clearly resented losing their chance to become the parliamentary leader; Attlee and Cripps had won and Dalton had lost by very small majorities. Dalton made no secret of his low regard for Attlee, calling him 'a little man', 'a nonentity', 'a mouse'. Furthermore, after the 1931 crisis Attlee and Cripps had become more radical, Cripps increasingly so, while Dalton and Morrison had become more moderate in their anxiety to prevent a violent swing to the left.

Historically the ILP had always provided the focus of left-wing criticism within the Labour party. However, after the 1931 election débâcle, a split developed within its own ranks between the majority led by Maxton, the radical 'Clydesider', who felt the continued political alliance with the PLP in the House of Commons was meaningless, and the minority led by Frank Wise, who wished to remain affiliated with the party. The Socialist League was formed by the amalgamation of SSIP with the ILP affiliationists, after a stormy meeting at the Leicester conference in October 1932. It proved impossible to agree on constitutional safeguards to prevent the new organization becoming a party within the party, so that most of the NFRB members of SSIP left, including Clark, Durbin and Gaitskell. Cole stayed on unhappily for another six months. He had promised Bevin the chairmanship of the new group, but he gave way to pressure for Frank Wise, as leader of the more numerous ILP faction. According to Bullock, the effect on Bevin was permanent; it confirmed all his old prejudices against intellectuals and he never tried to work with them again.[17]

At first the Socialist League worked loyally with the NEC, but it soon became increasingly critical. In retrospect the high point of its influence was the 1932 conference, when Frank Wise successfully introduced an amendment to include nationalization of the joint stock banks into Dalton's FTC-drafted resolutions on currency, banking and finance. Flushed with this success, the League tried to introduce a much more radical programme calling for abolition of the House of Lords, emergency powers, immediate nationalization and an economic

plan to end unemployment. But they lost heavily in successive conferences. Frank Wise died shortly after the 1933 conference, and Cripps
succeeded him as chairman. Later Dalton satirized his own role in this
period; he felt he was constantly moving resolutions to nationalize the
solar system at the party conference, only to have a Socialist Leaguer
get up and move an amendment to add the words 'and the Milky
Way'.[18] More disgustedly Dalton noted of Cripps in his diary for 19
January 1934: 'Tory HQ regard him as their greatest electoral asset'.

By the mid-1930s politics had become dominated by the threat of
world war, as wars broke out in Abyssinia, Spain and China, and the
League of Nations began to fall apart. The Labour party had a strong
pacifist element, as well as deep suspicions of imperialist warmongers.
Both Dalton and Bevin became convinced that Britain should rearm
after Hitler came to power; together they are credited with weaning
the party from its pacifist past and bringing it round to support
Churchill in the wartime coalition.[19] In the early 1930s the Labour
party, under the leadership of Arthur Henderson, formally adopted
collective security and support of the League of Nations. When the
Italians invaded Abyssinia in early 1935, the NEC strongly condemned
the Italians and supported the League; they presented a resolution to
this effect to the 1935 Brighton conference, which Dalton introduced,
strongly supported by Attlee. Lansbury reluctantly spoke against the
resolution from the depths of his belief in pacifism. When the motion
was carried overwhelmingly, Lansbury resigned as leader of the party.
Thus, Attlee, his deputy in Parliament, who had moderated his position
considerably since supporting the abolition of the House of Lords in
1933, came to lead the party in the election which followed shortly
afterwards. Although the party tripled its strength in the new Parliament and important leaders such as Dalton and Morrison were
returned, the results only gave Labour a disappointing 154 seats.

When Parliament reconvened, the PLP was immediately faced with
choosing a leader. In the fight which followed, the two leading
contenders were Attlee and Morrison. Dalton was a strong supporter
of Morrison and lobbied strenuously on his behalf, possibly doing
him more harm than good. Bevin's personal dislike of Morrison had
intensified their political battles. Although Bullock has argued that
Bevin was preoccupied with the Italian invasion of Abyssinia,
Donoughue and Jones concluded that he was determined that
Morrison should not be the leader.[20] Morrison was favoured by the
young, the moderate, the middle class and the intellectuals, particularly
after he led the London Labour party to a sweeping victory in the
1934 county council elections; thus, he was the candidate for all those
searching for a strong leader with practical experience of planning and

implementing a comprehensive social programme. But to others he appeared personally ambitious and insufficiently broad in appeal, because of his identification with London. In the final analysis it seems likely that Morrison's own vacillation swung the uncertain votes against him.

Attlee won 88 to 48 on the second ballot. Although Morrison's background was closer to the working class, the trade union members chose a bourgeois public-school leader. The death of Henderson and the resignation of Lansbury mark the passing of the 'old guard' from the party's leadership. The choice of Attlee and the rise of Dalton, both from the educated upper-middle class, and the rise of Morrison from the lower-middle class all symbolize the broadening of the party's electoral aims beyond its narrower working-class origins.

New programmes

At the 1933 Hastings conference the Labour party decided to draft a more concise version of its new programme which the various reports and resolutions of the previous two conferences reflected, and which would replace *Labour and the Nation* as the main statement of its policy. For *Socialism and Peace* represented this collective effort; it was debated and adopted at the 1934 Southport conference with overwhelming majorities, despite the strident opposition led by Cripps and the Socialist League.

The new programme called for the central planning of key industries, to include the immediate nationalization of the banking system, transport, coal and power, water supply, iron and steel and land and the drastic reorganization of electricity, gas, agriculture, shipping, shipbuilding, engineering, textiles, chemicals and insurance. Plans were also promised to extend social services, to provide medical care, to clear slums, to raise the school-leaving age, to abolish the means test and to give adequate maintenance for the unemployed. Finally, to deal with unemployment and not to be outdone by the Liberals, extensive plans were proposed to build roads, bridges, harbours, houses, schools and hospitals, to electrify the railways, to re-equip nationalized industries, to drain land and to plant trees, all to be financed by government loans.

The strategy behind this programme had been debated extensively in the policy subcommittee of the NEC. Dalton had pressed for a clear statement in an important memorandum written in March 1933; he had explained:

It is the mood of the Movement to be bold and definite; to learn

the lesson taught by the experience of the first two Labour
governments that timidity and vagueness and indecision pave the
road to failure; to face all the difficulties with clear eyes; not to
be content with criticism of the lamentable failures of the present
Government, but to offer to the electorate a positive, intelligible
and practical programme of our own.

Our primary task in domestic policy is rapidly to reduce
unemployment. By our success or failure in this task we shall be
judged as the present Government will be judged, and all the lines
of our policy must converge on this objective. It is as a means to
this end, and also as a means to a higher standard of life for our
people and to the reduction of social inequality, that we must
press forward rapidly with measures of Socialisation and Economic
Planning, both National and International.

Speed at the outset is essential. We must start off, as neither the
first nor the second Labour Government did, with a rush . . . .
We must begin with a comprehensive General Powers Act,
including the taking of various Emergency Powers, and enable
the next Labour Government swiftly to carry out fundamental and
necessary changes by means of Orders in Council . . . . We must
demand powers to win the war against unemployment, poverty
and economic anarchy. If we act boldly and in this spirit, we
shall have our best chance of a quick victory over any organised
forces of hostility or obstruction.[21]

Thus, Dalton articulated for the NEC the possibility of deliberately
using unemployment policy as an integral component of socialist planning through public ownership, and its priority over taxation and
social services as the means to move Britain towards socialism. It is
interesting that he was willing to contemplate the introduction of
emergency powers, although he had opposed the nationalization of
the joint stock banks.

Dalton's strategy was in marked contrast to that propounded by
Attlee and Cripps at the same time. In January 1933 they submitted
their conclusions to the NEC:

The moment to strike at capitalism is the moment of taking power
when the Government is freshly elected and assured of its support.
The blow struck must be a fatal one and not merely designed to
wound and to turn a sullen and obstructive opponent into an
active and deadly enemy.

The difference, as we see it, between those who believe in
immediate nationalisation and those who do not is not really on
the technical or economic issue. It is much more upon the general

issue of whether it is possible to persuade capitalism to hand over control to Socialism by gradual and restrained measures. We are convinced that to take such a course is to court disaster. So long as capitalism holds the power and the control, so long will it use every weapon to retain it. There will be a short time when Labour returns to power in which it will be possible to take this power completely or almost completely from capitalism and to show a beneficial result; if that opportunity is missed, as we think it would be if the Joint Stock Banks were not nationalised, we do not think that another opportunity is likely to occur for many years. The result of failure will be the immediate splitting of the Labour Party into fragments to the great and permanent advantage of the perpetuation of the capitalist regime. From these fragments will probably be built up – amongst others – a strong revolutionary party, and the eventual issue will be fought out between that party and capitalism.[22]

Understandably Dalton noted on his copy 'feverish', with 'no detailed plan'.

To control the banking and financial system, the FTC had worked out detailed plans to nationalize the Bank of England and the joint stock banks and to set up a national investment board to co-ordinate investment programmes and overall planning. These proposals were incorporated in *For Socialism and Peace*, but the fullest description is to be found in the earlier *Socialism and the Condition of the People*. This earlier statement had also included positive references to Keynes's recent expansionary policies outlined in his book, *A Means to Prosperity*, which first appeared as a series of articles in *The Times* in March 1933, when Dalton was writing his memorandum to the NEC. These references were dropped next year, and the party retained its cautious goal 'to stabilize wholesale prices at a suitable level in this country'.[23] In short, while opposing orthodox deflation, the party still did not support 'inflationary' expansion.

On exchange policy the party aimed 'to seek by international agreement the largest practical measure of stability in the rates of foreign exchange'. The party had endorsed the 1932 Exchange Equalization Act, but it was not prepared to trust fluctuating exchange rates to insulate Britain from outside pressures. Therefore, the Labour party's view on monetary policy – a stable, managed currency at home and abroad – did not differ significantly from the National government's practice. The party did differ on the question of protection, which they opposed, and they did advocate the public ownership of the monetary system as the means to control the economy.

Besides the specific industries marked for nationalization or reorganization, the Labour party had made important decisions on general
issues of organizational design, accountability, worker representation
and industrial legislation. During the 1930s the party produced
detailed plans for seven major industries and policy statements about
many others. The basic model for most of these plans was the public
corporation developed for the London Passenger Transport Board by
Herbert Morrison when he was minister of transport. This model was
not popular with the left wing, who advocated direct ministerial
control of the nationalized industries; and many of them still yearned
for an end to the class system through workers' control of their own
economic lives along guild socialist lines. Others warned that the
managers of the public enterprises would merely replace the private
managers, and that the work environment would be unchanged.

Workers' control was a sensitive issue for trade unionists. On the
one hand, they were outraged when Herbert Morrison submitted a
resolution on the appropriate forms for 'reorganization of industry' to
the 1932 conference which did not even mention workers (Morrison
was summarily sent back to the drawing-board). On the other hand,
given their collective bargaining agreements they were open to charges
of collaborating with the capitalist enemy and of postponing effective
socialist control. The left wing was defeated on the question of ministerial control. Morrison compromised to include union 'representatives' on the boards of the public corporations, although the workers
were excluded from management.

The left wing also lost on another matter of principle, the issue of
compensation to private stockholders in industries which were
nationalized. At the 1934 conference it was decided to pay full
compensation to the owners of private stock. Dalton in particular had
worked hard for full compensation, because he felt it was crucial to
prevent financial panic by capitalists during the transition to socialism.

The Labour party's programme as a whole has been described as
'unremarkable', 'ambiguous' and 'vague', particularly by those who
judge the degree of socialism by the extent of public ownership.[24]
However, even its critics consider that *For Socialism and Peace* was a
significant improvement on earlier statements, because it did include
specific plans and an overall strategy to introduce socialism. Ben
Pimlott feels that the weakness of documents such as *Labour and the
Nation* was not that they did not measure up as blue-prints for
socialism, but that 'they were not blue-prints at all'.[25] Howell found
the general tone of *For Socialism and Peace* 'more radical than its
predecessors or successors'.[26]

An unsuccessful campaign

For Socialism and Peace was used to draw up the 1935 election manifesto. The party moderates hoped that their pragmatic approach would win enough seats in the next election to gain a clear majority for their programme. They blamed the election defeat on the left wing for its noisy public demonstrations, revolutionary talk and collaboration with the Communists. According to Colin Clark, Dalton had been particularly enraged by the publication of G. R. Mitchison's book, *The First Workers' Government*, shortly before the election. Mitchison, a close friend of Cole and executive committee member of the Socialist League as well as the NFRB, had opposed the private ownership of houses among other radical positions; the Tory press had relished publicizing his opinions, many of them contrary to party policy. The left wing, in turn, naturally blamed the moderates for being too cautious.

In his later analysis of the election, Cole called it 'a thoroughly confusing affair'.[27] The Tories stole Labour's thunder by their sudden switch to support the League of Nations and collective security, and even managed to turn Labour's previous support for disarmament against them. On the domestic front, in another gallant effort to promote expansion, Lloyd George had worked out detailed plans for his version of the 'New Deal' for Britain; however, it did the Liberals little good at the polls. Most recent analysts seem to think the results had more to do with the changing climate of the times than alarm at Socialist League fulminations against capitalism.[28] They attribute the party's defeat to the gradual improvement in Britain's economy and Baldwin's personal popularity. In the late 1930s Britain preferred 'safety first', fearing that *any* radical change could precipitate dictatorship from the right or the left.

As a strategy to deal with unemployment and introduce social change, the party's programme might have worked in 1929. By 1935, however, it was to take the destruction and upheaval of world war with its drastic government intervention in the economy to convince the British electorate that the party's programme should be tried. Howell has suggested that, although the party had come up with a generally agreed programme centred around the nationalization of key industries, contradictions about its purpose lurked beneath the consensus: 'Was it to be an instrument of socialist transformation that would produce a significant redistribution of power, or was it really just a technique for modernising and rationalising an antiquated economy?'[29] Howell concluded that this question was not formally tackled by the party in the 1930s. However, the young socialist economists, who worked as back-room boys for the party, consciously addressed this problem in their own deliberations. Their arguments were to provide a rationale for the next generation of party leaders to suppose that such a programme could transform British society.

CHAPTER 5
THE NEW
GENERATION

Born in the first decade of the twentieth century, the new generation
of intellectuals in the Labour party were still children when the First
World War broke out. Thus, they had not been decimated in the
trenches as had the previous generation, of which Attlee, Cole, Dalton,
Tawney and Keynes were survivors. For the most part they enjoyed a
relatively carefree youth at school and university in the 1920s. The
major political event was the general strike; it became the turning-
point for many, which crystallized their socialist sympathies into a
commitment to the Labour party.

One important influence on this new generation was the 'Cole
group', started at Oxford after the general strike. This comprised those
undergraduates who had met at Cole's house during the late 1920s;
they became the ardent young workers for the New Fabian Research
Bureau (NFRB) of the next decade. The young economists amongst
them were also teaching, attending seminars and conducting their own
research in the academic world. Their professional connection to the
predominant schools of economic thought in Britain at the time was
the second critical influence on the development of their thought.
Finally, Durbin and Gaitskell gathered their friends and colleagues
into an informal socialist 'think tank', where they thrashed out their
own revisionist version of democratic socialism.

Oxford and the 'Cole group'

Throughout the 1920s and 1930s Cole, Tawney and A. L. Lindsay,
the Master of Balliol, cultivated an oasis of socialist discussion and
teaching in the desert of Oxford establishmentism. When he returned

to Oxford in 1925 as the university reader in economics, Cole would invite his students and others from the Oxford Labour Club and from Ruskin College (where the students were mostly on trade union scholarships) to his house on Holywell each week to discuss the burning socialist issues of the day. It was, therefore, natural that the Coles became an important focus for the university strike committee in May 1926. While most Oxford undergraduates were helping to run trains and man the docks, the members of the Oxford University Labour Club threw in their lot with the workers. As Margaret Cole has described it, they included 'a number of unusually able young men . . . Hugh Gaitskell, Colin Clark, John Parker, John Dugdale, Evan Durbin, Lord Listowel, Michael Stewart, John Betjeman and Wystan Auden'.[1] Ironically, considering the subsequent careers of many of these young men, two other members of the Cole group, Maurice Ashley and Christopher Saunders, writing a short history of socialism at Oxford University in 1930, noted that 'the University Labour Club has seen many theorists but few practical statesmen'.[2]

Hugh Gaitskell, who remembered Oxford in the mid-1920s as 'gay, frivolous, stimulating and tremendously alive', met the Coles first through the general strike.[3] He had been reading Tawney, the Webbs, Marx, J. A. Hobson and Hugh Dalton, and vividly recalled:

> The impact of the strike was sharp and sudden, a little like a war, in that everybody's lives were suddenly affected by a new unprecedented situation, which forced us to abandon plans for pleasure, to change our values and adjust our priorities. Above all we had to make a choice. And how we chose was a clear test of our political outlook.

Gaitskell sympathized instinctively with 'the miners, the unions, the Labour party and the left generally'. Thus, he became a driver for the strike committee, ferrying speakers to and fro, driving Margaret Cole to London to connect with the TUC and fetching the *British Worker*. He met Tawney in Mecklenburgh Square for the first time, and was fined for climbing into New College late one night, despite fierce protests about the Warden's bias against the strikers and their helpers. For Evan Durbin, it was a time of intense activity but deeper frustration; later that summer he wrote, 'It all seems feverish – ill balanced – now but then it seemed valuable and important'.[4]

One important effect of the general strike at Oxford was the enlargement of the 'Cole group'. John Parker has since described the post-strike meetings, which Cole organized in consultation with Colin Clark, 'one of the most original and striking Labour Club personalities':

To begin with we all had government posts allotted to us and were then asked to prepare papers as to what we should do over three years if members of a Labour government with a majority. Cole was surprised to find that despite a vague sympathy for guild socialism, we were all strongly parliamentary in our approach.[5]

He remembered that the first time Beatrice Webb attended one of these meetings, she absolutely demolished the paper read by James Meade. 'Then before anyone could reply she looked at her watch, said "It is 10 o'clock, my bedtime" and stalked out of the room.' Since the group members had all thought of the Webbs as 'a couple of old fuddy-duddies', they were dumbfounded. Besides the names already mentioned, Dame Margaret Cole later recalled other participants at these meetings, Anthony Bowlby, Robert Henriques (two of Durbin's closest friends at Oxford), Teddy Radice, Ivor Thomas, Geoffrey and Roger Wilson, and a group from Ruskin including Tom and Betty Baxter and E. H. Littlecott. Radice and Meade remember that A. T. K. Grant, A. M. MacIver and Gilbert Walker were active members.

The 'Cole group' and the Labour Club meetings provided important introductions to the leading socialist intellectuals and Labour leaders of the day. Colin Clark first met Ernest Bevin when he came to visit the Labour Club. John Parker has related that the Labour Club's membership doubled to 300 after the general strike and that speakers such as MacDonald himself, A. J. Cook, the miners' leader, Harry Pollitt, the Communist party leader, and the colourful Saklatvala, a wealthy Indian Parsee and Communist MP for North Battersea, addressed their meetings.

The leading lights of the Oxford University Labour Club in the late 1920s were Clark, Durbin, MacIver, Parker, Radice and Stewart, as well as the Wilson brothers and the Ruskin contingent. Many of the club leaders were also active in the Union, but they had difficulty winning office against the more numerous Tory and Liberal members. In 1925, they viewed it as a great victory when, by parliamentary manoeuvering, they managed to win a voice in choosing debating subjects. However, Stewart was later elected secretary, and Durbin librarian; eventually Labour supporters were also chosen as presidents, both Wilson brothers serving in the late 1920s. Gaitskell was not an active participant in the club or the Union. Douglas Jay followed Clark, Gaitskell and Radice from Winchester to Oxford two years later, with his close friend Dick Crossman. He spoke at the Union, but from his special vantage point as a Winchester and New College scholar he perceived the Labour Club, rather inaccurately, as consisting of 'three or four eccentric Wykemists', and did not join.[6]

Thus, Jay did not meet Durbin until 1934, when he contacted Gaitskell in London.

The Labour Club debaters also met their Cambridge counterparts in exchange visits. Lionel Elvin remembers that he first met Evan Durbin on such an occasion, when he and Donald Barber represented the Cambridge club and Durbin and Michael Stewart, Oxford's. On the lighter side, Oxford members established a tradition of producing political skits each term, after Cole had written and produced an operetta, 'The Striker Stricken', to hymn tunes and Sullivan melodies at a summer school in 1926.[7] The tradition of skits and singing these songs was continued in Fabian summer schools and conferences for thirty years. On the serious side, club members helped various local candidates in the 1929 election, Christopher Addison in Swindon and Colin Clark in North Dorset; however, according to Parker, the Oxford City candidate 'refused all undergraduate help as likely to damage his chances'. Only Addison succeeded; he became minister of agriculture in the Labour government and, later, chairman of the NFRB, when Attlee became leader of the parliamentary Labour party.

Finally, the role-playing as members of a future Labour government in the more intimate weekly sessions at the Coles' gave these young socialists an early confidence in their ability to perform as the responsible leaders which they later became. This practice was also continued after Oxford days, and friends remember that in the 1930s Gaitskell often took the part of prime minister, with Durbin as chancellor of the exchequer, in ordinary social discussions of politics.

Through Cole, Tawney and Lindsay, many of the young middle-class public-school socialists also had their first introduction to members of the working class. At Oxford they would encounter undergraduates from working-class backgrounds at Ruskin College; Durbin, for instance, met his lifelong friend, Reg Bassett, in this way. More important, through the Workers' Educational Association (WEA), they visited working-class groups all over the country. Hugh Gaitskell spent his first year after Oxford as a WEA tutor in the Nottingham mining district. Evan Durbin later wrote that he had found his own 'spiritual home' as a WEA lecturer in the north, and particularly in the Potteries, to which he travelled once a week throughout the 1930s.[8] Gaitskell recalled that Cole had once said to him that 'WEA tutors were in many respects the true missionaries of today – doing the kind of job which at one time the churches used to do'.[9]

The young Oxford socialists were all invited to one or more extra-ordinary weekends at Lady Warwick's Easton Lodge in Essex. They vividly remember the hostess herself, a Victorian grande dame, who had been a mistress of Edward VII and who still wore 'her Edwardian curls and her Lily Langtry smile', and her large house, its ill-kept park with peacocks on the terrace, four-poster beds dripping with dusty muslins and bows and bowers of fresh hothouse flowers. They also recall the fascinating people who went: H. G. Wells and his mistress, Lansbury, Cripps and Attlee from the House of Commons, Bevin for the trade unions, guild socialists such as William Mellor, Ellen Wilkinson and Tawney, WEA tutors and organizers, Labour lawyers, representatives of the co-operative movement, left-wing journalists and the famous cartoonist, Frank Horrabin; according to Margaret Cole, 'except for the dyed-in-the-wool Communists, scarcely a section of Labour was unrepresented'.

Elizabeth Harman, later married to Frank Pakenham and now Countess of Longford, who was a close friend of both Durbin and Gaitskell at the time, has described 'the mood of defiance' at these meetings; it seemed as though 'a sword of Damocles was hanging over us' with the terrible unemployment and poverty, and a totally ineffectual Labour government. She particularly remembers the marvellous contrasts between the Edwardian splendour and, for example, 'Colin Clark with his sandals and straw sticking out of his hair'. Many of the young men had to sleep in a ramshackle outhouse; Parker remembers being very impressed with a speech by Bevin on agriculture; Clark recalls giving a speech on devaluation; John Strachey attended once, but was so full of the Mosley manifesto that he was not invited again.

Besides organizing sessions for SSIP and the NFRB, the conferences discussed such policy issues as unemployment, education, the League of Nations, reform of Parliament, nationalization, protection, and imperial problems. The last two SSIP conferences, on banking policy and the causes of the 1931 election defeat, were held jointly with the NFRB in early 1932. The economic research programme for the NFRB was also debated, and many of its committees and subgroups initially met to decide their research agendas at Easton Lodge.

The Cole group joined the NFRB in force, serving on its committees and attending its conferences throughout the decade. Besides Durbin and Gaitskell, Colin Clark and John Parker also served on the executive committee. Radice became the first paid secretary, serving half-time for the Bureau and half-time for SSIP. When he left for a year in the USA in 1933, John Parker took his place and remained the secretary for the Bureau, continuing in that role for many years after the amalgamation with the Fabian Society. Besides Clark, Durbin and Gaitskell, James Meade was the other New Fabian economist who had also been a member of the Cole group in Oxford. He does not recall attending any NFRB meetings, although he well remembers the

SSIP conferences at Easton Lodge. Because he was living in Oxford, he did not attend regular committee meetings. However, he did organize an Oxford group of Bureau sympathizers; Roy Harrod, Robert Hall and Redvers Opie, among others, helped to draw up proposals for the Labour party's finance and trade committee and attended the 'Pink' lunch club. Clark organized a similar group in Cambridge, where he lectured on statistics. He was responsible for the capital supply subcommittee of the economic section, which included R. B. Braithwaite, Lionel Elvin, C. H. P. Gifford, Joan Robinson and G. F. Shove.

Economists in academia

The world of academic economics in the 1930s was small and close-knit compared to the far-flung thousands of today. In Britain it was dominated by the London–Oxford–Cambridge axis. Although there were influential outposts in the provinces, such as the Manchester/Liverpool school of empirical research, many of their staff were also Oxbridge graduates. Most economists knew each other, met regularly and read the major new books and articles as they appeared. Furthermore, publication was very fast, so that new ideas were disseminated quickly and discussed avidly. Economists knew what was going on in their field; there was no narrow specialization and little mathematics. Departments, where they existed, were small, and academic teachers were expected to cover a broad range of topics.

In the 1920s, with relatively few exceptions, the Cambridge neoclassical school of Marshall and Pigou still dominated the teaching and practice of British economics. Furthermore, with even fewer exceptions, the study of economics was quite insular; it was confined to British thought, with only passing regard for American or European scholars. All this changed in the early 1930s. There were major revolutions in thinking, not only in macroeconomics leading up to *The General Theory* (1936), but also in microeconomics. At Cambridge the work of Piero Sraffa and Joan Robinson, which culminated in the publication of *The Economics of Imperfect Competition* (1933), raised fundamental questions about the viability of the Marshallian system based upon perfectly competitive assumptions. At the London School of Economics (LSE), John Hicks was working out the elaborations of value theory which eventually appeared in *Value and Capital* (1939) and still form the basic apparatus for the study of microeconomics. Later important advances were made in the theory of international trade and of socialist economics. Finally, a start was made on the development of mathematical economics and econometrics. The NFRB economists and their colleagues were closely involved in all these developments.

Economics at Oxford

Most of the young men who organized the NFRB economic research had received their earliest training at Oxford. They studied economics as only one part of the newly instituted degree in philosophy, politics and economics (PPE).[10] This degree, peculiar to Oxford, had been designed to apply the same broadly philosophical approach to modern social science subjects which the traditional 'Greats' degree had applied to the study of the classics. Both were intended to provide a suitable education for the successive generations of eminent politicians, imperial administrators and civil servants for which the university was famed. Since 'modern Greats', as it was called, was such a recent innovation, many of the tutors and students felt inspired by their pioneering role. Others, such as Lionel Robbins, who was the economics tutor at New College from 1926 to 1929, thought that, although it was a good idea, its realization was 'truly lamentable'; the college system made standards difficult to apply, the philosophers dominated the teaching and were out of touch with the rest of the world; in short, 'the degree to which one could instil economics was not great'.[11] What students lacked in professional economics training, they gained in their wider sense of the historical, political and philosophical forces in society.

Oxford did not have its own independent tradition in economics at this time. Indeed, D. H. Macgregor, who succeeded Edgeworth as the professor of political economy, was a Cambridge man and a favourite of Marshall's. Cole was far better known for his work in political and social theory, and only took up the systematic study of economics in the 1920s because of its importance to the Labour movement. Thus, Robbins was an unusual tutor in this setting, a grammar-school boy with a degree from LSE, who was also well acquainted with American, European and especially Austrian economics.

Robbins was an important influence on the young men he taught in the late 1920s. All the NFRB economists, Clark, Durbin, Gaitskell and Jay wrote their early economic essays for him. He also gave tutorials to Durbin's close friends, Reg Bassett and Henry Phelps Brown, when they all three stayed on to study PPE and shared digs at 10 Worcester Street from 1927 to 1929. Other students included Frank Pakenham, David Eccles, H. V. Hodson and Gilbert Walker. James Meade went to his lectures, which he found very moving, and attended the Adam Smith Society, which Robbins ran in New College. Robbins took an immense interest in his students' fortunes. He recommended Colin Clark for a research assistantship at LSE; he recommended Durbin for the fellowship at University College (UC), and then hired him as a lecturer at LSE; he recommended Phelps Brown to take his own place at New College, when he was appointed professor of economics at LSE on the sudden death of Allyn Young in 1929. When Durbin wrote to Clark to congratulate him for being chosen as a research assistant to the newly formed Economic Advisory Council (EAC) in February 1930, he described the amazing accomplishments of Adam Smith Society members: 'Henry running Oxford economics, Frank Pakenham running the Conservative party, you and Harry [Hodson, also at EAC] running the country. Only Hugh and I remain in the obscurity of provincial academic life'.[12] No wonder Robbins later recalled these years 'as among the halcyon periods of my life'.

Economics at LSE

When LSE was founded in 1895, Sidney Webb had been determined that its economics should provide an antidote to the prevalent individualistic economics and to the Marshallian monopoly of the subject. But he was equally determined that it should not become a propaganda vehicle for collectivism and should include a wide diversity of opinion. When Robbins arrived as a student in 1920, Edward Cannan was professor of political economy, H. S. Foxwell, a Tory social reformer and 'an avowed enemy of the left', was professor of money and banking, and Dalton was one of two economics lecturers.[13] Cannan was quite sympathetic to socialism and strongly anti-Cambridge, a rebel against the classical Ricardo–Mill school. He was a great debunker of esoteric language and advocate of institutional economics; in his presidential address to the Royal Economic Society in 1933, he exhorted young economists not to avert their eyes from 'the disgusting mess' of the public mind, nor to 'run back to find contentment in neat equations and elegant equilibria', but 'to assist common sense to grasp the basic elements of economic science'. In the early 1920s Cannan also strongly opposed Keynes's analysis and his policy recommendations; he believed that prices should be reduced to their prewar levels by strong deflationary policies, and that the self-regulating monetary mechanism should be restored as soon as possible. Thus, with Dalton's socialism and Cannan's anti-Cambridge position, LSE's economics department did fulfil Webb's hopes until well into the 1920s.

The School itself changed dramatically under William Beveridge's forceful and ambitious leadership from 1919 to 1937.[14] The number of full-time staff and students doubled, while graduate students increased ninefold. In economics, new professorships went to Friedrich Hayek in economic science, to Arnold Plant in business administration and to Eileen Power and R. H. Tawney in economic history; besides Durbin, John Hicks, Richard Sayers and George Schwartz among others were retained as lecturers; R. G. D. Allen was hired to supplement the old-fashioned statistics taught by A. L. Bowley, the professor. In other departments, Harold Laski replaced Graham Wallas, Morris Ginsberg replaced Hobhouse; Bronislav Malinowski and, later, Karl Popper were also hired. Beveridge was deeply committed to empirical research and to the search for a natural science basis for social science; in his words, basing 'economics, politics and all the other social sciences on collection and examination of facts rather than on analysis of concepts'.[15] He felt this was the way to implement the intentions and the techniques pioneered by the Webbs. However, his ambitions were to be completely thwarted in economics, where high theory became the order of the day when Robbins returned to head the department in 1929.

Robbins was appointed with strong endorsements from Cannan and Dalton over the objections of their stuffier colleagues. Although not known for progressive political views in later life, in his youth Robbins had been a guild socialist, and he had worked on the 'Labour Campaign for the Nationalization of the Drink Trade' for the party. Dalton hired him as his assistant in 1920 ('I must take some responsibility for the academic birth and childhood of Lionel Robbins', he wrote in his *Memoirs*). While still an undergraduate, Robbins visited Vienna, falling in love with its setting, its culture and its economics. He studied the works of Gustav Cassel, Irving Fisher and Frank Feller; he met Ludwig von Mises, Schumpeter, Menger, Böhm-Bawerk, Wieser, as well as the younger generation, Haberler, Hayek, Machlup and Morgenstern.[16] In his inaugural lecture Robbins explicitly called for a return to the fundamental theoretical problems; his aim was to press ahead with theory and technique, in order to 'acquire the respect now given without question to the practitioners of the natural sciences'.[17]

In 1930 Friedrich Hayek was invited from Vienna by Robbins to give a series of visiting lectures; the following year he was offered a professorship. The two shared similar views on the importance of relying on theory in economic analysis and of keeping the government out of the market in practice. Together they dominated LSE economics in the 1930s, where, ironically, their outspoken stand against Keynesian intervention perpetuated the School's anti-Cambridge tradition. On Monday afternoons they held their 'grand Seminar'. Before a student body which contained such later prominent professionals as Maurice Allen, Harold Barger, Ronald Coase, Ronald Edwards, Nicholas Kaldor, Ludwig Lachmann, Abba Lerner, Arthur Lewis and Brinley Thomas, Hayek expounded his theories of the trade cycle and presented chapters from *The Pure Theory of Capital*, and Hicks spent two years outlining *Value and Capital*. The students made their own early contributions, and eminent foreign visitors included Haberler and Machlup from Vienna, Bresciani-Turoni from Rome, Knight and Viner from America and Lindahl, Ohlin and Frisch from Scandinavia.

For Robbins the experience was poetic; to describe his feelings later he quoted, 'Bliss was it in that dawn to be alive/But to be young was very heaven'. Ronald Coase, who was a student from 1929 to 1931 and a staff member after 1935, found the intellectual atmosphere 'extremely agreeable', with 'an openness to new ideas' and 'harmonious relations' within the department despite political differences.[18] Lord Robbins has recalled that there were intellectual squabbles, but with the mellowing of the years he has described them as the natural expression of unreserved talk, within 'our little family'. However, others remember serious friction within the department with at least a hint of political overtones.[19] While Hayek was the very model of the patient, courteous man of learning in pursuit of truth, Robbins was a much more emotional and passionate man, who could exude great warmth and enthusiasm, but who could also flare up in towering rages. Certainly Durbin, who had been very close to Robbins and dedicated his first book to him, came to feel that because of his political activities he was not offered the department's readership, which fell vacant when Dalton re-entered the House of Commons in 1935.

Much more obvious were the running battles between Beveridge and Robbins over the direction of the economics department and the political activities and strident Marxist views of Harold Laski. Although they collaborated in an organized attack on Keynes's renunciation of free trade in 1931, and had more in common with each other politically than either had with Laski, they clashed violently on the proper methodology for economics. Robbins, indeed, has gone so far as to attribute the failure to give Hicks a permanent appointment on the staff to Beveridge's 'insensate hostility to theory' and 'positive antipathy to economics as it was developing in the thirties'.[20]

As early as 1932, Dalton was writing in his diary about 'the possibility of intellectual friction at the School'; he attributed the problems to the increasingly right-wing views of Robbins:

> His intellectual development is a disappointment. He will do much
> distinguished work in economic theory. But he has stiffened in
> an old fashioned laissez faire attitude of approach to current

problems, he is bemused by modern Viennese theory, and by the personality of Hayek, in particular. He has no belief or interest in or knowledge of, the Planned Economy such as in the Soviet Union. He overcultivates his feud with Keynes .... He is exercising a powerful influence – for he has a powerful intellectual personality and much charm – on younger teachers and on students.[21]

More pessimistically, on a visit to Germany in the spring of 1933, he noted, "Geistige Gleichschaltung" [intellectual co-ordination] is the Nazi ideal in education. There is something of this, too, in the Economic Dept. at the School of Economics.' Others such as Tawney and Beatrice Webb commented on the difficulties of discussing politics at LSE, particularly after open warfare broke out over the acquisition of the Frankfurt Institute's library, a centre of Marxist study, and Laski's public utterances and political activities. The contemporary joke was that at LSE the market liberals, Hayek and Robbins, produced socialists in their economics seminar, while the left-wing Marxist, Harold Laski, produced liberals in his politics seminar. Certainly, Laski, an elected member of the Labour party's National Executive and a popular orator for the Socialist League, was largely responsible for LSE's vastly exaggerated reputation as a hotbed of red firebrands.

Economics at Cambridge

Colin Clark and James Meade were the two NFRB economists who were closest to Keynes in the early 1930s. Clark and Meade were also on friendly personal terms; they once walked down the Icknield Way together, staying in pubs and living on bread and cheese, which Clark insisted was the working-class thing to do. After a year in Liverpool, six months at LSE and eighteen months on the EAC, Clark was offered two jobs, one by Keynes as a lecturer in statistics in Cambridge, the other by Cole as secretary to the NFRB; he recalls that on the advice of Ernest Bevin he took the Cambridge job. Meade was offered a fellowship in economics at Hertford College, Oxford, when he finished PPE; he was given a year to pursue more concentrated work on economics before taking up full-time responsibilities. He was invited to go to Trinity College, Cambridge, by D. H. Robertson, whom he already knew through two of Robertson's maiden great-aunts, who were the Meades' neighbours in Bath; indeed, he had persuaded Robertson, to address an undergraduate society as his guest at Oriel College. Arriving in the autumn of 1930, he soon connected with the Robinsons' Richard Kahn and Piero Sraffa. Recognizing Meade's talents, the group admitted him to their inner discussions, or the

Cambridge 'circus' as they nicknamed themselves. They all met regularly that winter to thrash out the problems of Keynes's *Treatise*; their work helped to open up the road to *The General Theory*.

The economics atmosphere at Cambridge in those years has been vividly recaptured by Sir Austin Robinson.[22] It was a very small world, consisting of the aloof, remote Professor Pigou (despite fairly frequent contacts Robinson never discussed economics with him), the shy and scholarly Dennis Robertson as reader, ten university lecturers (of which only seven were active), one assistant lecturer, and half a dozen fellows scattered around the various colleges. Although Keynes dominated the intellectual debates, he held no official university appointment. Furthermore, he was only in Cambridge from Friday evening to Tuesday morning and had many additional duties as the bursar of King's College and the editor of the *Economic Journal*. Nevertheless, his occasional lectures, his tutorials for the chosen few and above all the Political Economy Club, which met on Monday evenings, have remained the highlights of their Cambridge education for the illustrious economics graduates and undergraduates of the period.[23]

Keynes was a son of Cambridge literally; he was born at 6 Harvey Road in June 1883. His father, John Neville Keynes, was a lecturer in moral science and a university administrator for many years; his mother was a justice of the peace, an alderman and, finally, the mayor of Cambridge. Brilliant, witty and vital, Keynes could be enormously warm and sympathetic to close friends, kind and patient with students and colleagues; but he could also be arrogant, sarcastic and ruthless to opponents, and quite rude and tactless at almost any time. Intellectually generous and open-minded, he was always ready to listen to criticism from those he trusted. Given to exaggeration to stress his opinions, he was combative in discussion, pouncing on weak spots: it was only later that he repeated the arguments of others as his own, or 'that the insuperable objections to the frightful rot one had been talking the other day had somehow melted away and were never mentioned again'.[24] Above all, Keynes was the renaissance man of affairs, constantly involved in the public affairs of his day. He also lost, but in the end made, a great deal of money on the stock market; he was a patron of the arts, a discerning collector of paintings, an avid collector of books and founder of the Cambridge Arts Theatre.

'A marvellous man', said James Meade, who as a young man was so in awe of Keynes's intellect that he could not bring himself to write a critical word to 'God'. Durbin, who appeared to some of his contemporaries too self-confident ever to fear rejection, had no such compunction; he boldly sought an interview with Keynes to explain his disagreements with *The General Theory*. According to Sir Michael Postan, he emerged three hours later somewhat shaken to announce that, although undoubtedly a genius, Keynes was also 'a megalomaniac madman'.[25] Lord Robbins, who was on the receiving end of Keynes's anger and renowned rudeness more than once, has summarized his mature assessment:

> What distinguished him rather and made him stand out above all his generation were more general qualities of mind and character: the swiftness of his thought and perceptions; the cadences of his voice and his prose style; his idealism and moral fervour; above all, the life-enhancing quality of his presence – as someone, I think it was Sir Roy Harrod, once said, when he came into a room we all cheered up . . . all in all, I would certainly regard Maynard Keynes as the most remarkable man I ever met.[26]

Very different was Keynes's fellow Etonian and close colleague of the 1920s, Dennis Robertson. Insecure and almost irritatingly self-effacing, Robertson was the epitome of the painstaking, erudite scholar. In many ways he was more approachable than Keynes; he took a personal interest in the work of the younger generation, carefully criticizing their efforts and championing his favourites. His relations with Keynes cooled slowly after their collaboration over *A Treatise on Money*. Later their personal relations became quite strained, when a younger generation of Keynes's enthusiasts seemed to usurp his place. In the early 1930s Robertson was still an important influence on Keynes. Indeed, in his recent assessment Robinson concluded that Keynes was 'only happy when Dennis had given his assent', for among economists in Cambridge at the time:

> In important ways Dennis Robertson was the best scholar of all of us. Pigou was conservative and could slip into mistakes. Keynes was the intuitive creator who could visualise a solution before he could formulate it. Robertson was less quick, less intuitive, less impulsive than Keynes. But in *Banking Policy and the Price Level* (1926) he was greatly original and creative and began much of our new thinking.[27]

Indeed, Sir Austin Robinson has argued that without Robertson Keynes might never have started *A Treatise* or *The General Theory*. In particular, many of Robertson's questions about the former helped to set the ball rolling for the Cambridge 'circus' activities.

Meade returned to Oxford in the autumn of 1931, and became an ardent proselytizer for the expansionary policies which Keynes had advocated for so long. Together with Roy Harrod, he spread the

Keynesian word among the younger economists, forming the nucleus for his group of NFRB researchers in the process. Harrod had also spent a year at Cambridge in close contact with Keynes before taking up his fellowship at Christ Church in 1923. Destined to make major contributions in the application of Keynesian models to international trade and economic dynamics, Harrod was better known for his political activities on behalf of the Liberal party; he attended the Liberal party summer schools in the 1920s, and in 1945 stood as a parliamentary candidate for Huddersfield. He was nevertheless also a close collaborator with Meade in missionary work within the Labour party during the 1930s, as well as in the broader arena.[28] In 1932 and 1937 they organized the collection of signatures for two letters to *The Times* advocating expansionary policies; in November 1933 they briefed Felix Frankfurter, a visiting professor that year, on what he should write to Roosevelt to urge a programme of public works.[29] In NFRB committees and conferences Harrod and Meade, in addition to Clark, undertook to convert their socialist friends and colleagues to the new 'Keynesian' economics.

Revolution and counter-revolution: Keynes and the LSE

The main centre of opposition to Keynes's policies and his new theories was the Hayek–Robbins nexus at the LSE. The most intense clashes between Keynes and the LSE were not, however, over *The General Theory*, but over free trade and government intervention in the very early 1930s. The major ingredients were Robbins's stand against the revenue tariff and public works in the EAC and Hayek's review of *A Treatise*. Relations were not improved by very different perceptions about economic methodology and the appropriate role of economic advisers.

Although Robbins has confessed to the error of his ways in the matter of public works, he has maintained his defence of free trade; in fact, he later thought that he and Keynes were not that far apart on the basic issue, differing only on tactics.[30] Harold Barger, who had been an undergraduate student of Keynes, has agreed; he feels now, as he felt then, that Keynes's opportunistic advocacy of the revenue tariff, which infringed the great principle of free trade for the sake of staying on the gold standard a few months longer, has to be counted 'a dreadful lapse', even amongst Keynesian enthusiasts. Colin Clark, who was in a position to observe both Keynes and Robbins in the committee of economists, thinks there was 'wrong on both sides':

Keynes was happily embracing protectionism and economic nationalism in their crudest forms. Lord Robbins refused not only to see the necessity of measures for increasing demand in such an emergency, but embraced a weirdly erroneous doctrine which claimed that this was the time actually to reduce consumption.

Furthermore, Robbins offended the British economists 'by saying that the committee ought to begin by seeking advice from the leading economists of Europe: "They will soon tell you what's wrong," he added, menacingly.'[31]

A more serious attack on Keynes's credibility at the time was Hayek's lengthy and critical review of *A Treatise*, which appeared in August 1931 at the height of the financial crisis.[32] While acknowledging his neglect of Wicksell and Böhm-Bawerk, Keynes rejoined with a scathing review of Hayek's *Prices and Production*:

[It] seems to me one of the most frightful muddles I have ever read, with scarcely a sound proposition in it beginning with page 45, and yet it remains a book of some interest which is likely to leave its mark on the mind of the reader. It is an extraordinary example of how, starting with a mistake, a remorseless logician can end up in Bedlam.[33]

Neither the language nor the assessment was improved in Sraffa's review for the *Economic Journal* the following year. It is understandable that, as a newcomer to Britain with a message for recovery of his own, Hayek would be appalled by this reception of his own painstaking research.

In any case, the bitterness of the arguments owed more to the political, philosophical and, some would add, personal dimensions of the controversy than the purely theoretical points would justify. Hayek and Robbins were, after all, defending the status quo, the City, the Treasury and all the other ramifications of orthodox finance in a volatile political setting. Other scholars have also suggested that the echoes of the Austrian methodological controversy lingered on in this battle.[34] Hayek and Robbins were archetypal proponents of the objective scientific base of an autonomous market system and the strict ends/means dichotomy between politics and economics, whereas Keynes luxuriated in his role of political adviser and man of affairs, pressing 'another tract for the times', in Hayek's condemning view.[35] Not only was Keynes 'unacademic' in his speculations, careless scholarship and extravagant views, he was also unreliable in his policy recommendations. Even worse, from the European liberal perspective, he was a proponent of state intervention, which to someone coming from a shaky political democracy seemed dangerously close to supporting totalitarian government.

In the short run the theoretical battle was won by Cambridge. Ludwig Lachmann, a student of Hayek's at LSE in the 1930s, says he felt like a junior officer in a war which was being lost. Yet many socialists, including Durbin, Kaldor and Lerner, were strongly influenced by Hayek's theories. However, Durbin was not comfortable with the militantly free-market, political implications of the support for orthodox policy, for Philip Snowden and for James Ramsey MacDonald. He and Brinley Thomas are remembered by many as the only 'socialist consciences' in the economics department at the School. They were both much more at home in the Wednesday seminar run by Hugh Gaitskell and Paul Rosenstein-Rodan at UC. Rosenstein-Rodan recalls that their 'pink' seminar was held in direct and conscious contrast to the activities in the 'Grand Seminar' at LSE. The atmosphere was pro-planning, and Marxists such as Kalecki were invited to speak.

The main forum for debating the theoretical issues was the joint London–Cambridge–Oxford seminars, which were held regularly during term time in one of the three places. Apparently everybody came, particularly the younger economists – Durbin, Gaitskell, Lerner, Hicks, Kahn, Sraffa, Joan Robinson, Harrod, Meade; occasionally the big guns would also show up – Keynes, Hayek or Robbins. Rosenstein-Rodan vividly remembers one meeting chaired by Dennis Robertson in 1935, in which he presented a paper on money and its different functions, arguing that both Keynes and Hayek were wrong because they did not take account of the role of time and its effect on anticipations. Hayek responded with a 'lengthy diatribe'; he was followed by Keynes, 'who rose to say he entirely agreed and that in his next book he dealt with it'. Postan recalled an important conference held in the summer of 1936 to win over the Londoners, who included Durbin, Gaitskell and Kaldor.[36] Joan Robinson played a leading role, but it was Kahn who 'crushed all remaining doubts'; only Durbin remained unconvinced.

Socialist 'think tank'

Throughout the 1930s Durbin and Gaitskell were the philosophical and social organizers of an extraordinary level of unofficial intellectual activity on behalf of the Labour party, for which there is no parallel before or since.[37] First, there was the New Fabian Research Bureau and, second, the XYZ Club, where the economic issues were thrashed out. In addition, two other groups were organized by Durbin at different periods and for somewhat different purposes; in a sense they were two stages of the same group.

The first stage, of which a report has survived, was a 'small group of university economists and politicians', which 'held a series of meetings during 1934 and 1935 to discuss the problems which face the English Labour Party in any attempt it may make to set up a Socialist Community by democratic methods'.[38] The group summarized its discussions in a set of resolutions on policy, most of which were adopted unanimously. Durbin was in the chair, Frederick Brown was the secretary, and the following took part at various times: 'Mr. Robert Fraser, Mr. H. T. N. Gaitskell, Mr. H. R. G. Greaves, Mr. Arthur Creech Jones, Mr. John Parker, Mr. M. M. Postan, Prof. Eileen Power, Prof. R. H. Tawney, Mr. Leonard Woolf, Mrs. Barbara Wootton'. A colleague at UC, Sir Michael Postan's chief recollection of these discussions was the enormous importance which Durbin and Gaitskell placed on working out the ideological basis of democratic socialism first; without the appropriate political framework they believed it would be impossible to develop practical policies of any kind for the Labour party.

The second stage consisted of the continuing discussions organized by Durbin until the outbreak of war. Although still centred around the group described above, more people were included and the meetings tended to become more specialized. Thus, one set of people might be invited for discussions of foreign policy, and another for economic policy. Although no documents have survived, a number of books were published which had their genesis in these meetings; they included two books of collected essays by group members edited by Professor George Catlin, *New Trends in Socialism* (1935) and *War and Democracy* (1938). In addition, Durbin's drafts for *The Politics of Democratic Socialism* were discussed at length; Durbin explicitly dedicated the book to six friends, Bowlby, Postan, Bassett, Fraser, Tawney and Gaitskell.

Besides these groups, their senior common rooms and the economics departments at UC and LSE, Durbin and Gaitskell participated in a wide variety of other clubs and discussion groups in the heady intellectual atmosphere of Bloomsbury in the 1930s. When he moved to London from Nottingham in 1928, Gaitskell had taken a flat in Great Ormond Street; he rented the back room to the Coles as a pied-à-terre. He joined the 1917 Club, a cheap social and political centre named after the earlier non-Bolshevik revolution, and the Cave of Harmony, a late-night dancing club; he was also a regular patron of Bertorelli's restaurant on Charlotte Street and the Fitzroy Tavern, better known as Kleinfeld's, where he first met Dora Frost after a political rally in early 1929. With Solly Zuckerman he was also one of the founders of Tots and Quots, a small dining club of scientists and other intellectuals, many of whom were committed Marxists.

Durbin, who eschewed the 1917 Club and Marxists, took a room during the week in John Bowlby's Camden Town flat, where he set about organizing this friend's social life when he arrived in 1929. Bowlby, a younger brother of Durbin's Oxford friend Tony, had already embarked on his psychoanalytic training; grinding his way through medical school, he was in search of light relief. Besides regular Tuesday dinner parties, Durbin persuaded Bowlby and a friend, Doris Austin, to join him in putting up the money for Bogey's Bar, a small café in the basement of the Royal Hotel, just off Russell Square and down the street from the flat where the Durbins lived after they were married in 1932. Durbin had apparently been very impressed with Colin Clark's success at supplementing a meagre academic salary with ventures as a pig farmer; he hoped to do the same, and also to provide an inexpensive and congenial gathering-place for colleagues, students and friends. The partnership lasted about five years, and although they failed to earn any profit, many of their fellow socialists, who liked to think out loud and in company, would drop by. Bowlby remembers that Dalton came on occasion; Sir Michael Postan recalled going there for a 'series of gatherings organized by Hugh and Evan in 1931 to discuss the economics of socialist society', some of which were attended by James Meade and Roy Harrod.[39]

Bowlby also arranged his own discussion group of medical students interested to learn more about psychology, of which Durbin was a keen member. He feels that the club, which met three times a term from 1929 to 1933, had a powerful influence on his contemporaries, many of whom became medical luminaries. Bowlby has never forgotten one evening when Durbin, drawing on his Oxford training as a zoologist, torpedoed a rather pretentious paper on the biological foundations of psychology given by a well-known child psychiatrist.

Sir Michael Postan and his wife, Professor Eileen Power, were themselves another Bloomsbury centre for socialist discussion, for they lived in Mecklenburgh Square and were friendly neighbours of Tawney, the other professor of economic history at LSE (his wife, Janet, was a sister of William Beveridge). In 1932 they formed a group 'to discuss the sociological and historical implications of economic problems', where papers were presented by Walter Adams and Denis Brogan, both in the politics department at UC, and by T. H. Marshall in social administration at LSE, a lifetime friend of the Postans and the Durbins. In the previous year Durbin had attended Postan's lectures on recent trends in the social structure of employment, the proliferation of elites and the relative decline of semi-skilled jobs; he then suggested that the group try to work out the implications of this trend for socialist policy. These meetings provided Gaitskell with the necessary evidence to enable him to reject the Marxian theory that the revolutionary army would be formed from the growth of a skilled working class – a major intellectual step, according to his biographer, Philip Williams.[40]

Gaitskell spent the academic year 1933–4 in Vienna on a Rockefeller research fellowship, in order to study Austrian capital theory at its source. In February 1934 Chancellor Dollfuss, head of a minority conservative Catholic government, with military support from Mussolini, attacked the powerful Austrian Socialist party and its private army, arrested its leaders, shelled the brand-new workers' flats and left 1,500 dead and 5,000 wounded after two days of street fighting. Gaitskell worked hard through the Coles to raise money in Britain and to smuggle prominent socialists out of the country before returning home that summer. He was transformed by this confrontation with violence into 'a proper social democrat', in the words of Noel Hall, his department chairman at UC. After the 1931 crisis Gaitskell had been more sympathetic than Durbin to revolutionary calls to abolish the House of Lords and to seize emergency power, but now he insisted on total support for parliamentary democracy and the rejection of revolutionary rhetoric.[41]

In Gaitskell's absence Durbin had taken his place as assistant honorary secretary on the national executive of the NFRB. When the Bureau's committees were reorganized in October 1933, Durbin was nominated to the research committee and placed in charge of the new financial policy committee of the economic section. When Gaitskell returned from Austria, he was appointed vice-chairman of the international section, and was duly elected to the national executive in the following year. They both remained in these positions until amalgamation with the Fabian Society in 1939, when they became joint assistant honorary secretaries.

Although there are no records, Sir Vaughan Berry and others think that sometime in 1934 Durbin and Gaitskell were invited to join the XYZ club. The earliest recorded evidence of their participation is a memorandum dated June 1935 and initialled H.V.B. and E.F.M.D. Through these activities Durbin and Gaitskell were also meeting City journalists, such as Francis Williams of the *Daily Herald*, Cecil Spriggs of the *Manchester Guardian* and Nicholas Davenport of the *New Statesman*. Davenport was a generous host to successive generations of 'levellers' in his lovely country house near Oxford, as he joyously recounted in his memoirs.[42] However, he was also considered wildly indiscreet by the secretive XYZ club members, who were not pleased to find large sections of their private papers appearing under his name in the weekly journals for which he wrote.[43] Davenport made substantial contributions to the Labour party's 1933 policy document, *Socialism and the Condition of the People*, but by the mid-1930s he was gradually being dropped from XYZ meetings.

Robert Fraser, a leader writer on the *Daily Herald*, was another new friend. An Australian, who had come to LSE in the mid-1920s, he had been strongly influenced by the Marxist thinking of his tutor, Harold Laski. As a member of the London University Labour Club, he had also been an active member of the New Fabian Group in the late 1920s. A splinter group of the Fabian Nursery for younger members, it had been formed in 1925 by W. A. Robson; while it lasted a number of pamphlets were produced of which Fraser wrote one, *A Socialist Philosophy for Fabians*. In 1930, his final year, Laski strongly recommended Fraser to William Mellor (Cole's guild socialist friend), who was reorganizing the *Daily Herald*, Labour's newspaper, as part of Odhams Press. Fraser took the job at nine guineas a week; he stayed there learning all aspects of journalism until he joined the ministry of information during the war. Sir Robert Fraser, who later became Director of Independent Television News, recently reflected that the crucial contribution from their debates in the 1930s was the commitment to political freedom and the redistribution of wealth. He feels now that they overrated the importance of nationalization and underrated the syndicalist effects of trade union power.

Douglas Jay became the financial journalist who worked closest with Durbin and Gaitskell at the XYZ club and on the party's policy subcommittees. Jay had gone to work for *The Times* in 1929, after getting a first in 'Greats' at Oxford. Later he won an All Souls' fellowship by writing a paper on neoclassical policical economy; he had been tutored informally by Lionel Robbins, who had him read Marshall, Pigou and Marx. One of his early subsequent assignments was to review Keynes's *Treatise on Money* for *The Times Literary Supplement*. However, he became disenchanted with the pro-Hitler bias of the editor, Geoffrey Dawson, and gladly accepted a job on *The Economist* in the spring of 1933. At the time only he and Graham Hutton were full-time staff writers, while Geoffrey Crowther worked part-time. Walter Layton, a Liberal who had worked with Keynes, was the editor, but he was very preoccupied because he was also the chairman of the *News Chronicle*. Hutton, a member of NFRB, briefly shared an apartment with Kingsley Martin, editor of the *New Statesman*, before getting his own flat in Bloomsbury; it was through him that Jay met Davenport, Thomas Balogh and Nicholas Kaldor.

On his honeymoon in 1933, Jay took for light reading the newly published *What Everybody Wants To Know About Money*, written by a number of NFRB economists; he was 'immensely impressed' with Gaitskell's chapter. Consequently, when he decided to become an active member of the Labour party, one of the first things he did was to contact the author:

> And when we lunched together I discovered that Gaitskell's feelings about the Nazis were as intense as my own . . . . We decided then and there to work together; and so began the closest working friendship of my life, which continued almost without a break and without disagreement, for close on thirty years till Gaitskell's death in January 1963.[44]

Jay's own book, *The Socialist Case*, was published in 1937; it has since been widely recognized as an important step in adapting Keynesian analysis to socialist goals for the Labour party.[45] Jay himself has said that the book owes most to Gaitskell, who read and criticized the typescript 'with great care and perspicacity', and to James Meade, whose book, *An Introduction to Economic Analysis and Policy*, published in 1936, influenced him more than any other printed work.

Conclusions

During the course of the 1930s this new generation of Fabians helped to redefine and to rearticulate the revisionist case for democratic socialism in Britain. Together they met the enormous challenge presented by Britain's economic collapse and the Labour party's political débâcle. It was an unparalleled situation in which the intellectual search for cures to economic woes merged with the party's internal consensus to rethink a practical socialist programme from first principles. To this task they brought their own special brand of social conscience. Looking back on their accomplishments fifteen years later, Gaitskell liked to think that they had succeeded in combining the influences of Cole's stimulating mind, of Dalton's political drive without 'his fierce intolerance', of Keynes's economics without his social philosophy and of Tawney's moral teaching with less of its emotionalism and its puritanism.[46]

In many ways their contributions also reflect the last great flowering of a particular kind of intellectual discourse, of social responsibility and of collective idealism. Apart from their teaching and writing, all their work for the party, for the NFRB and for the think tank was unpaid. Rarely can such talent and such energy have been rallied so willingly and so constructively. And despite the depression, they were optimists in many senses: they believed that problems could be solved rationally, that the state could intervene to correct and improve economic performance, that socialism represented the only ethical course to improve human society. Above all they had faith in their own abilities to tackle society's problems, to influence public decisions and eventually for some of them to win political power; they saw themselves as leaders in training.

In the early years Colin Clark was far the best known of the new generation amongst the party leaders. He worked closely with Attlee, Bevin and Keynes; he was a leading member of the Cole group and an important organizer for SSIP and the NFRB. He dined with Dalton fairly frequently, and helped to draft the party's conference resolutions and manifesto in 1931. Gaitskell was undoubtedly closest to G. D. H. Cole. Margaret Cole has described how Cole was briefly 'in love' with his pupil and protégé, feelings which both flattered and embarrassed the recipient, but which he did not reciprocate.[47] They worked together in the early months of the NFRB, but in June 1931 Cole was first stricken with the diabetes from which he died many years later, and his activities were considerably curtailed.

Durbin, who had never been as close to Cole, was rather impatient with his lack of economic rigour and his romantic nostalgia about the working class. He is still remembered for his unsentimental view of the reality of working-class life, as well as his unshakeable opposition to Marxist interpretations of the 1931 crisis and his extraordinary prescience about the inevitable outcome of the totalitarian Soviet regime. Durbin and Gaitskell were not widely known in the Labour movement until their work for the NFRB brought them to the closer attention of Hugh Dalton after 1933. Dalton first met Gaitskell when he came to speak in Nottingham during 1928, but after the 1931 crisis he was cool to anyone with connections to the dangerously militant Cole and suspicious of the economic influence of Lionel Robbins. Consequently, the first NFRB economist he approached directly was James Meade in November 1932. After 1933 their work for Dalton's committee brought Durbin and Gaitskell directly into the policy formation process within the Labour party.

Clark, Durbin, Fraser, Gaitskell and Parker were the most politically active among the new generation in the early 1930s; they all stood for election in 1935. But, as Dalton later wrote, 'nearly everyone I cared for in the younger generation had been beaten. John Parker was a solitary young victor'.[48] Although many recall Durbin's outspoken integrity and early leadership potential, it was not until the late 1930s that Gaitskell emerged in the same light. Douglas Jay, who had become increasingly aware of Gaitskell's 'penetrating common sense', only recognized 'his extraordinary reserve of underlying strength', his confident and accurate appraisal of political reality and his will 'like a dividing spear' during the Munich crisis in 1938.[49] But in the meantime, in crowded classrooms and leisurely senior common rooms, in stuffy committee rooms and the freezing NFRB office, in pubs and restaurants and coffee shops, in welcoming homes and country cottages, another, largely unheralded, Bloomsbury group argued out the economics and politics of a reformed Britain, which still echo in modern discussions of democratic socialism.

CHAPTER 6
COLE AND THE NEW FABIANS ATTACK TRADITIONAL POLICY

The New Fabian Research Bureau (NFRB) had already designed its programme of research and published its first pamphlet before the political and financial crisis of 1931. Part of its purpose was to repair two weaknesses in the government's performance, its inability to cope with mounting unemployment and its failure to introduce any significant measures of socialism. More fundamentally, the party's 'loyal grousers' were questioning MacDonald's conception of gradualism and a party programme of vague promises such as those contained in *Labour and the Nation*. In addition, Snowden's policies were under attack on two fronts. First, his insistence on orthodox deflationary policies to maintain the gold standard and to balance the budget was being challenged by all who favoured expansionary measures to combat unemployment. Second, his reliance on redistributive taxation to eradicate poverty was increasingly criticized by socialists, who doubted whether taxation alone would be sufficient to transform society and redistribute power between the classes.

At the Bureau's first executive meeting it was formally decided that only the author or committee doing the research was to be held responsible for the views expressed.[1] Therefore, unlike the Labour party, the NFRB did not face the difficulties of getting formal resolutions adopted as an official position. This so-called 'self-denying' ordinance was also included in the constitution when the NFRB amalgamated with the Fabian Society in 1939; it remains in effect to this day. However, the executive did have some control over research conclusions, for they decided what was to be published, and they appointed two readers to check facts and style and to make recommendations. In practice, a considerable amount of rewriting was often requested, and on a few occasions publication was refused, twice for fear of litigation.

The policy views discussed in this study are those of individual Bureau members or committees, which were not necessarily consistent with each other. Indeed, there were crucial differences between the Bureau economists, which reflected the diversity of economic opinion on theory and policy, and the relation between the two. Four main policy areas are explored: industrial policy, redistributional policy, macroeconomic policy and the theory of socialist planning. The first two represent the traditional means of nationalization and taxation by which the Labour party had proposed to bring socialism to Britain. The second two broke new ground in the theory and practice of economic policy for a Labour government. In this chapter the Bureau's vigorous, if somewhat muddle-headed, attack on traditional party policy in the early 1930s is explored; the first steps towards a new socialist economics are taken up in the following chapters.

The research record has been pieced together from the periodic research reports of the Bureau, which listed the memoranda submitted to the committees. Some of these memoranda have survived in the Fabian Society papers, and a few were located elsewhere. Fortunately, most of the final reports of committees were published as NFRB pamphlets; other submissions were published in NFRB books or elsewhere in the economics literature. There are some unfortunate gaps, particularly in the work by Meade and Durbin, but their views can be inferred from available sources.

Organizing the Bureau's economic research

The NFRB was a hive of organizational activity throughout the spring of 1931. There were lengthy committee meetings in Abingdon Street, weekend conferences at Easton Lodge and innumerable informal group discussions. After one such session in early March, Evan Durbin sent Colin Clark his proposals for a structure of economics committees based on 'the natural division of subjects' into 'the economics of control, the economics of equalitarian legislation and pure theory'.[2] He wanted to separate the control issues into 'productive industries' and 'banking and finance', for he felt strongly that the latter constituted 'a fruitful single subject for *socialist* research'. However, the executive committee led by G. D. H. Cole, its secretary, rejected this approach. Cole saw banking, monetary policy and especially the trade cycle as capitalist economics. For socialist economics he viewed planning and capital supply as the central questions, which arose from the need to organize production in the socialist state. This perspective prevailed in the Bureau's initial research design.

Cole had first expressed his implicit criticism of the party's official policy in his book, *The Next Ten Years of British Social and Economic Policy*, published in March 1929. In an about-face from his guild socialist days, he conceded that the state must have the authority to introduce socialism and to run economic policy. However, he emphasized the importance of establishing control over policy rather than taking over the ownership of industries for its own sake. His subsequent exposure to Keynes's ideas confirmed his faith in Hobsonian economics and convinced him that expansionary policies were essential to reduce unemployment. Thus, until the crisis of August 1931, Cole recommended that the socialist authorities devise programmes for the recovery of the capitalist system, not its immediate overthrow, before taking steps to introduce socialism.

In May 1931 the NFRB published its first document, *Memorandum on a Plan of Research into Economic Policy*, which Cole wrote. The purpose of its economic research, according to the author, was to seek

> fresh examination from the Socialist standpoint, . . . not only on the immediate measures which ought to be pressed forward and the reactions which may be expected to follow them, but also on the underlying conception of a socialist economic system and the way of working towards it. It is not the object to lay down hastily, and on the basis of mere opinion, any new or comprehensive policy, but rather to make use of research work and evidence concerning practical developments that are already available, to supplement them by fresh research and then to place in the hands of the members and of the Labour Movement a body of information designed to lead to clearer thinking and better formulation of policies for the future.[3]

Its emphasis, therefore, was upon formulating the right questions, providing information and, possibly, making recommendations; it was not meant to devise either specific legislative proposals or a blue-print for a socialist state.

The memorandum identified eight main topics, proposing to set up committees to work on each one. Cole elaborated dozens of questions to be addressed, the whole giving a good sense of the man who wrote to Beatrice Webb that he was 'bubbling with ideas just now'.[4] The eight sections were titled as follows:

1 Form and scope of State control and socialisation of industry, Rationalisation and the reform of commercial law;

2 The machinery of Economic Planning and the problem of Capital Supply;
3 Economic and Technical Research, in their relations to economic development, State organisation and control and working-class conditions;
4 Appointment and dismissal of managers and staff in socialist or State-controlled enterprises, questions of wages, hours and conditions, and the problem of workers' control in industry;
5 The Standard of Living in relation to wages and social services, the promotion of economic equality on these lines, including the problems of taxation and taxable capacity;
6 The Theory of Socialist Policy, including the problem of Price Regulation and the Distribution of Productive Resources;
7 Foreign Trade, including the question of control of imports and exports, the problem of State or collective trading, and the question of Protection v. Free Trade;
8 Financial and Industrial Fluctuations, including unemployment and the 'trade cycle', banking policy and the price level, and the possible nationalisation of the Banking system.

The research questions which Cole raised under each of these topics were strong on institutional and programmatic considerations, but weaker on theoretical connections. The problem of unemployment was given short shrift. There was no inquiry proposed into the use of public works to provide jobs, and little on unemployment insurance. The problem of the gold standard and the effect of international exchange rate policy on Britain's position was not mentioned, although under 'foreign trade' issues were raised about import boards, state control of trade relations, protection and imperial preference. Thus, the overall design reflected the Webbian organizational approach and Cole's long-term planning concerns. The immediate problems facing Britain's capitalist economy were added at the end.

At a general meeting held on 29 May 1931, the young economists, in particular Clark and Durbin, pointed out that long-term and short-term policies could not be separated so easily. In the end a compromise was reached; an economic planning and capital supply committee convened by Clark would deal with organizational and structural questions, including the socialization of banking; a price level and industrial fluctuations committee convened by Durbin would handle policy questions. Thus, the crucial internal debates on macroeconomic theory and Keynesian policies took place in Durbin's committee well before the publication of *The General Theory*. In practice the economists thrashed out the issues in many different arenas and regularly met to discuss each others' professional papers, as well as their memoranda for the NFRB.

The main burden of organizing the economic research fell to Hugh Gaitskell after Cole was taken ill in June 1931. He noted in exasperation at the time: 'so far the committee has spent its whole time appointing subcommittees.'[5] But in the end he managed to get nine active committees off the ground; their members wrote memoranda, which were circulated, they attended meetings and conferences, and by 1933 they had also published a number of pamphlets and books. Despite physical restrictions, Cole remained a busy organizer of the socialization committee, and eventually took over the workers' control committee as well. Thus, Cole was largely responsible for the Bureau's research on industrial policy in the early 1930s. Redistributional policy was tackled in three committees, one on wages convened by Gaitskell, one on social services convened by Barbara Drake and one on taxation chaired by Barbara Wootton. Socialist planning questions were covered in Clark's committee and in another on the theory of socialist policy also convened by Gaitskell. Finally, besides Durbin's macroeconomic policy committee, there was a foreign trade committee, which Leonard Woolf took over as chairman of the Bureau's international section.

There were three main effects of the 1931 crisis on the Bureau's research agenda. First, it added a sense of urgency and defiance to their tasks and deepened the need for critical reappraisal of the party's traditional assumptions and of economic orthodoxy. Second, it pinpointed the party's appalling ignorance of the operation of banking and financial markets, and convinced the leaders that they must be educated in the proper management of the system. Third, it cast grave doubts on the possibility of introducing socialism by a gradual process of squeezing concessions from capitalism. Cole, for example, as well as Cripps and for a while Attlee, became convinced that nothing short of a revolutionary take-over of the economic system would enable the party to achieve its socialist goals. Even party moderates such as Bevin, Dalton and Morrison were willing to contemplate the assumption of emergency powers, if capitalists refused to co-operate with a Labour government. The younger generation was similarly torn; however, the Bureau economists all remained loyal to the party's leadership, and none of them followed Cripps into the Socialist League.

Industrial policy

The socialization committee members examined an enormous number of specific industries to study the case and the appropriate form for their public control. They also wrote a series of memoranda and pamphlets on the general principles of socialization. Cole believed that 'the question of Socialisation and Social Control of industry can profitably be studied in detail only in relation to particular industries or services, as the appropriate ways of approach and forms of organization are bound to vary widely from case to case'.[6] He outlined four general problems, the definition of socialization, control by government or Parliament, the provision of capital and the time of compensation. He also raised questions about other forms of social control which should be investigated, such as marketing boards, compulsory reorganization or rationalization, and regulation of prices, profits and labour conditions.

In 1933 Cole wrote a long series of notes 'for the use of research workers in drawing up reports on the socialization of particular industries', who were warned that the notes 'may seem unduly formidable', but 'it is believed that the research worker will be able to get to work with greater confidence and promptitude if he approaches the study of the material with a fairly detailed idea in his mind of what he wants to get from it'.[7] These notes contained instructions on how to digest existing materials and how to draft a scheme of socialization, as well as a list of thirteen specific questions to address.

It is impossible to do justice here to the richness and diversity of the industry studies undertaken by the NFRB; indeed, they probably deserve a study of their own. During the 1930s, conferences were held on the socialization of banking (of which more later), of transport and of the iron and steel industry. The Bureau published pamphlets on the nationalization of five industries: West Country minerals, aircraft manufacture, milk, electrical supply, and iron and steel. Numerous other unpublished reports can be found in Cole's papers and the NFRB files, and many others were listed in the research reports; they included studies of gas, coal, flour milling, retail food distribution, electrical manufacturing and armaments, and references were made to studies of cotton, anthracite, chemicals, insurance and the motor industry. The 1935 research report noted that the reports on aircraft manufacture and armaments were 'used in preparation of evidence for Arms Inquiry'. The Bureau also set up two ad hoc committees on transportation and agriculture (land nationalization was a hot topic); conferences were held on agricultural policy by SSIP in 1931, and on food policy by the NFRB in 1938.

In 1937 Professor W. A. Robson, an influential member of the Bureau's political section, edited a volume, *Public Enterprise*, which drew on NFRB research into the various forms of existing industry organizations, such as the Post Office, the BBC, the London Passenger Transport Board, the Coal Reorganization Committee, and the Co-operative movement. In her history of Fabian socialism, Margaret Cole later noted that this book 'undoubtedly played some part in the formulation of Labour policy with regard to nationalization', and that 'its general tenor was to accept the idea of an independent corporation . . . sponsored by Herbert Morrison'.[8] Ben Pimlott has argued that the NFRB's 'contribution was in building up confidence in the viability of Labour's plans, offering detailed blue-prints where, in the MacDonald era, there had been vague generalities.'[9]

A considerable amount of research was conducted on the different forms which public control of industries might take, and on the relation of the government to them. Cole himself outlined a number in his research memorandum, and in the Bureau's first pamphlet, *The Essentials of Socialism*, he raised ten questions about the critical elements. Most of his concerns were administrative, but he also addressed the basic problems of capital supply, pricing policy and profits, which were central to the emerging debate over the appropriate economics for the socialist state.

In this pamphlet Cole argued that socialized undertakings should be allowed to charge prices sufficient to pay 'a reasonable return on capital', so that industries would not run at a loss.[10] In order to raise capital, Cole advocated a National Investment Board (NIB) to distribute the necessary funds for new capital development, although most industrialized industries should be able to finance their own capital development from their accumulated profits like private companies. This meant that nationalized concerns must be allowed to build up 'reasonable reserve funds' and not have their surplus incomes 'automatically appropriated by the Exchequer'. Such a policy was contrary to the traditional socialist opposition to profits, because they were assumed to depress wages and to benefit the rich at the expense of the poor. However, Cole explained that under a system based on economic equality, profits would serve an entirely different purpose:

> As we approach such a system . . . the community will distribute in wages and salaries only the amounts it means people to be free to spend, and not also the sums it wants them to invest; and funds for investment will be provided directly out of the product of industry before incomes are distributed to individuals.[11]

In addition to providing a reasonable wage and the necessary capital supply for investment, as long as there were substantial income inequalities, it was also important to reduce the prices of consumer goods. But, Cole did not think prices should be reduced 'in the case of industries producing producers' goods, providing services, or producing luxuries'. Thus, Cole wanted nationalized industries to charge prices high enough to accumulate reserves, because he thought it was by far the simplest way of raising the appropriate amount of capital.

The problems of profits and expenditure control were developed in an exchange of memoranda between Cole and Attlee at the end of 1931.[12] On the question of allowing profits to accumulate, Cole outlined three options with objections to each: the industry should keep all the surplus; the State should take it all; or they should share it. He was against industry getting all the surplus, but recognized the need for management to have 'an incentive for economical management'. He suggested that industries should present development schemes along with regular accounting to the NIB; through its power of approval and modification, the Board would in effect decide how much surplus could be kept. The Board would take the remainder for other projects, and lend it to industries not making any surplus. Cole noted as an aside at the end of his discussion that 'the amount of surplus a socialized undertaking earns will be affected by the prices it charges for its product or service'; he felt that some form of wage and price control by the State would be necessary, but that these issues were beyond the scope of his memorandum.

Attlee challenged Cole's whole approach, because he did not think that 'the subject can be dealt with adequately, until the two matters relegated to a "note" are more fully considered'. Cole had implied that the surplus was 'something arising more or less fortuitously in a particular year', while Attlee believed that:

> In practice, at any rate in public utility undertakings such as
> electricity supply and the Post Office, the production of a surplus
> depends on certain factors which are ascertainable within fairly
> narrow limits. These are demand, cost of materials, rates of
> interest and wages where machinery exists for their determination.

He concluded that the 'provision of capital assets out of revenue depends on how far it is right to deny advantages to present consumers and/or staff in the interests of posterity'. From his experiences as the postmaster general, he felt that the choice often depended on the influence of the minister upon the chancellor of the exchequer. In any case, price was not the only consideration; there was also the question of 'amenities' for consumers and for workers. For example, in the Post

Office he had to decide about extra deliveries, more, better and brighter post offices and better staff accommodation. Both price-fixing and wage-fixing State bodies would have to take such amenities into account.

Attlee did agree with Cole that State expropriation of the entire surplus would have 'a thoroughly bad effect cramping initiative'. However, he considered that the same objection applied to the approval of capital development schemes by the NIB. He preferred to have nationalized industries pay 'a certain sum to the state by way of rent' and keep the rest to spend as management saw fit. Attlee thought that it was undesirable for new capital investment to be provided from current revenue, because one industry might need far more capital equipment than another. He also pointed out:

> There is no reason why this capital should be provided at the expense of the present consumers of the products of that industry or instead of increased amenities to the workers in that industry for the time being. Further as between one industry which has provided capital out of revenue in the past and another which has been capitalised by the State and has presumably to pay interest to the State on that capital there may arise disputes as to the disparity of remuneration and conditions between different groups of workers unless of course we have reached a Shavian equality in this respect.

Attlee believed that the government should provide the necessary capital for industry; 'the State should be ground landlord and debenture holder but not ordinary shareholder vis à vis industrial undertakings'.

Durbin apparently also disagreed with Cole, but for entirely different reasons. In marginal notes on his own copy of this pamphlet, he commented that Cole had ignored 'the need for property' and 'the disposal of funds for investment according to a universal Rate of Interest'. This rate of interest, which the NIB should charge all nationalized industries, could only be secured by 'free saving in a competitive equilibrium'. Consumers were best protected by market pricing and free choice of occupation; workers should control 'conditions of production', but *not* prices, entry or wages. Thus, both Attlee from a knowledge of practical difficulties and Durbin from a concern with theoretical efficiency criteria shared an impatience with Cole's vague notions of industry control by State fiat.

It is also striking that Cole failed to include any criteria for nationalization in his list of general problems. In his outline for the Bureau's economic research, he listed a number of industries to be investigated because they were 'ripe for socialisation', without spelling out what that was supposed to mean. At the general meeting in May, Ben Greene had argued that 'a criteria of efficiency' should be used. The enormous number of industries which were investigated by the socialization committee does suggest that Cole considered all industries potential candidates. In his pamphlet he also stated that he presumed 'the final aim is the complete elimination of the private investor from the sphere of socialized industries and services' (Durbin strongly disapproved).[13] The choice of which industries to nationalize, and at what stage, became one of the critical policy choices made by the Labour party during the 1930s. The appropriate criteria for intervention remain a fundamental problem for governments wishing to regulate industries for the public good.

Redistributional policy

Cole's original research design addressed redistributional issues by posing the question 'How far is it an essential part of socialist policy to promote more equal distribution of incomes (a) by raising real wages, (b) by development of the social services?'[14] Elaboration of the research questions on the social services included such topics as the limits of taxation for financing social services and the effects of taxation on the accumulation of capital, on the costs of production and on profits. These problems were central to the Labour party's positions that inequality could be reduced by taxing the rich to pay for social services for the poor (Snowden's approach) and that trade union activity to raise workers' wages and conditions improved the distribution of income (the trade union view). Many Labour supporters also argued that unions should resist wage cuts during a depression and push for wage increases during a boom, in order to reduce inequality, to improve purchasing power and to maintain growth (the underconsumption theory of Hobson).

It was decided at committee meetings chaired by Gaitskell in the summer of 1931 to divide this work between three committees, one on wages, one on taxation and one on social services.[15] The social services committee further subdivided itself into a housing committee and an education committee, which were moved to the local government committee chaired by W. A. Robson in 1933. Pamphlets were published on housing, technical education, rent rebates, nutrition and adult education. In the late 1930s funded research projects were undertaken on unemployment compensation and on the national assistance board. Assisted by Bureau researchers, Robson published a book of essays, *Social Security*, at the beginning of the war, which became an influential source of evidence for the Beveridge Report. Many Fabians also served as staff for the Beveridge commission. Thus, although the NFRB later made important contributions to the development of the British welfare system of social services, in the early 1930s the main work on redistributive policy was undertaken by the wages and taxation committees.

The wages committee

The wages committee started work immediately, laying out an ambitious review of wage movements, cost of living, industry wage rates, rationalization schemes, wage-fixing machinery and union attitudes to new technology. Although the committee decided to approach some unions on these questions, there was no report of any factual findings on these matters. The only reported memoranda from this committee were by Gaitskell and Durbin and were highly theoretical.[16]

The two young economists worked out their position during a holiday in the Lake District in 1932. They stayed with the Postans in Patterdale; according to Durbin, it was Munia who convinced them of the hopelessness of 'eleemosynary socialism', that is, redistribution through government-financed services.[17] They assured their friends that they had solved the wage problem under socialism. Sir Henry Phelps Brown, one of their walking companions, has never forgotten his astonishment when Evan solemnly explained that wages must be determined by the marginal product of the worker, and that high wages might actually cause unemployment. Thus, as Durbin's comments on investment indicate and their joint work on the theory of socialist economics makes even clearer, the two comrades were systematically applying neoclassical principles to socialist policy questions; 'pure theory' meant Marshall.

Durbin and Gaitskell hoped to publish their work on wages as a book, but in November 1932 Faber and Faber rejected their manuscript.[18] Cole recommended substantial reworking before submitting to Macmillan; his basic criticism was that the manuscript was too academic and expensive for the lay reader and not comprehensive enough to sell as a textbook. Durbin suggested that they rewrite the book as an analysis of trade union policy in three parts; the first two parts would use their existing chapters and they would add a section on wage and tax policies. They evidently completed this version during the summer of 1933; however, only the introduction and first two parts have survived in the NFRB files and in Cole's papers. The book was never published, although Durbin used large portions of his section in his NFRB pamphlet, *Socialist Credit Policy*, which will be discussed in the next chapter.

It is not difficult to see why the manuscript was rejected, since it is an uneasy combination of political rhetoric and laborious theoretical analysis. Gaitskell's economic analysis was a worthy attempt to estimate the impact of union wage policies on wages and employment in particular industries; but it was neither as systematic nor as lucid as Hicks's *Theory of Wages*, which was published in 1932. Durbin's analysis tackled the relationship between production and the general level of money wages under capitalism, and the question of whether the capitalist system would inevitably break down. Nevertheless, the study provides a revealing glimpse into the early thinking of these prominent socialist economists about the relationship of economic policy to socialism. They also attacked the traditional aims of union collective bargaining to secure high wages for their members, which they perceived as misguided attempts to reduce inequality by piecemeal redistribution within industries. Nor were they afraid to raise the thorniest problem for Labour party policy, namely, the possibility that sectional union policies might actually subvert the public interest.

Although Gaitskell wrote the introduction, it expressed the authors' shared views on socialism, economics and distributional policy and outlined their opinion of the Labour party's approach to these questions. It opened as follows:

> To remove the economic injustice implicit in capitalist society is the ideal which all Socialist movements have in common. This injustice is in part caused by, in part identical with, economic inequality. Hence the destruction of this inequality, the creating and maintaining of a society in which it cannot exist becomes the essential and direct purpose of all Socialist policy.

Gaitskell contrasted the Marxist-Communist approach with 'the mild tempered evolutionary idealists' of the British Labour party. He rejected the Marxists' aim of a classless rather than an equal society, as well as their revolutionary tactics. He identified with the rational parliamentary approach, but warned of the inherent dangers of confusing the party's central goal of equality with electorally attractive 'subsidiary aims'.

Gaitskell was especially vehement that 'prosperity measures' to reduce unemployment and increase productivity must not be permitted to 'usurp the position of equality':

> Prosperity as an aim is important. No political movement can afford to neglect it. But, it must be stated emphatically, it is not

the distinguishing characteristic of the Socialist ideal. A Socialist party is different from other parties not because it offers a different mechanism for the same object, but because the object itself is different. Even economic planning, the institutional machinery of [the] Socialist State, is not a monopoly of Socialism and can exist without Socialism. Still more is this true of a particular monetary policy or the public control of an individual industry. But in the goal of equality, the determination to uproot the conditions of economic injustice, lies the true characteristic of a Socialist. All Socialist activity must ultimately be judged by its successes in achieving this end.

He went on to outline the two main lines of redistributional policy by which the British labour movement had pursued equality, progressive taxation through government action and improvements in wages and working conditions through industrial action. He argued that apart from these two methods ('whose achievements indeed should not be underestimated') little or nothing had been done to hasten the progress towards equality; 'nationalization has been discussed in speech and writing . . . but the attempts to put it into practice during the last decade can be numbered on the fingers of one hand'.

Gaitskell concluded that this reformist strategy of 'nibbling' and 'tinkering' had essentially been undermined by the failure of the two Labour governments to introduce socialism and by the onset of the world depression. He therefore called for a 'scientific' re-examination of the traditional approach to decide to what extent industrial action could succeed in transferring income from property owners to workers 'without leading to an economic situation which is quite intolerable to the workers'. Gaitskell felt that this problem had been ignored in the past because trade unions had been fighting for survival, but now that they were well established the effect of high wage policies must be explored. He warned that unionists might become 'very indignant' at the implied criticism of their past activities, but asked for their patience; he promised that the questions had been chosen for their political importance; they had deliberately avoided the 'preoccupation of Economic Science' with the long run, with problems 'in which the public was not in the least interested' and with answers 'which appeared entirely satisfactory to the expert [but] seemed to the layman to be either quite untrue or else beside the point'.

The remainder of Gaitskell's long manuscript provided only theoretical answers; on the last two pages contrasting examples of the coal and railway industries were presented as illustrations. The analysis was entirely based on microeconomic arguments about the nature of supply and demand in individual industries, which Gaitskell spelled out in semi-textbook fashion. He argued that the question of whether trade unions could raise wages without causing unemployment, and consequently alter the distribution of income between shareholders and workers, depended entirely upon the elasticity of demand for labour. Only if labour was a fixed cost or if the industry was a monopoly could trade unions expect to raise wages without causing serious unemployment; if unions succeeded in raising wages, they might also raise prices at the consumer's expense. Only where the union caused a reduction in capitalists' profits was a high-wage policy justified on redistributive grounds.

Although the surviving manuscript does not contain Gaitskell's conclusions, Durbin had suggested that 'we draw the conclusion that previous methods are played out and that the future lies with nationalisation'. It is perhaps not too surprising that this manuscript was never published as an NFRB pamphlet either. Dame Margaret Cole believed that some trade unionists were asked to review it and recommended against publication.

The taxation committee

While the wages committee attacked the traditional view that trade unions could extract concessions from employers, the taxation committee attacked the extent to which the government could extract social service concessions by increasing taxation to redistribute incomes. This committee was somewhat slower to get going. However, Barbara Wootton took over its chairmanship in early 1932, and in November it was reported to be meeting regularly; Harold Barger had drafted a section and Radice collected some statistics.[19] Barger has recalled some difficulties with Barbara Wootton; 'she had a vague idea that centralized planning could solve all problems'. Eventually a pamphlet, *Taxation under Capitalism: Effects on Social Services*, was published in late 1933 as 'a report of the taxation committee' and signed by the chairman, Harold Barger, E. A. Radice and Barbara Drake.

The pamphlet described the nature of taxation and taxable capacity; it provided an historical survey and statistics on direct and indirect taxes and the incidence of taxation by income group in Britain. Its main purpose was to explore to what extent taxable limits had been reached, because 'ability to expand the social services depends upon the possibility of raising the necessary money by taxation'. Their study drew some interesting and unexpected conclusions for the period. They pointed out that indirect taxes were highly regressive in their incidence; furthermore, beyond a certain point, their increase would only lead to a reduction in consumption. They discovered that a large part of national savings were made by the middle and working classes, not the rich. They therefore concluded that indirect taxes should not be increased. Turning to direct taxation, the committee argued that the maximum rates of income tax and death duties 'compatible with expediency' were determined by the incentives to work, to save and to invest, and by 'the use to which the funds raised in taxation are put'.[20] They reviewed the evidence and concluded that any further expansion of social services might well exceed the limits of feasible taxation. They summarized their case against traditional party policy as follows:

> If we conclude that the present burden of taxation offers no cause for alarm, it would nevertheless appear that the limits of redistributive taxation as an engine of social reform may soon be reached. It would seem in fact that taxation is no longer the 'cutting edge of socialism' which Lord Snowden at one time thought it.[21]

Since there was a limit to society's taxable capacity, the committee recommended that saving and investment should become public functions, in order to ensure the necessary funds to improve education, health and other social services. If the sources of wealth were largely controlled and owned by the State, there could be no disincentive effect of taxation on the willingness to save and invest; 'taxation merely becomes part of the apparatus whereby that wealth is distributed'.[22]

The taxation committee also suggested that socialized industries be required to run at a surplus, which could in part be used to finance the extension of social services: 'this form of taxation which is strictly neither direct nor indirect . . . will be made possible by selling the products of socialised undertakings at above cost price'. Their optimistic conclusion was that by linking taxation and social services with wage payments and the general level of economic activity, 'the State will be able to make accurate provision both for the saving of resources for the future and for the distribution of consumable goods'. Pressed by the chairman, Barbara Wootton, the committee ended its report as follows: 'As in Soviet Russia, private and public finance will no longer be separate, and there will at last be some guarantee that the community's resources will be fully used and distributed to the best advantage'.[23] Thus, the party's traditional expectation, that redistribution could be accomplished by financing social services from taxation, was demolished. Like the wages committee, the taxation committee urged extensive public ownership as the alternative. Unlike Durbin and Gaitskell, who relied upon a considerable degree of market pricing, the suggested model was the Soviet form of centralized planning.

Conclusions

The New Fabians attacked the Labour party's traditional nationaliz- ation and redistribution policies on various grounds. They were all agreed that the programme as a whole was insufficient to effect the transition to socialism; they also believed that many of the specifics were economically inefficient. The main contributions of the Bureau's research in these areas were the detailed industry studies and proposed plans for reorganization, and the emphasis on the social control of industry as the distinguishing feature of socialism. The Bureau econom- ists rejected arguments for winning piecemeal concessions from capi- talism through higher wages, taxes and social services as the effective way to redistribute incomes; they recommended nationalization of a significant segment of the economy instead. However, there was a wide divergency of views about how policy towards the nationalized industries should be used for redistributional purposes. At one end of the spectrum, the taxation committee proposed deliberate pricing above cost to raise revenues to finance increases in the social services; at the other end, Attlee advocated industry responsibility for its own pricing policy to take acocunt of consumer demand, workers' wages and conditions, although the state should plan new investment. In between, Cole called for central planning to decide upon prices, wages and investment, industry by industry.

One reason for the emphasis on nationalization was the dawning recognition that neither prosperity measures, nor increased taxation and social services, nor government intervention in industry, would automatically reduce inequality. The demands for government inter- vention in the free play of the market system by Liberals and maverick Tories, which were enhanced by the world depression, challenged Labour supporters to define the socialist content of their proposals more specifically. At the same time, the demand for practical proposals forced hard thinking about the realities of pricing, wages, taxation, incentives, investment and 'amenities', and the interrelationships between them.

While the Bureau researchers agreed that socialism would provide a more rational planning environment than the chaotic market system, their views on the specifics were often vague at this early stage. Never- theless, it is possible to detect two different approaches to the problems which their research uncovered. Durbin and Gaitskell were determined to use 'scientific economics' to theorize about policy effects and to apply allocative efficiency criteria in the socialist state. If their enthusiasm for intellectual rigour led to some rather naive and unrealistic conclusions in these early days, they must be credited as pioneers in their advocacy of market pricing. Their view contrasted sharply with that of Cole and Wootton, who believed that central planning authorities could resolve the complex problems of resource allocation with a judicious combination of economic efficiency and redistributional criteria.

As attacks on the Labour party's traditional economic policy, neither of these approaches provided a coherent alternative as yet. One continued the Fabian tradition of using neoclassical arguments to justify government intervention, although in the case of the labour market the logic was used against trade union intervention. The other replaced vaguely evolutionary socialism with vaguely planned socialism. The attack on incremental nationalization and piecemeal redistribution did uncover important problems for socialist policies, which needed to be tackled. The most important contribution was to destroy the assumption that socialism could emerge in the long run from a democratic process of transforming successful capitalism, and to face head-on the question of how a Labour government should deal with the failures of capitalism in the short run.

CHAPTER 7
THE NEW FABIANS
ATTACK
UNEMPLOYMENT

Despite universal agreement that unemployment was Britain's central economic problem in the early 1930s, there was total disagreement about the necessary theory to analyse its causes. As Evan Durbin wrote to Colin Clark in March 1931, urging theoretical research into the economics of control 'Economics is in such a muddle that anyone can say what they think'. Nevertheless, even at the time it was obvious that the most fundamental policy cleavage was between those allied with Keynes, who advocated government intervention to manage market forces, and those sharing the 'Treasury view', who did not. Socialists were naturally in sympathy with the interventionists on social and political grounds, as well as economic ones. However, when the New Fabian economists came to examine the problems more closely, they found that they too disagreed about the basic reasons for the depression, about the likelihood of recovery and about the proper way to intervene.

The exit of Snowden and the devaluation of the pound ushered in a new era of policy thinking within the Labour party; yet, the party remained cautious about unemployment policy. Although Snowden's deliberately deflationary policies to lower domestic prices had been rejected at the 1931 conference, Keynes's 'inflationary' recommendation to expand public works and to create jobs was not adopted. Nor did the party endorse underconsumptionist proposals to increase purchasing power by introducing family allowances and raising the minimum wage, because these were also viewed as fiscally irresponsible. One critical lesson which the Labour leaders had learned was that they must be able to deal with unemployment in the capitalist system, if they wanted to win and maintain electoral support. Socialist economists were also beginning to question how the socialist system itself would have to be managed in order to ensure the full employment of all resources.

During the 1920s Keynes's challenge to economic orthodoxy had been practical rather than theoretical. His essential message was to try to shift government attention from upholding the automatic regulation of the market, as represented for instance by the gold standard, to deliberate management with the policy tools available. He focused upon the stabilization of general prices as the policy objective, and recommended monetary methods of control. By 1928 he was also pressing for government-financed public works to expand the economy, but his argument rested on the special case of a country which needed high interest rates to maintain its exchange rate; the theoretical base was still monetary. It was not until his new theory of effective demand was spelled out that the theoretical case for fiscal intervention was fully articulated.

The interplay between Keynes's shifting policy positions and his developing theoretical ideas in this period makes the task of untangling who thought what when peculiarly complicated. Modern research is under way, but the findings are often as controversial as Keynes's own ideas and sometimes conflict with the recollections of important protagonists.[1] However, for the purposes of this study, it is possible to distinguish three separate stages, which do reasonable justice to all the evidence. In the first stage, the early work of the Cambridge 'circus', which gave birth to Kahn's multiplier, convinced Keynes and the participants that expansion was possible without inflation on theoretical grounds and that they were on the right track to formulating a new model to explain unemployment. However, it seems clear that they did not understand the full implications of the multiplier until 1933, when Keynes spelled them out in his pamphlet, *A Means to Prosperity*, and in an article on 'The Multiplier'. By the autumn of 1933 the shift from models explaining price levels to models explaining output and employment was apparent in Keynes's lectures, which, it has been argued, were the first time he presented a recognizable version of the theory of effective demand.[2] In the last stage up to the publication of *The General Theory* in 1936, Keynes systematically worked out the connecting links between the money market, the determinants of investment and the level of output as specified in the final version.

In order to appreciate the controversies of the early 1930s, it is important for analysts weaned on Keynesian concepts to understand that there were legitimate grounds to challenge the theoretical basis of Keynes's policy positions at the time. Besides arguments about labour market rigidities to account for structural unemployment, the accepted way to explain general unemployment was as part of the downswing of the business cycle. Thus, its causes were attributed to whatever factors precipitated the crisis which upset the boom period and brought about the slump. However, there was such a plethora of these theories, each using different notations, each bearing different policy implications, that it was difficult, if not impossible, to judge between them. Some emphasized monetary phenomena, others income distribution, and still others exogenous factors such as harvests and inventions.[3] Cycle theories usually raise broader issues than the current level of employment. For example, price changes affect real incomes, investment determines productivity growth and the amplitude of the cycle describes the relative stability of the system. Thus, the onset of the great depression raised theoretical spectres of long-term stagnation, intensified boom-and-bust cycles and the ultimate collapse of the market system.

At the London School of Economics (LSE) the recently appointed Professor Hayek was a business cycle expert. As a young man he had suffered through the postwar hyperinflation in Austria. He firmly believed that the crisis and the downswing were caused by an artificial credit boom in the producers' sector, which only the market system could correct.[4] Together with Professor Robbins, he provided the main source of theoretical criticism of Keynes's 'inflationary' expansionism. In his model, the cyclical process depended on the lengthening and shortening of the structure of production; the more 'roundabout' (or longer) this process, the more capitalistic its methods of production and the greater its potential for growth. Voluntary saving could sustain the higher capitalization because it would shift demand from consumers' goods to producers' goods, but a bank credit boom would distort the structure of production by creating excess capital capacity in the producers' goods sector and capital scarcity in the consumer goods sector. Thus, the crisis and downswing were brought about by insufficient saving and too much consumer demand, the very opposite of Keynesian analysis at the time. Furthermore, the upswing would only occur when the price mechanisms of the free market system had ensured that all the mistaken investments undertaken in the artificial credit boom had been written off. The government should not interfere with this process; it should encourage saving, raise the interest rate and above all refrain from increased investment by an 'injection of credit', which would only distort the structure of production further and cause a worse crisis. Thus, Hayek stood for deflation through automatic market forces, in direct and public opposition to Keynes's stand in favour of expansion through active government intervention.

When he first came to LSE in 1930, Hayek presented his findings in a series of lectures entitled *Prices and Production*, which was published as a book the following year. Their effect was 'magical' according to Ronald Coase, a student at the time; 'the audience was enthralled . . . After hearing these lectures we knew why there was a depression'.[5] It is almost certain that Durbin attended these lectures, and possibly Gaitskell; they were both to criticize and adapt Hayek's analytic techniques in their own studies. They wanted to understand the business fluctuations which appeared to be endemic to the capitalist system, so that they would know how a socialist government could control them. Durbin never lost this perspective, which remained the key to understanding his disagreements with Keynesians throughout his life.

Against this background the NFRB decided that Durbin should go ahead with his investigation of the theoretical questions in a committee designated tellingly 'on industrial fluctuations and the price level'. For two years Meade and Durbin thrashed out the appropriate unemployment policy for a socialist government. By 1933 Meade had convinced the doubting Fabians that expansionary policies were not doomed to failure; by 1935 he had also persuaded Durbin that budget deficits were essential in a severe depression. Thus, Meade laid the groundwork for the new generation of Fabians to accept the main principles of *The General Theory* and to apply them to socialist policy. Only Durbin entertained lingering doubts about the suitability of the new Keynesian models to solve long-term problems of growth and stability in the socialist state.

The New Fabians on industrial fluctuations and the price level

In an organizing memorandum dated 12 June 1931, Durbin identified the central purpose of his committee as to consider 'the policy of the banking system in the supply of credit, and its effect upon the price level'.[6] After preliminary work reviewing socialist thought on the control of credit and the opinions of experts, he proposed a two-part study of 'the relation between banks, the provision of credit, the price level and industrial prosperity' and 'the motive of industrial fluctuations under the capitalist system, and the probable nature of the phenomenon under socialism'. The first committee meeting was held on 29 September 1931, which James Meade, E. A. Radice, George Schwartz and Durbin attended. The committee decided to limit their inquiry to the effect of 'price level policy' on prosperity and to assume, among other things, that the banking system was socially controlled, but that industry was competitive. The minutes also appended an impressive list of books and articles 'taken as read', which included

Wicksell, Mises, Hayek, Robertson, Keynes, Hawtrey, Hobson, Foster and Catchings and Kahn's multiplier article.

The main contributors to this committee's work were Durbin and Meade. Meade wrote a lengthy memorandum on 'The Market Rate of Interest' early in 1932. It caused a flurry of letters, notes and memoranda. Unfortunately, it has not survived; nor has Durbin's response, nor tantalizing papers by Meade on 'Theory of Unemployment' and 'Price Level Policy'. Meade wrote a pamphlet, *Public Works in Their International Aspect* in January 1933; Durbin wrote another, *Socialist Credit Policy*, which used much of his chapter on wages and was published in December 1933. By this time Meade had also organized the 'Oxford Group' of Labour sympathizers, who attended NFRB conferences and helped to write the joint memoranda for Dalton, which were also discussed in this committee. Durbin and Meade were simultaneously pursuing their own lines of theoretical investigation in the field. Many of their disagreements on the committee reflected the contrary views of their mentors, Hayek and Keynes, as well as the confused state of theory in general, but they also had a different set of policy concerns.

Durbin and Gaitskell were particularly concerned to uncover and demolish what they saw as 'treasured dogma' in the Labour movement, the belief that capitalism was 'incapable of sustaining full employment and maximum output'.[7] Durbin argued in his draft on wages policy:

> Despite its periodical depressions, capitalism has grown and flourished, and although it has brought in its train a continual growth of the evils that are inherent within it, yet it is simply ridiculous to pretend that it has shown any signs of economic decay, or any steady movement towards collapse.

To attack the dogma, Durbin and Gaitskell focused on those heretical monetary doctrines which had strongly influenced the Labour movement. Durbin spent his Ricardo fellowship year at University College (1929–30) studying underconsumption theories including Hobson, Foster and Catchings, Major Douglas and Lt Col Powell. His critique was not published until 1933, by which time Gaitskell had also painstakingly analysed the monetary doctrines of Major Douglas, Professor Soddy, Silvio Gesell and Robert Eisler, to show their economic errors.[8] Gaitskell's attack on a high wage policy had also been intended to refute underconsumption arguments, as well as to question union tactics, in direct opposition to his mentor, Cole.

Durbin and Gaitskell worked closely together on this academically obscure and somewhat pedantic task, sharing a belief in its importance well summarized by Durbin, who recognized the appeal of 'golden

cures for poverty and distress, for unemployment and insecurity', but
who concluded:

> I believe with reluctance that this theory does not tell us the truth
> about the processes of monetary circulation or describe the real
> alternatives that are before us, and if we are to have the courage
> to live with open eyes and to accept the hard discipline of an
> uncompromising realism we must turn away from the false hopes
> of prosperity which the theory of under-consumption has
> everywhere called forth.[9]

On the technical level Durbin felt he successfully demonstrated that
underconsumption theories were quite wrong when they sought to
show that all types of savings were disastrous, 'and must *necessarily*
destroy monetary equilibrium'. He also correctly emphasized that the
theories did nothing to explain the trade cycle.[10] But the main force
of the argument against Hobson was to contradict his view that money
and monetary policy were unimportant. For Durbin and Gaitskell
firmly believed that money would have to be managed properly in
the socialist state; therefore it was crucial for socialist economists to
understand its role in the economy and not to be misled by 'funny
money' theories.

Meanwhile, Meade was hard at work in Cambridge. Keynes's *Treatise* had begun to receive serious criticisms almost as soon as it was
published in 1930, while Colin Clark and Richard Kahn were investigating the secondary employment effects of an increase in exports for
the Economic Advisory Council (EAC). These problems were taken
up by the 'circus' members that winter, when the multiplier effect was
further refined. Meade also worked out the complementary process of
savings accumulation, which they christened 'Mr Meade's relation'.
Kahn, who had easier access to Keynes at King's high table, would
relay their thoughts to him and return with his reactions, questions
and suggestions. His role has since earned him the nickname, 'the
angel messenger', for, as in a medieval morality play, he would appear
mysteriously with the latest word.[11] Sometimes they all met together
with Keynes. Meade has never forgotten one such occasion when
Keynes, being asked whether he knew 'Mr Meade's relation', looked
all round the room for the relative in question. Although modern
historians of economic thought doubt that the theory of income determination was properly understood before 1933, Clark, Meade and Sir
Austin Robinson still remain convinced that by the summer of 1931
they had identified the central questions and had visualized 'the essential framework' of the new explanation for persistent unemployment.[12]
Certainly, on the policy issue the theoretical breakthroughs were more

than sufficient to convince them that expansion, not deflation, was the correct course.

From the documents of the NFRB committee which do still exist, it is clear that Meade was presenting his understanding of Cambridge theory in support of expansionary policies, while Durbin struggled to understand countering with Hayekian arguments. In what proved to be a vain attempt to find an agreed set of conclusions, Durbin wrote a memorandum in the spring of 1932 in which he stated his view of 'the nature of the problem':

> I do not think that we are concerned with a short period policy of depression. As I see it, it is not our business to assume that there are unemployed men and machines, and to ask ourselves how credit creation can be used to set them to work. Our business is to ask what policy during a long period of saving the banks should pursue in relation to the Price Level. It is the maintenance, not the recovery, of equilibrium, realised in the full employment of the factors of production, that it is our business to consider.[13]

He elaborated the position he wished the committee to take concerning 'the complex structure of production' in straight Hayekian terms, although he did add further questions raised by his reading of Robertson and Keynes.

On rereading their correspondence, Professor Meade was especially struck with the difference in their theoretical positions, which he had forgotten. He was amazed at Durbin's insistence on starting the analysis of socialist economic policy with full-employment assumptions, when unemployment stood at three million. Although in his own work Meade did not assume full employment, at this early stage the Keynesian converts were still working with models which explained price levels, as well as output and unemployment levels. In a paper for the joint NFRB/SSIP conference on the socialization of banking in January 1932, Roy Harrod stated that stable prices should be the major objective of a socialized central bank; he also admitted that 'there may be something in currency cranks' view about the need for consumers' credit', in what proved to be an early suggestion for 'a planned budgetary deficit'.[14]

Surviving correspondence gives some flavour of the continuing debate. In February 1932 Durbin wrote that Meade's argument in his market rate of interest memorandum had 'driven me back to Keynes'; he suggested that Meade should write the second edition of the *Treatise* because 'you are an immense advance on him in lucidity and precision'.[15] In a postscript he summarized his understanding of Meade's main argument: that the market rate of interest may be held above (or below) the equilibrium rate of interest for any or all of three reasons. The three reasons described different investment and savings adjustments through 'the demand and supply curves for securities' and 'the existence of speculating'. In April Richard Kahn wrote from Cambridge to say that he had shown Meade's memorandum to Keynes:

> He was very much interested, and also put forward the criticism that you altogether neglect a very important question which he himself is guilty of having never dealt with; namely, the relation between the rate of interest and the price level of securities. (Do you mean ordinary shares, gilt-edged securities, or what? You see what I mean – I do not see how the difficulty is going to be dealt with, and I am sure Keynes does not).[16]

In an attached memorandum for 'your committee', Kahn explained the point further as the effect of a change in 'the degree of bearishness' on the prices of securities. Kahn also applauded Meade for refusing to discuss the problem of 'the injection of credit', in what was undoubtedly a dig at Durbin's Hayekian analysis.

In June 1932 Harrod and Meade organized a letter to *The Times*, which urged expansionary policies 'for the restoration of prices'. They appealed to 'the patriotic motive' of citizens and organizations to spend 'according to their capacity', to the banks to increase the supply of money and to the government to impose no additional taxation and 'to remit existing taxation, where that presses hardest'. Cole and Gaitskell wrote to Meade explaining why they could not sign, both balking at the commitment not to raise taxes. In a long and interesting letter Gaitskell explained his reasons:

> The forces likely to prevent any further imposition of Taxation are at the moment quite strong enough. The danger is that the government will do what is from the monetary view just as bad – that is cutting down current expenditure especially on the Social Services . . . . I think it would have been better to have argued in favour of not balancing the budget. As it is, the readers of the Times will assume that . . . you do believe in cutting down current expenditure. The correspondence in the Times has centred around the question of whether there should be Private as well as Public Economy. You are merely throwing your weight on the side of Private extravagance. From the moral point of view I should have thought there was more to be said for supporting Public extravagance . . . . If you now argue that business men are business men and do not like removing 'Means Tests' . . . I should reply

first that they probably won't like your proposals much better . . . and second that so long as we only do what the business world likes we shall never get anywhere near a classless society. These considerations would perhaps be outweighed, if I thought my signature would prevent the world from complete economic collapse.[17]

Thus, some New Fabians put a higher priority on enlarging the public sector through increased taxes for social expenditures than on expanding the economy by cutting them.

Meade finished his first book, *The Rate of Interest*, in January 1933. His purpose was to trace what happened to the rate of interest as output per head increased; his intention was *not* to discuss the causes of disequilibrium, because he felt it was crucial to understand 'the conditions of dynamic equilibrium as a necessary preliminary to a study of disequilibrium'.[18] In other words, until the effect of a change in output on the rate of interest was better understood, he did not think it would be possible to discover the reasons why the market was failing to maintain output at full employment levels. He concluded that the banking system would have to act to maintain equilibrium because the market forces do not automatically prevent unemployment. Joan Robinson, who reviewed Meade's book for the *Economic Journal*, thought that 'it represents a considerable feat of bold and independent thinking'.[19]

Durbin wrote to Meade after reading *The Rate of Interest*, which he had found a great help in preparing the lectures he was giving at LSE.[20] Durbin's chief concern was whether 'you make realistic assumptions about the determination of investment':

> It can never be known by how much an increment of capital will reduce cost, by how much prices will fall. The essential determinant – the margin between the new prices and the new costs – is ultimately a matter of guesswork – and this introduces an element of uncertainty which is, in my opinion, far more important than the Rate of Interest and which cannot be dismissed as though it were a minor divergence between the Market Rate and the Rate of Profits. It is the heart of the matter. As a result I am reduced to the position of doubting the existence of any simple relation between the Rate of Interest and the Volume of Investment.

In reply, Meade wrote that as far as he was concerned it was 'all a matter of emphasis':

> Doesn't it boil down to this? We would agree that the rate of

interest has some effect in determining the amount of investment on the lines of my analysis, and we would both agree that other 'psychological' factors are involved. I emphasize the former more than you do.[21]

Given all the interest in the development of the ideas for *The General Theory*, Meade recently looked through his book to see if it threw any light on the matter. His own conclusion was that it was not as Keynesian as he remembered; while it did not clearly support the view that he had understood the theory of effective demand, it did not dispute it either.

The theoretical uncertainty of the period was also apparent in Meade's NFRB pamphlet on public works. He showed that public works could be used to increase stability, which he defined in terms of price fluctuations, as well as employment changes.[22] In separate work on capital supply for the NFRB, Colin Clark took another aspect of the *Treatise* arguments to claim that the cause of the depression was an excess of savings over investment. Clark had understood that investment did not depend on savings, although he still thought savings were determined independently.[23] As progress was made from models explaining the determination of prices and investment to models of employment and savings, these young economists were often confused about cause and effect.

Durbin was struggling with a different synthesis, one between Hayek's *Prices and Production* and Keynes's *Treatise*. One scholar has noted that 'the result was strongly Hayekian in flavour and markedly pessimistic in its conclusions'.[24] In the introduction Durbin described his own theory as 'eclectic rather than original'; it differed from Keynes by attributing the cause of the trade cycle to efforts to stabilize prices when costs were falling and by denying that inflationary prices could cure the trade cycle, but it also differed from Hayek by insisting that the relation between capital investment and the demand for consumption goods was determined by excess capacity and unemployment in the producers' sector. Thus, Durbin used Hayekian imbalances between the producers' and consumers' sectors to provide a structural explanation of the trade cycle, but Keynesian unemployment arguments to refute Hayek's view that capital scarcity caused the depression. However, he still concluded that 'trade depression is due to an excessive supply of money' and that expansionary policies 'would merely cause the Trade Cycle to appear':

If pursued with sufficient vigour during the period of depression it will start the recovery but it will sow the seeds for the next boom. If pursued at any other time it will merely accentuate the process of cyclical fluctuation . . . . It is not possible for us to enjoy an easy road to salvation in the cure of the Trade Cycle.[25]

Together Durbin and Gaitskell were developing a schema based on Hayek's stages of production, which demonstrated that the additional costs in successive stages added up to the final prices to the consumer.[26] Gaitskell used it to refute Major Douglas's social credit programmes, and Durbin to describe cyclical processes. It was quite ingenious, and had enough similarities to the multiplier process to be confusing. However, its purpose was rather different, as Durbin realized when he struggled to incorporate the new savings/investment analysis into his own models during 1933. In this process he finally became convinced that expansion was necessary to cure depression unemployment, but, true to his Hayekian heritage, he remained cautious about its inflationary potential.

In his NFRB pamphlet, *Socialist Credit Policy*, published in 1933, Durbin fully acknowledged his debt to Meade in an appendix on capitalist trade depression and the relation between savings and investment. He distinguished between 'the correct long term credit policy' and 'an immediate monetary programme', defining the long run in terms of rising output, increased productivity and full employment.[27] Durbin posed the policy problem for long-run growth as a choice between stable prices (the Labour party's official position) and stable money incomes. Durbin chose the second, because it would ensure rising real incomes as falling prices reflected productivity increases. By contrast, stable prices with falling costs would be inflationary and would cause the recurrence of slump conditions, which his policy was designed to avoid. In the short run, however, a policy of stable monetary incomes would be 'political suicide', if there was substantial unemployment. In this case a carefully controlled monetary expansion through public works and increased private investment was 'essential'. Durbin argued that such a policy would initiate a capitalist boom, which would continue until there was full employment in consumer goods industries. To prevent the inevitable collapse which would follow as inflationary pressures built in this sector, Durbin recommended that the government hold down consumption through increased taxation, the opposite of Meade's advice. This revenue should be used to continue investment in the under-utilized producers' (or capital) goods sector, where there was still unemployment. In short, Durbin believed the Hayekian imbalance between consumers' and producers' goods could be circumvented 'by a double process of taxation and investment which is not unstable and which can be prolonged indefinitely'. He felt that he had finally discovered how a socialist government could 'cure the unemployment problem for ever and succeed as no capitalist policy could ever do, in stabilizing the capitalist boom indefinitely'.

Durbin was keen to share his new insights, so a session on money and prices was organized for the NFRB conference on socialist planning, which was held in November 1933 and was attended by Clark, Harrod, Cole, Dalton, Berry and Spriggs (two XYZ members), among others. In a paper outlining the appropriate long-term policy for a Labour government, Durbin recommended falling prices during prosperity, expansion in a depression and stabilization of the boom by monetary means.[28] Harrod in reply supported long-run price stability, and emphasized public works and consumer credits to increase employment in a depression. Although the New Fabians now agreed about expansion through cheap money and public works, their theoretical reasons were still quite different. Meade and Harrod were close to the Keynesian arguments for increasing effective demand, but Durbin was only prepared to use expansion to get out of a severe depression.

In an exhaustive study for the lay reader, which G. D. H. Cole edited, a major effort was made to fill the enormous knowledge gap in the Labour movement about the role of banks, other institutions and money in the existing system. It was titled *What Everybody Wants to Know About Money*, and, according to Margaret Cole, flippant critics said the book failed to tell everybody what they really wanted to know – how to *make* money.[29] Although the nine contributors were billed as 'Oxford economists', their collective connection to the university was rather tenuous, since only three of the authors actually held university appointments, but they were all NFRB members. In an important way the book summarized the positions of the Bureau economists in 1933; it included chapters by Cole, Clark, Durbin, Harrod, and Gaitskell's study of monetary heretics.

Cole, who had worked closely with Hobson in the 1920s, was very sympathetic to the underconsumptionist approach. In 1930 he wrote that 'the development of production on the one hand, and the right distribution of income on the other, are the essential foundations of socialist economic policy', for which a nationally controlled banking system was indispensable.[30] Hobson's analysis enabled Cole to combine a long-term strategy for the elimination of unemployment with a short-run policy to ameliorate poverty conditions. But under Keynes's influence he also supported public works and the 'monetary palliatives' which Hobson deplored. His theoretical arguments were eclectic; unlike Hobson, he included traditional monetary explanations of the role of banks in credit formation and the role of savings as a determinant of investment funds. But he did not always follow the complicated issues which Keynes and Robertson were tackling; for instance, in an otherwise careful appraisal of British social and economic policy in 1929 he wrote that the trade cycle was 'mere Mumbo-Jumbo' as a universal explanation of unemployment.[31]

After the 1931 crisis Cole changed his mind about mitigating the effects of unemployment before introducing socialist controls. In a series of articles that autumn he questioned both the stability and the 'squeezability' of capitalism.[32] By 1933 he had incorporated some of the new work under way at Cambridge, although he still focused upon price levels as the regulator of employment. In the new book Cole recommended monetary management for a Labour government, proposing different price policies in different circumstances. If there was full employment, price levels should be allowed to fall as productivity increased; but if there was a depression, prices should be raised; in both cases higher wages were also desirable to redistribute income. True to his Hobsonian heritage, Cole thus sought a macroeconomic price policy which meshed productivity changes with a higher wage policy, so that both growth and redistributive goals could be met at the same time.

The major disagreement among the New Fabians at this stage was over Keynes's proposal for deliberate budget deficits, which had an important impact on New Fabian thinking when it appeared in *The Times* early in 1933. In his chapter on currency and banking Harrod promoted their use to cure unemployment. Durbin, whose task was to spell out the quantity theory of money and its relation to money, purposely avoided recommending them in his chapter. Surprisingly, Colin Clark, whose position was usually closer to the Keynesians than to Durbin, preferred to increase consumption by raising taxes and spending the revenues on improved social services. He concluded that this was 'a much less hazardous policy than that of deliberately unbalancing the budget', which might cause an internal crisis 'due to fear of inflation'.[33]

By this time Durbin and Gaitskell had already expanded Hayek's conception of the structure of production and sectoral imbalance in their attack on underconsumption and their formulation of a socialist investment policy. They questioned what it meant to say the structure of production was too long, and why it mattered whether savings were voluntary or 'injected'. In Vienna Gaitskell pursued these problems in his most innovative contribution to economic theory, although his findings were not published for some years.[34] He demonstrated that the average period of production (the indicator of capital intensity) could only be defined when the system was in equilibrium. Thus, if there was any imbalance between the sectors, their relative prices could not be calculated.

By 1934 Durbin had already started work on a new book, *The Problem of Credit Policy*, which expanded his ideas about credit policy; it was published a few months before *The General Theory*. Building on his earlier trade cycle analysis, he focused on the theoretical problems of investment expansion and contraction and on the implications for government banking policy. He extended Hayek's structural analysis to include the role of the money market, and his own analysis to assess the impact of rigidities on confidence and 'the preference for liquid resources'. Thus, Durbin pursued the line of thought started in his controversies with Meade and foreshadowed Keynes's use of uncertainty in *The General Theory*. In a more systematic exposition of policy choices, he repeated his earlier recommendation that in a depression his goal should be met by expansionary policies: 'in such a situation ... it is a pedagogical impertinence to advocate deflationary measures'.[35] As before, the recovery boom could then be maintained by a taxation policy to control consumption and by an investment policy to maintain capital growth. Durbin finally accepted the use of budgetary deficits as an important part of his overall strategy to control prices. In a final section he went beyond the theory of short-run expansion to outline the possibility that the cumulative impact of such policies could cause increasing distortions in the structure of production, and eventually more severe business fluctuations. Again, Durbin concluded that 'there is an inherent or institutional defect in an advanced capitalist order which prevents the cure of the Trade Cycle by ordinary credit policies', which only a central authority could control: a Hayekian diagnosis with a socialist cure.

On the whole the book was well received, although R. G. Hawtrey was quite critical and Harrod, who found the policy proposals 'interesting and courageous' and applauded his excellent dismissal of the gold standard, felt that its theoretical base was only partially satisfactory with too many ad hoc assumptions.[36] In particular, he challenged Durbin's assumption that full employment and inflationary pressures arose first in the consumer goods industry, in an argument which he used to dismiss Durbin's gloomy prognostications about the destabilizing effects of successive short-run expansions. Its contemporary impact, however, was swamped in the deluge of debate and controversy following the appearance of *The General Theory*, during which Durbin's own views evolved considerably.

The New Fabians and *The General Theory*

In February 1936 the long-awaited book, *The General Theory of Employment, Interest and Money*, was published. It is difficult for post-Keynesian students educated in the new orthodoxy to imagine its effect on the professional world of economics. Keynes himself described his intellectual effort as 'a long struggle' to free himself 'from habitual modes of thought and expression'.[37] In reply to early reviews he claimed that his book differed in two fundamental respects from traditional theory. First, it introduced the effect of uncertainty on investment decisions and demolished the tacit assumption that monetary policy could maintain an interest rate compatible with full employment. Second, it asserted the importance of aggregate output and rejected Say's Law, which emphasized the automatic adjustment of the market to full employment.[38]

Although the value and accuracy of Keynes's original formulation has been increasingly questioned in the light of modern failures in macroeconomic management, there remains a general consensus about its main components. Fashioning elegant new functional concepts for aggregate consumption, for the efficiency of capital and for liquidity preference, Keynes built a model to explain the important determinants of aggregate output and employment in a closed economy. The main building blocks can be described as follows: (1) the marginal propensity to consume, which states that consumption will rise as income rises but not as fast; (2) the multiplier, which depends upon an elastic supply of output at less than full employment and whose size is derived from the marginal propensity to consume; (3) the marginal efficiency of capital, which is the expected return on a capital investment and determines the volume of investment at the point where it is equal to the market rate of interest; (4) a theory of the rate of interest based on the speculative motive for holding money and determined by future expectations expressed by the preference for holding liquid reserves. Roughly speaking, the first two building blocks make up the theory of effective demand as the determinant of output, income and employment; the second two introduce uncertainty in the form of expectations and provide the connecting links between the production system and the money system, between real and money prices.

From the theoretical point of view, the new model accomplished a number of important tasks, which seem to have been recognized fairly soon after publication. First, it spelled out systematically for the first time how an economy could be in equilibrium at less than full employment, demolishing faith in the automatic adjustment mechanisms of the price system. Second, it demonstrated that investment, not saving, was the chief independent factor determining income changes. Similarly investment, not saving, was influenced by the rate of interest, and it was saving which became the residual tail. The rate of interest was dethroned as the adjusting price mechanism; instead, income changes ensured the equalization of savings and investment through the multiplier process. Finally, Keynes introduced a new speculative motive for holding money into the demand function of money; his 'liquidity preference' schedule now determined the rate of interest. Since businessmen's expectations about the uncertain future also affected their decisions whether to invest or not, there was no longer an automatic relationship between savings decisions and investment opportunities.

From the policy perspective the new model was used to provide the theoretical justification for major shifts towards a new orthodoxy for employment policy. First and foremost, through the theory of income determination, it explained why there could be substantial unemployment and justified the use of expansionary policies to increase aggregate or effective demand. As a corollary it identified increases in investment and consumption as the key variables to increase output and employment in a depression and underscored the negative effects of an increase in savings. Second, one effect of including uncertainty in the model was to demonstrate why monetary policies could not be relied upon exclusively; they had to be supplemented by fiscal policies to prevent further declines in income and to force output back up again, before businessmen would be willing to undertake their own investment programmes. Finally, both these policy imperatives called for a substantial degree of government intervention to reduce unemployment successfully.

The most immediate impact of *The General Theory* within the economics profession was to silence the antagonism to expansionary policies in Britain. Hayek did not comment; as he explained later, 'I feared that before I had completed my analysis he would again have changed his mind', which had been Keynes's response to Hayek's criticism of the *Treatise*.[39] Robbins, who had just published his own analysis of *The Great Depression* along Austrian lines, was to become an enthusiastic supporter of the new Keynesian full-employment policy during the war. He later confessed that it was the only one of his books which he wished he had never written; he blamed 'mistaken theoretical concepts', such as Hayek's, which were 'as unsuitable as denying blankets and stimulants to a drunk who had fallen into an icy pond, on the ground that his original trouble was overheating'.[40]

Many of Robbins's brightest protégés from LSE, including John Hicks, Nicholas Kaldor and Abba Lerner, were among the new converts. Lerner had already spent the 1934–35 academic year in

Cambridge on a fellowship, where he was exposed to the new developments. When he returned to London, he held intense seminars for his colleagues, which many still remember as their first introduction to Keynesian macroeconomics.

Among the New Fabians, James Meade carried on his role as the foremost evangelist. In 1937 he published an important article which outlined 'a simplified model of Mr. Keynes' System'; he remembers that he had first presented his version to the Econometric Society at Oxford some years before.[41] He felt then that Keynes had opened up a new way to resolve the world's economic problems, a faith which he holds to this day. After 1936, as others took up the cause of convincing Labour supporters, Meade devoted his time to expanding the theoretical and practical applications of the new economics. Together with Richard Stone he later pioneered the development of official national income statistics, and won the Nobel Prize for his contributions to international trade theory. In his mind his only significant difference with Keynes was over the direct subsidy of consumption. In 1938 Meade published a book on the subject, *Consumers' Credits and Unemployment*, which Keynes reviewed, rejecting its main recommendation because he believed the employment effects would be less than direct investment.[42]

Douglas Jay, who was soon the strongest advocate for Keynesianism among the active participants in Durbin and Gaitskell's discussion groups, has acknowledged Meade's central role in his conversion. In 1935 he had already begun work on his own book, *The Socialist Case*; he remembers spending the following summer reading *The General Theory* on the beach in the afternoons, while writing 'before lunch and after tea'. In his autobiography, he outlined the three main theses of his book:

> First that the case for greater social justice rested on Alfred
> Marshall's 'broad proposition' that 'aggregate' satisfaction can
> *prima facie* be increased by re-distribution of wealth, whether
> voluntarily or compulsorily, of some of the property of the rich
> among the poor, and had been sadly distorted by Marx's obsession
> with ownership and outdated theory of value. Secondly that there
> was no rational ground for believing re-distribution could not be
> peacefully and democratically achieved. Thirdly that
> unemployment and cyclical depression were monetary phenomena
> which could be overcome by intelligent management of what I
> boldly labelled 'total effective demand'.[43]

The book had an important impact in demonstrating the relevance of Keynesian management policies for achieving socialist economic goals.

Pimlott has argued that the process of 'dressing up Keynes in socialist clothes' begun by Dalton's *Practical Socialism for Britain* was completed by Jay.[44] G. D. H. Cole commented on Jay's book at the time: 'there is very little in it of what most people habitually think of as Socialism', because it gave such a low priority to nationalization.[45] Jay himself feels that 'the main weakness in the book, not fully apparent to me till the 1970s, was my failure to see that, given vigorous collective bargaining on pay, the effort to manage demand without managing labour costs (pay rates) could generate cost-push inflation'.

At first Cole himself was an enthusiast for *The General Theory*. In a review for the *New Statesman* he welcomed it because it justified the underconsumptionist view that purchasing power must be increased to solve the unemployment problem.[46] He applauded the book for giving 'the critics of economic orthodoxy solid ground on which they can set their feet'; he thought it the most important book in economics published since Marx's *Das Kapital* or Ricardo's *Principles*. However, after the war Cole became disillusioned with the likelihood of achieving socialism by Keynesian management; he also felt that 'most of the non-Marxist socialist economists swallowed Keynes whole, and became his most fervent disciples'.[47] He was afraid that the Labour party was giving up its socialist goals for a mess of aggregate pottage:

> For I continued to believe that, great as was the advance made by
> Keynes in the techniques of economic manipulation, his
> conclusions were partly vitiated by his habit of reasoning in terms
> of global demand and supply, or at any rate of 'capital goods'
> and 'consumers' goods' as global divisions of the total product of
> industry, instead of breaking up the productive system into much
> smaller and more differentiated groups of real persons and things.

Thus, Cole was also concerned with structural problems in a socialist economy, which *The General Theory* had ignored. Furthermore, he maintained that the State must own 'a large part of the apparatus of production', even though it was not necessary to nationalize everything 'heaven forbid!'. In short, 'the Keynesian revolution in economic thought is to be welcomed and accepted by Socialists up to a point, but cannot be taken as a substitute for Socialism, or for a socialist economic theory which goes a long way beyond it'.

More cautious colleagues in the profession were at a distinct disadvantage in this exciting dawn for economic science. In retrospect Dennis Robertson was probably closest to the mark in a rearguard attempt to maintain the business cycle perspective. Unfortunately, insecurity about his own judgment and insistence on his own idiosyncratic terminology obscured the main force of his arguments. He often appeared to be fussing over minor issues and remote possibilities when the need to tackle the immediate problem of deficient demand seemed so obvious. Hicks has since confessed that he can now see that Robertson was right to perceive the weaknesses of Keynes's 'quasi-static' model, 'but he was too much occupied with its weaknesses to perceive its strengths'.[48] Unlike defenders of the orthodox faith, Robertson was not bothered by Keynes's disequilibrium approach, but he did mind when Keynes drew conclusions without due regard for all the theoretical implications or the relevant facts.

In his critique, Robertson insisted on the importance of introducing lags into the system, because savings were related to previous income.[49] He also pointed out that liquidity preference only determined the rate of interest on the short-run assumption that money supply was constant and capital stock was fixed. Thus, in the longer run the interest rate could affect both savings and investment. Robertson may well have been the first to articulate the now generally accepted fact that *The General Theory* was a short-run-demand analysis of output changes, with serious limitations for dealing with long-run supply problems, particularly capital formation.

What was probably less clear at the time was the extent to which Robertson was trying to analyse the process of change and its relationship to the various structural elements of the system. For example, he argued that investment would have to be maintained over a longer time period than suggested by Keynes. He was worried about the effect of unanticipated change during this process, about the proper balance of investment between cyclically stable and unstable industries, the possibility of inflationary pressures from maladjustments between the consumption goods and production goods sectors before full employment was reached, and the inherent instability of the system as a whole. He did not believe that one could assume that the marginal propensity to consume would not change within the investment time frame and had serious doubts about the assumed elasticities of other crucial relationships. In short, while he recognized the potential for long-term growth through Keynesian prescriptions, he could also foresee the possibility of serious structural problems, increasing instability and an eventual trade-off between growth and stability.

Despite Robertson's emphasis on dynamics, his approach was rather different from the models which the disciples were busily constructing from the Keynesian system. Harrod, in particular, was incorporating change as part of a feedback mechanism between the determining variables of the static model in what proved to be a prelude to later growth models. By contrast, Robertson was exploring the effect of ignorance and error, and of equilibrium positions which shifted before they were reached. Agreeing with Hicks's earlier assessment, Michael Danes has recently concluded that in fact Robertson was not really looking for a dynamic theory, or a cycle theory, but for a theory to explain trend.[50] In the 1930s, he was preoccupied with the possibility that cumulative cyclical phenomena could eat away at long-run growth potential, a view which he expounded in 'The Snake and the Worm' address at Harvard in 1936. Keynes's discoveries had renewed his own faith that the system could be made to work, and that active and intelligent management could save the day. By contrast, the depression had confirmed Robertson's fears that the system was inherently unstable and that even well-intentioned government policy could also make things worse. In short, Robertson was concerned with unexpected change, not system-induced change; he was more pessimistic, the Keynesians were more optimistic.

One New Fabian economist who never swallowed Keynes whole was Evan Durbin. Partly because of his own work on economic fluctuations, partly because of his deep suspicion of Liberal palliatives, Durbin was critical of some aspects of *The General Theory* from the start. On 4 February 1936 he wrote to Dennis Robertson as he read Keynes's preface: 'I must register here my belief before I read the book that I do not think that any man really gets back beyond or wholly invalidates a century of scientific thought'.[51] He also complained jokingly to his LSE colleague Brinley Thomas that after paying fifteen shillings for *A Treatise on Money* he now had to pay another five shillings to find out what was wrong with it.

Durbin's primary concern was that *The General Theory* did not provide an explanation of the trade cycle. In an exchange of letters with Keynes in 1936, he spelled out his criticisms of *The General Theory* model, arguing in essence that expansionary policies do not offer a cure for the trade cycle:

Let us imagine the Trade Cycle boom to be sufficiently strong to reduce general unemployment to zero . . . . Now you may have good reasons for believing that the Trade Cycle movement is quite different in kind from the larger inflations that accompanied the war. We know that it is possible for upward movements in monetary expenditure to proceed through the condition of full employment to a rise in prices. Unless there are such reasons – and I do not find them in the 'General Theory' – you have given no reason for supposing that your 'cure' would not simply lead to an accelerated inflation, and ultimately rise in prices, and the continuous dilemma between allowing the movement to gain further impetus or checking it. And if the movement is checked the disappointment of expectations is the crisis and produces the depression . . . . I fail to see how you propose to stabilise the boom without allowing the expansion of money to go on after full employment has been reached.[52]

Keynes replied that he would not use further expansionary policies once full employment was achieved and that he could not accept the argument that such policies would cause inflation when existing measures were not maintaining full employment.

Interestingly, Durbin's challenge drew from Keynes an early statement of his attitude to policy once full employment was reached:

On the other hand, I agree that our methods of control are unlikely to be sufficiently delicate or sufficiently powerful to maintain continuous full employment. I should be quite content with a reasonable approximation to it, and in practice I would probably relax my expansionist measures a little before technical full employment had actually been reached.

The following year, in a series of articles for *The Times*, Keynes dealt with the inflationary potential of increased government expenditures, particularly rearmament.

However, Durbin's apparently prescient prediction of stop/go inflation should be seen in its proper context. In the mid-1930s the British economy was very far from anything remotely resembling full employment. It was Durbin's focus upon price changes and business cycles which gave rise to his criticism. In recent conversation Professor Meade argued that, if he was right, it was for the wrong reason! Many of Durbin's friends feel that the efforts he expended on mastering Hayekian theory were a waste of his time and talents. Scholars familiar with the 'Austrian' perspective are more aware of his positive contributions. Drawing on his own unpublished work, Professor Laurence Moss, for instance, argues that Durbin and Gaitskell clarified the relation between capital formation and equilibrium in important ways and identified a crucial growth problem, that of maintaining sufficient savings without causing sectoral imbalance. In his first book, Durbin remarked that much of Hayek's theory amounted to the claim that 'you can't have your cake and eat it too in the matter of saving and consumption'. Moss believes:

In a profound sense, Durbin was trying to merge Hayek's description of the production process with the general socialist vision that central control could result in an economic order in which the participants could have and enjoy a steadily growing cake.[53]

Durbin's 1935 book provided the theoretical base for this position, and his policy work the necessary practical programme for a socialist government to fulfil its promise.

Durbin also criticized an entirely different point in *The General Theory* from his socialist perspective. Keynes had written that, even with one million unemployed from a labour force of ten million, there was no evidence that the nine million employed were misallocated; indeed, he raised no objection to classical theories of market allocation in this case and argued that it was not important for the State to assume public ownership of the instruments of production. Durbin asserted:

> These views of yours may be correct or not but I think I am at liberty to criticise them because I think that a case has been made out for rejecting the laissez-faire analysis on these grounds as well as others – and of course it is a vital point to make clear to a Labour public because it is the main difference between yours and the Socialist Movement – or at least one of them. When you speak of a 'Control of investment' I think that in the light of these passages it is obvious that you are chiefly referring to the volume, rather than the detailed direction, of expenditure on capital.

Durbin thus held that competitive models were to be rejected on both aggregative and allocative grounds, and that Keynes was confusing the two separate arguments for intervention with a political judgment about public ownership.

Durbin never did accept the Keynesian models expressed in *The General Theory* as the complete answer to the problems of full employment and growth in socialist economies. Although *The Problem of Credit Policy* was to be Durbin's last published writing on macroeconomics, his continued doubts can be gleaned from his correspondence and his notes for 'The Economics of Democratic Socialism'. His own position was closest to Robertson, as both recognized in an exchange of letters and visits in the late 1930s. Robertson felt that Durbin's book had made an important contribution, despite an inordinate number of misprints and some rather tortuous logic; he wrote, 'Otherwise, I think I am in accord with all your major conclusions.'[54] In particular, he shared Durbin's 'scepticism about the efficiency of the rate of interest', welcomed his discussion of consumer credits and liked his analysis of the cumulative effect of short-run monetary expansion on the structure and stability of employment. When Harrod criticized the last item in his review, Robertson stoutly defended Durbin's position, which may well have presaged his own Harvard address.[55] None the less, Durbin felt he could not answer Harrod's criticism and wrote dejectedly to

Robertson, 'I feel now that the wretched book is so full of ambiguities, omissions and positive errors that it is a pity it was ever written or published.'[56]

Durbin cannot have helped feeling that *The General Theory* had rendered his own efforts painfully obsolescent. He never relinquished his view that the trade cycle was the heart of macroeconomic problems in advanced capitalist economies, which only socialist control could eliminate. In his unpublished notes, he emphasized the limitations of Keynes's 'psychological' theory among others, because they had no explanation whatever 'of why a cumulative movement in one direction – why a movement away from liquidity and a cumulative improvement of expectations and turnover – should suddenly (as they all admit) – turn into a depression crisis'.

Like Robertson, Durbin was concerned with long-term growth and stability. He believed that policy should be designed to mitigate, even completely offset, the effects of fluctuations in expectations through monetary and fiscal policies. Once the Labour government had gained sufficient power over the economy, it would be able to replace the vagaries of business confidence with clear-cut policy rules for prices, incomes, employment and money supply. Then the chief planning problem would become the proper allocation of investment between capital and consumer goods to prevent supply-side inflationary or deflationary pressures from upsetting steady growth. While Keynes's new model was enormously useful for stabilizing demand, it had little to contribute to Durbin's supply questions. Although Durbin had built on Hayek's cycle model, he had reached opposite theoretical and policy conclusions. He had also incorporated Keynesian arguments to explain the cumulative downswing, which was missing from Hayek's original formulation. Thus, neither Keynes nor Hayek provided the appropriate model for Durbin's concern. However, both Durbin and Robertson exaggerated the destabililzing danger of expansionary policies. For twenty-five years after the Second World War full employment and built-in stabilizers, such as unemployment benefits, brought stability and growth to industrialized democracies. Only recently have the problems of stagnation, unstable currencies and deepening depressions returned to plague the world economy.

The major impact which *The General Theory* had on Durbin was to change his mind about the need to nationalize the joint stock banks. By the summer of 1935, he only supported their nationalization if they circumvented expansionary policies by withholding loans for investment and could not be forced to comply; by December 1936 he had dropped the entire idea.[57] By demonstrating the importance of expectations on business behaviour and of total investment on income and employment changes, Keynes had shifted the focus of practical attention from the commercial banks to the role of the central banks and government policies to maintain consumption and investment levels, in order to restore confidence. This did not require control over day-to-day banking operations, and the national investment board would come into its own as the allocator of investment funds. Furthermore, as long as there was considerable slack in the economy, the effect of government lending on interest rates and security prices was less crucial, and the banks were more likely to comply.

There is less direct evidence of Gaitskell's reaction to *The General Theory*. Jay recollects that the book had a tremendous impact on their joint work for the Labour party. Although Gaitskell worked closely with Durbin on their theoretical and policy approaches to macro-economic problems, at University College he was not as caught up in the extreme partisan controversies. Consequently, he was probably more open to the new Keynesian theories than his friend, even though they shared the same policy concerns. In 1937 he visited Sweden as part of a NFRB team. On his return he wrote the chapter in the NFRB report on Swedish banking and monetary policy, which drew heavily on Brinley Thomas's work for Hugh Dalton.[58] Gaitskell was particularly struck by the conscious interweaving of exchange rate policy, the public works programme, deliberate deficit budgeting and a cheap money policy. He concluded that Sweden's remarkable prosperity had not been entirely due to government policy, nor had Sweden learnt the secret of preventing cyclical fluctuations: 'But the combined efforts of academic economists, experienced bankers and sagacious Socialist politicians have secured for her the pursuit of what in an imperfect world was probably the best monetary policy available'.

Hugh Dalton had been strongly influenced by Keynes's *Means to Prosperity* in 1933, which convinced him of the need for expansionary policies. However, it is not so clear that he had understood (or even read) *The General Theory*, since he was so preoccupied with foreign affairs at the time. Professor Brinley Thomas, who had worked for him in Germany and Sweden, feels that Dalton had all the theory he needed to justify expansion from their joint work for the unbalanced budgets study in the early 1930s.[59] Thomas himself wrote a comprehensive book on the Swedish contributions to theory and policy, *Monetary Policy and Crises*, published in 1936; it had a preface by Dalton extolling the virtues of the Swedish recovery, 'based largely on the theories of Gunnar Myrdal, and executed with great political skill and economic foresight by Ernst Wigforss, the brilliant Finance Minister'. Indeed, Thomas has been credited with bringing the ex-ante/ex-post identity from Stockholm to London in 1935. He argues now that the Swedish models were quite sufficient to justify short-term expansion and that they avoided all the complications of 'forced savings' and 'loanable funds', which were being hotly debated in England at the time.

Conclusions

The great depression had threatened the political and economic stability of capitalist systems. Keynes discovered the key to restoring economic health to market economies, if governments were prepared to take his advice. His advice justified intervention to bolster invest-ment and to increase expenditure without relinquishing total economic authority to the state. In the early 1930s Keynes was searching for mechanisms to solve unemployment. Thus he was led to attack misguided establishment orthodoxy in order to preserve the market system. The New Fabians were searching for mechanisms to enable a Labour government to control market forces, as part of their design for short-term and long-term socialist economic policy. They attacked misguided socialist orthodoxy for assuming that substantial redistribu-tion or drastic nationalization alone would solve the unemployment problem in the socialist state.

Durbin and Gaitskell also went to some lengths to demolish the underconsumptionist arguments, which had exerted a strong influence on many socialists. In general, they were unsympathetic with simplified solutions to complex problems, which may also account for their lingering suspicion of quick Keynesian demand fixes. They believed that through control of the production side of the economy, inequality could be reduced in the long run, not vice versa. They were adamant that the socialist state would need to work out appropriate short-term monetary policies. As they also struggled to define long-term growth policies, they became convinced that only a socialist state, which had the power to modify and enhance the performance of the market system, could overcome the trade cycle and achieve maximum growth.

The new Keynesian theory shifted the main emphasis of economic policy from microeconomic problems to macroeconomic, from monetary management to fiscal, from savings and efficiency policies to investment and consumption, from long-run structural approaches to short-run demand. Keynes demonstrated conclusively that full employment could not be assumed, that automatic market mechanisms could not restore full employment and that increased government expenditures would not cause inflation when millions were out of work. For most professional economists, *The General Theory* made their subject seem relevant to world problems once again; for many others it carried radical implications about the role of government, the redistribution of income and the possibilities of economic growth and stability in a properly managed system.

For democratic socialists the new analysis provided an obvious answer to the problem of dealing with capitalist collapse; the disaster of 1929 could be avoided. Furthermore, the Keynesian message reinforced their redistributive goals, indicated the ways in which full employment could be maintained in the socialist state and provided another forceful argument for central planning. The new understanding of the economic system defined the crucial elements to control, reduced the need for a massive take-over of private institutions and opened up new options. Specifically, while they believed that nationalization of the Bank of England was still necessary to control the total volume of investment, the emphasis on investment directed attention away from the joint stock banks towards government and business expenditure. The new approach clarified and underscored the path already chosen by socialists opposed to the revolutionary overthrow of capitalism and in favour of parliamentary reform.

However, most democratic socialist economists, particularly Cole, Durbin and Gaitskell, were fully aware that full employment policy was not socialism. Furthermore, *The General Theory* had little or nothing to say about the changes which would be necessary to accomplish Keynes's policy objectives. The NFRB economists worked hard for the Labour party on the institutional reforms to control the banking system; Cole, Durbin and Gaitskell had insisted that the public sector must be increased through taxation, as well as nationalization. In the aftermath of *The General Theory* only Durbin, and perhaps Gaitskell, seemed to have recognized that, while the new macroeconomics was invaluable for the immediate policy problem, it had serious limitations for coping with inflation under full employment and it had little to say about the causes of the trade cycle, long-term growth and stability, or the relation of short-run to long-run policies.

Durbin and Gaitskell were also aware that they did not share Keynes's social values. Keynes had written that in the private enterprise system, 'dangerous human proclivities can be canalised into comparatively harmless channels'; 'it is better that a man should tyrannise over his bank balance than over his fellow-citizens'.[60] Durbin, who found this 'bizarre and unconvincing', wrote passionately to Keynes:

Although it is to be expected that economists will disagree about political matters it is difficult for me to understand how the author of 'The Economic Consequences of Peace' – familiar in part with the world of Labour and the history of Trade Union emancipation – can argue that one advantage of a *laissez faire* system lies in the freedom it gives to certain privileged persons to exercise their sadistic impulses in the control of industrial workers. It is as though you argued that it was one advantage of possessing an Empire that we could get rid of our cruellest countrymen in Kenya. Free enterprise with the whip. After all, the sufferers are only black! The petty tyranny of the employer-employee relationship – irresponsible, hidden, without redress – is surely not a lovely thing? As Tawney says, the religion of inequality seems to make it possible for even men of generous good will to forget that workmen are also men.[61]

In short, Durbin recognized that Keynesian policies alone would lead to a continuation of the system of private enterprise, to which he was opposed on political and humanitarian grounds, rather than economic.

CHAPTER 8
THE NEW FABIANS
PLAN FOR SOCIALISM

Although socialists were beginning to recognize that a Labour government would need to know how to deal with unemployment under capitalism and socialism, planning still remained central as the socialist alternative to the market system. Yet the justification for planning was often a vague belief that somehow the state ought to be able to manage things more efficiently than the creaky and chaotic free market. Furthermore, many others who were not socialists also believed in planning for the same kinds of reasons. Therefore, democratic socialist thinkers in the 1930s needed to identify, on the one hand, the organizational structure necessary to carry out effective economic planning and, on the other hand, the principles of planning which would ensure the introduction of socialism. While public ownership was one of the necessary ingredients to make the transition to socialism effective, socialist economists were becoming increasingly sensitive to the problem of how they would allocate resources efficiently. At the same time the existence of the Russian five-year plan and the apparent Soviet success at eliminating unemployment presented another kind of challenge to democratic socialists, who rejected Marxist economics and non-parliamentary politics.

In the aftermath of the 1931 crisis the Labour party engaged in extended public discussion of the reforms necessary to enable the next Labour government to gain sufficient power over the economy to meet its political goals. It was agreed that a centralized financial system and the nationalization of specific industries would form the main apparatus of control. While legislative proposals were being debated in party committees and conferences, the New Fabians were conducting their own research into the theory and practice of socialist planning. Their work raised more general questions about the nature of planning, the form of government intervention and the role of the price mechanism than the party's practical agenda has suggested to historians.[1] It also uncovered fundamental disagreements on many central problems. The recommendations which the young economists later made to the party's policy subcommittees were shaped in significant ways by the economic and political controversies generated in these early discussions.

At the NFRB Colin Clark's committee was assigned the task of investigating planning machinery, while Hugh Gaitskell's committee studied the theory of socialist economic policy. These committees made important contributions to the definition of democratic socialist planning and to the practical implementation of socialist economic policy. They clarified the relations between machinery and policy, between the form and purpose of planning mechanisms, and the political implications of these distinctions.

In the early 1930s the debates were largely confined to pro-planners, socialist and non-socialist. It was only after 1935 that the anti-planners, led by Hayek and Robbins at the London School of Economics, joined the fray to attack the economic foundations of central planning. Before this diversion, the research process within the NFRB had revealed substantial diversities in approach, which were later reflected in different rationales for the 'mixed' economy.

The machinery for socialist planning

Despite the ambitious plans for Clark's committee, the members worked extensively on only two topics, the supply of capital and the control of investment. In a pamphlet on national planning for SSIP, Clark explained that he was not interested in 'an elaborate paper scheme of Committees and Councils', because he thought that unemployment was the major planning problem.[2] He estimated that the decline of export industries accounted for a two million increase in unemployment; since the actual increase was only 1.6 million, he boldly asserted that 'there has not really been any depression in the internal market' and that consumption was 'actually increasing'. He did not repeat these conclusions in any of his subsequent work, so it seems safe to assume he thought better of them. As for the necessary machinery, Clark argued that the main vehicle to solve the unemployment problem should be a national investment board (NIB) which would 'regulate the flow of new capital into industry . . . and accommodate it to the savings available'.

Clark also tackled the problem of area redevelopment through the geographical distribution of new industrial development, expanding on Tawney's arguments in *Labour and the Nation*. He provided data on unemployment and new industrial development by area, and discussed the dispersion of London and the planning of new cities. He also suggested a state planning department as a third tier on top of existing town and regional boards, which would be a 'thinking' body to co-ordinate and direct industry and area development with the activities of the NIB. Further thoughts on the location of new industry were later developed by F. J. Osborn in a pamphlet, *Transport, Town Development and Territorial Planning of Industry*, published by the NFRB in October 1934. An NFRB conference on the problems of depressed areas was also held in 1937, to which Osborn contributed a long paper on the location of industry.

Thus, although some general questions about the appropriate form of a 'Supreme Economic Authority' (SEA) were discussed at conferences and in memoranda, little systematic work on the overall planning machinery was done at the Bureau before 1935. Their main effort was directed towards the institutional structure necessary to control the banking and financial systems, the main economic preoccupation of Labour party conferences and policy subcommittees at the time. Everybody participated in this debate. The most heated controversy arose over the nationalization of the joint stock banks, but there were also strong differences of opinion about the appropriate role of the NIB.

A nationalized banking system

Control of the money and credit systems was central to socialist plans to regulate the economy. However, opinions about the extent of public ownership necessary to ensure control varied enormously. Everyone accepted that the Bank of England should be nationalized (as did many non-socialists); other candidates included the joint stock banks, the acceptance houses, the discount houses, the insurance industry, building societies and investment houses. The diversity of opinion was well reflected at a joint SSIP/NFRB conference held in January 1932.

This conference was opened by Roy Harrod; he provided an outline which stressed that national control of central banking was important, not only in its own right, but as an example of the benefits of nationalization in general.[3] For example, if the first industries to be nationalized were coal and railways, which showed 'no tangible benefits', the whole policy might be discredited with the public, and 'universal socialization put off till doomsday'. He proposed expansionary policies, for which he believed the nationalization of the Bank of England would be essential. Although the new central bank would need to be 'linked' with other institutions responsible for supplying long-term capital, he did not suggest any further nationalization.

In reply, Cole insisted that the form of socialization was vital. The conference report recorded that 'Cole was against the representative system suggested in *Labour and the Nation.* . . . the Board must consist of technically qualified full time officials'. In the second session, E. A. Radice, secretary of the NFRB, in contrast to Harrod, was doubtful 'whether the financial system was of great importance, as compared with nationalisation of the land'.[4] He felt that Harrod's 'financial juggling' would not 'put matters right', and that the joint stock banks would have to be nationalized in order to provide more capital for home investment. A. T. K. Grant raised the problem of lending criteria; he thought 'that the allocation of credit should be done by a National Planning body'. He urged caution, but dismissed problems about the constitution of the socialized banking system because it was 'less a matter of paper than of getting hold of the right people'. G. R. Mitchison criticized the past policy of the banks for allocating too much credit to foreign markets at the expense of home production.

On the second day Vaughan Berry, the organizer of XYZ, spoke on the short-term capital market, and his colleague, Nicholas Davenport, on the long-term capital market. Both described the existing system in some detail. Berry focused on the discount houses and international bills, and Davenport on the means for directing savings into investment. Neither suggested nationalizing the joint stock banks; both recommended various reforms. In explicit opposition to Keynes, Davenport reportedly concluded:

> In general the best organ of control would be a loans council
> linked up with the Cabinet Committee for Economic Planning, and
> it is doubtful whether a national investment board as advocated
> in the Yellow Book would serve any additional purpose.[5]

He strongly disapproved of Keynes's proposal to allow the NIB to issue its own bonds; he was afraid such a body would over-extend its loaning powers and damage the government's financial credit. Both Colin Clark and Mitchison attacked Davenport's recommendation, which gave the NIB only the power to deny projects and no positive means to direct new development. Cole agreed with Clark that any loans council must be 'part and parcel of a much wider scheme for the national reconstruction', with positive powers to plan new industries. He warned that the NIB must be independent of the Treasury, 'as it is essential that the general needs of the industry should never be subordinated to the monetary financial requirements of Treasury officials'.

Although Durbin, Gaitskell and Meade were not reported in attendance at this conference, until 1935 Durbin and Gaitskell both supported the nationalization of the joint banks in the next Labour government. Meade agreed with Harrod; his priorities were 'the socialisation of the Bank of England, the institution of the National Investment Board and the reform of financial and budgetary policy'.[6]

A national investment board

The main research on the problem of capital supply and the form and powers of the NIB was carried out in Cambridge, where Clark and G. F. Shove were co-conveners of the Bureau committee. R. B. Braithwaite, H. L. Elvin, C. H. P. Gifford and Joan Robinson were the most active members. There was already a SSIP chapter in Cambridge; the two groups collaborated on annual reviews of 'recent capital issues', which were duplicated and available for a penny ha'penny. In a memorandum to the Bureau's overall economic committee in June 1931, Shove suggested that the two main research questions should be to consider: (a) how far the 'socialist policy of equalizing incomes' can be reconciled with 'securing an adequate supply of new capital'; (b) 'how far and in what ways should the State itself undertake the provision of new capital'.[7] Clark wrote two pamphlets based on the committee's work, *The Control of Investment* (1933) and *A Socialist Budget* (1935).

On behalf of the committee Clark elaborated the notion of the NIB, which had originated with Keynes and the Liberal party in the 1920s. Unlike Davenport, he sought broad powers for the board to issue its own bonds. But unlike Keynes, he wanted more control over other institutions, particularly the joint stock banks; however, he stopped short of demanding immediate nationalization. Furthermore, he explicitly avoided commitment on questions about the control of insurance companies and building societies as suppliers of new savings. Clark listed the seven powers he thought appropriate for the NIB. The committee also proposed that 'a substantial sum to be raised by taxation should be set aside annually out of the Budget for the use of the National Investment Board'.[8] Finally, Clark discussed the composition and control of the board briefly; he advocated ministerial responsibility for the banking system and the board, but was vague on details. He was clear that 'it is certainly undesirable that Parliament shall attempt to exert control over the day to day administration of either'.

Other NFRB members called for even more radical measures. At its 1933 conference on socialist planning Mitchison presented the left-wing view of ministerial responsibility for economic planning.[9] He proposed the creation of a ministry of finance to control central finance, the credit system, regional finance and the NIB. Half the board members should be politicians and half experts; it should issue its own stock, raise its own bonds, license other transactions 'which it thought fit' and control all foreign issues and exchange strictly. Dalton was strongly opposed to having politicians on the NIB; he was also doubtful about allowing it to issue its own bonds. Two XYZ members who attended, Berry and Spriggs, supported Dalton; indeed, Berry argued that banks could handle credit better than a separate board. By contrast, E. S. Watkins, who had written a memorandum for the capital supply committee on building societies and their role as savings institutions, wanted the NIB to have more powers; the building societies should be nationalized, and their savings invested in the public interest.

In the Bureau's collective work, *Studies in Capital Investment* (1935), Radice explained that 'for socialists the state control of savings and investment is of course an essential part of their programme of public ownership and economic equality'.[10] He put forward the most comprehensive and radical view of investment planning. He called for the nationalization of insurance companies and building societies as well as the banks; he wanted all forms of taxation to be partially earmarked for investment, not only undistributed profits, but also personal taxes and death duties. In short, the NIB would 'co-ordinate and socialise a large proportion of the national savings and investment'.

In the same book, Francis Williams, city editor of the *Daily Herald* and a member of XYZ, argued for the 'absorption of the functions' of insurance companies and investment trusts into the NIB, particularly if the board was to issue its own bonds and finance industrial development.[11] Sir Vaughan Berry later recalled that nationalization of insurance companies was discussed in some detail at XYZ meetings, until someone realized that the companies had 10,000 door-to-door salesmen whom it would be electoral folly to antagonize; the idea was quietly dropped. In another chapter Watkins concluded that, while the building societies would have no role if land was nationalized, they must be 'controlled and directed' under a national housing corporation to finance housing and to collect a considerable portion of the national savings during the transition.[12]

Socialist banking and finance

After 1933 the appropriate financial institutions for the socialist state were elaborated by individual NFRB members in direct response to requests from Dalton as chairman of the Labour party's finance and trade committee. All the issues were discussed at length in XYZ club meetings to which Durbin, Gaitskell and Jay were first invited in 1934. However, the NFRB did hold a conference on banking and finance in May 1935, which most of the XYZ attended and which provides an interesting glimpse of the reasons why so many moderate socialists continued to believe in the nationalization of the joint stock banks, as well as other institutions.

The conference was held in Maidstone, Kent, a popular choice at Whitsun because everyone enjoyed unwinding at the local fair. It must also have been a lively conference, for the participants recall it well.[13] Apart from Dalton's domination of the proceedings, the most dramatic confrontation was between the voice of orthodox banking, in the person of Charles Lidbury from the Westminster Bank, and the socialist reformers.

George Wansbrough, from Robert Benson and later chairman of Reyrolle, opened the first session with a paper on 'Central Control (Form and Essentials)'.[14] An affluent Etonian member of XYZ, he is remembered as a generous host in his exotic flat, which featured a parrot and a kinkajou, as well as high-minded discussions of socialist finance. He emphasized the importance of the NIB to stimulate the economy and of nationalization of the Bank of England, for under Montague Norman it was a 'totally irresponsible body'; he also advocated nationalization of the joint stock banks because they could sabotage an expansionist policy 'by expanding their cash ratios'. In reply, Charles Latham, chairman of the finance committee of the London County Council, a close associate of Herbert Morrison and another XYZ member, argued against allowing the NIB to raise its own capital. He wanted it to have only a licensing authority; he also questioned the wisdom of nationalizing the joint stock banks, for he thought that to reduce speculation it would be better to take over the stock exchange, 'since it was the house of panics'.

In the general discussion, Berry, Durbin and James Lawrie all spoke, as well as McLaughlin, a rather handsome, young 'social crediter', whom Lawrie recalls received patient and kindly attention from Dalton, much to the amusement of Durbin and Gaitskell, who were accustomed to the short shrift such ideas usually got. Pethick-Lawrence, a member of Dalton's committee, sounded the most conservative and orthodox note. It was reported that he 'wanted to know what would be the essential difference when the Bank of England had been socialized'; he feared 'the change could be nugatory', and felt that the governor of the bank 'would ultimately toe the line, to a determined Chancellor of the Exchequer'. It is not clear from the report that anyone gave him a direct answer.

In the second session Lidbury presented his paper on 'Joint Stock

Banks (Their Organisation and Function)'. He gave the standard line that banks were providing a public service, and was reported to have said:

> There was no justification for the socialist supposition that the banks would be obstructive to a Labour administration. The Joint Stock Banks were concerned only with the administration of the funds deposited with them by the general public. In carrying out this job they were not concerned with politics. The soundness of the borrower was their sole criterion in lending; it was their duty to judge credit worthiness.

A Labour government would have no trouble borrowing from the banks, he insisted, as long as it maintained its credit worthiness. Apparently he quoted Cripps, Cole, Laski and Mitchison to show that it was socialists themselves who had little confidence in their own government, since they were constantly assuming there would be financial panic if the Labour party was elected. Finally, he caused an uproar by insisting that nationalization was quite unnecessary, and that 'the Profit and Loss account was the only real and safe criterion of the efficiency and safety of any bank'.

Douglas Jay has never forgotten Lidbury slowly waving his finger to and fro over 'Profit and Loss'; Berry remembered sitting next to Pethick-Lawrence, who said, 'Good God, I thought we were living in the twentieth century'. Gaitskell replied that 'it was absurd to suggest that confidence depended entirely on the government: the Joint Stock Banks themselves would be largely if not mainly responsible for any panic through their refusal to take up government bills'. Therefore, he argued it was 'absolutely necessary that a Labour Government should socialise the Joint Stock Banks and be prepared to deal with any panic that might arise'. Various XYZ members spoke in the general discussion. Francis Williams pointed out that 'while Lidbury was against mixing banking and politics, 46 directors of the big Five were Conservative members of Parliament' and 'no avowed Socialists were on the board of any bank'. John Wilmot thought 'that Lidbury's speech was the strongest statement he had heard in favour of the socialisation of the Joint Stock Banks'. Lawrie thought socialisation of the Joint Stock Banks was inevitable; Durbin said 'that an expansionist policy would necessitate the socialisation of the Joint Stock Banks as well as the Bank of England.' Even Pethick-Lawrence reportedly said he 'believed that the nation demanded a planned economy and that the Joint Stock Banks must fit in with this'.

In summarizing the conference, Dalton maintained that the central question was whether the joint stock banks could prevent an effective expansionist policy. Although the Labour party officially supported their nationalization, the appropriate time had not been settled. Dalton himself felt that the banks should be given a chance to see if they would co-operate with the Labour government. He thought 'the control of the National Investment Board much more important than the Joint Stock Banks', because it would 'mobilise savings and stimulate and direct investment'. The board would be concerned with the provision of long-term capital, while the banks controlled only short-term funds. In reply Durbin said that short-term funds were 'the life blood of industry'; if a Labour government wanted to carry out an expansionist programme and control the boom, it would have to control the joint stock banks.

In short, the New Fabians were agreed that the major institutions necessary for macroeconomic control were a socialized banking system to regulate the volume of savings and investment and a national invest-ment board to allocate the funds among industries and areas. However, they disagreed widely about the actual form and powers of these institutions. There was unanimity about the nationalization of the Bank of England. An influential group, including Cole, Durbin and Gaitskell, advocated nationalizing the joint stock banks as well; however, the XYZ club leaders, Berry and Davenport, and the Keynes-ians, Meade and Harrod, thought that it would be unnecessary. More radical Fabians called for nationalization of insurance and building societies. There was also general agreement about the need for a NIB; but opinions about its role ranged from a loans council with licensing powers to full-scale responsibility with power to raise investment funds and to allocate them over a broad spectrum of activities. With the exception of Davenport, the New Fabians went further than the Liberals in favouring a larger share of national savings for the NIB and in contemplating broader public ownership of savings and investment institutions.

The theory of planning

The most innovative work on the principles of socialist planning at the NFRB began under Gaitskell's direction. For the first time in Britain socialist economists dealt with the problems of allocation. The New Fabian economists were concerned with the practical issue of pricing in nationalized industries, the place of the private market in the socialist state and the relevance of neoclassical economics. But they were deeply divided on the question of free-market pricing versus government-controlled pricing. The research on market pricing evolved into a full-blown controversy among professional economists, for which the initiators are rarely given credit. Within the Bureau, Gaitskell and Durbin were committed to market pricing, Cole and Barbara Wootton to a significant degree of controlled pricing. In the course of their debates broader political problems of democratic planning emerged, revealing very different conceptions of its role under socialism.

Market pricing under socialism

As early as the summer of 1931 Gaitskell wrote a memorandum proposing seven research questions for his committee:

1 A criticism of the Individualistic Method of directing and organising Economic Resources.
2 A Discussion of Possible Rival Methods and their Relation to Socialist Ideals.
3 The Use of the Pricing System under Socialism.
4 The Operation of the Pricing System under Socialism.
5 The Problem of Material Resources (the quantity of saving and the direction of Investment).
6 The Problem of Wages, Mobility and Employment.
7 The Place of Private Enterprise under Socialism.

His aim was

to point out the various methods which might be employed to direct and organise the economic resources of a socialist community, and to discuss in full the implications and difficulties of these various methods and their relation to socialist ideas. No attempt should be made to decide categorically what *is* the best method, for in fact decisions about what is best in this matter lie partly outside the realm of scientific inquiry altogether and belong more properly to Ethics or Social Philosophy.[15]

The main contributor to the committee's research was H. D. Dickinson, an economist from the University of Leeds with an abiding passion for trains (he knew Bradshaw by heart), who would travel down for intense discussions with Durbin and Gaitskell. He had already published an article on the economic basis of socialism in 1930.[16] For the committee he drafted a paper, 'Failure of Economic Individualism', which was being revised in July 1932. He also circulated an article, 'Price Formation in a Socialist Community', which was later published.[17]

In his first article Dickinson posed what he considered 'the crucial problem of all socialist projects, how the government, once it has nationalized all industries, would allocate labour and capital to the different branches of production?' He argued that one part of the problem, the allocation of goods between consumers, was best accomplished through the market-place. However, this could only be done fairly if there was equality of income. The allocation of factor resources between different branches of production could be determined by the price mechanism. Unfortunately, as Dickinson pointed out, incomes could not be equal, because that would be 'incompatible with freedom of choice of occupation' and would probably be 'unfavourable to a high level of production'. Therefore, he felt that some departure from equality would have to be allowed. However, inequality would be substantially reduced because a large part of private wealth would be collectivized, and equal educational opportunities would prevent the accumulation of inequalities possible in the individualistic market system.

Dickinson's second article has since been credited with introducing the concept of marginal-cost pricing to welfare economics.[18] He also proposed that increasing-cost industries should be taxed and decreasing-cost industries subsidized. Although Dickinson used neoclassical efficiency criteria, he was fully aware of the limitations of this model for social purposes. His memorandum on the failure of economic individualism provided a systematic exposition of market failures; unfortunately, it was not published until 1935, and is rarely referred to in the literature. He summarized the threefold defects of the market, those which occur even under perfect competition, those arising from monopolization and finally the dynamic disturbances caused by the monetary system.

Meanwhile, Maurice Dobb, a Cambridge lecturer and a convinced Marxist, had attacked Dickinson for using the neoclassical model to evaluate a socialist economy in an article published in December 1933. He raised three main criticisms, which were immediately challenged by Abba Lerner, Robbins's young protégé at the LSE.[19] Dobb first criticized Dickinson's reliance on 'the sacredness' of consumers' preferences; he did not believe that a competitive market could provide an economic democracy similar to parliamentary democracy, where 'in the one votes are cast by offers on a market, in the other by crosses at a polling booth'. Dobb argued that the analogy was false because those with higher incomes had more votes in the market-place. Second, Dickinson was unclear about what was being maximized, because the actual optimum depended on an implicit value assessment, not a 'scientific' solution. Finally, Dickinson's pricing rules would not work because of the inability of static market conditions to allow for dynamic changes in technology and tastes.

Lerner sprang to Dickinson's defence in the first of his seminal articles on the economics of socialism in early 1934. Although he admitted there were some errors in Dickinson's analysis, they should not detract from its pioneering merits, but 'rather emphasize the extreme difficulties of investigation in a vast unexplored region'. He believed with Dickinson that one important principle for democratic socialists was to give people 'what they wanted when there was no good reason for a contrary policy'. Indeed, to do otherwise in a planned socialist society would supplant the democratic assumption 'by the much more suspect proposition that somebody else (the Government, Mr. Dobb?) knows better than the people themselves what is really good for them'. Lerner depicted the bureaucratic tyrannies of Dobb's own Russian-based system in passionate terms. He also berated him for not helping to refine Dickinson's adaptation of market pricing to socialism, but only attacking 'with the sword of Midas in the left hand and the club of Hitler in the right'. Finally, true to his Robbinsonian education, Lerner disputed that there were any value judgments implied in the neoclassical Pareto optimum.

In a subsequent reply Dobb maintained that a scale of relative values, and not just quantities, was involved in choosing the appropriate mix of outputs.[20] Planners could construct their own priorities, but they could just as well use 'judgement and inference' to provide a scale which was responsive to consumer basic needs and 'the simpler comforts of life'. He also questioned whether the market system actually provided a geniune choice: 'the masses have dangled before their eyes the illusion of free choice – freedom to have what they want *if* they had the money – and are then handed over to the rack devised for them by the advertising agent, the commercial salesman, and the social conventions of a ruling class'. In his rejoinder Lerner restated his belief in the democratic merits of free consumer choice, which could only be urged on political, not scientific, grounds.[21] However, he still maintained that no system, whether based on consumer preferences or planners' priorities, could 'achieve its ends with any reasonable degree of efficiency without the use of a price system'.

By this time the level of argument had developed far beyond Dickinson's use of marginal-cost pricing as a simple rule to maximize production in the socialist state. Dobb's criticisms and Lerner's elaborations had raised questions about choices between different optimal positions, the appropriate means to scale economic priorities and eventually the need for making interpersonal comparisons. In short, this controversy had moved into the higher realms of welfare economics, far from the practical motivations behind Gaitskell's socialist economics committee.

Controlled pricing under socialism

G. D. H. Cole found price theory useless for socialist systems, but for different reasons than Dobb. In an essay 'Towards a New Economic Theory' written in 1932, Cole outlined some of the main problems for working out an economics 'appropriate to a socialist community.[22] He rejected the neoclassical price system because it failed to take account of social cost or to ensure the full employment of all available productive resources. His argument relied on Hobsonian ideas of the separation of the theory of distribution from the theory of production, not on the macroeconomic relationships between savings and investment. Thus, while Cole accepted the importance of free consumers' demand, he argued that 'a realistic Economic Theory ... will set out from a study of the character and organization of the available productive resources of modern society, from the standpoint of production itself'. He thought that such a study should start with a taxonomic description of all forms of productive organization including Russian planning schemes. He concluded:

> What I am certain is that it will mean giving to Economic Theory
> a totally new shape, based far more on the study of real
> productive forces and of the right relationship between the
> productive and distributive systems, and far less on prices, which
> will come to be regarded much less as data than as controlled
> expressions of the results of concrete decisions about the
> organisation of production and the distribution of real income.

Although Cole's arguments were quite vague at this stage, their Hobsonian antecedents contrasted sharply with Dickinson's neoclassical approach.

In the summer of 1932 there were two Fabian visits to Russia to observe socialist planning at first hand. In May the Webbs sailed for Leningrad, to be treated as 'minor royalty'. In July an NFRB team also set out, and enjoyed a less-regal 'whale of a time', according to Margaret Cole, one of the members.[23]

In the 1920s the Webbs had recognized that Britain's parliamentary institutions would not be able to cope with the complexities of the state's planning function, which they envisaged in their new world. They had proposed a 'social parliament' to complement the existing political system which would draw up the overall plan and implement it. True to their lifelong faith in experts and administrative efficiency, they suggested that this parliament should be elected in the same way as the political arm, but that its operations should be carried out by a hierarchy of standing committees along functional lines. While the Webbs outlined a democratic form of planning, the potential conflicts between the two parliaments underscored the difficulties of combining majority rule with economic efficiency and social consistency. Their combination of nationalization, municipalization and central planning by committee provided a schema for the socialist control of the economy, but no specifics about how the economy should be run. Nevertheless, just as Sidney Webb's 1918 policy outline for the Labour party described the accepted framework for all subsequent programmes, even though it contained no specific legislative proposals, so the Webbian kind of system became the general party view of how planning would have to be conducted.

At first the Webbs had been hostile to the disruptive tendencies of the Bolshevik revolution, but ten years later, in the midst of capitalist depression, they returned from Russia convinced of the superiority of the Russian economic system. *Soviet Communism: A New Civilization?*, the final intellectual fruit of their partnership in the collective cause, was first published in 1935. It was republished, this time without the question mark, in 1937. Beatrice herself described their 'love affair' with the Soviet system. Margaret Cole felt that, although aware of 'the disease of orthodoxy', their hearts were 'in Russia and Russia alone' thereafter, and they tended 'to judge all political characters – and all their visitors to Passfield Corner! – by the amount of interest they showed in Soviet affairs'.

The New Fabians returned impressed, but not as committed as the Webbs. The group included Hugh Dalton and Pethick-Lawrence as financial experts from the Labour party, Mitchison, Beales and Pritt from the NFRB, and other assorted experts such as John Morgan, a farmer, Graeme Haldane, an electrical engineer, Redvers Opie, Meade's colleague at Oxford, and Naomi Mitchison, the novelist. They wrote a report, *Twelve Studies in Soviet Russia*, published by the NFRB in 1933, and gave a series of lectures. One of the earliest appraisals of the first five-year plan, its findings were mainly positive, in some cases 'lyrical', although Morgan 'wrote with unhappy honesty of the conditions on the farms'. Margaret Cole later recalled ruefully:

The investigators, like the Webbs, rejoiced to see what they wanted to see – the 'Spirit of the Revolution', the sense of collective purpose and planning so notably lacking in Europe and America in 1932; and like the Webbs again did not see, or minimised, what they did not want to see. They were in good company; the cold war, and the revelations of the Twentieth Congress, have made it difficult for this generation to understand the unique and compelling force of the Soviet appeal in the dark years of the depression.

Dalton, who wrote the chapter on planning, was particularly impressed with the enthusiasm and the apparent flexibility of the Soviet planners. He found little connection between Marxist theory and practical experience; he summarized their objectives as follows:

> To avoid the economic crises and trade fluctuations of capitalism; to keep the whole working population in continuous employment and to raise their standard of living, without permitting the growth of large inequalities, to a level higher than that of workers in capitalist countries; to achieve a large measure of self-sufficiency and, as a means to this end, to stimulate to the utmost the industrialization of the country.[24]

Although he noted that Russian planning was handicapped by lack of industrial experience, he could not help concluding that 'most of the Russians I saw looked better fed than my unemployed Durham miners and their families'.[25]

Dalton recognized that planning was not the same thing as socialism: 'socialism is primarily a question of ownership, planning is a question of control or direction'.[26] He defined planning, 'in its widest sense, as the deliberate direction, by persons in control of large resources, of economic activities towards chosen ends'. Dalton judged planning not by efficiency or democratic criteria, but 'according to who directs, toward what chosen ends, by what means, and with what skill'; none the less, 'a good plan, well executed, is always better than no plan at all'. Thus, by concentrating on the goals of planning, he avoided the tough economic and political questions being raised by his democratic socialist comrades.

In his book *Practical Socialism for Britain*, which was primarily concerned with the Labour party's programme, Dalton included a section on planning. He outlined four stages of 'social planning', two national and two international, which started with separate plans for nationalized industries and then developed an overall plan co-ordinating them. But his discussion of planning mechanisms was descriptive and fragmented rather than analytic and coherent. His positions were derived from widely accepted views about the need for planned development of jobs, geographic planning, industry location, national parks and the importance of a supreme economic authority (SEA) to be responsible to the government and to Parliament, and to consult 'with the legimate interests affected by its decisions'. The SEA must be efficient, 'in the sense that it applies well understood and intelligently formulated rules to the material with which it deals, and is competent both for current administration and for fresh thinking and research'. On the formulation of the rules, Dalton had nothing further to add.

On the use of the price mechanism Dalton was equally imprecise: 'in so far as we retain prices at all in our economic system, and a price mechanism – and on grounds of practical convenience we shall certainly retain it, though possibly its range will be narrowed – we must study the workings of this mechanism, lest its unanticipated movements defeat our purposes'. Despite the vagueness of this statement, Dalton was clearly against market pricing under socialism, and in favour of controlled prices. He was bitterly opposed to worship of 'the God of the Free Market', which was based on gross inequalities of income, to privately planned capitalism, which allowed private monopolies free rein, and to rationalization schemes, which allowed society to be 'more planned against than planning'. Harold Barger has never forgotten an NFRB conference in 1935 at which he supported competition between socialized sectors, only to incur the wrath of Dalton, who thundered, 'You want me to write a book called "Unplanned Socialism for Britain"?'

The growing divergence between market and control planners was already reflected in the 1933 NFRB conference discussions on 'Some Aspects of Socialist Planning'. In one session on existing marketing and price-fixing machinery, the main speaker concluded that national marketing boards had had some success, but export boards had been a failure. Other speakers were highly critical of price-fixing machinery and monopolistic standardization, which kept prices higher than they would be under perfect competition, and also deplored industry representation on price-fixing boards. Hugh Dalton opened the next session on price fixing in nationalized industries under socialism. He proposed to limit Treasury subsidies to socialized industries and to plan prices centrally; 'the matter could not be left to industries to fight out for themselves (laissez faire socialism)'. Dalton thought that as long as there was great poverty, planners should decide output and prices rather than allow the free market to reflect consumer preferences. He reasoned that divergences in tastes were not important among the poor and that they did not apply to public goods such as health and education. Dalton wanted a cabinet committee to be responsible for price fixing. In the discussion Durbin claimed that poor people did have different consumer preferences; Cole held that consumer preferences would only be important in an egalitarian society; Mrs Cole urged the necessity of ministerial responsibility for price-fixing policy, and Harrod the use of marginal-cost pricing.

Durbin's Principles of Planning

Shortly after this conference, in response to Dalton's earlier request to the NFRB, Durbin submitted a long memorandum on 'The Principles of Socialist Planning' to the Labour party policy committee.[27] It is an important document; for the first time it spelled out principles of planning for democratic socialism which systematically applied economic principles to evaluate social policy. It summarized the work of the socialist economics committee, which disbanded thereafter; Gaitskell had left for Vienna in the autumn of 1933. The memorandum was divided into two parts: part one discussed in some depth 'the purpose of planning and the economic tasks of a Labour government'; part two outlined 'the necessity for and the constitution of a Supreme Economic Authority (with suggestions as to the economic principles according to which it should operate)'.

Durbin expounded his own view of planning in part one. He saw it as a form of economic organization, which provided a central authority to make decisions about the course of economic development and to act as an alternative to the individual decision making of capitalism. However, he raised two unusual questions for a socialist: 'Is planning an efficient type of *economic* organization? Is it superior to private enterprise in its power to raise the general standard of living?' Durbin proposed three standards for judging system efficiency: (1) whether the system ensured full employment of labour and capital; (2) whether it provided for investment in new technical inventions; (3) whether it adjusted production to the needs and tastes of the public. Durbin felt the last was 'often neglected in current Socialist discussions because it is incorrectly assumed that the problem of production has been largely solved in our own generation'.

In theory, Durbin pointed out, capitalism could meet these standards, but it depended on three social institutions, competition, inherited private property and private banking; these in turn caused inequality and maintained a social class structure. Thus he concluded:

> Capitalism is to be condemned far more on the grounds of the social system to which it leads than on any inherent weakness in the institutions by which an active capitalism attempts to solve the economic problem.

Durbin believed that planning was a 'way of life', although it was not by itself 'a new social order'; indeed, 'it is increasingly possible in these days to be a "planner" without becoming a Socialist'.

To constitute *socialist* planning, a Labour government would have to pursue three critical policy goals: it must cure unemployment by monetary policy before the main instruments of socialist control were undertaken; it must extend control beyond banking and finance to industry and trade; it must undertake a 'clear and unambiguous equalization programme'. Durbin rejected both the Marxist solution of dictatorship by the proletariat and the traditional Labour party policy of redistribution through taxation and social services. The latter still depended on the rich to save, it ran the risk of discouraging investment and it 'saddles the economic system with a weight of obligations which destroys its flexibility'. He concluded that equality could only be secured under a planned economy with enough control to enforce the equalitarian policies in ways which were still consistent with 'the maintenance of democracy and the constitutional guarantees of personal liberty'.

Durbin argued that the extension of central control beyond financial institutions into industry required the formation of a supreme economic authority (SEA). The second part of his report spelled out the reasons why, its appropriate constitutional form and the principles for its operation. In general, the plan itself should never be 'fixed or rigid', but should be sensitive to changes in the free-market price of goods and the accounting costs of their production. On governmental relations, Durbin was in favour of a small body directly responsible to the cabinet.

This memorandum broke new ground for the theory of socialist economic planning in a variety of ways. First, it separated out the macroeconomic policy issues from the microeconomic problems of allocation. Second, it used economic efficiency as one criterion to judge the effectiveness of socialism. Third, it outlined two principles of the emerging school of thought on the use of market pricing under socialism, the use of the free market for consumption goods and the use of marginal-cost pricing in nationalized industries. Durbin agreed with Dickinson that 'apart from a limited number of social services, the production of no final commodity should be subsidized out of general funds'; if people were not willing to pay what it cost to produce goods, they must really prefer to buy and consume something else. Finally, Durbin was unusually frank about the difficulties facing a Labour government in its attempts to allocate efficiently. In particular, he pointed out that nationalized industries might build up their own vested interests and resist the SEA, those industries with increasing demand would want to raise prices to get their workers higher wages and those with falling demand would try to secure subsidies and resist contraction.

It is not easy to imagine what the Labour party's policy subcommittees made of this theoretical approach to their practical problems and its categorical rejection of their earnest endeavours to redistribute incomes. Since Dalton was opposed to its pricing policies, he may well have buried it in oblivion. While Durbin's document was being finished, Gaitskell was presenting, in German, a paper 'demonstrating a workable price system under socialism' before von Mises's awesome private seminar in Vienna. He boldly challenged von Mises's well-known thesis that such a system was impossible; he reported afterwards, 'I was a little nervous for, of course . . . Mises is not exactly good at taking criticism. However, it went off better than I expected. He was very polite, and Haberler and Strigl both came firmly to my rescue'.[28]

In the same year Lionel Robbins published *The Great Depression*, a blistering attack on Keynes's expansionary policies and on planning in general. Although he later regretted his mistaken analysis of the unemployment problem, the book provided a foretaste of the revised Austrian case against socialism. Robbins equated socialism with a centrally planned collectivist state, which he opposed on liberal political grounds; he also challenged the piecemeal reorganization of industry, which non-socialist planners also supported, claiming that it was not planning, but syndicalism. In the following year Durbin took up the gauntlet, refining his thoughts on the importance of planning for socialism in the most systematic analysis he published during the 1930s.[29] Because the term 'planning' was applied to such a wide variety of activities, Durbin distinguished between intervention and overall planning as follows:

1 Planning, meaning simply the *intervention of the Government in a particular industry* at a time when the greater part of the economy still remains in private hands, and
2 Planning which results in the *general supersession of individual enterprise* as the source of economic decisions.

He rejected the idea that general planning was simply 'the sum of a large number of interferences with a private economy'. What mattered was the source of authority; general planning was very different if it was carried on by an inter-industrial body, which reflected social interests, rather than by the restricted interests of one industry. Durbin identified the common element of all new forms of control constituting planning as 'the extension of the size of the unit of management and the consequent enlargement of the field surveyed when any economic decision is taken'.

Durbin believed that planning was essential to socialism, if it was to replace capitalism successfully. First, a socialist government must gain control of investment, in order to take over the function of private property in capital formation. Second, the system must work efficiently from the start 'if socialism is to be obtained by democratic means', because he held:

the man in the street judges the economic efficiency of any system by the degree of security in employment and the level of real wages it brings to him. To him planning will 'work' if it brings about a sustained rise in employment and a noticeable increase in the general standard of living.

Durbin argued that a planned economy was more efficient, because it would see the consequences of its actions over a broader spectrum of industry and further into the future, and because it alone could control business fluctuations through a centralized monetary policy. Moreover, if planning was genuinely perceived to be for the good of all, it could increase the co-operation of workers and reduce trade union resistance to the removal of their obstructive regulations.

Durbin laid down three conditions for the successful operation of a planned socialist system in Great Britain:

> In the first place it will be essential to set up some kind of Central Authority with power over industry and finance . . . In the second, it is of great importance that an Authority with general powers should proceed upon the basis of a reasonable pricing and costing policy . . . . The third, and perhaps the most important, requirement of efficient Planning is therefore the supersession in the Trade Union and Labour Movement in practice as well as in theory of the last element of Syndicalism.

He concluded that planning was crucial to the success of democratic socialism. First, the social control of industry was 'the prerequisite political condition for any stable advance to a more just society'. Second, planning was necessary to establish a more efficient economic system, and to make the approach to equality popular. In response to Robbins, he acknowledged that trade union practices were 'one of the real problems of socialist planning'. However, he thought they could be tackled if workers felt they had more to gain from the increase in society's well-being and efficiency than from the pursuit of their own narrow group interests:

> The organized workers who claim with justice that the interests of the community should not be over-ridden for the profits of the few should go on to add that those same interests must not be over-ridden for the wages of a few.

Thus, while being more judicious in tone than in his wages manuscript, Durbin maintained his unfashionable concern about the monopoly potential of trade unions in a centralized economic system.

Wootton and Cole on planning

In an influential book published in 1934, Barbara Wootton systematically compared the nature, achievements and possibilities of the unplanned economy with those of the Russian planned economy.[30] Although Wootton did not break any new theoretical ground in her analysis of the price mechanism or of Russian planning techniques as methods for allocating economic resources, she raised important questions about the problems of democratic control for both systems. Besides the usual socialist arguments against the market, she also pointed out that its much-touted political freedoms were severely limited by Parliament's inability to cope with economic problems:

> There is no part of their job which parliaments do worse than their economic work, and no department of affairs in which the theory of democratic control is further removed from actual practice; and no wonder, when one considers on the one hand the amount of technical knowledge that constructive economic planning demands, and on the other hand the means by which members seek and gain election. So already this pathetic inability of amateur Ministers and members of Parliament to handle extremely complex technical questions has become an old story and one which agitates every school of political reformer; and, thanks to this, theoretical democracy is visibly degenerating into a mere pull of rival vested interests.[31]

Although in her view the Russian economic system was clearly superior in its provision of collective goods, in its greater equality and, above all, as 'the land of no unemployment', she recognized that its average standard of living was still low. More importantly, she distinguished Russia's economic accomplishments and possibilities from its revolutionary techniques and class rhetoric, which she argued had arisen from the political and social systems peculiar to Russia.

Her major contribution to the intellectual debates about planning was to think through the conditions of successful economic planning, which would combine political freedom, social justice and economic efficiency. Besides detailed work on planning processes, she concluded there were three critical ingredients, expert economic knowledge and the ability to use it, control over the instruments of production and a central planning authority with 'the power both to draw up plans and to supervise their execution'. Control by professional planners was essential for positive direction of the economy and to avoid the tyranny of vested interests. Wootton has been characterized as the greatest supporter of the economic expert, with a willingness to accord 'economic expertise an almost unfettered freedom'.[32]

Wootton remained vague on the role of the price mechanism: 'this, of all aspects of planning, seems to me most urgently to call for investigation'. Clearly there would be an important role for pricing, particularly to express the content of the plan in general directives and to provide the economic incentives to allocate workers between jobs without compulsory direction. Nevertheless, Wootton was insistent that a planning authority will not be *wholly and automatically* guided by the readings of the price mechanism'; however, it would be 'silly to set up a cumbrous organisation merely to do what can be actually done better without it'. She was willing to accept that planning would involve some degree of 'arbitrariness' from planners and some 'negative compulsions' in the labour market, such as refusing recruits in oversupplied occupations and requiring minimum performance levels. Wootton's work represented a natural development from the earlier vision of administrative efficiency advocated by the Webbs, and reinforced the conventional socialist expectation that planning would require a complex system of controls.

In contrast, G. D. H. Cole's contributions to the planning literature were an adaptation of his own earlier guild socialist yearnings to the economic and political context of the 1930s.[33] In 1935 he published *The Principles of Economic Planning*, which was to remain his most ambitious statement on the theory and practice of socialist planning in Britain. Although Cole represented the left-wing end of the spectrum on many issues, he was in full agreement with his fellow democratic socialists on the centrality of planning, on the necessity for extensive social control of the economy and on the need for a combination of monetary plans to maintain full employment and microeconomic plans to allocate resources and distribute incomes. However, he differed from them in two fundamental ways. First, he not only rejected both neoclassical and Marxist economics, he tried to build up an alternative, the 'new economics'. Second, in designing the machinery for drawing up and executing the national plan, he stressed worker participation and democratic control over planners and Treasury officials.

The roots of Cole's economic theory, already briefly stated in his 1932 book, were Hobsonian. By focusing on the essentials for practical planning he developed a more comprehensive schema of the relation between economic analysis and distributive goals. He introduced economic and social priorities as an explicit part of the planning process not wrapped in a vague humanistic jumble. He argued that the existing distribution of incomes, based on enormous differences in wealth and opportunity, could not be used to value outputs through the price mechanism; the resulting price relatives would only measure the structure of demand generated by the existing distribution, not social need

or social cost. Socialist planning should obviously 'seek to plan production, at least to some degree, according to conceptions of social expediency and social cost'.[34] Need, rather than demand, would become 'the
primary criterion of the worthwhileness of productive effort'. Thus, 'a
satisfactory minimum of food, fuel, clothing, housing, education and
other common services' would constitute the first social claim which
'a planned economy must meet'. Cole thought that the basic needs
would not be difficult to estimate because they are 'neither highly
subject to individual caprice nor very liable to rapid change'; furthermore, many could be provided free or at very low cost, which would
reduce the need for wages to cover the 'social dividend', thus defined.
Earnings would become 'pocket money' available for the goods
produced in addition to the necessities. These goods would vary in
demand depending on consumer preferences and the planned distribution of incomes, and could best be allocated through the normal
pricing mechanisms of supply and demand.

In one sense Cole's social dividend was an obvious descendant of
the national minimum, which Sidney Webb had written into the
Labour party's constitution, of the 'Living Wage', and of Major Douglas's 'social credit', and a forerunner of the minimum incomes provided
in most modern welfare states. Yet Cole's contribution was unique in
its recognition of the need to synthesize social policy with economic
planning of production and incomes. While it was less new economic
theory, and more sophisticated planning analysis, it included important
new insights into the appropriate use of neoclassical analysis for the
practical planning of income distribution, largely unappreciated at the
time and still not resolved to this day.

His work on the machinery of planning and workers' control has
achieved more recognition, particularly as demands for decentralization and participation have grown, and Britain's class structure has
failed to wither away. Cole wanted a 'Minister of National Planning'
of cabinet rank to be responsible for presenting the national plan to
Parliament, 'much as the Budget is now brought forward'. The plan
would be drafted by a representative national planning authority, with
advice from experts appointed to a national planning commission. The
commission's task would be to co-ordinate the plans drawn up by 'all
the sectional agencies', industry boards, government departments and
so forth; 'but it would have no power to enforce its own plan against
those of the sectional bodies, but only the right to submit its proposals
and comments to some other body of a more representative character,
with which the power of decision would rest'.[35] An independent department of economic inspection would be responsible for checking that
plans were implemented. Finally, Cole was adamant that workers

should be included in the process of drawing up plans for individual industries; 'on this issue I remain an unrepentant Guild Socialist, though I am conscious that the way to industrial self-government in any full sense may be longer, and more difficult than I used to think'.[36]

Conclusions

In the early 1930s the only practical planning issue tackled systematically by the New Fabians was the necessary machinery to control the banking and financial systems. While they agreed that a centralized bank and a national investment board were the essential mechanisms, they disagreed widely about the extent of nationalization, the form of control and the appropriate powers for their operation. Although nothing like the same kind of energy was put into studying the overall planning machinery, the attempt to define the relation of planning to socialism introduced important new dimensions to the debate over socialist economics and the general theory of planning. Despite their differences the New Fabians agreed on the fundamentals, the case against capitalism, the need for a central planning authority and the importance of specific socialist policies to maintain employment, to allocate resources (especially capital) and to distribute incomes.

The chief socialist arguments against the unplanned capitalist system were its gross inequalities of income and wealth based on private ownership, its inability to deal with the allocation problems raised by extensive externalities in the form of social costs and the provision of collective goods, and the recurrent unemployment problems associated with the business cycle. It was recognized that capitalist planning might succeed in reducing general unemployment and tackling the structural problems of distressed areas and industrial inefficiency. Socialists were united in their belief that it was impossible to increase social justice without a major offensive against the institutions of private property and social class.

On the economic principles for socialist systems, there was a major cleavage between those who thought that the scientific criteria of economic efficiency could be applied and those who believed that other criteria were necessary. In a departure from the traditional assumptions that capitalism was by nature wasteful, was heading for collapse and would be replaced by rational socialist planning, questions had been raised about the efficiency of socialism itself. The role of the price mechanism became the dividing issue. At an NFRB conference on socialist planning in June 1935 attended by such experts as Abba Lerner, Cole took the position that 'it was absurd to say that pricing could not be planned, for wages and salaries could be fixed and other costs controlled'.[37] Gaitskell completely disagreed, arguing that there was no need for price control and that 'rigid price fixing might lead to a wastage of resources'. On this question there was no compromise, and, as it turned out, no final resolution. One school, led by Cole, Wootton and Dalton, continued to advocate some form of administered prices, although their theoretical work on prices did not progress. As professional economists, the young socialists in favour of market pricing went on to make their own contributions to the emerging field of socialist economics.

The New Fabians also had rather different conceptions of the problems for democratic control raised by the institution of a central planning system. Wootton has been credited with being the first to raise the problem, but everyone immediately recognized its importance.[38] They were all agreed, for instance, that subordinating vested interests to the central plan would pose major problems for planned capitalism. Therefore, their designs for socialist planning machinery were intended to make sure that organized sections could not exploit their monopoly powers at the expense of the general welfare. However, the democratic socialists differed in their diagnoses, as well as their solutions; they all had their own special bugbears, in addition to the usual wicked capitalists, landlords and financiers of socialist demonology. For Cole the danger arose from the bourgeoisie, particularly in the form of conservative civil servants and pompous experts. For Wootton it was the amateur politician, and for Durbin the self-interest of organized labour. Cole's solution was to give workers substantial powers in economic decision making at the industry level, with a representative planning authority to make the final decisions about allocations between the industries. Wootton assigned the responsibility for balancing special interests to the planners and economic experts. Durbin wanted to use the price mechanism to allocate resources as far as possible, with a supreme economic authority responsible to the cabinet as a safeguard against the abuse of monopoly power.

Nevertheless, despite these differences, the New Fabians were all convinced that planning was the essential ingredient in the socialist economic alternative. Their major contribution was to open up the Labour party's thinking from its narrow focus on structural organization and public ownership to a fuller consideration of policy options, relevant criteria and the relation between policy and institutional reform. They all understood that the appropriate planning mechanisms and principles were the necessary, but not the sufficient, conditions for successful socialist planning. Durbin undoubtedly spoke for them all when he concluded his 1935 chapter on planning with the following exhortation:

> The efficiency of Planning depends in the last resort upon the breadth and consistency of the Socialist faith which animates us .... The interests of the whole are sovereign over the interests of the part. In society we are born; in society we must live. To the centralized control of a democratic Community our livelihood and our security must be submitted. It is the business of society to secure the welfare of all. To do so it must be able to set limits to the welfare of each one of us.

CHAPTER 9
THE NEW GENERATION RETHINKS ECONOMIC STRATEGY

Concern with immediate practicality has always been a trade-mark of British democratic socialism. Despite their excursions into abstract economics and planning theory, Durbin and Gaitskell were no exception. Indeed, their choice of economic theory and focus was determined by its relevance to their political concerns, not the reverse. Although Gaitskell wavered momentarily after the 1931 crisis, his experience in Austria reconfirmed his commitment to democratic parliamentary methods. Thereafter, he and Durbin became the intellectual leaders of a group among the new generation, who thought through the appropriate revisionist strategy for the Labour party in the altered circumstances of the mid-1930s.

Their belief in democratic methods is fundamental to understanding the kind of socialist economic policy which emerged from this process. On the one hand, they repudiated all Marxist policies and systems which depended upon the dictatorship of the proletariat and were considered by definition undemocratic. They also rejected armed revolution, which placed the group firmly in the reformist tradition of the Fabians. On the other hand, this commitment meant that their economic policy was shaped by political priorities. The primary political goal was to get a Labour government elected with plans for the first stage to establish a socialist society in Britain; the next goal was to get re-elected to complete the transition.

While their democratic methods distinguished the New Fabian economists from Marxists, their socialism distinguished their philosophy from those of other social and economic reformers. They believed that a major shift in power from the private to the public sector was necessary to replace the capitalist system. Although they might agree on many issues with the broad spectrum of reformers, who advocated interventionist policies to reduce unemployment and/or inequality, they still sought to abolish capitalism, not to make it work better. Their strategic problem was how to devise an electorally viable programme to accomplish these goals. Betrayed and disillusioned by the events of 1931, they had rejected the traditional piecemeal approach represented by MacDonald and Snowden. They had confirmed their belief in a determined programme of nationalization, but its exact form remained vague.

In their earliest work the NFRB economists directed their efforts to discovering the appropriate economic principles to direct socialist planning. In the process they had discovered that they disagreed, sometimes fundamentally, about political aims and about the role of private decision making in a socialist economy. Durbin and Gaitskell, in particular, were drawing away from Cole, and through Dalton were becoming directly involved in party research. As a consequence, although their work at the Bureau continued, the two organized less formal discussions to thrash out political priorities with like-minded friends and colleagues.

As well as being anti-Marxist, Durbin and Gaitskell emphasized the parliamentary aspects of democracy, rather than the participatory decentralization which Cole espoused. Durbin, in particular, was strongly influenced by his Oxford friend, Reg Bassett, who published an important book, *The Essentials of Parliamentary Democracy*, in 1935. The book was a strong indictment of the Marxist perspective and revolutionary rhetoric of the well-known professor of political science at LSE, Harold Laski, which, as it turned out, did not help Bassett professionally. Bassett had been an ardent admirer of Ramsay MacDonald since his pacifist stand in the First World War; he continued to revere him, even after 1931, and to devote much of his career to exonerating the prime minister's actions.[1] Durbin's closeness to Bassett was a matter of controversy among his friends. For instance, Professor Sir Michael Postan deplored Bassett's MacDonaldite influence; but Sir Robert Fraser later appreciated the importance of his parliamentary perspective, which was firmly grounded in British institutions.

In a review of Bassett's book, Durbin described this view of democracy as follows:

Democracy is not a state of society but a method of taking decisions about the state of society. Democracy cannot be identified with social equality or personal freedom or their opposites, or indeed with any general condition of the social order whatever. Any form of society is compatible with the method of resolving differences within it by discussion, a search for agreement, mutual toleration, and freedom of political association. It is the method which is the true definition of democracy and the most fundamental thing in the political constitution of the state. The most important question which arises when powerful groups disagree is not what they disagree about, but whether or not they can agree as to the method by which their disagreement is to be resolved . . . the only 'agreement about fundamentals' which is necessary is the agreement not to resort to force in the settlement of disputes.[2]

Durbin later incorporated this analysis into his discussion of the politics of democratic socialism. In the meantime, the use of force was one of the critical criteria discussed in the development of Labour strategy.

The principles of economic policy and planning which Durbin and Gaitskell had worked out in their NFRB committees had been summarized in Durbin's memorandum for the Labour party delivered in January 1934.[3] Their research had convinced them that, despite the severe world depression, capitalism was not on the verge of collapse; nor would a gradualist policy of squeezing concessions bring about a meaningful redistribution of power. By late 1933 both believed that a Labour government must engage in a vigorous expansionary policy to reduce unemployment; in the midst of acrimonious professional controversies they were endeavouring to work out the correct macroeconomic policy for the Labour party. At the same time they were concerned about the appropriate long-term policies for the socialist state. They had defined three main economic objectives – the reduction of industrial fluctuations, the transfer of power from private to public control through nationalization and the efficient use of resources through full employment and market pricing mechanisms. Control of the financial system was a crucial first step; they believed that it would require nationalization of the Bank of England to control the overall volume of activity, nationalization of the joint stock banks to distribute short-term investment funds in the national interest, and the creation of a national investment board (NIB) to plan overall industrial development. A supreme economic authority (SEA) was also necessary to set policy and to co-ordinate the financial and industrial plans, in order to prevent vested interests from subverting the public interest.

After Gaitskell returned from Vienna, he and Durbin turned the attention of their discussion group to the political strategy for achieving these economic goals. By the summer of 1935 they had a much clearer view of the essentials, which, it is argued, led Durbin to reject an alternative programme presented to the NFRB by James Meade.

Economic programmes and political strategy

During the autumn and winter of 1934–5, a group of economists, political and social theorists, and assorted socialist practitioners held a series of meetings, 'to discuss the problems which face the English Labour Party in any attempt it may make to set up a Socialist Community by democratic methods'.[4] The economists were Durbin, Gaitskell, Barbara Wootton and Frederick Brown, a statistician at LSE; the economic and social historians included Michael Postan, Professors Eileen Power and R. H. Tawney, the political theorists, Robert Fraser, Richard Greaves, also from LSE, and Leonard Woolf. Arthur Creech Jones, a research officer for the Transport and General Workers Union, and John Parker, secretary of the NFRB, also took part. Durbin was the chairman, Brown, the secretary; they made notes of the meetings and a final summary of their discussions in a set of resolutions, which, with a couple of exceptions, were accepted unanimously.[5] The resolutions fell into two groups: (1) those concerned 'with the objectives of Social Democracy, the political instruments by which those objectives can be secured and the methods by which [an] attack on democracy can be repelled'; (2) those which 'set forth a programme of action in the economic sphere which in the opinion of the group it will be advisable for the next Labour Government to pursue'.

In the face of the threat of fascism in Europe and Gaitskell's recent experience in Austria, the group led by Tawney examined the risks of repression of the party in opposition, of sabotage once elected to power and of Tory attempts to rig elections. They discussed at great length the justifiable circumstances for resorting to revolutionary force. They concluded that it was important to pursue an active campaign against fascism and in favour of democracy, and that the Labour party should state in no uncertain terms its commitment to constitutional procedures. Early on they had decided 'that a programme of wholesale socialisation and rapid redistribution of wealth would provoke extra-Parliamentary opposition'. Therefore, in the final report they agreed that the Labour party should base 'its case for Socialism in so far as it could upon grounds of social justice and efficiency'.

The group report marks an important step in the development of the definition and strategy for democratic socialism in Britain, and is worth quoting at length. The report distinguished four kinds of social and economic measures:

1 *Ameliorative* measures whose purpose is to benefit certain groups such as the aged, the children, the unemployed, or particular groups of workers by the use of the budgeting or other powers of the Government;
2 *Transfer of power* or *Socialisation* measures whose purpose is to transfer economic power to the Government and to Society;
3 *Prosperity* measures whose purpose is to improve employment or productive efficiency so as to increase the real national dividend;
4 *Equalitarian* measures whose purpose is to establish economic and social equality.

In light of the problems facing a Labour government, the group unanimously agreed to the following six resolutions on strategic imperatives:

1 The Power Measures must take precedence in time during the first period of office over all Ameliorative Measures except such as constituted in themselves the acquisition of economic power and those which were necessary to the retention of political power;
2 Prosperity Measures stood in a separate category to purely Ameliorative Measures and that the case for such measures taking precedence with Power Measures should be discussed;
3 Such Equalitarian Measures as prejudice the execution of Power Programme must wait until the first stage of the Power Programme – estimated to last for at least the first period of power – was completed;
4 Full Compensation will be politically necessary;
5 A special Planning Authority of some kind must be established;
6 The general *tempo* of the whole Programme should be such as to maximize the possibility of achieving a second period of office by peaceful means.

For the critical power measures, the following order of priorities was accepted:

1 It was *first* necessary to take such steps in the direction of financial control as will reduce to a minimum the probability of a sharp decline in the external value of the pound sterling.
2 It was desirable to acquire the Bank of England, the Joint Stock banks, and the other main present institutions first in the normal process of socialisation because:

    i general financial confidence could then be controlled.
    ii the Banking structure was in intimate contact with the great body of industry.
    iii the financial machine was necessary for the execution of the Prosperity Programme.
3 It was then necessary to proceed to the socialisation (ownership and control) of a group of basic industries into which it was agreed that Transport, Power, Coal, Iron and Steel should be included.

Creech Jones wanted to add cotton, and Professor Tawney, land, life insurance and building.

For the 'early economic programme', it was considered wise to distinguish between an immediate financial panic, or sterling crisis, and reactions to a 'later stage of internal credit and employment policy'. The appropriate policy would be determined by the phase of the capitalist trade cycle in which the Labour government took office. The probability of achieving the party's political goals would be greatly increased if economic policy successfully reduced unemployment and increased national income. However, it was also resolved:

that the execution of a Prosperity Programme was almost certain to be a complex and difficult business, lasting for a period of two or three years and that for this purpose the Civil Service would not be fully equipped to provide the necessary advice or the existing Bankers the necessary co-operative will. It was consequently desirable to have some responsible Minister advised by an economist (such as Mr. Keynes) during the whole period of the programme.

The group as a whole agreed to a series of general principles for central planning machinery. First, they thought it 'essential for economic efficiency' to have a central body, or structure of bodies, to co-ordinate policies between nationalized industries, between production and monetary policy, between internal and external economic policy and between economic and social policy. Second, they emphasized the distinction between these 'major decisions of economic policy', the day-to-day administration of public industries and the general principles of their regulation. They discussed the form of the planning machinery at some length, opting for 'a Cabinet body of some kind' to decide the major economic issues and superintend their implementation; they assumed that a specialized planning commission or civil service department would grow up to serve the responsible minister.

The group seem to have been more tentative about the principles for planning production in the socialist state. They noted two views: one held that 'Planning should preserve the existing distinction between industries which are commercially self supporting and social services which are not'; the contrary view was that 'industries and social services should be planned as a whole without reference to the commercial position', but 'take account of broad social considerations'. However, they did not reach any definite conclusions on which approach to recommend. Although they discussed the relative merits of 'cost' and 'non-cost' planning, the report only noted what was 'generally agreed', namely, that cost calculation was 'desirable', and that social cost should include 'certain important personal elements', such as 'ill health suffered by workers' and 'aesthetic losses endured by the community'. Finally, they decided that 'the principle of *controlling* production by margin of price over cost was not unacceptable'; however, the report specifically mentioned that the group had not discussed how this could be done. There may have been quite a lot of disagreement on these issues. Durbin and Gaitskell were certainly in favour of market pricing for consumer goods and the application of marginal-cost pricing for production, while Barbara Wootton advocated the inclusion of social considerations in pricing and planning decisions. In short, even in this select group the division over market and controlled pricing lurked between the lines.

In addition to the group report, Wootton and Durbin as 'the technical economists', provided an appendix with their agreed conclusions on the nature of the 'Prosperity Programme'. They analysed the causes of the trade cycle in terms of the balance between savings and investment along the lines which Durbin had presented to the NFRB. They agreed to the following three proposals about policy:

1 During the phase of *crisis and early depression* it is difficult to believe that the downward movements of confidence and velocities can be checked except by extreme measures of currency inflation – measures which are not politically desirable.

2 During the phase of *late depression and early recovery* it is essential to distinguish between the periods – during the first of which the full influence of the Government should be used to press up the Rate of Investment – and during the second of which the Government should seek to increase the Rate of Saving and ideally to stabilise the monetary expenditure on consumption goods. To do this it should maintain investment by taxation and interest guarantees of various kinds.

3 During the *phase of boom and crisis* the only practicable

programme is to press ahead with the nationalization of those industries which will enable the volume of direct Government investment to be increased.

They disagreed about the possibility of judging when the second phase of the cycle began. Durbin thought an index of unemployment in consumption-goods industries could be constructed to predict when to switch from increasing investment to increasing savings. Wootton was less optimistic that the correct moment could 'be foretold with any great precision'. They agreed on the appropriate methods for controlling savings and investment, and concluded:

> In general it is plain that the phase of the Trade Cycle is one circumstance, among others, which should be taken into account in deciding the order of industrial priorities in the Power Programme.

To summarize, the group designed an economic programme to meet their political goals of avoiding armed rebellion and ensuring a significant redistribution of power from the private market to public control. According to Postan, they borrowed Lenin's phrase, 'control of the commanding heights', to express this aim. They gave nationalization of financial institutions and basic industries priority over the extension of social services. They wanted to set up central planning machinery to establish economic policy goals and direct macroeconomic policy, but to leave the administration of nationalized industries to their own boards. The aim of macroeconomic policy was to reduce industrial fluctuations by systematic intervention, but its precise nature would have to depend upon existing conditions. The group were committed to efficiency, as well as social justice, but they were divided on a thoroughgoing use of market pricing. Although the report did not spell out the criteria for nationalization, in a later article Gaitskell outlined the three tests which Tawney suggested in his 1931 book, *Equality*, which it seems reasonable to suppose the group discussed.[6] Tawney's criteria were: (1) Were the industries basic? (2) Were they monopolies? (3) Did they require to be reorganized? The group were committed to full compensation for the private owners of nationalized industries as a crucial part of their strategy to prevent political or economic sabotage, and, therefore, to maintain democracy.

As part of their political strategy, the group tackled the problem of devising a programme which was attractive to the majority of voters, was feasible for a first term and forestalled the possibilities of armed rebellion or sabotage by the forces of capitalism. As a growing menace, the threat of fascist take-over had been added to fears of another bankers' ramp. They worked out a two-dimensional strategy: to maintain democracy they underscored the importance of full compensation to capitalist shareholders and an immediate prosperity programme; to introduce socialism, they recommended nationalization of basic industries and the priority of power measures over ameliorative measures.

In comparison with the Labour party's programme which had just been adopted, these recommendations included fewer industries to be nationalized; they also ruled out extensive gains in social services. A more specific rationale was given for the means to reduce unemployment and increase national income; the analysis used the new savings and investment criteria, and not the level of prices. Both programmes were committed to nationalizing the financial system as the means to accomplish their aggregate policy. However, the party was silent on industrial pricing policy, while the group asserted the central government's responsibility for major policy decisions and the importance of using efficiency criteria.

The report was evidently sent to the party's Finance and Trade Committee (FTC) because one member, H. B. Lees-Smith, responded with comments which Gaitskell pencilled on the back of his own copy. These comments remain the only evidence of any outside reactions to the group's efforts. Lees-Smith noted presciently, 'that the T. U. wing would insist on ameliorative measures at early stage, e.g. Trades Disputes, 40 Hour Working Week, Worker's Compensation . . . also Compulsory Holidays with Pay'. Of the prosperity programme, he asked, 'Have we anything new? More light required on the less obvious points of Expansionist policy'. Finally, he thought land would be nationalized before the joint stock banks, and he was bothered about the amount of time central planning would take from cabinet ministers.

Yet the group must have made some impact. When Dalton was chairman of the party and responsible for designing the party's platform after its failure in the 1935 election, he wrote to Durbin asking for his suggestions.[7] The party's 1937 'Immediate Programme' was much closer to these earlier group recommendations.

Economic policy for a Labour government

James Meade had been the important influence in introducing Keynesian analysis to the NFRB deliberations, convincing Durbin and Gaitskell that expansionary policies were necessary and significantly altering Durbin's own trade-cycle theory. However, important areas of disagreement remained. At the theoretical level, Meade was exploring the reasons why the economy was not operating at full employment, while Durbin was searching for an explanation of fluctuations in real incomes. At the policy level, while Durbin and Meade were propounding similar monetary and capital development components of their expansionary policies, Durbin still stopped short of recommending deliberate deficit budgeting.

It is not clear exactly when Durbin changed his mind, but in June 1935 in a memorandum to Dalton's FTC he did finally recommend 'the possibility of using *Budget Policy* as an instrument of recovery and financial control', referring to Meade specifically.[8] He also stressed that 'it is vital after a period of two or three years to take steps to prevent the inflation becoming cumulative and getting out of control'; the steps proposed were those which Durbin and Wootton had worked out for the strategy committee. Meade had discussed the need to prevent the boom, in order to avoid a crisis followed by a slump, but it was to become evident that this problem was not Meade's immediate concern.[9] Since he was writing for the FTC, he may have included the discussion to forestall orthodox criticisms of the inflationary dangers of expansion; he may also have been persuaded by Durbin and others of the political importance of allaying the fears of the more cautious FTC members. He may even have accepted the logic of Durbin's arguments, although this is less likely, given his disdain for Hayekian analysis. None the less, on this documentary evidence, by 1935 Durbin and Meade seem to have been in substantial agreement on the correct financial policy for a Labour government.

In the spring of 1935 Meade completed an eighty-foolscap-page 'Outline of Economic Policy for a Labour Government'.[10] An impressive and detailed document, its argument combined macro and micro analysis and set four main policy objectives: (1) 'to cure unemployment and then to preserve a high level of employment'; (2) 'to devise a foreign exchange policy and tariff policy' to ensure full employment and maximum trade without foreign exchange repercussions; (3) 'to socialise certain industries which are in need of reorganization in order that they may be more efficiently managed'; (4) 'to increase the equality of distribution of the national income'. Meade suggested that the fourth objective should come last, 'not because it is the least important', but because the first and third were designed to increase the national income to be divided up, which would take some time. The rest of the monograph spelled out these objectives in considerable detail with an analysis of the causes of unemployment and the relation of socialization to unemployment, to 'the efficient service of consumer needs' and to equality. He, too, was concerned with the institutional structure necessary to carry out these objectives, and he discussed a national development board, the organization of the banks, the unemployment assistance board and the 'Supreme Economic Authority'.

Meade recommended expansionary policies and fluctuating exchange rates; he analysed the causes of the depression to include the reduction of consumption, as well as a decrease in investment. A year before *The General Theory* was published, he described the depression as follows:

> The money demand for consumption goods is small; this causes unemployment and reduced production of consumption goods. Moreover, because the demand for consumption goods is low, the profitability of industry is small and there are few profitable opportunities for capital development. This is so in spite of the fact that interest rates are generally low in times of depression; profits are so depressed that low interest rates do not stimulate fresh capital development. The small demand for capital goods means that those engaged in the production of capital goods have small incomes and are therefore unable to spend much on consumption goods, which in turn explains in large measure the fact that the demand for consumption goods is abnormally low.

Meade was now clear that low interest rates could fail to generate sufficient investment, and that the level of effective demand was critical. Meade recommended increases in both consumption and investment as unemployment cures, the former by a scheme of unemployment benefits paid from borrowed funds when unemployment rose above 5 per cent, the latter by the familiar combination of monetary, budgetary and development policies. He pressed for nationalization of the Bank of England, but not of the joint stock banks, because he thought that the government would be able to determine the amount of available credit with a constant reserve ratio and control of the central bank.

A new element in Meade's presentation was his extended discussion of socialization policy. He outlined four main arguments for nationalization: (1) to help cure unemployment; (2) to satisfy consumer needs better by planning to meet wants rather than make profits; (3) to increase productive efficiency and avoid the wastes of competition; (4) to remove income inequality. Meade briefly discussed the control of industry as an additional tool to maintain employment. He also pointed out, as Durbin had done already, that socialization did not necessarily alter the distribution of incomes; indeed, compensation to capitalist owners would hinder it, until the government either bought up the compensation bonds or acquired them through other income-redistributive methods such as death duties. After a textbook exposition of the ways in which perfect competition maximized consumer satisfaction and productive efficiency, Meade suggested that one of the strongest arguments for socialization was the lack of market competition arising from natural monopolies, product differentiation and imperfect markets. Using these recently developed models, Meade concluded that 'in those industries in which there is least perfect competition . . . there is greatest need for state control of industry'. The government should therefore 'choose those industries in which there is the widest discrepancy between the price paid to factors of production and the price offered by consumers for the extra product of the factors'. For similar reasons Meade also offered competitive-pricing criteria as the appropriate principles for planning and operating socialized industries. In particular, he advocated free consumer spending, marginal-cost pricing of goods and marginal-revenue pricing of factors. In those industries whose average costs were below marginal costs, he applied Dickinson's principle to suggest subsidization by allowing the relevant industry to borrow from the revenue budget below the prevailing interest rates.

Meade sent a copy of the manuscript to Roy Harrod, and also submitted it to the NFRB for publication. In April Harrod wrote back; in general, he thought it was 'splendid' and, indeed, that 'it would make an enormous difference to the attitude of a large part of the electorate to the Labour Party', if it was published 'in a very simplified form'.[11] However, he feared that the party was 'still very far from adopting the principles relating to unemployment'. Harrod's only substantial criticism was on Meade's principles for socialization. He felt they were 'rather unrealistic', because they left out the administrative problem; the practical issues must be tackled, 'otherwise a Labour leader such as Morrison might view it as hopelessly academic. In October the minutes of the NFRB's economic section record that on the subject of Meade's report, 'both Cole and Durbin had recommended against its publication'.[12] No reasons were given, and the manuscript remains unpublished.

In addition to Harrod's contemporary criticism, Professor Meade now suggests two other possible explanations for this rejection. First, he notes that his second objective of flexible exchange rates was contrary to official Labour party policy at the time. More fundamentally, Professor Meade believes that there was a basic difference in policy emphasis, which was not as obvious at the time. He saw himself as a 'Lib/Lab', and Durbin and Gaitskell as 'real socialists'. He had learnt from Keynes that the world could be spared the evil of unemployment by expansionary policies, which was why he emphasized its cure as the first policy objective. He was also in favour of removing inequality (he thinks he gave it more importance than Keynes, for example), but he was less concerned with fundamental alterations in the structure of society of the kind envisioned by Durbin and Gaitskell. Meade saw his role as one of convincing others of the correctness of the Keynesian view; since he felt 'a substratum of loyalty to Labour, having hitched my star to the Labour Club', it was through Labour party channels that he worked, much as Keynes worked through Liberal party channels.

There were two main aspects to this difference in emphasis; one concerned nationalization criteria, the other, expansionary policy. In determining the criteria for nationalization, Durbin and Gaitskell were predominantly influenced by the political considerations which they had thrashed out in the strategy discussions. Since Meade was not present at these, he had not thought through the same set of political ramifications. Therefore, he relied upon the 'hopelessly academic' efficiency criteria, much as Gaitskell had in his wages manuscript. The political criteria adopted by Durbin and Gaitskell reflected their fundamental concern to establish a socialist power base, which in terms of economy meant a significant increase in government control of its financial and industrial sector.

From the memoranda they discussed and developed for Dalton's committee, it seemed as though Meade and Durbin were in substantial agreement on expansionary policy. In this new outline, however, Meade made one significant omission from Durbin's perspective; he did not mention policies to prevent a boom. Durbin made a few marginal comments on Meade's manuscript, all of which express scepticism about his suggestions to control the banks in order to enforce expansionary policies and to reduce unemployment. For instance, Meade argued that the joint stock banks would not have to be nationalized, if they agreed not to alter their cash reserve ratio; Durbin noted, 'does not give you the essential control over the *distribution* of assets'. Thus, on the one hand, Durbin and Meade differed in their political estimate of the degree and kind of direct controls over the financial system that would be necessary to enforce government policy. On the other hand, Meade focused upon the reduction of unemployment as an end in itself, while Durbin saw the trade cycle as the root problem. Meade concentrated on the immediate problem; Durbin was searching for the key to control capitalism's booms and slumps.

New trends in socialism

By 1935 the original strategy group had expanded and the meetings had become more specialized.[13] Economic subjects were argued out at the XYZ club; foreign policy received increasing attention in sessions which included George Catlin, Dick Crossman, Frank Hardie, Douglas Jay and Ivor Thomas among the new recruits. The flavour of these discussions and their positions at the time can be gathered from their joint production, *New Trends in Socialism*, edited by Catlin and published in 1935. As Arthur Henderson explained in the preface, 'there is a British political principle of freedom, experiment and social justice which these writers emphasise'; he applauded it because 'the more intelligently active Democracy is and the more efficiently its institutions are made to function, the more surely and rapidly will socialism be achieved'.[14]

The book contained chapters on foreign and colonial policy by Crossman, Hardie and Parker, on liberalism and on fascism by Thomas and Fraser, on trade unions and the Labour party by Catlin, Ellen Wilkinson and representatives of the TUC. Durbin, Jay and Gaitskell covered economic policy. Durbin's contribution on the importance of planning has already been discussed in the context of New Fabian controversies on the subject; it outlined the essential political and economic framework for conducting economic policy in the socialist state. Jay wrote on the economic strength and weakness of Marxism, while Gaitskell dealt with the immediate problem of the transition to socialism, focusing on the appropriate financial policy.

Jay presented the case against the Marxist theory of surplus value on neoclassical grounds, drawing explicitly on Barbara Wootton's book, *Plan or No Plan*. He also demolished Marxist arguments that exploitation led to trade depressions and the inevitable collapse of capitalism. For this he used Durbin and Gaitskell's arguments to attack underconsumption theory and to predict the continued existence and probable recovery of capitalism. He concluded:

> The economic strength of Marxism consists in its emphasis on the injustices of unequal and unearned incomes; its weakness consists in its facile analysis of value and profits, and in its assertion that Capitalism is inevitably doomed for some fundamental economic reason. Capitalism will be ended only when those who suffer from [its] cruelties realize that they are unnecessary, and consequently set out to remove them.[15]

On the reasonable assumption that an extra pound was worth considerably more to a poor person than to a rich one, Jay demonstrated the democratic socialist case for the redistribution of incomes in succinct neoclassical economic terms. Finally, he argued that if capitalism was to be replaced by something better, not something worse, the political leaders must be guided, 'not by fanaticism and pseudo-metaphysical jargon, but by a clear, balanced, and rational understanding of the economic forces that confront them'; 'otherwise injustice will merely be followed by chaos'.

To these economic arguments against Marxists, Gaitskell added his rejection of their political view that revolution was necessary to ensure the transition to socialism; he asserted the Labour party's faith that the transition could take place within the framework of normal parliamentary democracy. However, this meant that socialist financial policy took on 'a special significance', because a Labour government would have to improve economic conditions in order to face opposition criticism and to win re-election for the second stage of constructing a socialist society. In particular, it was crucial to reduce unemployment and to cope with any financial reaction to Labour's policies. The rest of the chapter spelled out in some detail the issues raised in dealing with exchange currency and/or banking crises.

On the matter of financial panic Gaitskell separated three questions – its different forms and their likelihood, its effect on industry and employment, and the necessary action to meet each situation. He then traced the impact of Labour electoral victory on three centres in the financial system, the foreign exchange market, the capital market and the joint stock banks. He concluded that a slight depreciation might be necessary to ensure a successful expansionary programme to increase employment, but that with the proper controls the pound was unlikely to collapse. Gaitskell emphasized the importance of co-ordinating monetary and investment policies; he thought that public works financed by government loan were needed, as well as low interest rates, and that the Bank of England must be nationalized. While he explained that the nationalization of the joint stock banks was still controversial, he personally believed that in the long run it would provide 'a much simpler and more effective form of control'.[16] He also argued that, since the Crown had monopolized the minting of new money many centuries ago and bank credit had replaced coins and paper notes as the largest source of money, it was 'ridiculous' for a modern government to be blocked by private institutions in its efforts to increase the money supply. Thus, Gaitskell maintained that the moral case for nationalizing the joint stock banks was 'overwhelmingly strong'.

Conclusions

The main outlines of the Durbin and Gaitskell political and economic strategy had been worked out by 1935. With their deep faith in parliamentary procedures, they believed it would be possible to introduce socialism to Britain by getting the Labour party elected to power with the right programme ready to go. Their main effort had been to determine the political constraints and to devise the appropriate economic policies to achieve an orderly transition.

In a review of Dalton's book, *Practical Socialism for Britain*, Durbin summarized those constraints as follows:

> The difficulty of achieving democratic socialism by peaceful means consists in devising a programme for the Labour party which will fulfil three conditions: (1) It must, at the very least, include a transfer of a substantial increase of economic power to the government, otherwise it will represent no real advance towards the establishment of a socialist democracy. (2) It must not provoke the opponents of socialism to appeal to force or frighten them into an uncontrollable financial panic. In either case there would be a breakdown in the normal processes of peaceful government. (3) On the other hand it is equally essential that the programme of the Labour party should retain the loyalty of a very large proportion of its followers.[17]

This strategy fitted in well with the moderate leaders of the party. Dalton in particular turned to these protégés for advice after 1933.

On economic strategy Durbin and Gaitskell had further clarified their short-, medium- and long-term goals. They thought that, immediately after winning the election, it would be crucial for the Labour government's survival to prevent financial panic and to reduce unemployment. For this reason they worked hard on defining and outlining the appropriate strategies to cope with these problems. The main work of the next Labour government, however, must be to achieve the first stage of the transition to the new socialist economy. To accomplish this it was essential to gain control of the commanding heights of the economy by establishing the government's control over the financial system and by nationalizing a limited number of basic industries to gain a strong public sector and to make the national investment programme effective. Although improvement in social services and reduction in inequality were vital to a just society, they must take second place to securing control of the economy. Amelioration of conditions and equality would follow from prosperity and power, not the reverse. The second stage would complete the transition; central planning would replace the market system and the full range of social goals would be implemented. Even when socialism was fully established, it would still be necessary to work out the appropriate policies to maximize economic growth through the reduction of industrial fluctuations and the efficient allocation of resources.

Although moderate and emphatically non-Marxist, this strategy was in some senses more radical than the party's, and in some senses less. More than forty years later, in a conversation comparing the Durbin/Gaitskell position with his own, Professor James Meade described their joint work for a practical socialist economic programme in the 1930s as 'the road to the New Jerusalem'. Meade himself was willing to accept that road 'as the Holy City itself', because it explicitly included Keynesian expansionary policies to reduce unemployment. But Durbin and Gaitskell had their sights set on a more drastic transformation of the economy and of British society.

CHAPTER 10
DALTON ORGANIZES HIS EXPERTS AND LABOUR'S FINANCIAL POLICY

Hugh Dalton exercised a crucial role in the formation of the Labour party's foreign and domestic policy, as a leading member of the national executive committee (NEC) throughout the 1930s. His chief ally on the NEC was Herbert Morrison; he also worked closely with Bevin through the joint council on economic policy. This triumvirate organized the research, drafted the resolutions, led the debates and won overwhelming support in the party for the programme outlined in *For Socialism and Peace*, which was adopted at the 1934 annual conference.

As chairman of the finance and trade committee (FTC), a standing subcommitee of the NEC's policy subcommittee, Dalton was directly responsible for the research and resolutions on the party's financial policy. Three other members of the NEC, Walter Smith of the National Boot and Shoe Operatives, T. E. Williams from the Royal Arsenal Co-operative Society and Barbara Ayrton Gould from the women's section, were appointed, and F. W. Pethick-Lawrence was co-opted each year. At various times Attlee, William Mellor, John Wilmot and H. B. Lees-Smith were also co-opted. Grant McKenzie from party headquarters was the committee's secretary, and Jim Middleton, the assistant party secretary, would often attend the meetings.

In the immediate aftermath of the 1931 crisis, feeling within the Labour party was very hostile to the banking community. After the party voted against the NEC to nationalize the joint stock banks in 1932, Dalton organized a research programme on a broad range of economic and financial topics. A moderate himself, who knew that the party must attract middle-class votes, he deplored inflammatory rhetoric and irresponsible resolutions. Although he did not try to overturn the 1932 banking resolution directly, he managed to tone down some of its radical potential in the specific proposals for its implementation.

While the Socialist League clamoured for emergency powers and immediate nationalization, and unemployed workers marched and demonstrated, Dalton and Bevin tried unsuccessfully to win their more cautious NEC brethren over to an aggressive Keynesian expansionism. The NEC had little trouble winning approval for its unemployment programme at the annual conference, but in truth it was not radically different from the National government's efforts. Dalton drew heavily on the assistance of his 'experts', the XYZ club, the NFRB committees and its individual members, and a group of young scholars, whom he sent to study financial policy in European countries through the Acland travelling fund of the Labour party. The XYZ provided the most informative and consistent approach to the design of the new socialist financial institutions. Dalton attended half their monthly meetings, and kept their memoranda in his active files. As the controversies over Keynesian policy came to the fore, Dalton relied more on the young economists, Colin Clark and James Meade at first, but increasingly on Evan Durbin, Hugh Gaitskell and Douglas Jay.

Nationalization of the joint stock banks and the triumph of the left

The first recorded meeting of the FTC took place on 26 February, 1932 with Dalton in the chair.[1] The committee laid out an eight-point work programme covering banking, currency, company law, regulation of external trade, state development of trade, empire trade, international economic policy and taxation, with memoranda to be invited from a variety of people, including Sidney Webb on Russian methods of trade regulation and Barbara Wootton on taxation. The minutes identify a number of policy memoranda submitted to this committee, of which only a few survive in Dalton's papers.

One of the most interesting, written by Vaughan Berry in April 1932, was probably the first XYZ paper circulated to the FTC. It concentrated on the short-term funds available in the London market and the relation of the market's operations to the 1931 financial crisis.[2] Berry believed that 'the London money market does not consider that it is concerned with financing the internal trade of the country'; he continued:

Until last August, the operations of these institutions were a complete mystery to most Englishmen . . . . The ordinary Englishman then became aware that the discount and acceptance

houses occupied a key position in our monetary system and that
their operations were capable of dislocating the whole currency.
Without joining in all the accusations which have been levelled
against this section of the City of reckless international financing,
there is not the slightest doubt that its methods are open to serious
criticism and still more that its whole outlook needs to be
readjusted.

Berry charged that recent practice had led to carelessness about the
security of loans, lack of co-ordinating information and the support
of foreign investment at the expense of domestic employment. The
Bank of England had also rallied to support the banks and discount
houses, when their customers, particularly those in Germany, Austria
and Hungary, appeared likely to collapse. 'What right have private
banks to expect national support?' asked Berry. Although he opposed
abolishing the discount market, he did recommend that 'a small supervisory committee . . . would be sufficient to control the market in the
sense desired'.

On 12 May, the FTC met to discuss the resolutions which they
should put to the October conference to implement the 1931 currency,
banking and finance conference decisions. The meeting was attended
by all the committee members and secretaries, Ernest Bevin, Emil
Davies, Charles Latham and '6 members of City Group'. The six
must have been Berry, Davenport, Williamson, Spriggs, Quigley and
possibly Francis Williams. They agreed on the following six points:
that there should be no return to the gold standard; that currency
policy should control the domestic price level; that foreign exchange
rates should be stabilized; that a ministry of finance should exercise
control over the banking, credit and financial systems; that the Bank
of England should be nationalized; that a national investment board
should be set up, under the general supervision of the minister of
finance, 'to control the amount and direction of home and foreign
investment, to authorise new issues, to secure priority for enterprises
of social importance and to assist in the work of National Planning'.
The minutes make it clear that the committee was undecided about
who should control the Bank of England, and whether to nationalize
the joint stock banks. They also tabled consideration of any other
institutional changes.

Word of this meeting evidently leaked out, for three days later
Dalton wrote to Pethick-Lawrence telling him that Cole, as well as
'our friend Wise', had been lobbying him; 'I am of the opinion that
we should not yield to these people – though there is much further
"City" detail to be explored after Leicester, in which we should, I

think, take counsel with many more people than we have called in so
far'.[3] In early June, Cole wrote to Pethick-Lawrence expressing his
strong feelings that the joint stock banks would have to be nationalized
right away. He doubted the effectiveness of open-market operations
to expand industry, if the banks were hostile, and he felt that the Bank
of England could not direct the dispersion of investment funds, so
'indispensable' to socialist policy. Cole wanted the party 'to make our
intentions clear at once'. He thought it would take 'a long time to get
our own people to the point of intelligent propaganda on this issue',
as well as 'to combat the fears which the policy will arouse in the
minds of certain large sections of the electorate'.

In a long reply Pethick-Lawrence argued that a socialist government
would simply have no personnel to run the banks, since 'at the
Treasury at the present time there is practically no direct knowledge
of banking, either of central banking or joint stock banking'. Furthermore, 'I cannot envisage the minister who is controlling the Bank of
England having any time or brain left to perform this colossal task
for the Joint Stock Banks.' He also felt that it would take valuable
parliamentary time from 'other measures which the Socialist Government will want to carry'. He did not think the banks would oppose
expansionary policies; the real problem in the past had been the Bank
of England, which had pursued a deflationary policy in opposition to
the government's attempt to expand through borrowing. In reply, Cole
explained that he expected to use existing bank personnel. He still
hoped to convince the committee because, if the party did not mean
'real socialism now', he concluded ominously, 'I am afraid I shall not
be the only person to lose interest'. Pethick-Lawrence sent a terse
response by return of post:

> In reply to the last paragraph of your letter, it is just because I
> want the next Labour Government to begin Socialism in earnest
> next time that I want us to tackle a definite job we *can* do, rather
> than embark upon a large scheme of nationalisation which looks
> well on paper but, as you appear to expect, will not amount to
> very much in practice.

Finally, in July, after a number of drafts, four resolutions were
drawn up to present to the conference and a background report,
'Currency, Banking and Finance', was published, which drew heavily
on the work of XYZ.[4] The resolutions called for a policy of stable
domestic prices and stable foreign exchange rates, as far as possible.
It was proposed to control the financial system in three ways, by
nationalizing the Bank of England under a 'Minister of Cabinet rank'
with day-to-day business carried on by the governor and his staff, by

appointing a national investment board (NIB) to 'exercise control over all new public issues on the capital market', and by all necessary emergency powers 'to deal with any attempt by private financial institutions to obstruct a Labour Government, damage national credit, or create a financial panic'. Not only did the resolutions omit any reference to the joint stock banks, the NEC had also dropped the earlier proposal for a minister of finance.

As Keynes pointed out in a review of the resolutions for the *New Statesman*, the party had opted for 'a managed sterling currency', rather than 'a managed, or more probably half-managed, international currency which would certainly turn out to be based on gold'.[5] Keynes believed 'this is the right decision'. He also approved of the other resolutions, with the exception of the one demanding 'vague' and 'undefined' emergency powers. He felt that the party had 'wisely and prudently' left in abeyance the former proposal to nationalize the joint stock banks, because it was not necessary for 'handling the vital controls'. The resolutions set forth 'a moderate and quite practical monetary policy for adoption by the political party which represents the only organised body of opinion outside the National Government'. Keynes's only reservation was that the proposal for the NIB did not go far enough. He wanted the board to have the power to control the volume of total investment and the amount of new lending going to foreign and domestic borrowers: 'the grappling with these central controls is the rightly conceived socialism of the future'.

On 4 October, 1932, Hugh Dalton rose to put the NEC resolutions on currency, banking and finance to the party's annual conference in Leicester.[6] In his speech he emphasized the interim nature of the resolution, stating that the NEC needed more time to work on the problem of short-term credit. In this way he hoped to avoid a confrontation with the Socialist League over the joint stock banks, which he felt lacked 'electoral merit' and should not be given a high priority.[7] Dalton's argument in favour of price stability was rather muddled and repetitive; but he rallied to demand the emergency powers to carry out Labour's policy:

> We must ask for power, and we must all of us acquire
> understanding; and if we have both power and understanding,
> and if with these we have courage and comradeship, then I do not
> believe anything can stand in the way of the triumphant forward
> march of this Party to power and to the reconstruction of the social
> system of this land within as short a space of time as may be
> necessary to carry through the schemes we are now elaborating.

However, the speech did not convince the left wing. An amendment was put down to include the nationalization of the joint stock banks with the Bank of England, and to nationalize or control the other finance, acceptance and banking houses.

Among the supporters of the amendment, Frank Wise of the Independent Labour Party gave the most cogent speech:

> The transfer of the Bank of England to public ownership and control is a first step, but only a first step. There is nothing very socialistic about making your Central Bank a nationalised bank. The Bank of France and the Central Banks in Germany and in Austria, and even in the capitalistic United States, are nationally owned and controlled . . . . It is the Joint Stock Banks and not the Bank of England which decide whether money shall go to this industry or that industry, whether credit shall be easy, cheap, and available for this enterprise or that enterprise, and in allocating their resources they primarily use their deposits and their capital, and only to a minor extent are they dependent on the Bank of England.

In the debate Bevin pleaded against undertaking plans which could not be accomplished and taking over 'a moribund out-of-date banking system'; John Wilmot warned that 'you are going to mobilise against the entire Labour programme, hundreds and millions of small depositors'; and Pethick-Lawrence reminded the audience, 'You all know how many votes and how many seats we lost by the Post Office lie'. Nevertheless, the Socialist League won the day, although by a fairly close margin (1,141,000 to 984,000).[8] Thus, nationalization of the joint stock banks and all other financial institutions of the City became official party policy over the objections of the leadership. The proposals on domestic price stability, foreign exchange stability, the NIB and the use of emergency powers in a financial crisis passed without question.

Labour's financial policy and the reassertion of moderation

During the next three years the Labour party came up with a succession of policy statements, reports and pamphlets outlining its new programme. In the financial field the three most important documents were *Socialism and the Condition of the People*, debated at the 1933 conference in Hastings, *For Socialism and Peace*, debated at the 1934 conference in Southport, and *Labour's Financial Policy*, published as a pamphlet in 1935, which summarized the party's official views on economic policy and on its recommendations for institutional reform.

Despite the setback to the forces for moderation at Leicester, Dalton was soon hard at work drawing up specific plans to implement the conference decisions. In March 1933 in a long memorandum to the NEC's policy subcommittee, Dalton outlined his views on the party's overall finance and trade policy, which formed the basis for those sections of *Socialism and the Condition of the People*.[9]Among other matters, he dealt with the financial institutions necessary to carry out this plan. He felt that the resolutions approved at Leicester were sufficient for the Bank of England and the NIB, although the latter needed further elaboration. But more research was necessary on appropriate plans to implement the resolution on the joint stock banks, to decide about other financial institutions and to examine the problems of 'intermediate credits, panic and exchange control'. He drew up a five-point programme to reduce unemployment and he spelled out plans for national development, because 'socialisation is, indeed, in many cases a necessary condition of collective economic planning'. He listed the various programmes for development which the party had to work on, and stressed the importance of geographic planning, for 'here, worst of all, laissez-faire has let us down'. He recommended financing these projects by loans in the first instance until socialized industries had time to build up surpluses, referring to Keynes's recommendations in *The Means to Prosperity*. For this reason, he strongly advocated not dealing harshly 'with expropriated capitalists', whose goodwill would be essential to the success of the plan.

Meanwhile the FTC had regrouped after the Leicester conference and co-opted Attlee. On 10 November, 1932, they met in consultation with 'three representatives of the City Group, which was invited to assist in the following matters: Joint Stock Banks, London Money Market and position of London as financial centre, National Investment Board, Short term financing of publicly owned basic industries and Emergency financial powers'. Attlee and Frank Wise were also invited to prepare memoranda on the joint stock banks; it was decided to seek the views of the co-op movement, the Co-operative Wholesale Society Bank and Birmingham Municipal Bank on banking practice, and of Emil Davies and C. Latham on 'the finance of public administration'.

Attlee and Wise wrote their 'feverish' piece on banks, but the XYZ club members wrote most of the memoranda on financial institutions. On rereading some of these documents not long before his death, Sir Vaughan Berry wrote to the author:

I really feel quite proud of them! They seem to me quite well-written, clear, to the point, few words wasted and I can imagine

> they began to open a new world to the NEC. Is that claiming too
> much? . . . I suppose the great value was that it started Labour
> party thinking about money machinery. We, the XYZ, were not
> among the Captains of Finance but we knew the machinery! And
> we had plenty of publicity for our views.

The club became in essence a cadre of specialists upon whom the
party's leaders could rely for advice, a crucial development in the
party's ability to handle financial affairs.

At the same time Dalton was initiating research into the broader
questions of the policy options confronting a future Labour government. In November 1932 he wrote to James Meade: 'I am delighted
to hear that you and Opie [who had been on the NFRB trip to Russia
with Dalton that summer] and others are going to do something, as
a NFRB group, on Financial and Economic Relation of this country
with the outer world, including the control of panic'.[10] This group
produced a series of reports over the next two years on ways to deal
with financial panic, exchange rate policy and unemployment, which
provided an invaluable background resource for the FTC. A year later,
for instance, Dalton described their financial panic memorandum as
'most valuable for what I call the live pigeon-hole'; Lees-Smith thanked
Meade for his 'very penetrating memorandum' and commended him
for providing material 'which will clear our minds and shape the
nature of our policy reports without being a part of them'.

More formally, Dalton supervised a research project on 'recent state
policy with special reference to public finance', using the Acland travelling fellowships of the Labour party and a Rockefeller research grant
through the London School of Economics.[11] In the academic year
1932–3, three students were sent abroad, T. J. Hughes to Italy, J. N.
Reedman to Switzerland and Brinley Thomas to Germany; the
following year Thomas went to Sweden as well. Dalton travelled round
to visit them, meeting government officials and scholars and discussing
different ways to tackle unemployment and undertake economic reconstruction. In Italy he was most impressed with Mussolini and the
Italian public works schemes; in Sweden he met the new socialist
prime minister, Per Albin Hansson, and had long talks with Ernst
Wigforss, about the Swedish recovery.[12] In Germany, he saw the perse-
cution of Jews, socialists and intellectuals by the Nazis, which he
describes eloquently in his *Memoirs* and which made him an early
convert to British rearmament.

The transition to socialism

At Leicester Dalton had demanded powers to enact the financial provisions of Labour's plans, but the NEC had steered clear of any explicit statement. At the Hastings conference Sir Stafford Cripps moved an amendment asking the NEC 'to specify the means to be adopted by the next Labour Government 'for a rapid and complete conversion of the Capitalist to the Socialist system'.[13] In particular, the resolution called for the immediate abolition of the House of Lords, the passage of an Emergency Powers Act, revision of the procedure of the House of Commons and an 'Economic Plan for Industry, Finance and Foreign Trade designed rapidly to end the present system and thus to abolish unemployment and poverty'. Cripps firmly believed that there could be a fascist take-over in Britain. Since Attlee and others supported these proposals, it is clear that this fear was widespread. To Bevin, however, the reverse was true; in his biographer's words, 'it appeared certain that the logical conclusion of Cripps' campaign, if it succeeded, would be to create the political climate which Mussolini and Hitler had exploited to establish their own dictatorship'.[14] Therefore, during the emotional debate Bevin rose to denounce the amendment, and it was sent back to the NEC for further study.

Although Dalton did not speak in the debate, Meade's research reports on financial panic being written for the FTC presented a more sober study of how to avoid disastrous reactions to the socialist programme or other financial crises. Their work influenced the Labour party in two important ways. First, careful analysis of internal and external panic, and of the mechanisms available to counteract withdrawal of capital, provided the necessary knowledge for crisis management; the new generation of Labour leaders could feel more confident that they would not be at the mercy of banking and Treasury officials. Second, the Oxford group's study emphasized the different effects of different situations, and they linked the party's electoral programme to possible reactions in each case.

The report began by distinguishing between a panic arising after an election in which Labour won a majority in normal times and one which occurred during a period of economic crisis.[15] The authors argued that the second was more serious; thus, if the right plan could be devised to deal with the crisis, it would be easy to adapt it to ordinary circumstances. They continued:

The intensity and to a large extent the probability of a crisis will depend on the character of the policy which the Party puts forward during the election; and also on the form in which it is stated. For example, during a time of incipient crisis or depression it would be better to emphasize those constructive parts of the Party's proposals which aim at a more conscious control of those parts of the economic system which are functioning badly, rather than to deliver a frontal attack on private property.

In the event of a flight from the pound, the group recommended suspension of the gold standard rather than being driven off it. They concluded 'that the aim should be some measure of exchange control without fixed prices', a policy contrary to Labour's official policy of maintaining stable prices and exchange rates.

Dalton himself was deeply involved in writing *For Socialism and Peace* for the 1934 Southport conference, which contained the NEC's response to Cripps on emergency powers. Although the official statement committed the party to abolish the House of Lords, particularly if it sought 'to wreck its essential measures', and to reform House of Commons procedures, this was not enough for the Socialist League. They wanted to circumvent Parliament to forestall a capitalist take-over. In a show-down at the conference, the League lost heavily. They also lost on the question of compensation, which raised similar issues and had preoccupied the FTC for much of the year.

In November 1933, Dalton had asked the NFRB formally to submit memoranda on the issues involved in compensation to the expropriated owners of nationalized industries. In order to pursue his national development programme to reduce unemployment as quickly as possible, Dalton wanted to come up with a formula which would prevent massive withdrawals of capital, and yet ensure sufficient loans for the Labour government to begin reconstruction.

Cole sent the FTC an extensive report in December after receiving internal comments from Durbin, Mellor and Mitchison.[16] He argued that a crucial consideration was the speed of transition to socialism, because the faster it was introduced, the less relevant the form of compensation. He recommended against both full market-value compensation and no compensation at all, seeking a middle position of granting some expedient relief for a limited period. Cole thought that the current plans to nationalize a wide range of industries in two or three years would make full cash payment impossible, and might undermine capitalist 'confidence' in a socialist government.

From the FTC Dalton wrote to Meade asking for his 'views on Compensation to Expropriated Capitalists'. Lees-Smith explained more fully, 'Your argument for full compensation is very important as many of our people have a hankering after a partial confiscation, e.g. Cole.' Meade outlined the same options as Cole, but he argued that full compensation was the only alternative which was fair; it would also reduce 'the probability of serious political and economic sabotage to a minimum'.[17] Taxation could then be used to redistribute wealth. Durbin had also commented to Cole that he did not believe arbitrary and unequal expropriation was just, or 'consistent with the gradualist nationalization policy'; thus, full compensation was 'necessary for the preservation of democracy'.[18]

The final draft of For Socialism and Peace called for 'the payment of fair compensation to existing owners' on a basis of 'net reasonable maintainable revenue'. G. R. Mitchison, the treasurer of the NFRB, who had approved Cole's memorandum, moved an amendment to exclude 'rights to capital repayment' from the compensation formula.[19] Cripps and Mellor for the Socialist League both spoke for the amendment, while Lees-Smith, Morrison and George Ridley of the Railway Clerks' Association spoke against it. A card vote was taken and lost by 149,000 to 2,118,000, an important victory for the moderate economic programme and for a non-revolutionary transition to socialism through the parliamentary process.

In 1935 Dalton organized a series of summaries of the research completed for the FTC, one of which was on financial panic.[20] Described as the work of a subcommittee of the FTC, the report 'was not intended for publication but is submitted to the policy committee and to the National Executive as part of the private preparation for the tasks of the next Labour Government'. The members of the subcommittee are not identified, but Meade and Gaitskell were certainly major contributors, and it is quite likely that Gaitskell wrote the report.[21] Using all the previous reports to the FTC, which despite different authors were described as 'in all essentials unanimous', it began:

> The general conclusion reached by the subcommittee is that financial panic may take a number of different forms, but that all of these can be effectively dealt with by appropriate administrative and in some cases legislative action. It is however important that these methods of action should be clearly worked out beforehand and swiftly and confidently applied in case of necessity.

The rest of the memorandum spelled out five forms of panic and the appropriate means to combat each. The first, a foreign exchange crisis or severe 'flight from the pound', was thought 'most probable'. To handle the problem a series of steps were recommended; these included leaving the gold standard (if appropriate), *not* using the bank rate to prevent depreciation, using the exchange equalization account, prohibiting the export of capital, and establishing a foreign exchange control board to enforce the prohibition of capital export and to regulate the exchanges. To deal with the collapse of internal security prices, they recommended that the Bank of England intervene by buying securities in the open market.

The report gave an impressive and detailed account of the various options which the next Labour government might have to face very soon, if the party was successful in the pending election. Obviously the main intention was to provide Labour leaders with the knowledge and confidence they lacked in 1931. The decision to keep this document 'private' was a more immediate reaction to the left-wing prophets of sabotage and doom to whom Lidbury had tellingly referred at the NFRB conference on banking and finance that summer. Douglas Jay remembers that at the same conference Robert Fraser attacked what he called 'the inferiority complex wing' of the Labour party, those who went around assuring everyone that Labour would not ruin the country. Fraser pointed out that brewers do not put up large placards announcing, 'There is no arsenic in my beer'.

Socialist control of the economy
Control of finance was regarded as central to the ability of a future Labour government to gain command of the economy at any early stage. As long as monetary policy was viewed as the only government tool available to influence economic activity, it seemed that control of the banking system was essential, and that nationalization was the quickest and simplest way to accomplish this goal. However, after the party's overwhelming rejection at the polls in 1931 amid charges of financial irresponsibility, moderates were anxious to keep state take-over to the minimum, although their hands were somewhat tied after the 1932 resolutions. The party still had to come up with a specific plan to implement those resolutions. This became the major task of the FTC and its advisers at XYZ.

Attlee and Cripps furnished a joint memorandum in early 1933, but Dalton found it useless because it lacked specific proposals. Frank Wise evidently provided a more detailed plan to nationalize the joint stock banks, which was later described as putting the case for early nationalization 'especially comprehensively', but 'against early nationalization of the other financial houses'.[22] Davenport wrote a detailed report on the national control of investment, and Berry one on banking. Their ideas were incorporated into the NEC statement on banking, finance and investment included in *Socialism and the Condition of the People*. This part of the report spelled out the role of the NIB to provide long-term credits more fully than before. It proposed to set up a banking corporation which would amalgamate the 'Big

Five' banks under public ownership and control the direction of short-term credits. It specifically recommended against extending nationaliz-ation to the discount and acceptance houses because sufficient control could be exercised through the central bank and the banking corporation.

Berry had had second thoughts about his earlier opposition to the nationalization of the joint stock banks.[23] Although he still believed it was unnecessary on technical grounds, he felt it was important for party unity. He also pointed out that the problem had changed considerably. Under the second Labour government the Bank of England had pushed a policy opposed to government, but since then it had substantially lowered the interest rates; now it was the commercial banks who were not distributing funds and were making it difficult to borrow. Davenport, by contrast, did not budge from his view that the role of the NIB should be confined 'to planning, co-ordinating and mobilising the capital requirements of the country'.[24] Evidently the NEC shared this cautious approach; the party's description of the NIB explicitly stated that the board 'should not have the power to issue national investment bonds, nor should it attempt directly to finance any activities, public or private, for its function is not to finance industry but to co-ordinate finance'. In short, the Labour party was less radical than the Liberal party on the methods for financing capital development.

Dalton proposed the new banking plan to the Hastings conference. Although Wise tabled a minor amendment, he agreed to its reference back to the NEC, and his speech was full of praise:

> I would like to express appreciation for the handsome way in which the Executive has carried out the mandate given to it by the Conference last year in regard to the nationalisation of the Joint Stock Banks.

The League had produced its own policy document, *Forward to Socialism*, which called for a national economic plan, price and foreign trade controls and effective workers' control. Wise himself had been advocating greater powers for the NIB to the FTC, but he seems to have been content to win NEC approval of the banking corporation. Unfortunately for the continued dialogue between the left wing and moderates in the party on financial questions, Frank Wise died shortly after this conference, and Cripps, who knew little finance and less economics, became the League's chief spokesman.

Meanwhile, economic research at the NFRB revealed new policy tools, such as public works and budget deficits, which could be used to promote recovery, but which did not require the kind of direct control of banking operations suggested to socialists by earlier theory. James Meade was one of the first to spell out the relation between the new policies and administrative change in an important memorandum written for the party's policy subcommittee in December 1933. His main purpose was to discuss the financial policy necessary 'to avoid economic chaos and unemployment, while the Government is taking over and reorganizing the major industries on the lines laid down in the Party's Policy Reports'.[25] But he also dealt with 'the administrative control necessary to carry out this financial policy'. He did not believe that a Labour government should take over any more administration of the financial system than was 'essential for the carrying out of its financial policy'. More fundamentally, he did believe:

> There is a danger that the Labour Government will be more occupied with changing financial organization and administration than with changing the financial policy of the bodies which it takes over. It cannot be too strongly emphasised that in the financial sphere it is not so much administrative machinery and ownership of existing organisations which needs altering, as their financial policy

Since the government already controlled the budget, Meade argued that the only essential reforms to carry out his policy would be the nationalization of the Bank of England and the establishment of the NIB. He did not think it would be necessary to nationalize the joint stock banks, unless they tried to nullify the government's policy. He thought that the NIB should administer loan flotations, but the government should decide the volume of borrowing and approve or disapprove specific projects. He did not think the NIB would have much effect, unless the government had already carefully planned its development programme. Again he emphasized the importance of policy over organizational structure.

Discussion of these issues continued at XYZ club meetings, and members sent their reports on specific issues to Dalton. Dalton was searching for ways to achieve the necessary control of the economy without having to resort to nationalization of the joint stock banks, even though it remained official policy. In 1935 Durbin and Berry furnished two long memoranda on the nationalization of the English banking system, in which they laid out in great detail how this might be accomplished.[26] They outlined three main purposes for controlling the banking system: to control panic, to cure unemployment and to obtain power over investment. The essential powers were to determine the volume of credit creation and its distribution. Their central conclusions were, first, that no new powers were necessary to control internal and external panic; as long as the Bank of England followed orders from the Treasury, the influence of its foreign exchange department on the London bankers' foreign exchange committee (set up after Britain left the gold standard) and control over the customs were sufficient for an informed Labour government to cope with the immediate effects. Second, nationalization of the Bank of England and formation of the NIB were sufficient to pursue expansionary policies by orthodox means. Third, only less orthodox and more powerful methods for curing unemployment required new financial machinery.

Berry and Durbin defined orthodox banking and financing methods as 'running the banks on a business, profit-making basis with traditional demands for security, traditional balancing of the Budget, etc.' They outlined three unorthodox methods, which they called security policy, budget policy and power over industry. For budget policy they referred to Meade's memorandum on deliberate deficit budgeting by the Treasury. By power over industry they meant nationalizing basic industries and planning their capital development as an integral part of national policies to control the volume and direction of investment. Security policy was forcing banks to lend freely in a depression against their natural inclination. Nationalization of the joint stock banks was one way to accomplish this goal; as such it represented the one case for extending socialist machinery beyond the Bank of England and the NIB. However, Berry and Durbin pointed out that even in this case nationalization was not necessary if the government had the power to guarantee advances. Finally, they spelled out various reforms to facilitate central control, most of which had already been recommended by Keynes in the Macmillan report.

At the same time Dalton prepared an FTC memorandum, which outlined the main headings of a bill of finance to incorporate the party's 'declared policy on finance, in respect of monetary and banking policy and the methods of finance'.[27] Berry furnished Dalton with a copy of section 27 of an 1844 Bank Charter Act on termination and detailed notes on the Macmillan committee's recommendations. He also probably wrote the much-annotated rough outline remaining in Dalton's papers. This outline started with the Bank of England Board, proceeded to list the duties and powers of the Board and ended with a series of observations. The observations concluded:

The whole scheme outlined in these pages is a half-way house between nationalisation of the central bank and nothing else, and nationalisation (i.e. purchase) of the Central Bank and the Clearing Banks. If we limit ourselves to buying out the Bank of England, appointing a new Board, and doing nothing else, there is no need at this stage to specify duties and powers. Similarly if we decide at once to buy the Bank of England and the Clearing Banks and constitute a single Banking Board according to programme, there is also no need to specify powers, but if we are seeking to nationalise the Central Bank and obtain as much control of the rest of the Banking system without compulsion as we possibly can, giving the other side a reasonable chance of co-operation, then I think the duties and powers outlined cannot be rejected as unreasonable, and will certainly be accepted by the better half of the City.

This outline included all the Berry and Durbin recommendations for the reform of the central banking system. Dalton's final memorandum incorporated most of these ideas under three main proposals: (1) to nationalize the Bank of England (but not the clearing houses); (2) to set up the national investment board; (3) to amalgamate the joint stock banks under a national banking corporation. If Labour had won the election in 1935, they had the draft of a bill to implement these financial reforms all ready to go.

Socialist unemployment policy

At the national level unemployment had remained a volatile public issue. On the one hand, the National Unemployed Workers Movement led by Wal Hannington had doubled its membership since 1931 and was organizing mass demonstrations and hunger marches up and down the country. This caused much embarrassment to the TUC and the Labour party, 'which made no serious attempt to set up a rival body, yet refused to co-operate with it or give it recognition', because of its Communist party affiliations.[28] On the other hand, the National government had also bestirred itself; in 1934 both the Special Areas Act for the distressed areas and the Unemployment Act to take unemployment assistance out of the old poor law administration were passed. The latter caused a great deal of agitation when it was discovered that the new rates, due to come into effect in January 1935, were in many cases lower than the previous rates, particularly in the depressed areas. Although the lower rates were never put into effect, they remained a continuing source of bitterness and concern among the working class.

Dalton and Bevin together designed the national job development and unemployment plans included in *Socialism and the Condition of the People*. With statistical help from Colin Clark, Bevin published a pamphlet in early 1933, *My Plan for 2,000,000 Workers*, in which he made five proposals to provide this number of jobs: (1) a State pension for all aged sixty-five and over who retired; (2) an optional pension at sixty; (3) invalidity pensions for the disabled; (4) an increase in the school-leaving age to sixteen; (5) a forty-hour work week.[29] He estimated that the first three methods would release 600,000 jobs, the fourth 560,000 and the last the remainder. In May, Dalton wrote to Clark that the figures on the cost of the pension schemes seemed 'suspiciously low'; however, he thought the estimated cost of raising the school-leaving age was 'on the high side'.[30]

Socialism and the Condition of the People included an explanation of unemployment which referred to Keynes's figures and the savings/investments and multiplier analysis in *The Means to Prosperity*. While the 1932 FTC report had implied that guaranteed loans would be used for national development, this new version omitted any reference to loans or budget deficits, in fact it stressed 'revenue-producing' public works. Although Dalton was open to Keynes's prescriptions at the time, others were obviously working to remove any explicit references to expansionary policies, such as guaranteed government loans or budget deficits. This was even clearer in *For Socialism and Peace*, which no longer contained the savings/investment model or Keynes's statistics, although the description of the multiplier remained.

In 1935 the party conference debated the unemployment question. A resolution was presented by Arthur Greenwood on behalf of the national executive.[31] It deplored the National government's policy and called 'for a comprehensive and constructive policy'; 'such a policy necessitates a co-ordinated plan based upon the public ownership and control of the great basic industries and services, the development of organized marketing both at home and abroad, and international arrangements aiming at the expansion of the world's purchasing power and thereby world trade.' The resolution roundly condemned the 1934 Unemployment Act and the hated means test.

In the debate moving speeches were made about conditions in Durham, 'a concentration camp with a vengeance', in South Wales, 'a graveyard', and by Ellen Wilkinson, one of the Jarrow march organizers. Apart from the unanimous opposition to the means test, the only other practical suggestions to free more jobs were Bevin's proposals to raise the school age and to introduce pensions. Mr. D. McHenry from Whitehaven, however, proposed that the party should send investigators to the distressed areas, in order to develop its own policies; it should not rely on reports prepared 'by people who, however good intentioned, are Tory-minded and have no use for the Socialist outlook'.

The only debate on financial policy at the 1935 conference was on a report, *Socialism and 'Social Credit'*, commissioned by the NEC after a request from delegates the previous year. A small committee was appointed which consisted of W. R. Hiskett, a railway clerk, who had written a book on socialism and social credit, and two economic experts, Evan Durbin and Hugh Gaitskell. Working with Jim Middleton, the group interviewed Social Credit representatives at length, reviewed party research in the 1920s on Douglas's credit scheme (in which Dalton and Cole had participated) and wrote their own report. Fred Montague of the Social Democratic Federation moved a motion to introduce the report, which Hiskett seconded. He explained that the social credit schemes were incompatible with socialism because they explicitly rejected the necessity of administrative change in financial or industrial systems. In his first conference speech, Durbin argued that simple monetary expansion was not enough, that there must be financial control to maintain full employment: 'It is that which no private institution can secure; it is that which alone the socialisation of the banks can secure'. The party published the report as a pamphlet, explaining that the NEC did not accept some of its policy proposals. The unacceptable proposals were presumably the report's endorsement of unorthodox methods, such as budget deficits and subsidized food and necessities.[32] The authors were in great demand to explain social credit to Labour party groups across the country. It was the first time Durbin and Gaitskell became more widely known within the Labour movement.

Meanwhile, at the unofficial level, Dalton continued to request memoranda for his 'live pigeon-hole' on employment, exchange rate policy and planning. James Meade wrote his memorandum on financial policy, in which he discussed the appropriate policies for the prevention and cure of unemployment; Durbin's complementary memorandum on the principles of socialist planning was delivered in January 1934.[33] That summer, with help from Harrod and Opie, Meade extended his analysis to include its relation to exchange rate policy. In a further memorandum he argued forcefully for fluctuating rates to protect the domestic market from the exchange repercussions of pursuing a more vigorous expansionary policy than other countries.[34] The XYZ club provided additional memoranda on the control of investment, concentrating on the role of the stock exchange.[35]

Dalton also organized more research on Labour's proposed budget, focusing in particular on appropriate and feasible ways to finance Labour's proposed development plan to reduce unemployment. In November 1934 he wrote to Colin Clark telling him that he was going to be asked 'to do us a memorandum on the *Next Labour Budget* with statistical estimates of revenue and expenditure, in accordance with our programme'.[36] He explained that:

There's a constant demand from some of my colleagues for an 'honest Labour Budget' to be sketched. I tell them that nearly all the elements, on both sides of the Budget, are variable within such wide limits that one can't really do much with this. But I daresay one can do something, – very roughly.

The report was to be for 'private preparation', not for publication by the party. Dalton was also running into heavy opposition to unorthodox Keynesian budgeting proposals on the FTC. He confided to Clark that Pethick-Lawrence in particular was 'frightfully opposed to doing development out of taxation' and that he was doing his own study, in which '*he* thinks he can't raise more than, say, 30 million pounds a year, and so can't afford to spend more than an extra few halfpence on anything'.

Clark responded with a lengthy memorandum in February 1935, which was published by the NFRB in May.[37] Clark made rough estimates of the cost of Labour's proposed social services, and he detailed proposals to introduce Dalton's variation on the Rignano scheme for death duties. He also proposed the division of the budget into revenue and capital accounts and cyclical variations in the ratio of loans to taxation for financing public works, along the lines already outlined by Meade. However, he disagreed with Meade on the matter of nationalizing the joint stock banks, because he thought their control by the government was necessary to keep down the rate of interest, which large government loans could drive up. For this purpose 'the nationalisation of the Bank of England is not enough'.

Keynesian recommendations for expansionary policies were substantiated by the findings of Dalton's travelling scholars, and described in *Unbalanced Budgets*, published early in 1934. Dalton wrote the summary and conclusions; he noted that in the fifteen countries studied few new ways to raise taxes had been devised, but public works had been pursued 'with greater or less energy and persistence' in nearly every country. On the choice between balanced budgets and deliberate deficits, Dalton concluded with a personal opinion:

Those who advocate the expansionist doctrine have the better case but that their policy, in order to be fully effective, needs to be pushed a good deal further than most of them seem willing to push it. I believe that freedom from the plague of recurrent booms and slumps can be found only in a Planned Economy.[38]

On a prophetic note, he ended:

Behind today's Financial Crisis looms the dark shadow of another graver still, a War Crisis, which may tomorrow completely destroy the civilisation which we know, and finally burst asunder the framework of economic relationships which the Financial Crisis has so harshly strained.

In short, while Dalton may not have followed all the intricacies of the Keynesian professional debates among economists, he did understand that to be successful Keynesian policies required substantial institutional reform. Ironically, rearmament probably did more for employment than any other government efforts to stimulate the economy and finally end the great depression.

Conclusions

By 1935 the Labour party was far better prepared than ever before to manage the country's economic affairs, to take control of financial policy and to begin serious planning efforts. Legislation had been drafted to nationalize the banking system; important leaders such as Dalton, but also other NEC members, were well briefed on banking options and policy operations; a loyal group of trained young professionals were eager to make their contributions.

From the economic perspective the official programme was a strange mixture. The party had firmly rejected Snowden's deflationary policies and voted to take over the banks. Yet, its monetary and employment policies were still couched in fairly orthodox terms. At Bevin's insistence it had accepted the rationale for monetary management recommended by the Macmillan committee. But in continuing to press for stable domestic and exchange prices the party avoided committing a Labour government to inflationary dangers thought to be inherent in deliberate expansion. The arguments for a comprehensive national development plan emphasized the structural problems of depressed industries and areas and offered ways to reduce the labour force by raising the school-leaving age, shortening the work week and encouraging early retirement. Furthermore, while the party wanted more control over the banks than Keynes, it proposed to restrict the powers of the NIB and not to allow it to issue guaranteed loans or its own bonds. Thus, in the history of economic thought, the official position was still based on orthodox ideas of controlling the price level through conventional monetary mechanisms. In the history of socialist policy, it relied upon the traditional methods of nationalizing the major institutions of the finance market, in order to achieve its socialist goals of public control.

In March 1935, Dalton published his own version of the party's new programme in his book, *Practical Socialism for Britain*. He described his approach as 'very British' and specifically aimed against 'our melodramatists of the Socialist League': 'I discount heavily, in this commonsense and politically mature country, all panic talk, whether from Right or Left, of an "inevitable crisis", and all theatrical nightmares of violent head-on collisions, wrecking the train of democracy'.[39] Roy Jenkins later referred to the book as 'the first swallow of the post-1935 summer', marking 'the beginning of the return of self-confidence'.[40] In a review at the time Durbin described it as 'the only book in existence which contains a careful, sober and highly persuasive defence of the broad principles of the policy of the Labour party'.[41] Durbin stressed the importance of party unity and rejected 'the use of a half-baked Marxian jargon and the elaboration of revolutionary force', of which the Socialist League presented 'a sickening intellectual spectacle'. He concluded that Dalton's approach met his three conditions for achieving democratic socialism. The financial reforms and nationalization programme ensured a significant transfer of power; the provision of full compensation and 'the correct administrative steps' would prevent armed revolt or financial panic. The party had rallied to support a platform of determined but moderate socialism.

Thus, the election of 1935 was a bitter disappointment to the Labour movement, to the leaders who had worked so hard to devise a significant programme for social change, and to the political aspirants of the younger generation. Durbin and Gaitskell ran a joint campaign for the adjoining constituencies of Gillingham and Chatham in Kent, with a lot of help from their friends, colleagues and students. However, they both lost; of their immediate associates, only John Parker of the NFRB and John Wilmot from XYZ entered the House of Commons. They were not to get another crack until 1945.

PART III
SOCIALISM IN OUR TIME

CHAPTER 11
THE NEW SOCIALIST
ECONOMICS

By the mid-1930s economists were clear that the failure of market capitalism raised two quite separate issues. One was the failure to generate sufficient economic activity to provide for the full employ-ment of all resources, the macroeconomic problem. The second was the failure of the system to allocate resources efficiently, the micro-economic problem. By the end of the decade socialist economists in Britain were convinced that they had found theoretical solutions for both these problems. *The General Theory* contained the necessary framework to analyse the aggregate problem and the new socialist economics outlined its allocational counterpart. Together these discoveries constituted the theoretical basis for believing that socialist planning could not only solve capitalism's failures, but that it could also yield the appropriate criteria for judging its own economic performance.

In the early 1930s the microeconomic reasons for government inter-vention had been expanded and refined along two distinct but comple-mentary lines: a general attack on the assumptions of perfect competi-tion, and a socialist search for the economic justification to expand the public sector and to redistribute income. For one hundred and fifty years economics had elaborated the theoretical and practical benefits flowing from a competitive market system based on private property; but faith in its validity was faltering. Its theoretical apparatus was attacked as indeterminate in many realistic cases and as irrelevant to the behaviour of giant corporations, powerful labour organizations and international cartels. Harold Barger first met Durbin in 1931, when they tried to put together a syllabus to teach economic principles to University College students; he recalls, 'I can still see Evan in my mind's eye saying, "What shall we do? There is nothing to teach out of." ' Microeconomics was in as much disarray as macroeconomics.

In 1933 two influential books were published simultaneously, E. H. Chamberlain's *Theory of Monopolistic Competition* in Cambridge, Massachusetts, and Joan Robinson's *Economics of Imperfect Competition*, in Cambridge, England. These books spelled out systematically the analytic implications of product differentiation, limited numbers of firms, price discrimination, decreasing-cost industries and all the other exceptions to Marshallian market models. This 'second revolution' successfully breached 'the complacency of the 1920's and the attitude, enshrined in Keynes' first preface to the Cambridge Economic Handbooks, that Marshall had done all the necessary thinking and it was just for us to apply it', according to Sir Austin Robinson.[1] Socialist economists used these arguments to add to their indictment of the waste and inefficiency of capitalism. H. D. Dickinson, Evan Durbin and Barbara Wootton elaborated the policy implications of monopoly capitalism and increasing externalities. James Meade recommended using the new analytic tool, the marginal-revenue curve, to identify those industries which should be nationalized, because the manufacturers exercised a substantial degree of monopolistic control over the prices of their products. As the New Fabians had articulated their own version of a democratic socialist planning alternative to the capitalist market muddle, they had been drawn into theoretical arguments about the role of the price mechanism in the socialist state. But they were split between those who advocated market pricing and those who belived in controlled pricing.

In 1935 Professor Hayek, who had withdrawn from intellectual combat with interventionists on the monetary front, turned his attention to the broader question of socialist planning. He published a volume of papers, *Collectivist Economic Planning*, whose general conclusion was that efficient planning was not possible in the socialist state.[2] Whether it was intended or not, the book enraged socialist economists, particularly those struggling to convince fellow socialists of the importance of market pricing on democratic, as well as efficiency, grounds.

The reactions and controversies spawned by Hayek's challenge, sometimes referred to as the great planning debate, helped to crystallize thinking on the economic issues raised by the socialist goals of collective ownership, central planning and income equalization. The result was a consistent body of thought identified for the purposes of this study as the new socialist economics, although some would argue that it was not new, and others that it was scarcely socialist. Oskar Lange, a Polish economist, and Abba Lerner have been credited with providing the most systematic expositions, in which they defined the conditions for efficient allocation under socialism and the famous marginal-cost rule.[3]

Although these economic controversies lack the high drama of the Keynesian revolution, they are important because they enabled socialists to demonstrate that central planning of resource allocation and income distribution would not cause the allocative chaos which their critics charged, just as Keynes wrote *The General Theory* to prove that expansion would not bring the dire consequences predicted by existing theories. Furthermore, the debate among the democratic socialists in Britain, who did believe in market pricing, revealed critical differences between them. It was in this area, not in the Keynesian controversies, that the relevance of economic analysis to socialist systems was questioned. During the 1930s when the aims of the Labour party seemed so modest in comparison with the task to be accomplished, such disagreements may have seemed largely academic. But they turned out to be the cutting edge between two quite distinct ways of thinking about the role of government, economic policy and socialist goals by economists, who otherwise all accepted the traditional tools of microeconomic analysis and the virtues of market pricing.

Socialist economics in theory

In the late-nineteenth century, Pareto had first shown how the conditions for achieving optimal allocation could be reached under the static assumptions of Walrasian general equilibrium analysis.[4] Briefly, these conditions describe the optimal position as one in which no goods can be reallocated between consumers without making another consumer worse off, and no factors of production can be reallocated to a different firm or to make a different good without reducing output or making another producer worse off.

Since the marginal revolution, the central focus of microeconomic analysis has been to show how the market system solves the allocation problem by setting prices in product markets and in factor markets, which reflect consumers' preferences for goods and producers' technical production possibilities. These relative prices become the scales of valuation within individual markets that enable both consumers to make the rational choices to allocate their income between goods, in the way which maximizes their satisfaction, and producers to allocate their funds between factors, in the way which minimizes costs and maximizes their profits. The assumptions of perfect competition ensure that the marginal-utility calculations of consumers match the marginal-cost calculations of producers. Firms also produce at the point where their marginal costs are equal to the market-determined price, and choose the plant size where average costs are at their lowest. However, any particular optimal solution depends upon the given distribution of income and wealth, the given consumer tastes and the given set of technical possibilities. If these change for any reason, the relative prices also change and, through market adjustments, a different optimal allocation is reached.

In an article published in 1908, Enrico Barone, Pareto's student, had shown that while Pareto optimality required all the assumptions of perfect competition, it did *not* require the private ownership of the means of production.[5] In other words, the price system was not a capitalist institution, but a theoretical construct. It enabled information to be conveyed between buyers and sellers, so that each could make the rational choices to maximize their own economic position. According to Barone, it was theoretically possible for a central planning board to gather the necessary information and to solve the equational system, which would satisfy Pareto's conditions. However, he suggested that it might be very difficult to accomplish in practice.

Shortly after the Russian revolution, Ludwig von Mises, Hayek's Austrian mentor, published an influential article, which set out to prove that it was logically impossible to allocate resources efficiently in the socialist state.[6] The main burden of his attack was directed against Marxian economics, in particular the naive versions which ignored the problems of allocation under scarcity, and even suggested that socialist states could function without money. Positing a completely collective society in which the state owned both consumption goods and production goods, Mises demonstrated that the central planning authority would be unable to calculate the imputed value of production goods. Although he allowed that it was 'conceptually possible' for a socialist state to simulate the allocation of the competitive market under static assumptions when all variables are known, he believed this could not happen because the transition to socialism would equalize income distribution, altering all the market-determined prices in the process. Thus, he concluded: 'We have the spectacle of a socialist economic order floundering in the ocean of possible conceivable economic combinations without the compass of economic calculation . . . . There is only groping in the dark. Socialism is the abolition of rational economy.' The economic confusion of Russia in the immediate post-revolution, post-war era, and the lack of any framework to address problems of allocation and efficiency in Marxian economics, added considerable force to Mises's arguments in 1920.

In 1935 the article appeared in English for the first time, in Hayek's revised Austrian philippic against planning. By then, of course, capitalist countries certainly appeared to be in a worse economic mess than Russia. Furthermore, the socialists Hayek attacked were all well versed in allocation problems, most were dedicated democrats, and some, such as Durbin, were outspoken anti-Marxists. Nevertheless, Hayek began his evaluation of the contemporary debates by blasting the Russian experiment and dismissing the mathematical solutions based on Barone's system, specifically including Dickinson's proposals in this category. He then attacked both Dobb's stand against consumers' sovereignty, which he knew other socialists did not share, and capitalist planning, which was irrelevant to socialism. He concluded with the arrogant claim that the critics had done more to solve the socialist allocation problems than any planning advocate.

Rather than engage in theoretical debate Hayek conceded the static case ('it must be admitted that this is not an impossibility in the sense that it is logically contradictory'), and concentrated on the practical impossibilities.[7] He emphasized the almost unimaginable quantity of detailed information the central authority would need to have in order to replicate both the quantity and quality of knowledge which individual entrepreneurs possess. To undertake the collection of the data necessary to solve a comprehensive system of equations would be difficult enough. But Hayek also argued that it was certainly an absurd idea to use such information for price fixing, when 'almost every change of a single price would make changes of hundreds of other prices necessary.' Even the simpler notion of marginal-cost pricing would assume 'a much greater precision and definiteness than can be attached to any cost phenomenon in real life'. In any case, Hayek believed that costs were themselves determined by the equilibrating force of market profits, which enable the economic system to adapt to dynamic change.

Hayek also thought that there would be major problems in identifying the appropriate industries, business units, managerial responsibilities and evaluation criteria. The problem of managerial incentives without the individual profit motive would be insuperable, and he predicted that managers would be less willing to undertake risky ventures and unlikely to follow central directives. In short, Hayek suggested that even the pseudo-competitive solutions, such as Dickinson's, raised issues which could not be dismissed as 'minor administrative problems'. He therefore concluded that the recent efforts to find a practical socialist system were doomed: 'It must be said that in their present state, even considering their very provisional and tentative character, these proposals seem rather more than less impracticable than the older socialist proposals of a centrally planned economic system.' Indeed, he went further to suggest, 'today we are not intellectually equipped to improve the working of our economic system by "planning" or to solve the problem of socialist production in any other way without very considerably impairing productivity'.[8]

By this time British socialists, including Hayek's colleagues at LSE, were busily tackling the allocation problem and were in the midst of arguing about the appropriate valuation scales. In published works they had made a broad case for planning to cope with capitalism's failures; they included unemployment and the extent of monopolization as obvious examples of the current waste of existing resources. Their main planning goal, however, was to remove the inequalities of the capitalist system, which Mises had recognized as an understandable aim of socialism, even if he did not agree with it. To satisfy the requirements of neoclassical allocational efficiency as well, and to meet their perception of Hayek's challenge, the socialist economists still faced two theoretical problems. One was to agree on the appropriate scales for the valuation of goods and of resource inputs; the other was to find a practical and theoretically correct set of instructions to give to the managers of socially owned enterprises. The solutions developed as answers to these questions formed the framework of a new socialist economics, which yielded a coherent theoretical justification for central planning based on traditional microeconomic criteria.

The British socialists who believed in market pricing were committed to the idea that citizens should choose their own purchases in a free market for consumption goods and their own jobs, occupations and amount of work in a free labour market. Thus, the valuation scale for goods and for the use of labour in such a socialist state would be determined in the same way as in the private market. What remained to be determined was the valuation of resources in the production of goods and the allocation of factors between goods. For this purpose instructions for plant managers would have to be designed which met efficiency criteria. The solutions which were provided in the 1930s differed on both theoretical and practical grounds.

Durbin's main contributions were contained in two articles, 'The Social Significance of the Theory of Value' and 'Economic Calculus in a Planned Economy', published in 1935 and 1936 respectively, which some students remember as more influential than Lange and Lerner because they dealt with the broader allocative issues. Durbin later explained that his dual purpose was to show: (1) 'why the institutions of competition do not, and in my view cannot, lead to a wise direction of our economic life'; and (2) 'if this negative proposition is accepted, how can the theory of value be applied within the institutions of a planned economy'.[9] Building on Dickinson's earlier analysis, Durbin argued that competition could not lead to optimal allocation, because it only covered 'part of the economic field', namely 'atomistic' or private goods such as boots. Public goods, or ends which must be shared (Durbin's example was 'the enjoyment of equality'), could not be priced in the market, and, therefore, the allocation of resources for their production could not be decided either. Even within the private sector, Durbin argued that competition broke down for many reasons – the lack of long-term foresight, the instability of competition as producers realized the benefits of monopoly, the customary laws which prohibited certain products, and the whole range of social costs caused by unregulated business practice, from factory smoke to Durbin's special nightmare, the destruction of beautiful countryside by speculative builders. Durbin concluded with a prophetic plea for an extension of economic theory to include criteria which would help to achieve the proper balance between public and private activities, and 'to formulate and solve the problems of rational calculus in an integrated economy'. He believed that in a mixed economy which contained significant public and private sectors, the logical distinction between individualist and collectivist economies disappeared: 'we are left with the much more difficult problem of choosing the principles of social selection and resolving the problems of economic calculus in a fundamentally collectivist economy'. His own solution was based on the equalization of marginal products, although he recognized that the technical problems of implementation might be very complicated. He rejected Hayek's dire predictions of widespread refusal to obey planning instructions as psychological problems, which 'the professor of economics is not competent to discuss'.

Lange's two articles appeared in late 1936 and early 1937; they are generally regarded as the authoritative answer to Mises, Hayek and Robbins, commonly referred to as the 'competitive solution'.[10] To dramatize his achievement in using the perfect-competition model to benefit socialist allocation, Lange proposed that 'a statue of Professor Mises ought to occupy an honourable place in the great hall of the Ministry of Socialization or of the Central Planning Board of the socialist state'. His own solution explicitly used the Walrasian system to describe the determination of equilibrium in a competitive market, and applied it to the socialist allocation problem as suggested by Pareto and elaborated by Barone. Indeed, Lange himself believed that he had 'scarcely gone beyond' Barone, except on the question of leaving capital accumulation to the saving of individuals; he drew on the new Keynesian analysis to indicate the possibility of stagnation under capitalism.

Lange's major contribution to the debates among socialists was his elaboration of the 'trial-and-error' procedure to allocate resources in a socialist economy, which was designed to meet Hayek's challenge that socialism could not replicate the market process. Although he himself believed in the free choice of goods and of occupations under socialism, he argued that this procedure was also applicable to cases where the central planning board made all the decisions. In making the general case for socialism Lange pointed out that, although Chamberlin and Robinson described the actual capitalist system much better than Walras or Marshall, 'the work of the latter two will be more useful in solving the problems of a socialist system'. Indeed, Lange suggested that Chamberlin and Robinson were in danger of losing their jobs under socialism, 'unless they agree to be transferred to the department of economic history to provide students of history with the theoretical apparatus necessary to understand what will appear to a future generation as the craze and folly of a past epoch'. Of all the new socialist economists, Lange was the least questioning about the application of the static assumptions of perfect competition to the socialist state.

Lerner, by contrast, was quite clear that reference to the perfectly competitive model created serious methodological and practical problems.[11] Rules, which depended upon the conditions of perfect competition, would require those conditions to be met before they could ensure allocative efficiency. For this reason, Lerner found the partial analysis of Marshallian economics far more useful than the Walrasian system used by Lange or the 'Austrian' marginal analysis favoured by Durbin. Instead, he proposed that the socialist state aim directly at '*the most economic utilization of resources*'; this could only be done by setting marginal cost equal to price. This rule would ensure that factors were moved into the places where they yielded their greatest productivity and that goods were valued by the extra satisfaction they provided to consumers; resources would still be allocated efficiently, even if there were imperfect competition or other dynamic changes in the market. In short, an efficient solution did not require conditions of perfect competition. Lerner concluded, 'Price must be made equal to marginal cost. This is the contribution that pure economic theory has to make to the building up of a socialist economy.'

In subsequent work Lerner pulled together all the ideas he had generated during the debates on the new socialist economics into a generalized application of economic principles to 'the exercise of conscious control over the economic system'; he called it *The Economics of Control* (1944). In the introduction he confessed that when he had started in this field he had believed in a completely collectivist form of socialism; the 1930s had convinced him of the overriding importance of democracy and freedom, and he no longer felt that state ownership of the means of production was crucial. For instance, central control without democracy was not socialism; indeed, it was 'much further removed from socialism than socialism's "opposite", capitalism'. Therefore, he wrote about the general principles of government intervention, that is,'the deliberate application of whatever policy will best serve the social interest, without prejudging the issue between collective ownership and administration or some form of private enterprise'. Although still largely concerned with the principles of allocation, the book included chapters on taxation, unemployment, growth and foreign trade, in what is still widely regarded as one of the most comprehensive treatments of commonly accepted theoretical grounds for government intervention and the criteria for its evaluation.

To summarize, the new socialist economics used existing microeconomic theory to spell out the economic tasks which a collective system would have to perform in order to allocate its resources efficiently. The theory also helped to define the appropriate social ends, which would then determine the scale of values in a socialist economy. Once these scales were decided, the optimum conditions spelled out the rules which would determine how to allocate resources efficiently to meet those ends.[12]

Theoretically there are three choice components in establishing the valuation scale of any economy, which are based on subjective judgment, that is to say, they cannot be explained by economic theory. They are preferences about the provision of goods, public and private, preferences about the use of resources, for example, how much to work or to play, and societal choices about the distribution of income and wealth. A capitalist economy based upon the private ownership of the means of production allows consumers to express their preferences for private goods and for the use of those factor resources through the market price mechanism; the state's role is to decide the scale of public goods and social services through the political process. The income distribution is only implicitly chosen as the end result of the market valuation of factor resources and their initial distribution among citizens.

Socialists, who advocate replacing the market system with central control of the entire economy, are implicitly assuming that state planners will determine the components of the valuation scale for the collective benefit of society. However, various combinations of consumers' and planners' preferences are possible; indeed, the arguments between advocates of market and controlled pricing were often disputes of this kind. Under the so-called competitive solutions devised by Dickinson, Durbin, Lange and Lerner, the socialist state would allow consumer preferences to set prices for private goods and for labour services through the market, explicitly rejecting the totally collectivist state. However, the state would expand the role of government planning in the valuation process through collective decisions to reduce income inequality, to extend the public ownership of industry, to increase the use of subsidies and taxes to handle social benefits and costs, and to set a societal rate of interest through its central control of savings and investment. Having thus determined the socialist scale of values, the optimal use of resources in production would be ensured by requiring production unit managers to follow the marginal-cost rules. The marginal-cost rules, as elaborated by Lerner, Meade and others, would enable planners and managers to decide what size plant to construct, what level of output to produce in each plant, what combination of factors to use and how to adjust to changes in demand or technology.[13]

In short, socialist central planning would supplant the capitalist market as the integrator of household and production decisions.[14] Not only would the new socialist state be able to replicate the market's efficient allocation of private goods, it would be able to *improve* efficiency through its planning powers in those situations where competition broke down. In particular, it would be able to direct the appropriate allocation of resources in the cases of public goods, social costs, monopoly, imperfect competition and decreasing-cost industries, which the market system could not handle. Furthermore, the socialist state would be able to enforce a fairer distribution of income and wealth. Thus, in theory, as a later analyst put it, 'not only could a socialist economy be "rational", but it could be much more "rational" than *laissez-faire*, the imperfections of which were admitted'.[15] Despite their theoretical differences, many of which were ironed out in the controversies of the late 1930s, these economists were convinced that planners could improve the microeconomic performance of the economy, as well as its macroeconomic efficiency. However, there was less agreement about the practical implications of this analysis than there had been over Keynesian expansionism to lick unemployment.

Socialist economics in practice

Some socialist economists, such as Durbin, had never believed in the practical possibility of implementing massive equational systems. Lerner's marginal-cost rule seemed to circumvent the problem by providing a simple method to make the major production decisions of the new socialist economy, which did not require any assumptions of perfect competition. Furthermore, it also appeared that Lerner had discovered a practical way to solve the pricing problem in decreasing-cost industries, which arises under any system.[16] These industries are able to cut their average costs and lower prices as they expand their scale. Because average costs are falling as output increases, marginal costs are lower than average cost; if output is set where marginal cost equals price, the firm will be running at a loss (the average cost of a good will be greater than its price); if price is set equal to average cost, the price will be higher and output lower than they should be to meet the optimal allocation criteria.

In practice, one of the main benefits of mass production has been this reduction in prices, but the pricing problem also applies to industries with enormous initial investments such as railways and electricity supply systems. Historically, such cases usually end up as virtual monopolies, or are taken over as public utilities. The choice of an efficient price arises whether the industries are public or private. Following Marshall and Pigou, Dickinson had first suggested that in the socialist state, unlike capitalism, the optimal criteria could be met by enforcing the marginal-cost pricing rule. Then, the government could subsidize the decreasing-cost industries, which were making losses, and tax increasing-cost industries, where excess profits were being made.[17] Lerner's analysis had generalized and reinforced this argument. However, as the debate continued in the late 1930s, it became less clear how the rule could be administered in practice. These practical problems of marginal-cost pricing merged with the general concerns of Hayek and others, and some analysts began to question its theoretical viability.

In his economic calculus article Durbin had proposed that plant managers in socialized industries be required to calculate the marginal products of all factors in different plant sizes and to choose the plant size which minimized costs, that is, the point at which price equalled average cost, not marginal cost. He further argued that, if demand decreased, thus lowering price, managers should produce to the point where marginal cost equalled marginal revenue (which would be less than price), until a new plant at the appropriate minimum average cost could be built. Durbin recognized that it was 'theoretically desirable' to set marginal cost equal to price; but he argued that his rules were more practical to administer, because it was difficult to measure marginal products with any certainty or to distinguish between fixed and variable costs.[18] Even though these rules would cause waste in the short run, 'such a general instruction would have the great advantage that it would enable the management to meet changes in the market conditions independently, and without the complex system of taxes and bounties required by the other instruction'.

Lerner raised strenuous objections to Durbin's use of average-cost pricing.[19] He pointed out that Durbin had confused long-run and short-run marginal-cost curves; in selecting the correct plant size, long-run average cost would equal long-run marginal cost at its lowest point. He also demonstrated that Durbin's optimization rule actually implied perfect competition, in which case average cost would equal marginal cost and price anyway. In answer to Durbin's practical concerns, Lerner argued that estimation would be improved by better predictions, not by tinkering with the rules for efficiency. He concluded that Durbin did not need 'to quail before the necessity' of a complicated system of subsidies, because in the socialist state individual firms or industries would not have to cover their costs; there would be 'no taxes or bounties', only differences in total revenues and outlays which would simply be collected as statistical information.[20]

In his reply at the time, and in his posthumous essay on the problems of the socialized sector, Durbin acknowledged all Lerner's theoretical points, but remained an adamant advocate of 'anticipated *future* average costs as the appropriate guide to pricing policy and investment because all these costs (with negligible exceptions) must, sooner or later, be paid'.[21] He gave two main reasons: first, the marginal-cost rule reduced 'the status of accountancy and the principle of accountability to empty formularies', with serious consequences on the incentives of workers and managers; second, it caused confusion in price policy because of the complexities of choosing the appropriate time frame for estimating marginal costs and for deciding on the maintenance or replacement of fixed capital stock.[22] In his notes for a chapter on economic calculus in his proposed 'Economics of Democratic Socialism', Durbin expressed his feeling that Lerner had failed to answer his practical objections: 'he tries to say that I did not understand the theoretical criterion ... he misunderstands the point about fixed capital ... he does not discuss the value of financial independence'.

Durbin also believed that Lerner had avoided the real difficulties of operating a partially socialized system, if the nationalized industries were suffering serious losses. Lerner had suggested such temporary losses added to the 'already imposing list of economic arguments in favour of a *speedy transition* from Capitalism to Socialism'; Durbin had countered that 'Mr. Lerner's technique of administration is not a technique of administration until the "transitional period" is wholly finished'. In a footnote Durbin commented 'that it is only if the socialized section happens to be, on balance, profitable that his use of theoretical conceptions is really a practicable rule of administration'.[23] He also added somewhat snidely that, had Lerner troubled to read the Labour party programme, he would have seen that it did include proposals to nationalize two 'very profitable industries', electricity and transport.   At the theoretical level, James Meade was the first to point out that the losses generated by subsidizing decreasing-cost industries could cost more than total property income.[24] Furthermore, use of the income tax to raise the necessary funds could seriously affect other choices, for example, how much people were willing to work. He, therefore, recommended nationalization of decreasing-cost industries. Others generalized this point to show that application of the marginal-cost rule could affect the distribution of income, and therefore could not be used to allocate factor resources objectively without also making implicit value judgments about the distributional outcome. Others have questioned whether the marginal-cost rule does ensure optimal allocation. After the war Little went so far as to state that 'the general case against marginal cost pricing is overwhelming'.[25] Interestingly, a recent analyst has suggested that average-cost pricing may well yield a third-best solution in a suboptimal world.[26]

Conclusions

The economic revolutions of the 1930s underscored and expanded the theoretical reasons why government must intervene to correct the economic failures of the market system. For many they provided the rationale for systematic planning of the economy, although not everyone accepted that policies to ensure allocative efficiency were as important as policies to enhance aggregative performance. Keynes himself believed that economic management of the policy instruments which determined national income and employment was 'the rightly conceived socialism of the future'; he did not think that the market necessarily misallocated resources, and he was certainly against large-scale nationalization.

For socialists the policy implications of the new economic thinking confirmed their own concerns to maintain full employment, to enlarge the public sector and to redistribute incomes. The new socialist economics provided theoretical grounds for supposing that the government could both correct market imperfections and improve upon its social efficiency. Today few economists believe that the welfare analysis on which this 'economics of socialism' was based can provide clear-cut and objective solutions to the problem of measuring efficient allocation, for many of the reasons which the socialists were the first to raise. At the time the so-called competitive solution certainly seemed to have successfully defeated the Hayekian challenge to its theoretical viability and to its practical possibility.

Many economists believed that the new marginal-cost pricing rule developed by socialist economists yielded a more general criterion than the narrower assumptions of perfect competition would allow. Socialist economists also succeeded in broadening the dimensions of the allocation question by making explicit the impact of public goods, social costs and benefits, and the distribution of income on the use of factor resources. Furthermore, by combining macroeconomic and microeconomic policy as complementary functions of central planning, they laid the groundwork for a more generalized conception of the economic role of government. Thus, their policy analysis foreshadowed the postwar 'neoclassical synthesis' of macroeconomics and micro-economics. James Meade's 1935 textbook, *Economic Analysis and Policy*, which drew heavily on the two economic revolutions, was one of the first to take on a recognizably modern shape.

Although the theoretical arguments raised by members of the Austrian school were valid criticisms of simplistic Marxian analysis, they were less relevant to the mixed systems proposed by the non-Marxist socialists of the 1930s. Hayek's practical objections were closer to the mark, but his own approach was, if anything, more irrelevant. He ignored the allocation problem posed by monopolization and his trade cycle analysis interpreted unemployment as a long-run adjustment to past malinvestments. What was really at stake was a nineteenth-century liberal distrust of government interference of any kind. Having failed to make much headway against the theoretical foundations of macro or micro planning in the 1930s, he launched a new offensive against the political foundations of socialism in 1944; he called it *The Road to Serfdom*.

Some analysts, notably Ian Little, consider these economic contro-versies about socialism quite irrelevant. It is even slightly odd to find socialists battling to prove that their system meets the efficiency criteria of the despised perfectly competitive model. Political scientists under-standably find the whole exercise 'highly esoteric', and rather unimpor-tant in the case for or against planning.[27] But it would be a mistake to relegate these arguments to the history of economic thought as having little political significance. This view misses three important ingredients of the debate itself. First, the free choice which the pricing system enables consumers to express was considered the economic complement to political freedom by *both* sides of the dispute, with the noted exception of Marxists such as Maurice Dobb. Second, for democratic socialists, this freedom was the chief distinguishing political characteristic of their economic system in contrast to the dictatorial methods of a system of planning by controls. Third, the whole context of the debate was political; Hayek and Robbins thought that socialist planning would destroy political freedom, whereas Durbin and Gaitskell believed that capitalist non-planning created and maintained social injustice.

Finally, the controversies between socialists on practical matters revealed significant differences in their approach to the use of economics for the analysis of social concerns. Although ostensibly about specific questions such as industry subsidies, marginal-cost calculation and the speed of transition, their differences had more to do with the limits of economics for relevant policy analysis. Lerner advocated the marginal-cost rule not only because it was theoretically correct, but because it seemed to him methodologically simpler and more elegant; it required fewer assumptions and special conditions. Durbin, by contrast, was concerned with administrative simplicity, institutional feasibility and practical repercussions. Could plant managers carry out their instructions? Could central planners control the whole system? Where would the money come from to pay for losing public enterprises? Durbin worried about fiscal responsibility, administrative chaos and bureaucratic red tape, particularly after five years in Whitehall during the war. His rejection of capitalism rested on the ethical case against its social injustices, not on theoretical or empirical arguments about the logic or relevance of different economic models.

None of the market economists questioned the use of the existing tools of microeconomics for the analysis of a socialist system, unlike G. D. H. Cole or Maurice Dobb. They all agreed that the socialist state would allocate resources more efficiently, and the new socialist economics used orthodox principles of welfare economics to demonstrate how. However, many of them became more interested in the general principles for government intervention than in its specific application to socialism. Durbin, by contrast, only used economic theory to help illuminate the means to achieve his socialist goals of equality, public control and central planning. If economics did not serve this purpose, then other disciplines must be brought to bear on the crucial planning issues. Thus, Lerner and Lange, and to a lesser extent Meade, regarded the problems of democratic control, management incentives, administrative feasibility and political priority as non-economic, and therefore as peripheral to their search for a systematic, theoretical analysis of market failures. To Durbin, once the economic efficiency questions were settled, these issues became central to his search for an economics of democratic socialism, which would provide a systematic and realistic policy alternative to the existing institutions of market capitalism.

CHAPTER 12
LABOUR'S NEW
PROGRAMME

For Socialism and Peace, adopted at the 1934 conference, remained the most fully articulated statement of the Labour party's overall aims before the war. However, their platform was altered in significant ways in the years following the election defeat in 1935. Although the left wing continued to demand radical take-over of the economy, the bulk of party members recognized that their only chance of victory lay in presenting a strategic plan of feasible reforms; the moderate leadership had been vindicated. The economic and political climate had also changed; the rise of fascism and the threat of war coupled with falling unemployment were shifting policy priorities from the economy to defence.

Hugh Dalton, along with Herbert Morrison and 154 other Labour members, was returned to Parliament in 1935. He was also elected chairman of the party's national executive commitee (NEC) at the 1936 Edinburgh conference, which meant that he was automatically chairman of the party in the following year and responsible for organizing the 1937 conference at Bournemouth. He later explained that previous policy statements were thought to be 'too complicated, too miscellaneous and too long'. He therefore spent the early months of his chairmanship carrying out a conference pledge to produce 'a Short Programme of primary measures of Socialism and Social Amelioration to which legislative effect will be given by the next Labour Government'.[1] The new official platform, called *Labour's Immediate Programme*, was adopted unanimously at the Bournemouth conference.

The preamble to this document affirmed the party's commitment to socialism, peace and democracy. The heart of the new programme was to propose 'four vital measures of reconstruction' and 'four great benefits'.[2] The industries to be rebuilt were finance, land, transport and energy (coal and power), the social benefits were 'abundant food, good wages, leisure and security'. The party committed itself to remedy conditions in the distressed areas immediately, and to support the League of Nations and collective security. Besides being considerably shorter than the comprehensive measures contained in *For Socialism and Peace*, the programme included the nationalization of the Bank of England, but excluded the joint stock banks; it called for national planning of the land, but not its public ownership; it only referred to the House of Lords obliquely, while earlier its outright abolition had been proposed.

Dalton retained the chairmanship of the influential finance and trade subcommittee (FTC) of the party's policy committee after the 1935 conference. He saw to it that Colin Clark, Evan Durbin, Hugh Gaitskell and Douglas Jay were co-opted onto this committee, and appointed to other advisory panels and policy subcommittees.[3] He continued to prepare resolutions for the party conference and to keep his pigeon-hole active on financial institutions, financial panic and unemployment policy. Through these channels the young economists had direct access to the party's policy making, where they played a significant role in spelling out the policy implications of Keynes's *General Theory* and in articulating an appropriate party position on employment, financial, exchange rate and foreign trade policy in the late 1930s. The XYZ club, as before, provided the forum for thrashing out the problems.

Following the Bournemouth conference, the policy subcommittee of the party's NEC unanimously elected Dalton chairman. Besides Jim Middleton, who became general secretary in 1935, W. A. Nield was hired away from the NFRB to be the director of research.[4] John Nairn from the parliamentary Labour party (PLP) assisted as secretary to several of the advisory committees of the party. Thus, the party's research department was more effective in the late 1930s, producing many useful documents. Its main task was to set up the necessary research to implement the new platform.

In a document presented to the policy committee in November 1937, *Labour's Immediate Programme* was broken down into thirty-one policy questions, with the work which the policy committee had decided needed to be done on each; the structure of subcommittees and their research responsibilities were also listed.[5] The whole gives a good sense of the enormous amount of serious work behind the party's new platform, about which little seems to be known. The party's research plan called for redrafts of the party's bills to nationalize the coal industry and to reform workmen's compensation, for drafts of bills to nationalize railways and gas, to set up a national transport board, to acquire land, to restrict rents, to raise the school-leaving age, to revise pension schemes and to help distressed areas, and for further consultation with the TUC on wages, shorter working hours and workmen's compensation; the necessary work for the reform of parliamentary procedure had already been completed.

This chapter concentrates on the economic policy issues which were explicitly delegated to the FTC and 'the City group'; they included the Bank of England, monetary policy, national investment board (NIB), public works, stability of trade and industry, the stock exchange, taxation and 'obstruction by vested interests'. The FTC was also asked to engage in new work on foreign trade policy and the coming slump, and, later, to provide 'a general co-ordination of economic policy', when all of the other questions had been worked out. At the NFRB an economic research programme was organized to meet some of the party's needs. Durbin supervised three projects, one on financial policy, one on unemployment services and another on food policy. G. D. H. Cole wrote a lengthy monograph on the machinery of planning for the NFRB's planning committee. It was submitted to the party's consti-tutional committee, which had been made responsible for the subject in November 1937.

There was no annual conference in 1938, because it had been decided to switch from the autumn to Whitsun and to hold the next one in June 1939. In late 1938, using the implementation reports for the immediate programme as their base, the party's policy subcom-mittee started to draft the necessary documents for a possible election in the following year. Although few of the resulting reports were debated at the 1939 conference, which was preoccupied with defence and the impending war, most were formally endorsed by the NEC, and others by their responsible subcommittees. For example, the FTC's final report on the outline for a bill of finance was approved by the NEC, but their more sensitive report on financial panic was kept confidential. Thus, by the outbreak of war, the Labour party had worked out all the legislative proposals necessary to carry out its new programme and had developed a set of unofficial positions on a number of other issues.

Labour's Immediate Programme

In his year as chairman of the party, Dalton worked hard on four critical matters – the shortened party programme, the distressed areas commission, defence and rearmament policy and a revision of the party's constitution. The first defined a viable set of legislative proposals, the second, the party's response to Britain's lingering unemployment problems; the third ensured a realistic position towards the impending European war, and the last, broader constituency representation on the NEC. In no small measure Dalton can be credited with finally bringing the Labour party out of its own post-1931 slump. The new constitution increased the number of constituency representatives on the NEC, reasserted the power of parliamentary leaders in Transport House, and infused headquarters with vigour and talent; it was 'a revolution', according to Ben Pimlott, which he credits Ben Greene and his Constituency Parties Movement for bringing to a head.[6] Looking ahead, the party's acceptance of rearmament ensured its place in the wartime coalition, and the new programme provided the basis for the party's successful 1945 platform.

In his *Memoirs* Dalton recalled that he wrote to Evan Durbin asking him to outline an appropriate short programme. Durbin sent 'a sketch' dated 26 December 1936, which Dalton used to draft a memorandum for the policy subcommittee. Although Durbin's letter cannot be found, Dalton himself said that his first draft did not differ 'in substance' from Durbin's proposals. In his memorandum Dalton proposed dividing domestic policy into two broad categories: '(a) some measures of Socialism and (b) some other measures of social improvement'.[7] Under the first, he listed five areas for consideration, financial institutions, coal and power, transport, armaments and land; under the second, he outlined seven main points, adequate maintenance for the unemployed, employment by financial and monetary policy and public works, school-leaving age, pensions, industrial legislation, agriculture and distressed areas. Thus, the shortened list reflected the earlier concern of Durbin's strategy committee to limit nationalization and not to go overboard with 'ameliorative measures'. It seems safe to assume that Durbin had discussed his letter with his fellow strategists. The addition of some social service provisions and the substitution of land for iron and steel were the only major departures from their 1935 resolution; these changes followed Lees-Smith's advice at the time.

On finance Dalton's memorandum recommended 'public ownership of the Bank of England, with powers to control the quantity and direction of new investment (National Investment Board) and the quantity of short term credit (Macmillan Report recommendation)'. Dalton noted that heads of a bill on this subject were ready. He specifically recommended against public ownership of the joint stock banks because 'this is bad politics, and at this stage unnecessary economics'; he said the same about land nationalization. Referring to the December 1936 letter, Dalton later commented that Durbin had changed his mind about the joint stock banks: 'He did not want their nationalization in the Short Programme'.[8] Apparently Durbin was also 'very keen' on a universal statutory period of holiday with pay each year, a proposal which also found its way into the programme.

As the party leader Attlee was naturally closely involved in the drafting process, and evidently contributed his own version. After discussions in the policy subcommittee, Dalton rewrote the proposals in February, acknowledging that Attlee had been 'very helpful in providing a continuous thread of argument to hold the programme together', which was 'much better than a bare list of items'.[9] This second draft, with some editorial rearrangements and rewording, and one significant omission, became *Labour's Immediate Programme*. In short, there was a good deal of unanimity about the party's general strategy among the moderate leadership, but some important differences on the appropriate emphasis.

Dalton's version had included an introductory paragraph on a national plan, which directly attributed the present economic evils to the grave defects of the capitalist system and proposed 'to plan the economic life of the nation, both industry by industry and district by district, and on a co-ordinated whole'. This introduction was omitted in the final copy. Dalton had also written that the purpose of credit control was 'to prevent deflation and restriction, leading to unemployment', and that budgetary and monetary policy would be combined 'in seeking the greatest possible stability of trade and employment, price levels and rates of foreign exchange'. This section was rewritten as: 'Every effort will be made to ensure the greatest possible stability of Trade and Employment'.[10] Thus, any specific commitments to expansionary policies and the new Keynesian techniques of fiscal and monetary management were cut out in the drafting stage. However, the force of the strategy committee's argument to gain the commanding heights of the economy was retained: 'the community must command the main levers which will control the economic machine. These are *Finance, Land, Transport, Coal* and *Power*'. The agreed financial measures were to nationalize the Bank of England, to set up the national investment board, to undertake large schemes of public development and to remain off the gold standard.

The final draft was published in March 1937, and had already sold 300,000 copies before the annual conference in October. Attlee, who as prime minister was to preside over the programme's postwar adoption, opened the debate moving formal acceptance of the party's policy document. He characterized it as 'practical idealism', which 'necessarily combines both ameliorative measures and fundamental changes'.[11] He defended its shortness as the result of intensive work to find the right programme of action on which to seek a democratic mandate. He did not spell out the details, but argued that the proposals on the control of finance were 'fundamental for reconstruction', 'for laying the foundations of a new order' and 'also vitally necessary for dealing with immediate measures of amelioration'. As the acknowledged leader of a new moderate programme, Attlee had come a long way from his 'feverish' collaboration with Sir Stafford Cripps; his underlying common-sense view of public management had reasserted itself.

Ironically, at the same conference, an NEC decision to expel the Socialist League from the Labour party for participating in the United Front with the Communist party was overwhelmingly upheld, despite Cripps's earnest plea to refer the report back to the NEC. *Labour's Immediate Programme* itself was accepted unanimously. Ernest Davies urged the nationalization of the joint stock banks in the debate, but did not force a division on the issue. In his contemporary assessment of the party's new programme Cole regretted the omission, emphasizing that it remained part of the official policy adopted in *For Socialism and Peace*.[12]

Employment and trade policies

Although much preoccupied with important and necessary institutional reforms, the Labour party had not formally debated its positions on employment, trade or financial policy before 1935. It had condemned the gold standard and committed itself to stable domestic and foreign exchange prices after the 1931 crisis. The Labour opposition had voted against the Import Duties Act in 1932, but the party had remained neutral on the protection issue. Furthermore, while it vowed to reduce unemployment, its actual programme emphasized the structural problems of depressed areas and efforts to reduce the labour force. Unorthodox budgeting had been firmly rejected in the committee stage. The Labour party was no exception to the generally confused policy making of the mid-1930s, as microeconomic approaches were applied to macroeconomic problems. However, the young economic researchers were helping the party's policy committees to sort out the complex interactions between domestic and foreign policy, between macroeconomic and microeconomic problems, between market realities and socialist aspirations.

Meanwhile, the National government had itself introduced some measures in a reluctant effort to bring order in chaotic market conditions. The 1934 Unemployment Act set up the Special Areas Reconstruction Association to provide loans to firms locating in depressed areas and a national scheme of unemployment compensation to relieve local responsibility. Since 1932 the import duties advisory committee (IDAC) had administered the new protective tariffs and the system of imperial preference inaugurated under the Ottawa agreements a year later. The government had also expanded the powers of the agricultural marketing boards set up by the second Labour government, and had initiated a subsidy system to maintain farmers' incomes. These measures, in conjunction with import quotas on meat, butter and bacon, and a 'levy subsidy' for wheat, meant that British agriculture was also enjoying selective protection for the first time. As a result, British agricultural production increased, reversing the secular trend. Finally, a series of controls had been introduced after the 1931 crisis, which effectively pegged the exchange rate, scrutinized foreign investments, controlled the acceptance houses and provided export credits. Furthermore, the Bank of England was explicitly working with the Treasury to promote government policy; the most dramatic evidence of this new relationship was the sharp reduction in interest rates and the war loan conversion of 1932.

Dalton continued to refine the FTC's confidential work on financial panic, using the young economists to explain the policy implications of the new macroeconomics and the XYZ to keep him up to date on the practical changes. Despite the resistance of some committee members, he also sought further elucidation on employment policy, exchange rate policy and the connections between the two. Meanwhile, the NEC policy subcommittee set up its own advisory committee on the Ottawa trade agreements to explore their impact on the party's position. Durbin, Gaitskell and Jay were co-opted in January 1936.

At the 1935 conference, the party had voted to set up a distressed areas commission to investigate conditions for itself. Politically important as Labour and union strongholds, their economic plight was a policy priority for the Labour party, as Tawney had already recognized in drafting *Labour and the Nation*. However, the National government seemed to be stealing the party's thunder with its area development policies, so that the commission was conducted with an eye to maximizing publicity. In contrast, the work of the policy committees was often deliberately kept confidential. As a result, the party's achievement in developing more sophisticated approaches to economic policy in the late 1930s has not been fully recognized, and the contribution of the new generation of young economists to this process has been neglected.

Employment policy

The distressed areas commission held a series of conferences in West Cumberland, South Wales, Durham and Tyneside, West Scotland and Lancashire. Written evidence was taken from the local movements, and the commissioners visited each area for several days. Besides the interim report, *Labour and the Distressed Areas: A Programme for Action*, which came out in January 1937, five regional reports were also published. The actions proposed included a minister of cabinet rank in charge of distressed areas, special Treasury grants to the local authorities to reduce public assistance, control over the location of new industries by the minister and various plans to improve communications, holiday facilities and decentralized trading estates. Dalton commented in his *Memoirs*:

> These reports attracted wide press notice. . . . They are well worth re-reading today. Since we wrote them, we have seen a revolution in these areas, and we have helped to make it. I look back on nothing in my public life with more joy and pride than my part in bringing about this great change, first as a propagandist without power, then as President of the Board of Trade with power in war-time, then as Chancellor of the Exchequer with power in peace.[13]

The report was carried unanimously at the 1937 conference. Jim Griffiths, Ellen Wilkinson and others from the various areas spoke eloquently on their plight and praised the work of the commission, particularly the attention it had brought them from Tory politicians and government officials.

The combination of the party's overall policy of financial control and public development with its specific proposals for the distressed areas provided an integrated attack on the problems of structural unemployment. The commission reasserted the Labour party's commitment to these areas, while providing a complementary unemployment programme to the macroeconomic policies designed to reduce the general unemployment level. There were no further debates on economic policy at the annual conference before the war, so that these proposals represent the party's final official word.

Although the party avoided discussion of unorthodox finance and explicitly expansionary policies in public, the unofficial debate continued at XYZ meetings, among the professional economists and increasingly on the FTC. An important turning-point in the development of unofficial economic policy was the publication of Keynes's *The General Theory* in February 1936. In June, Clark, Durbin, Gaitskell and Jay wrote a memorandum for the FTC after poring through the new book. Their report surveyed Labour's existing programmes, discussed the relation between investment and employment and estimated the employment effects of the party's proposals and their own recommended investment programme.[14]

Douglas Jay still vividly remembers their excitement, as they designed a new Keynesian policy for the Labour party. The report itself is interesting as the earliest attempt to spell out the implications of the new economic analysis in layman's terms, although in keeping with the views of its audience on the FTC the conclusions were cautious. For instance, the authors noted that, 'In so far as employment in a capitalist system depends on the vague anticipations of business men, we cannot hope that the winning of a Labour majority at a general election will lead to any "psychologically favourable" factors.' They recommended low interest rates, guaranteed loans for private investment and direct public investment to reduce unemployment; yet they were only prepared to propose unorthodox budget deficits in exceptional circumstances, 'when economic conditions were not merely bad but rapidly becoming worse'. In addition, their statistical appendix (presumably written by Clark) estimated a high rate of structural and frictional unemployment. They concluded that the current two million unemployed could only be reduced by 400,000 through 'general measures', or macroeconomic policy; in fact, unemployment fell by 700,000 within a year. Although their report seriously underestimated the potential of the new policy instruments, the authors were right to stress the need for additional policies to deal with structural problems. Nor were they alone in thinking that industrial countries could expect continuing high levels of unemployment and long-term stagnation.

Trade policy
Foreign trade policy has always presented a problem to the Labour party's policy makers. Because trade is so vital to Britain's economic well-being, any party wishing to take office must understand the policy options and hold a viable position. Yet, it is not at all clear what socialist principles, if any, are involved in trade policy, nor even, more narrowly, what impact different policies have on Britain's working class. Before 1931 the party was traditionally free trade. Economic leaders, such as Snowden and Dalton, agreed with the Manchester-school Liberals that free trade maximized world trade to Britain's advantage; they also believed that low prices on unprotected food imports benefited the working class. However, there was an influential group, including the Webbs, who assumed that foreign trade would have to be organized by the state as part of the socialist plan to replace

capitalism. During the 1920s Frank Wise and E.M.H. Lloyd of the ILP had first proposed import and export boards as planning mechanisms for foreign trade, along the same lines as the marketing boards they proposed for domestically produced agricultural products. This school of thought had more in common with Tory protection, particularly when combined with plans to rationalize British industry to make it more competitive with foreign producers.[15]

The issue was further complicated by the gold standard problem during the late 1920s and by Snowden's refusal to contemplate a revenue tariff as one way to save the pound in 1931. After the 1931 crisis, the Labour party had adamantly opposed a return to the gold standard, but it had also committed itself to stable domestic prices and exchange rates. Some Labour leaders, notably Ernest Bevin, had realized that foreign trade policy had a direct impact on domestic employment, as well as on prices. The younger generation led by Roy Harrod, James Meade, and later Durbin, were urging the adoption of fluctuating exchange rates, in order to pursue domestic expansion without causing balance of payments problems.

After 1932 the increase in world tariffs and Britain's own protective position made a completely free trade position too unrealistic for most Labour politicians. They also recognized that Britain was dependent on foreign trade to maintain its standard of living and employment in the vital export industries, and that the export industries also required substantial imports of raw materials. Bevin, who had persuaded the general council of the TUC to consider the revenue tariff in 1931, remarked at the 1932 TUC conference, 'I do not think Free Trade and Protection is a thing that a Socialist can get overenthusiastic about'.[16] However, he met with considerable resistance from his fellow unionists, who bitterly attacked the Ottawa agreements at the same conference. Nevertheless, at its 1934 conference, the Labour party formally adopted a proposal to establish import boards for the following purposes:

1 To provide abundant and acceptable supplies through an orderly and economical system of marketing; and
2 To see that the home producer, in contributing his share to these supplies, is assured of a reasonable standard of life.

As one speaker argued in the debate, the boards were seen as an alternative to both free trade *and* tariff reform.[17] However, nothing was said about how many boards should be set up, nor which products should be subject to them. The main opposition came from the members of the co-operative movement, who had deep reservations about the whole idea. They were promised representation on the boards, special rights to continue their own foreign purchasing arrangements and protection against future amendments to the boards by non-socialist governments.

Following the 1935 election, the NEC appointed a special joint subcommittee for two of its advisory committees, those on international questions and on imperial questions. Its purpose was to examine whether Britain as an 'imperialist' power was denying other countries access to the raw materials produced in her colonies. Durbin, Gaitskell, Francis Williams, city editor of the *Daily Herald*, Graham Hutton and Douglas Jay, both from *The Economist*, and Ernest Bevin were co-opted. At the same time, the policy subcommittee of the NEC set up its own advisory committee on the Ottawa trade agreements to explore the policy issues raised by imperial preference. Hugh Dalton was the chairman, and John Parker, secretary of NFRB and recently elected to Parliament, served as the secretary. Durbin, Gaitskell, John Wilmot, and later Douglas Jay, were co-opted onto this committee.

In the midst of continuing controversy, the Labour party was beginning to face the question of how a Labour government should conduct a coherent foreign trade policy in the existing capitalist world. Some regarded it as a political matter; a socialist government should only trade with socialist countries, the USSR being the obvious candidate. Others saw it as a planning issue, both in the aggregative sense of using trade policy to promote export industries and in the allocative sense of directing imports to the appropriate industries. The pricing of exports and imports presented another problem, because British goods would have to compete in world markets. Still others felt that foreign trade was not an ideological question at all, but simply a problem of managing Britain's position in the world economy. The economists were struggling to understand the connections between trade and employment policy, and to translate their knowledge to practical and viable party positions.

In July 1936 the NFRB published a pamphlet, *Foreign Trade*, by Harold Barger, which marked an important step in sorting out the different issues involved in determining an appropriate socialist trade policy.[18] The most innovative section spelled out why the value of the pound would affect foreign trade policy, whatever planning schemes for exports and imports the government might adopt. The pamphlet also recommended that socialist foreign trade should follow 'free trade principles', because it was the only way to increase Britain's standard of living, the ultimate test of socialism's effectiveness. Barger recalls that Leonard Woolf and Richard Greaves of the Bureau's international section were active participants in the research (in fact, he thinks they wrote it). Since Woolf was an influential member of the party's international committees, this position was well represented in the policy-making process.

In October 1936 John Parker organized an NFRB conference on international commercial policy as part of his investigation of trade questions.[19] Sir Arthur Salter, a Liberal, who strongly supported planning and the League of Nations, was invited to open the proceedings. Parker himself gave a paper, which favoured building up a group of democratic countries with lower tariffs between them. But Gaitskell was critical of the idea; he argued that it would not work with current import restrictions, and that the party's nationalization priorities precluded further extension to other industries. In another session Graham Hutton emphasized the importance of preventing pressure on the pound and recommended removing quotas, reducing tariffs, linking foreign trade policy to internal recovery and making financial arrangements to carry the likely import surplus. He remembers that he was heckled by those in favour of quotas and the party's support for trade boards, in particular both the Coles and Dick Mitchison. Cole disputed whether existing market forces could be trusted to decide which countries should produce what goods. He believed that planning was essential in foreign trade, and in his own paper he discussed at length the appropriate import and export board machinery for this purpose; in response to a question by Gaitskell, he acknowledged that he would use price controls.

Although there are few records of the party's committee discussions on trade policy, the final reports reflect their preoccupation with trying to understand its political and economic implications and to work out a consistent position. For instance, the Ottawa trade agreements report signed in November 1937 by E. Shinwell (chairman), John Parker (secretary), Hugh Gaitskell and Douglas Jay, among others, described the opposition's disarray in Parliament:

> Sometimes it opposes and sometimes it ignores the orders of the Import Duties Advisory Committee. Its action or lack of action seems to depend upon the varying opinions of certain members of the Party and, if the Executive consider the matter and reach a decision, the result is not always conveyed to the members of the Party. Members frequently follow Liberals into the Division lobby upon 'Free Trade' amendments without any previous decision on the matters. On the other hand, members for agricultural and iron and steel divisions usually support proposals for the protection of the dominant industries in their constituencies, and members for mining divisions frequently back suggestions for coal subsidies and export bounties.[20]

The advisory committee urged that in Parliament the party should support any steps towards building up low-tariff groups, but should not be doctrinaire about import duties or trade agreements. They also recommended that, once in power, the party should aim to socialize foreign trade. Until the appropriate planning mechanisms were set up, the party should abolish all quotas, but proceed more cautiously with tariffs because of the revenue consequences. The committee did not support export subsidies, and urged more research on foreign lending, on planning machinery in general, and on the future of British agriculture.

In late 1937 the FTC received two other reports, one on subsidies signed by H. B. Lees-Smith, MP (chairman), Arthur Greenwood, MP and John Nairn (secretary), and one on 'The Rise in Food Prices and Government Food Policy' written by Douglas Jay.[21] At its meeting on 12 January 1938, the committee decided to consider all three together, asking their assistant secretary, W. A. Nield, to prepare an introductory document. They also decided to invite Lord Addison, Sir Walter Citrine, John Parker, Emanuel Shinwell, Francis Williams and other experts to attend. Unfortunately, the minutes of this meeting have not survived, but Nield's report has.[22] It is an interesting document, for it reveals that the party's policy makers had a fairly sophisticated knowledge of the relationships between trade policies and domestic policy, but also that they had significant differences of opinion. In particular, the subsidies report, which condemned their use to prop up the failures of capitalism, clashed with the food prices report, which recognized their necessity as part of an adequate nutritional programme.

Nield himself advised the party to emphasize the aims of its economic policy, 'rather than much talk of machinery, and long term plans for "socializing" foreign trade'. He supported Durbin's advice to the Ottawa trade agreements committee that domestic expansion with fluctuating exchange rates was the only cure to prevent the international deflationary spiral of the early 1930s. But he warned that the terms of trade were moving against Britain and that the long-term balance of trade might be a more serious problem than these short-term considerations. Finally, he outlined a short-term programme which stressed the need for special financial arrangements, if trade barriers were to be lowered.

Meanwhile, on the joint subcommittee on colonial trade, Douglas Jay remembers that he hurriedly put together a paper arguing that, far from obstructing exports, most British and other colonial powers were desperately trying to sell the copper, rubber, tin, cocoa and coffee from their colonies in a deflated world market. He was most impressed when Attlee, one of three 'assiduous' committee members, pointed out all the weak points in his argument; the other two were Leonard Woolf, 'a grave and gloomy figure' but the best informed on colonial questions, and the enthusiastic Philip Noel-Baker, a fervent supporter of the League of Nations. In 1936 the Labour party published a report, *The Demand for Colonial Territories and Equality of Economic Opportunity*, presumably the result of the committee's deliberations. The report recommended removing preferential duties from colonial products and improving access to colonial markets by other countries, particularly the United States. This was the only official change in the party's pronouncements on trade policy before the war.

In short, the party's official policy remained a commitment to stable exchange rates within narrow limits maintained through the Exchange Equalization Account. The proposed import boards represented the party's attempt to compromise between free trade and protection, as well as between market forces and socialist controls. Although most of the party leaders supported free trade in principle, they had come to terms with the fact that some of their members benefited from protection, and had also realized that the tariff system could not be dismantled instantly. But the leadership was divided on the question of committing the party to the long-term socialization of trade, and whether to set up an elaborate system of controls. In its policy work the FTC had clarified the complex relations between foreign trade balances, exchange rates, internal expansion, agriculture and cheap food policies, and had pointed out some of the party's conflicting aims. Clearly, the younger generation were well informed about Britain's trade position, the economists in particular understood the value of fluctuating exchange rates in international policy and a few were prophetically concerned with Britain's long-term trade position.

Implementation of *Labour's Immediate Programme*

A year after the research work to implement the party's new platform had been allocated, the policy subcommittee of the NEC was informed that progress had been made in three areas, trade, food and finance policy. In December 1938 it was reported that 'a start had been made on the task of getting the Policy items of the Immediate Programme put into the form of Heads of a Bill'; finance was nearing completion, electricity and coal were in progress, and further work would be undertaken 'as speedily as possible'.[23] In January 1939, it was decided that only defence policy and fishing policy would be presented for debate at the party annual conference at Whitsun. Consequently, none of the implementation plans were formally debated before the war.

However, the policy subcommittee of the NEC announced in the 1939 annual report:

> The process of completing the work of detailed preparation of the various legislative and administrative measures required to give effect to all items in 'Labour's Immediate Programme' has been continued, and work has now been subsequently completed in respect of Finance, Defence, Transport, Electricity, Coal and Pensions. Considerable progress has been made with the work on the following items of the 'Immediate Programme': Land, Food and Invalidity Pensions.

Since the FTC had prepared the outline of a finance bill, it would appear the party had similar documents for transport, electricity, coal and pensions, even though they have not been preserved at party headquarters. Apparently the backs of mimeographed sheets were very useful during the wartime paper shortages.[24]

The main task of the XYZ club was to revise its earlier reports on financial panic and financial policy in light of later developments. Starting at the NFRB in September 1938, Christopher Mayhew was asked to go through the Labour party's official and unofficial statements on financial policy, to summarize the major gaps and conflicts, and to make recommendations for future research.[25] In his final report he concluded that official employment policy was inadequate, that the constitution of the national banking corporation and the functions of the NIB needed to be defined more clearly, and that the party had no policies towards the stock exchange and insurance companies. However, he also found several memoranda in the files at Transport House and the NFRB, 'which go far to remove these criticisms'. In particular, plans to deal with financial panic had been covered 'very thoroughly' (he recalls waiting for Gaitskell to finish a rewrite). He also thought that unofficial employment policy was well developed, and that Berry and Durbin's 1935 memorandum went a long way towards outlining bank nationalization policy.

Gaitskell's revised memorandum on financial panic drew heavily on the 1935 report, indeed much of it was unchanged. The most interesting additions were a discussion of the exchange problem and a much longer section on the long-term market for securities and the measures for its control. Gaitskell stressed the vital importance of coping with the exchange problem, for in his opinion:

> The failure of the Popular Front Governments in France is largely to be traced to their inability to handle it firmly and intelligently. We believe that a similar weakness here might easily make the

position of a Labour Government impossible. The export of
capital has been the chief weapon by which the right wing anti-
socialist elements in France have frustrated both the employment
policy and the social reforms of left wing governments.[26]

The French experience led Gaitskell to recommend control over the
export of capital, so that an expansionary monetary policy of buying
securities in the open market could not be subverted by converting the
proceeds into foreign currencies. In this revised memorandum, he also
gave greater emphasis to the control of prices in the long-term gilt-
edged market than he had earlier. Indeed, he now argued that with
the Exchange Equalization Account the problem of short-term interest
rates was not very serious.

At the same time another memorandum was being drawn up, 'to
serve as a basis for a general discussion of Labour's financial policy
and preparedness for power in that respect'.[27] Although the authors
were not cited, it is likely that Durbin, Jay, Nield and possibly Berry
had a hand in it; they used the earlier documents, particularly Dalton's
heads of a bill on financial policy, to describe the changes since 1935
and to review existing party policy. The memorandum concentrated
on two important factors, the decision to drop the nationalization
of the joint stock banks and the new monetary control mechanisms
introduced by the National government. After reviewing existing
policy, presumably using Mayhew's work, they suggested that four
matters needed to be considered: whether the joint stock banks needed
further controls; whether the powers of the NIB should be extended
to allow for more than licensing and surveying; what the budgetary
implications of Labour's policies on taxation were; whether some
decisions should be taken to reform the stock exchange.

Drawing heavily on Berry's NFRB pamplet, *The City Today*, and
Jay's recent Labour party pamphlet, *The Nation's Wealth at the
Nation's Service*, the report spelled out the new developments in
Britain's financial system and their implications for party policy.
Besides the altered attitude of the Bank of England to the government,
demonstrated by its co-operation to lower interest rates, Berry had
summarized the critical governmental changes as follows:

A Bank of England bowing down to the Treasury, an Exchange
Equalisation Fund dominating the Exchange Market, a Foreign
Investments Committee supervising longterm foreign lending, and
an Export Credits Department invading the domain of private
bankers – such a few words are the outstanding changes since
1931 in the international machinery of the City.[28]

Furthermore, a number of committees had been developed within the Bank of England, which ensured an adequate flow of information about all the important financial institutions. In particular, the foreign investments committee had extended its operations towards a more 'positive control of foreign investments'. Indeed, Berry suggested establishing a similar domestic advisory body; the nucleus of the NIB could then be formed by appointing a limited number of government representatives to both the foreign and domestic committees. After the war, as the new Labour government prepared to act on its prewar proposals, Berry, who had also written the party's pamphlet, *Why the Banks Should Be Nationalised* by 'A Bank Manager', and who had feared for his career in the City if his political affiliations were known, took great pleasure in presenting these anonymous contributions to his bosses, when they demanded to know 'what these Socialist chaps plan to do'.

At a meeting of the FTC on 25 November 1938, the two new memoranda and the 1935 version of Labour's finance bill were reviewed and discussed. Besides Dalton, W. H. Green, MP, and Nield as secretary, all the co-opted members (Durbin, Gaitskell, Jay, Pethick-Lawrence and John Wilmot) were present. The minutes record that 'a thorough review of the present state of preparedness for power was undertaken', and the secretary was asked to complete work on the Bank of England, NIB and other financial controls. By December an entirely new version of the heads of a bill of finance had been drafted with legal advice from Sir Stafford Cripps.[29] The main differences from the 1935 draft were the exclusion of the joint stock banks and the inclusion of the power of the NIB to 'itself undertake on behalf of approved borrowers the issue of invitations to subscribe for or purchase securities'. At last the NIB was to be given power to raise loans and undertake a constructive investment plan along the lines suggested by Keynes and pushed by the young economists.

At its monthly meeting in February 1939, the policy subcommittee of the NEC discussed the final draft of the finance bill:

> Finance Policy No. 6 was considered, and it was agreed to report to the Executive Committee that the Heads of Bill on Finance had been prepared in accordance with the policy of the Party and that the Policy Committee was satisfied with this draft as being in accordance with Party policy.

Finally, the NEC itself noted that 'the Financial Policy of the Party (including the question of a National Investment Board) had been considered, and Heads of a Bill were now ready for use by a Labour Government'. Although Dalton did not keep this final draft in his papers, it is safe to assume that it did not differ drastically from the version he had worked out in the FTC with the help of the XYZ club.

The machinery of socialist planning was one item conspicuously absent from the party's official platform. Some historians have concluded that the matter was simply not considered, but evidence suggests otherwise.[30] Dalton's very general statements about planning were deliberately excised and the recommendations of the Ottawa trade agreements committee were ignored. According to the NEC minutes, the policy subcommittee considered the question, and asked its constitutional committee to investigate. In June 1938 the progress report on research for the immediate programme stated: 'the consideration of questions of Machinery of Government was left over pending the completion of research on various other subjects, decisions on which would involve Machinery of Government'. Nothing further was reported in the minutes. However, correspondence between Attlee, Morrison and Cole reveal that there were basic disagreements amongst these policy leaders, which undoubtedly represented similar divisions within the policy committees.

In 1936 G. D. H. Cole had finally activated the NFRB's planning committee, for which he wrote a lengthy monograph published as a book, *The Machinery of Socialist Planning*, in 1938. Besides discussing general planning problems, he outlined various options for cabinet control of planning. His own recommendation was for a minister of planning directly under the prime minister, because 'he alone could have sufficient authority to settle departmental confusions and conflicts of jurisdiction, and to secure that other departments should work in effectively with the new department'.[31] Such a minister would have a similar relation to the prime minister as the secretary of the Treasury had to the chancellor of the exchequer. Cole also suggested supervisory commissions with planning authority over groups of related nationalized industries, rather than the independent public boards already in operation. Existing departments would be responsible for this co-ordinating role in the first instance, but later ministers might prefer to set up commissions, which would be directly responsible to themselves.

In August 1937 Cole's monograph was sent to Attlee and Morrison, among others, for their comments. Their replies reflect the deep divisions which existed on the appropriate form of democratic control within the British system, in addition to the disputes over pricing policy already discussed at length. Morrison wrote in a friendly holiday mood, but Attlee was quite sarcastic: 'I do not find myself much in agreement with the proposals in the pamphlet.'[32] Neither liked the commissions nor their relation to ministers, but for opposing reasons.

Morrison thought the boards would have 'no real sense of responsibility and will evade when troubles arise', Attlee that a minister who could hide behind a commission was not really responsible. Nor did they approve Cole's suggested relationship between the prime minister and the minister of planning. Morrison believed 'P.M. control would be an illusion – he should have too much to do in *leading* the Government and the Party and keeping his hand on *all* big matters'; he preferred to divest the board of trade of its regulatory powers and modernize it 'as the Department of Economic Planning, functioning for industrial affairs as the Treasury does for state finance'.

Attlee felt Cole did not appreciate 'the differentiation of function between large-scale planning and departmental carrying out of a plan':

> My conception of the work of the Minister of Economic Planning is that of a general with the H.Q. Staff to whom the heads of administrative departments are as Army commanders. It is the function of the Min Planning to take general decisions which must be implemented in the departments. He would be one of several ministers charged with the general direction of specific functions, e.g. Defence, Social Services, exter(nal) affairs, etc. These would form the inner cabinet with the P.M. etc. The Min Planning would preside over a Committee of ministers who are in charge of departments concerned with economic functions. He would be the interpreter to them of Cabinet decisions and to the Cabinet the representative of the group of Ministers dealing with economic affairs. Its general staff would be in touch with the general staff of his colleagues who are in charge of other functions.

In short, the party did consider planning machinery, but it was deeply divided on the appropriate form and functions.

Conclusions

By the outbreak of war the Labour party had travelled light-years in the depth and sophistication of its knowledge of British financial institutions and economic policy options since the dark days of 1931. In a long process of research and debate, a practical programme of institutional reform had been officially adopted, which would ensure central control over the forces determining money supply, exchange rates and investment. The party had also committed itself to a series of proposals to reduce general unemployment and to direct particular investment projects to the distressed areas. A complementary programme to nationalize railways, coal and electricity had been thrashed out simultaneously, which would substantially increase the public sector. Unofficially, detailed and systematic plans to cope with negative banking, business or speculative reactions to the election of a Labour government had been worked out by the party's powerful finance and trade committee. Neither the financial crisis of 1931 nor the failure to deal with depression unemployment was likely to be repeated out of ignorance. Furthermore, the education of its leaders and the establishment of an informed and professional group of financial and economic experts had greatly increased the party's competence to handle overall economic policy and its flexibility to meet new situations.

Despite these enormous strides, the party's view of fiscal and monetary policy remained fairly orthodox. Although the young experts pushed for Keynesian prescriptions to reduce unemployment, such unorthodox methods as budget deficits or fluctuating exchange rates had been deliberately excluded from the 1937 election programme. The party had avoided mentioning the role of planning; it had no proposals to set up planning machinery, other than the nationalized Bank of England, the national investment board and the regional authorities to assist depressed areas. Finally, although the principle of full compensation to the existing owners had been established at the 1934 conference, little or no thought had been given to the problems of pricing, wage negotiations or working conditions within nationalized industries, nor to the management of surpluses or government subsidies between industries, the crucial allocative role of government in a planned economy.

The party's policy subcommittee finally adopted Keynesian full-employment goals in April 1944, when they accepted with minor amendments Dalton's paper on 'Full Employment and Financial Policy', which Durbin and Gaitskell had helped him to draft.[33] As chairman of the economics committee of the Fabian Society (amalgamated with the NFRB in 1939), Durbin had induced many prominent disciples of Keynes to participate in the background research for this position paper.[34] Nicholas Kaldor, who was working for the Beveridge committee on social services at the time, served on this committee, and on another with Richard Kahn and Joan Robinson to explore the national income implications of providing a wide range of social services; Joan Robinson wrote a pamphlet on planning; they all attended a Fabian conference on full employment. Consequently, Dalton could claim that his final report was 'largely Keynesian'. He wrote triumphantly, 'So the Labour Party won the race on full employment. We were in print first, with His Majesty's Government second and Beveridge third.'[35] James Meade helped to prepare the government

White Paper and Kaldor drafted Beveridge's report on full employment. The Labour party's nationalization programme to expand the public sector, its use of progressive taxation to redistribute income and wealth, Beveridge's comprehensive social service network to eradicate poverty and Keynesian economic management became the major ingredients of the British version of the mixed economy after the war.

In addition to their direct contributions to party policy, the young economists were particularly important for focusing attention on the necessary means for managing the capitalist economy to achieve the party's short-run and long-run goals. Their approach was rooted in the practical realities of existing institutions and problems. Its intellectual rationalization was itself to form the basis for the new political and economic revisionism of the next generation. Beside Hugh Dalton's exposition and justification of the party's 1934 programme in *Practical Socialism for Britain* (1935), the other crucial contributions to emerge from this process of rethinking were Douglas Jay's *The Socialist Case* (1937) and Evan Durbin's *The Politics of Democratic Socialism* (1940). Jay outlined the rationale for the redistributive measures and the macroeconomic policies necessary to alleviate poverty; thus, he incorporated the new Keynesian analysis with the traditional socialist approach to the progressive taxation of income and wealth. Durbin provided the revised political theory for democratic socialism, building on the continuing work of the Durbin–Gaitskell discussion groups in the late 1930s. In the mid-1950s John Strachey wrote to Gaitskell that these works, together with Keynes, had converted him from Marxism to the view that 'a way through did exist'.[36]

Hugh Gaitskell believed that Durbin's contribution best summarized the views of that group. Shortly before he became leader of the Labour party himself, he wrote the preface for a 1954 edition, in which he elaborated as follows:

The most fundamental ideal of those who shared this outlook was social justice. . . . They were equally devoted to democracy and personal freedom. They believed in tolerance and they understood the need for compromise. They were for the rational and the practical, and suspicious of large general ideas which on examination turned out to have no precise content. . . . They wanted to get results. . . . They were realistic in politics and critical of armchair politicians. Above all, while accepting the ultimate emotional basis of moral evaluation, they had great faith in the power of reason, both to find the answer to social problems, and to persuade men to see the light.

They shared the belief that society could be transformed through democratic parliamentary procedures, that social injustice could be removed through redistribution and that economic planning could replace the capitalist system.

CHAPTER 13
THE NEW ECONOMIC
REVISIONISM

The apparent collapse of capitalism in the great depression precipitated an extraordinary intellectual search for policies to solve the economic problems and for political alternatives to the spectre of revolutionary take-over by the right or by the left. This book has examined in depth the contributions of a group of democratic socialist economists in the British Labour party who met this challenge. They all believed that changes in the economic order, compatible with efficiency and justice, were only realizable through democratic methods of persuasion and compromise. They all believed in the power of central planning to overcome the failures of the market system, to usher in a new age of prosperity and to redistribute income and wealth. Yet, they also disagreed profoundly on the nature of planning in general and on the appropriate use of economics for socialist planning in particular. Although there was reasonable agreement about the proper economic programme for the next Labour government, it is possible to see now that their intellectual differences reflected different visions of the 'New Jerusalem', that is, the character of the reformed British society to which they all aspired in principle.

In Britain, despite (or perhaps because of) the lethargy of the National government, a number of groups within and without the major political parties worked to redefine the economic role of government. Thus, although the 1930s were marked by serious social and political divisions, there was a growing consensus behind 'the middle way', which provided the basis for bipartisan acceptance of the mixed economy after the war. Nevertheless, socialists and non-socialists still entertained very different ideas about the purposes of government economic planning, which gave rise to rather different rationales for the mixed economy. Furthermore, anti-planners, led by Hayek, continued to deplore all these developments, calling them undemocratic as well as inefficient.

While planning purposes differentiated socialists from non-socialists, it was the use of economics, in particular conceptions of efficiency, which distinguished democratic socialists from each other. The emerging clash between socialist economists who were willing to adapt neoclassical economics and those who were not has been one of the major themes of this book. As the new socialist economics was thrashed out in professional circles, Cole and Durbin pursued their own concerns about various administrative problems. In the process each developed a different way to handle the methodological dilemma of applying market criteria to socialist systems, which they consciously contrasted with the ends/means dichotomy elaborated by Robbins in his influential 1932 essay, *On the Nature and Significance of Economic Science*.

The economic discussions among democratic socialists in the 1930s provided the intellectual basis for their subsequent adoption of the mixed economy, although the interweaving of policy goals and theoretical models resulted in different implicit rationales. There were four main strands to the policy imperatives of British democratic socialism. There was the traditional argument for extending the public sector on the production side by nationalizing some industries. To this had been added the necessity for government intervention to maintain employment and growth. These imperatives were tempered by two other considerations, the political logic of a transitional stage and the commitment to consumer choice. Democratic socialists differed in the relative weights they attached to these strands, in the choice of economic models for specific policies and in the use of conventional economic analysis as the criterion for evaluating socialist economic performance. The concluding section of this chapter, therefore, distinguishes three quite distinct perspectives, each with its own implications for the theory and practice of socialist planning, each based on a different vision of the new society.

The new political revisionism to emerge from the complex process of rethinking the Labour party's platform was carefully articulated at the time; it has been discussed, dissected, attacked, defended, rejected and re-revised ever since. In contrast, the new economic revisionism was often implicit, rather than explicit, and has to be gleaned from the surviving record. In his introduction to *The Politics of Democratic Socialism*, Durbin promised to write a complementary study on the economics of democratic socialism, which would be 'concerned with the economic organization of a democratic and socialist economy'. The unpublished notes for this book were rediscovered amongst Gaitskell's papers after being 'lost' for twenty years. Together with his published work they provide a good idea of his economic perspective, which Gaitskell evidently shared. In April 1949 Hugh gave a speech on the economics of democratic socialism which drew largely on Evan's notes.[1] This chapter distinguishes their approach from more centrist positions to the right and from more radical views to the left.

The mixed economy, planning and democracy

In an important article Arthur Marwick has described the contributions of various groups, PEP (Political and Economic Planning), the Next Five Years Group, the National Labour Committee and the peace ballot movement, to the discussions of the mixed economy during the 1930s.[2] Although he did not include the New Fabians in his discussion, some of the important figures he identified were also members of the NFRB, and others attended NFRB conferences. Marwick argued that the similarity in the conclusions reached by the different groups often transcended their political positions. Thus, after the war there was general recognition of the government's responsibility to intervene in the economy, particularly at the macroeconomic level.

PEP was founded in March 1931 on the day after the NFRB: the Next Five Years Group started at an Oxford congress in 1933. The main effort of the group was to come up with a programme which could be put into effect in one parliament. Their first manifesto, on 'Liberty and Democratic Leadership', was signed by many influential Labour leaders including Bevin, Lansbury and Dalton. Their final report, subtitled 'an essay in political agreement', was based on two fundamental principles, the planned reorganization of British industry and the end of war by collective action. In this early effort the rationale for government intervention in industry was based on microeconomic efficiency considerations. It was only after the publication of *The General Theory* that macroeconomic policies were incorporated, as for example in Harold Macmillan's *The Middle Way* (1938). Macmillan, a member of the Conservative party, was an active leader of the group, together with Clifford Allen, Geoffrey Crowther, Julian Huxley and Sir Arthur Salter among others.[3] Keynes himself contributed most directly to Liberal party thinking, particularly to Lloyd George's 'New Deal' for the 1935 election. This programme built upon his ideas for macroeconomic intervention, as well as American experience.

Whether justified on macro- or microeconomic grounds, the primary purpose of all these programmes and planning efforts was to revitalize capitalism, not to replace it. Liberals remained vague on the possible need for institutional reforms to ensure the implementation of their economic platform. In 1931 Keynes signed the recommendations of the Macmillan committee for the reform of Britain's financial institutions; he also supported the nationalization of the Bank of England and the formation of a national investment board. But there is nothing in *The General Theory* to indicate which reforms he thought essential to carry out a successful expansionary programme. Progressive Tories were explicit that their programme was designed to save Britain from socialism. Their pursuit of industry rationalization and import protection was designed to increase British competitiveness in world markets, but its effect was to encourage monopolization at home. Thus, ironically, their paternalistic view of government's role had more in common with the Labour party's marketing and trade boards than with free-market enterprise.

The democratic socialists were united in their determination to avoid the disasters which befell the second Labour government, and, in studied contrast to Liberal and Tory versions of the planning alternative, to institute a significant step towards socialism. Since they were also committed to the British parliamentary system, the Labour party, at the urgent prodding of its moderate leaders, had come to the realistic conclusion that socialism would have to be introduced in stages. Thus, at one level a mixed economy was simply the logical outcome of this political necessity; it represented a first step on the road to the socialist planning solution. The party was also determined not to repeat the mistakes of 1931, and to come to grips with the unemployment problem. Many of the economic leaders were convinced that expansionary intervention would be necessary during the transition. Furthermore, the young economists were insisting that the socialist state would need to have its own policy to maintain full employment and growth, in order to justify the voter's confidence in the benefits of socialist planning.

Given these political grounds for accepting a transitional period and interventionist policies, the economists agreed that the market-pricing mechanism would play some role in the socialist state. Where the line was to be drawn between market forces and state control distinguished the democratic socialist approach from Marxist forms of planning to the left and from non-socialist rationales for planning to the right. The new socialist economics was an innovative contribution to the general development of thought about government intervention. It reflected a dual commitment to economic efficiency and to individual freedom, particularly in choosing jobs in the labour market and goods and services in the consumer market.

In 1944 Professor Hayek launched his new polemic against all forms of planning under the contentious title, *The Road to Serfdom*. Since he had failed to convince his economic colleagues that government intervention would worsen both the trade cycle and allocative inefficiency, he frankly broadened his attack to include its political dangers and to insist that planning inevitably led to the suppression of political liberty. Furthermore, he held that the partial planning of a mixed economy might actually be worse than a completely centralized authority, for it allowed independent monopolies to run industries along syndicalist lines.[4] His dire warnings of 'the totalitarians in our midst', including the Labour party's support of policies 'which must lead to the destruction of democracy', certainly weakened his case with those planners who were concerned about political implications. Most British planners, however, dismissed Hayek; they believed that central planning problems were irrelevant to their own recommendations, that Hayek wildly overstated 'the power of the planner over our private lives', and that he had not shown 'any appreciation of the evils which have given rise, at least on the part of public-spirited persons, to a demand for planning'.[5]

Some democratic socialists, notably Barbara Wootton and Evan Durbin, went further to suggest that planning in fact enhanced political freedom. Wootton propounded this thesis at length in her book *Freedom under Planning* (1945). She modified her previous faith in experts, and accepted that Parliament must have the ultimate responsibility. But she also raised what seemed to her the two major political dilemmas of planning in Britain: one was the conflict between planners' priorities and the traditional freedom of collective bargaining; the other was 'that economic planning demands continuity, and political freedom appears to imply instability'.[6] Wootton predicted that regulation of wages would be 'the most stormy' of the two, and argued that the dilemma could only be solved if a national 'wages policy' were administered by a reformed trade union movement, which renounced its advocacy of particular group interests, or by compulsory arbitration; either alternative would require only a small loss of liberty compared to industrial conscription of the Russian variety. On the second she believed that planning was only possible without sacrificing political freedom, 'if the limits of any plan which is to be exempt from continual disturbance fall within the boundaries of general agreement on the purposes which the plan is to achieve'. In short, Wootton disagreed with Hayek that political agreement on all planning decisions was necessary to preserve freedom, but she did recognize that there would have to be bipartisan agreement on extra-parliamentary planning powers; the difficult task would be to set the appropriate limits.

Durbin, who reviewed *The Road to Serfdom* for the *Economic*

Journal, basically agreed with Wootton. In marginal notes on her book, he pronounced her analysis of the wage dilemma 'brilliant'. In *The Politics of Democratic Socialism* he had demolished Hayek's and Robbins's arguments that the state should intervene only to remove monopolies and to protect competition. He had pointed out that their proposals were in fact contrary to the expressed political will of the majority, for a vast array of specific measures had already been enacted to mitigate the insecurity of the capitalist system; in other words, 'their political theory is incompatible with their economic policy'.[7]

Durbin's new attack focused on Hayek's assumption that economic planning meant 'the imposition of a complete budget of production' by a central authority over which the ordinary citizen would have no control. Durbin explained that this was not what most planners meant by economic planning: 'We use that term to indicate a *principle of administration and not an inflexible budget of production*'.[8] Since there would be no specific plans, there would be no need to obtain political agreement on detailed economic decisions, only on the method for making such decisions. (In his unpublished notes Durbin criticized his fellow socialists, Cole and Dalton, for making the same mistake.) He also rejected Wootton's second dilemma, writing in the margin, '(a) planning does not imply continuity in the sense of inflexibility over long periods of time (b) political freedom need not result in instability – the element of reversal or repeal is very limited in our political history.' Unfortunately, contemporary history is busily proving him wrong on this particular score.

More fundamentally, Durbin saw economic planning as a '*change in the direction of responsibility*':

> Instead of looking towards small and unrepresentative minorities
> of shareholders, the persons or Corporations directing production
> would look upwards, or towards a Central Economic Authority,
> for guidance on the larger questions of output, prices, investment
> and costs.

Durbin viewed planning as a technique for organizing the economic system, not as a blue-print with specific objectives. He saw democracy as a method for resolving political conflicts; he saw planning as a method for solving economic problems, which he believed was superior to the capitalist method. Hayek wanted the government to act as the enforcer of a highway code for the economy, but not to tell people how, when or where to drive. To borrow Hayek's analogy, Durbin wanted the government to change the code, to build a better highway system, to regulate safety and speed, to fine polluters, and to allocate the necessary resources to meet citizens' demands about how, when and where they wished to drive.

Finally, as Durbin pointed out, at the heart of this debate were very different conceptions of freedom. He found Hayek 'guilty of a strange inconsistency about personal liberty'. 'The absence of it, in the political sphere, appals him. The absence of it, in the economic sphere, leaves him quite unmoved.' Quoting Hayek's definition of political freedom, 'freedom from the arbitrary power of other men, release from the ties which left the individual no choice but obedience to the orders of a superior to whom he was attached', Durbin continued:

> It never seems to occur to him that *economic* liberty means exactly the same thing, and that one man employed by another, or by a large Corporation, is denied exactly the freedom in his economic relations that Professor Hayek wishes to preserve for him in his political life. Professor Hayek is perfectly aware that political liberty does not mean the absence of political authority and laws. We are politically free because we share in forming the laws, not because we can do what we like. If we are to become economically free, the same principle must apply – that we share in making the economic rules and determine the economic methods by which we are controlled. The social government of industry represents an expansion, and not a contraction, of the liberty in which we live.

To summarize Durbin's position, socialist planning could not only surpass capitalism's economic record by ensuring full employment and socially efficient allocation, it could improve upon democracy as well. He saw the state as a benevolent force for improvement, in contrast to Hayek's suspicion of any government interference and fear of its potential for authoritarian rule.

Socialist planning and efficiency

The most obvious difference between socialist economists at the time was the question of whether to use price controls or market pricing as the allocative mechanism under socialist planning. There were less obvious, but equally important, differences among the new socialist economists, who did accept orthodox microeconomic tools, about how to evaluate efficiency in the socialist state.

The new orthodox economics to emerge from the theoretical break-throughs of the 1930s combined the notions of aggregative efficiency, that is, the full employment of all resources, with allocative efficiency, that is, the optimal deployment of those resources between economic activities. There were grounds for intervention when the market failed to meet those conditions for any reason. Thus, it was generally agreed that the government should undertake the responsibility to restore and maintain fulll employment, to prevent inflation and to ensure growth through its macroeconomic policies. It was also called upon to supply public goods, to correct for externalities, and to intervene when and where monopoly power threatened efficient allocation. Socialist econo-mists could thus use the newly honed criteria to answer three planning questions, how to solve unemployment, which industries to nationalize and what prices to charge.

It is perhaps ironic that Robbins, one of the arch-antagonists of the new planners, should have helped to resolve the dilemma of applying neoclassical criteria to socialist systems. In his methodological study he clarified the distinctions between positive and normative economics, which has informed the conventional approach to the role of econ-omics in policy formation ever since. He firmly believed that economic science had no part to play in choosing between political goals; in Durbin's phrase, he was 'the most outspoken champion of pure logic'.[9] Robbins's approach had two important implications for socialists. First, they could use market economics to trace the economic conse-quences of their interventions or to work out the most efficient ways to meet their objectives. Second, economics could not and should not be used to evaluate the two central questions for socialists, the degree of income inequality and social injustice. The relative merits of such goals had to be judged on other grounds, social, political and moral, but not economic.

Despite these clarifications, Cole continued to reject neoclassical economics; he wanted to integrate economic and socialist goals, which he attempted to do in his own theory of the economics of planning. Building on his earlier work he developed the conceptual framework for a centralized planning system in his book, *The Machinery of Planning*, which he had written for the Labour party's policy committee. He began with an exposition of the six basic economic questions which the machinery must be able to handle. He had evid-ently learned from the new socialist economics, for these essentially spelled out the efficiency criteria and evaluative standards defined by Dickinson, Durbin, Lange and Lerner.[10] In a short chapter on price controls, he also considerably softened his views on the use of market pricing, at least in the early stages, and admitted that there should not be 'in general, any divergency of state price-fixing policy from the principle of marginal costs'. But Cole remained a price controller; he expected that eventually 'boards of control' would be established for non-socialized industries, which would institute actual price controls, 'where necessary'. He was greatly influenced by Henri de Man, a Belgian socialist, who drew up a comprehensive 'Plan du Travail' for the Belgian Labour party. Cole translated the plan, and persuaded the NFRB to publish it with his introductory explication in 1935.[11] A reformist plan, it proposed to take over the banking system, in order to ensure prosperity, as well as all privately owned monopolies. Thus, although Belgian captialism was significantly different from the British system, the political and economic imperatives of the period led to a similar socialist planning strategy.

After the war, in a final attempt to outline an operational Hobsonian model, Cole argued that socialist economics must take 'due account of all the factors, in accordance with value judgments based on the socialist principle that in the last resort all men have equal rights to the means to happiness, as far as these depend on the use of human effort in production and on the distribution of the products of such effort'.[12] More specifically, he rejected orthodox economics because it postulated 'the private ownership and control of the means of production, the private appropriation by the owners of the rewards accruing to those factors, and the determination of these rewards by the laws of the so-called "free market", in which both goods and services, including the services of men and women in every sort of labour, are sold for what they will fetch'. In contrast, he explained:

> Socialist Economics set out not merely from a different set of postulates, but also from postulates of an essentially different kind. Socialist Economics is not merely an attempt to describe and analyse what happens under certain underlying conditions, but also to discover what ought to happen in the interests of the general well-being of society and of its members. The socialist postulates are not unanalysed facts derived from current capitalist practice, but *norms* – that is, fundamental objectives which the economic factors, as far as they are under men's control, are to be deliberately shaped to further.[13]

Cole catalogued twelve main postulates which outlined these fundamental objectives; in subsequent chapters he spelled out their implications for planning, employment, production, economic democracy and international economics. Although more explicit about the socialist objectives, the valuation system was still sketchy. As a 'new' socialist economics, Cole's analytic apparatus had not developed greatly beyond his 1935 *Principles of Economic Planning*.

In the late 1930s Durbin pursued his own concern to devise realistic pricing rules and appropriate incentives for nationalized industries in further informal think-tank discussions. He explored the practical details of economic planning at the factory level, especially the use of cost accountancy and management incentive schemes. His old Oxford friend, Sir Anthony Bowlby, has recalled coming to London from Birmingham to talk to the group about his experiences as a manager at Guest, Keen and Nettlefold. Another important contributor to these discussions was Austen Albu, an engineer and works manager for Electrolux, who had joined the ILP and the Fabian Society in the 1920s under the intellectual influence of Tawney's *Acquisitive Society* and the rhetorical eloquence of Sir Oswald Mosley. He had participated in NFRB discussions as early as 1933, when he was reported to be working on 'costings', and in later conferences. He remembers becoming very impatient with the endless group discussions of Keynesian policies and their complete ignorance of the technical problems of management. He later wrote a pamphlet, *Management in Transition* (1942), which Durbin kept in his file of notes for the economics of democratic socialism. These discussions were crucial for introducing Durbin to the contemporary literature on the managerial revolution, which figured prominently in his diagnosis of the development of capitalism and his prescriptions for socialist management.

Under the threat of war with the fascists, Durbin was also concerned about the personal motivations which led to aggressive behaviour. In close collaboration with John Bowlby and George Catlin, he pursued research into its psychological causes. They organized a symposium on war and democracy, and invited contributions from their friends and fellow discussants. The result was published as a book in 1937. According to Bowlby, all the reviewers remarked on the very varying quality of the papers. Consequently, in 1938 the publisher decided to reprint only the Durbin and Bowlby papers under the title, *Personal Aggressiveness and War*. It is an impressive study, the first of its kind. Bowlby is still proud of its contribution, although he now thinks rather differently about the content. In the *Politics of Democratic Socialism*, Durbin built on this work to identify the social institution of government as 'a potent cause of peace' and to emphasize the unconscious emotional education and the irrational motivations of social groups. He concluded that 'the categories of rational thought and conscious purpose are not sufficient by themselves to make social behaviour intelligible or the choice of policy well grounded'.[14]

It is clear from his rediscovered notes that Durbin defined efficiency more broadly than did orthodox economists, and more scientifically than Cole. Under a chapter heading, 'The General Conditions of Economic Efficiency', he listed six problems which any system faced: the distribution of human resources including such matters as training, selection and 'the random distribution curves of human gifts'; the provision of the best incentives; the best organization of the production units; the principles of sound and economic accountancy; and the preservation of adequate investment, full employment and foreign trade. The most innovative contribution in these notes is undoubtedly his lengthy discussion of the necessary forms of organization and motivation to make the system operational; even today its approach is unique and many of its conclusions prophetic.

Durbin considered that the questions of organization and motivation in the planned economy were inseparable, and raised four main problems:

1. How the representative production unit is to be organized;
2. How will the central machinery of planning be constructed;
3. The general problem of incentive;
4. Particular problem of workers' control.

He also believed that these questions were all fundamentally psychological in origin, and that their answers were dependent upon the existing nature of political institutions. Thus, Durbin introduced psychology and political science to his analysis of efficiency. However, he hastened to point out that as yet there were no general theories of individual or group behaviour; in particular, he warned economists against dogmatism on the issues, taking Professor Robbins to task for assuming that 'people will always behave stupidly in the mass' and resist changes in the common interest. Since the contemplation of dictatorship of the communist or fascist type made him 'feel sick', Durbin concentrated his own analysis upon democratic forms of incentive and control.

For the purposes of his investigation Durbin assumed that planned democratic economics would preserve the principle of 'earnings differing according to ability', and that discipline in the workplace could not be solved by the direct election of workers (democracy does *not* mean that 'the unruly crowd elects its own policemen, criminals elect their own wardens'). Managerial efficiency would require decentralized administration to provide responsibility and a central inspectorate to assess efficiency, to guard against bureaucratic red tape and to ensure accountability. He concluded that the necessary machinery and incentives for individual production units were clear. He also believed in a comprehensive system of consultation, an extension of the works councils, and even some workers' involvement in 'the normal conduct of discipline'. However, he was adamant that on all cost matters of common social concern, such as wages, hours and the mobility of labour, 'the last word must rest with the representatives of society – and not with the sub-groups of economic interest within it'.

On the question of a supreme economic authority (SEA), the central planning mechanism, Durbin distinguished two questions about which there was little consensus among socialists. The first concerned the urgency of setting up the SEA. Although many Labour politicians believed that it should have a low priority, because it could become 'a delaying organisation', Durbin disagreed. He argued that it was crucial to prevent nationalized industries from establishing their own syndicalist power and to secure the co-ordination of industry and finance, which was 'the greatest advantage of planning'. The second was the actual form of the planning machinery. Durbin recommended a single responsible minister in the early stages ('otherwise nothing will be done') and a cabinet advisory body along the lines of the committee for imperial defence. The SEA itself would be responsible for macroeconomic policy and for co-ordinating the policies of the nationalized industries with the central plan. Its final form would emerge slowly as the socialized sector expanded.

'New Jerusalems' and the mixed economy

The different perspectives on the question of efficiency gave rise to three quite distinct socialist rationales for the mixed economy. They also suggested different methodological approaches to the use of economics in policy making. In this concluding section it is argued that different visions of British society inspired these conceptions of government intervention in the economy and of the role of economics in social policy.

The first rationale rested upon the new orthodox economics, as it emerged after the theoretical breakthroughs of the 1930s. Thus, it combined Keynesian arguments for intervention to maintain full employment with microeconomic arguments for intervention in industries or activities where the market failed. Socialist economists could use orthodox criteria to solve those 'technical' problems, and then add their own political and social concerns to reduce inequality and to promote social justice. This was essentially the economic justification behind Jay's *Socialist Case* and Meade's 1935 'Outline of Economic Policy for a Labour Government'; they both adapted Keynesian analysis and the economics of imperfect competition to meet their socialist goals.[15] This position was generalized by Abba Lerner in *The Economics of Control* (1944), and further refined by James Meade in *Planning and the Price Mechanism* (1948), and by Sir Arthur Lewis in *The Principles of Economic Planning* (1949), which was written for the Fabian Society.

This rationale for the mixed economy was the practical forerunner of the so-called neoclassical synthesis after the war. The synthesis connected the macroeconomic conditions for full employment of all factors of production with the Pareto conditions for optimal allocation, in order to establish the necessary conditions for full system efficiency. It provided the intellectual basis for government intervention in the economy of western democracies for twenty-five years after the end of the war. More recently this approach has been attacked on practical and theoretical grounds.[16] Keynesian remedies have fallen into disrepute, macroeconomists argue about the theoretical foundations of *The General Theory*, and modern welfare economists have undermined many of the theoretical assumptions of Pareto optimality.[17]

G. D. H. Cole completely rejected this rationale; he thought it confused socialism with state economic planning and with the distribution of national income. Indeed, he argued that it produced 'a diluted socialistic doctrine which is little more than Keynesian Liberalism with frills'.[18] Although he had welcomed *The General Theory* enthusiastically, he began to have serious doubts about its application to socialist economics after the war. Cole was primarily concerned with the conditions of production, rather than its gross amount, and with structure rather than growth. Thus, he became increasingly critical of the Labour government after 1948, as it pursued Keynesian full-employment policies and, in his view, neglected the true socialist purpose to replace the capitalist economy. He was still searching for the way to build a new system of social relationships within the productive process and a valuation scale for judging performance which was not based on market criteria. Although he had been one of the first to recognize that social control of industry could take many forms and was opposed to the nationalization of all the means of production, he also refused to accept Britain's postwar version of the mixed economy 'as a permanent resting place'.[19]

Durbin did not reject orthodox tools of analysis, because he recognized that the socialist state would still have to resolve the micro and macro problems of efficiency. He believed that the new system could succeed with a central planning authority dedicated to socialist goals by using those tools to improve upon the employment and growth record of capitalism and upon its ability to allocate resources in the social interest. He also remained 'an unrepentant believer' in the principle of 'consumers' sovereignty for democratic and for efficiency reasons.[20] Nevertheless, Durbin was sceptical that Keynes had solved cyclical problems or that marginal-cost pricing was a practical way to make production and allocation decisions in a socialist economy. Furthermore, he moved beyond the narrow definitions of conventional economic analysis to include political, psychological and sociological insights into the determinants of operational efficiency. Finally, in Durbin's world, the synthesis between the macro- and microeconomic functions of government was to be accomplished by the supreme economic authority. It arose from strategic policy imperatives, not from the theoretical consideration of the conditions for economic efficiency.

Although these three schools of thought on the economics of democratic socialism each provided a rationale for the mixed economy, they rested on quite different conceptions of the use of economics in policy formation. The first, which applied the new version of orthodox economics, implicitly accepted the conventional dichotomy between economic theory and political goals as presented by Lionel Robbins. Cole, who rejected orthodox economics, had essentially outlined a revised and streamlined version of Hobson's heretical system, which merged what ought to be with what is. While he recognized that he could not hope to achieve 'such "elegance" of presentation as is open to those who, setting aside value judgments, are content to move solely in an abstract world of purely market values', he emphatically preferred to be 'an untidy social moralist than leave out half the relevant factors in order to achieve a speciously scientific conclusion'.[21]

Durbin, while maintaining a moral faith in socialism, believed that economics was a science because it employed the scientific method; that is, it proceeded from observation of the facts to the construction of theoretical explanations, which could themselves be verified empirically. However, unlike natural sciences which sought to explain the behaviour of separately identifiable phenomena, such as 'sticks and stones, liquids and gases, stars and electricity', economics was only one among the social sciences, each of which sought to explain some aspect of human behaviour. Durbin was a firm believer in the reforming tendency of all the sciences:

It is the fate of the true scientist – at once sad and challenging – that his work is never done, his results are never final. A theory may stand for three hundred years. But one day it will be replaced. It was always wrong, too limited, eternally provisional. The mystery of the universe still remains. The questing mind moves on – farther and deeper – to a receding goal. Science, in a word, is progressive.[22]

In this optimistic frame of mind, Durbin sought in his own work to apply the disciplines of economics, politics, psychology, history and management to his central concern, 'the happiness of ordinary men and women'. It was a methodology which sought to link the blended approach to economics with appropriate scientific criteria, Hobson's jumble with Robbins's logic.

In the conclusion to *The Politics of Democratic Socialism*, Durbin elaborated his approach to policy:

> It is, in our view, the supreme social duty, the one enduring achievement, so to think and so to act that men and women may sing at their work and children laugh as they play. . . . There is no easy road to social salvation, no gate around the corner that we may simply unlatch, and walk into a garden of peace. We can only deal with each social problem as it arises, and try to preserve the circumstances within which democracy may survive, and the slow but curative processes of a new emotional education bring men nearer to the full stature of their rational humanity.

In what may have been his most pioneering intellectual effort, Durbin was fashioning a new methodology, one appropriate to the analysis of social policy broadly conceived.

Finally, these different rationales were clearly animated by different visions of the kind of society which their protagonists hoped to achieve in Britain. Those democratic socialists who rested their case on the new economic orthodoxy were primarily motivated to remove unemployment, to reduce inequalities in wealth and income and to provide economic and social opportunity for every citizen; they were less concerned with major institutional change, and least involved with changing individual motivations. Those who joined with Cole in rejecting market economics were seeking to revolutionize social power relationships through some combination of the public ownership of industry with the active participation of workers in economic decision making. Those who agreed with Durbin and Gaitskell rejected both the Webbian vision of administrative control and the guild socialist faith in workers' control. They shared the market economists' belief in the freedom of choice and economic efficiency afforded by the market-pricing system. But they were also convinced that without a strong central planning authority sectional powers could subvert the public interest by creating inflationary pressures in a fully employed economy and by exploiting their monopoly position to allocate resources in their own interests. Furthermore, without the abolition of private wealth and privilege, the lower classes were denied full access to positions of power and prestige, and without significant changes in education and at work the class system would be perpetuated.

CHAPTER 14
CONCLUSIONS

The essence of the revisionist case for socialism is that the capitalist market system can be transformed into a collectivist state without recourse to violent class struggle. Since 1900 democratic socialists in Britain have looked to the Labour party as the political force which would instigate the necessary changes through the parliamentary process. Each generation has had the responsibility for articulating and justifying the policies appropriate to the existing social, political and economic reality which it faced. Until the Second World War the level of government intervention in the private market system was so minimal that there was broad agreement to support a substantial extension of the public sector in the production of goods and services and in the redistribution of income and wealth. Indeed, many non-socialists supported more government intervention, particularly to deal with the effects of the great depression. The socialist intellectuals of the 1930s helped to define the logic, the strategy and the appropriate programme to ensure substantial progress towards a socialist system, even though they disagreed on many of the specifics.

Before the 1930s there had been two contrasting traditions of revisionist philosophy and political strategy in Britain. One was based on MacDonald's gradualist view that socialism would evolve out of the success of capitalism; it stressed short-run concessions, piecemeal reform and political compromise. It foundered with the apparent collapse of capitalism in the depression and the breakup of the second Labour government. The other, which was articulated most forcefully by the Webbs and their fellow Fabians, advocated the gradual expansion of collective activities undertaken by the government through the take-over of existing market institutions and the development of new state ones.

The evolutionary approach lacked any explicit economic rationale. Although Snowden, for example, believed that progressive taxation and increases in social services would eventually achieve more equality, he did not question orthodox methods for handling the country's financial situation. The impetus for reform came from the inspired vision of a new and harmonious society freed from the disastrous consequences of untrammelled individualism. The Fabians, in contrast, had worked out an economic justification for their socialism. Originally it was based on the appropriation of unearned rents from the factors of production; Dalton extended the analysis to cover the redistribution of personal income and the gradual abolition of inherited wealth. Socialism would be achieved by deliberate state action to extend the collective ownership of industry and to reduce vast family fortunes. Eventually an entire structure of boards and commissions would run the economy in the collective interest. Planning would become the alternative to capitalism, because it would provide political control over economic institutions and administrative efficiency in place of the unregulated market.

The new revisionists firmly rejected the Webbian form of planning for many reasons. They believed in the mixed economy on economic and political grounds. Although they were committed to eradicating its social evils, Durbin and Gaitskell did not think that capitalism would inevitably collapse, or that it was some kind of intractable muddle. They wanted planning to improve upon capitalism's economic performance through the control and manipulation of policy instruments, rather than through detailed administration of the entire economy. In collaboration with other socialist economists, they were responsible for important and innovative contributions to the theory and practice of the socialist alternative in Britain. First, they insisted that aggregative and allocative efficiency in the economic sense was essential to the success of socialism. Second, they helped to introduce the Keynesian concepts of economic management to the arsenal of socialist policy instruments. Third, they expanded the notion of allocative efficiency to include all major sources of market failure which required collective action, thus providing a more comprehensive justification for intervention than the nationalization of specific industries. Finally, by disassociating the grounds for intervention from the ownership of factors and by concentrating on policy issues, they broadened the available options for socialist planners; and they went one step further to raise explicitly the question of how economic growth and stability were to be achieved in the socialist state.

Durbin and Gaitskell were clear that socialist economic policy could not be separated from the party's political imperatives or the existing state of the economy. They therefore worked out their political goals and strategy as an integral part of economic policy formation. They also emphasized the democratic importance of specific policies, such as full employment, market pricing, full compensation for the private owners of nationalized industries and methods to cope with financial panic. They were fully aware that by themselves an expanded welfare state, increased real incomes and planning did not constitute socialism. The abolition of poverty, social injustice and class hatred were their socialist goals; prosperity, social services and a supreme economic authority were some of the means for achieving those ends. In the context of the 1930s they sought the necessary instruments to control the economy, to redistribute power from the private to the public sector and from the rich to the poor, and to remove, in Gaitskell's words, 'the three major evils of an individualist system – inequality, insecurity, inefficiency'.[1]

Since democracy was intrinsic to their idea of socialism, Gaitskell and Durbin had faith that a majority could be persuaded that the Labour party's programme was in their interest. Under Tawney's influence they also believed that the kinds of industrial reform they proposed would begin to alter social relationships in Britain, and so reduce class hatred. They identified education as the key to increase equality of opportunity and to release 'immense resources of ability now running to waste'.[2] Their view of the classless society combined Dalton's thrust to remove income inequalities with Tawney's attack on capitalist institutions and his pursuit of the social conditions to create equality of status.

From their analysis of British society and its economic problems, the new revisionists redefined their socialist aims, as well as the appropriate methods for reaching them. Drawing on the Fabian tradition of intellectual leadership, as well as the moral and visionary force for socialist fellowship, they were moving towards a new conception of the state's role. The government was to be responsible for establishing the political, economic and social conditions which would expand horizons and enable citizens to make their own choices freed from the chains of economic necessity and social tyranny. It would not presume to make those choices, only to persuade people what was in their best interest.

Durbin and Gaitskell believed that a socialist government could use rational analysis to solve a wide range of problems. They de-emphasized the Webbs' stress on administrative efficiency and Cole's on direct worker participation, although they recognized their importance for the operational efficiency of public decision making. The newly defined concepts of economic efficiency were key components of their approach to the role of government. Durbin was also searching for appropriate ways to broaden the scientific use of other disciplines, such as psychology, in the planning process. They saw planning as a beginning, not as a panacea; there were still many pitfalls and dangers. They were concerned about the potential monopoly power of vested interests, they worried about inflationary pressures and proper public pricing, and they knew that planners must often make unpopular decisions.

Until the early 1950s, the political consensus within the Labour party behind the programme put into effect by the postwar Labour government disguised underlying differences about the nature of the new society to which they were all committed. In the threatening atmosphere of the 1930s, the New Fabians felt themselves 'a band of brothers' in Sir Vaughan Berry's words, working as comrades to design a realistic socialist future for Britain whatever their differences on specific issues. Since then, this sense of unanimity and purpose has proved elusive. Some seem willing to rest the case for socialism on the combination of welfare services and nationalized industries accomplished after the war; others have reverted to earlier visions of class struggle and workers' control. It has become more difficult to fashion a viable middle ground to provide a programme and rationale for the next stage of socialism in Britain. The roots of the party's intellectual and political schisms are clearly to be found in the different versions of the 'New Jerusalem' identified in this book.

There are many ways in which the discussions of the 1930s seem to come from another planet. The universal faith in the powers of progressive science and enlightened government, the sometimes naive analysis of complex intellectual and social questions, and above all the moral fervour and political passion may appear refreshingly positive, dangerously simple-minded or simply out of touch to this disillusioned and jaded generation. Their elite status as public-school Oxbridge intellectuals and their peculiarly British concerns may seem a far cry from the modern issues of nuclear arms, international finance and multinational corporations. Social science itself has altered beyond recognition; hundreds of thousands of scholars and experts are pursuing ever-more-specialized interests behind artificial disciplinary walls, as they try to climb the greasy poles of academic, corporate and bureaucratic life.

Yet, there are other ways in which the problems of the 1930s have returned to haunt western democracies. As I write, in January 1983, unemployment in some countries has reached prewar depression levels, while vast industrial tracts stand idle and boarded up, ghostly reminders of 'the distressed areas'. Government retrenchment is in, as hard-won gains in social services are slashed and educated professionals join the lines at employment offices. At a recent conference of socialist leaders in Paris, it was reported that they felt frustrated, because 'the economic downturn that helped them win power was now impinging on their proposals for social change'; there was no consensus on what could be done to restore prosperity: 'Each party is itself divided into wings that favor more or less state intervention and different kinds of intervention. And in power, the parties have pursued very different economic strategies.'[3] Once again, economic 'science' is at a loss; there is no agreement about what has caused the current combination of stagnation, inflation and unemployment.

In some respects the world is so different that it would be unrealistic to expect to find specific solutions by an examination of experiences in the 1930s. The public sector, then negligible, now dominates many market economies; a wide range of social services cushions the impact of economic failure on individuals, while it threatens governmental finances. No economist regards the present situation as a simple problem of low levels of effective demand curable by expansionary policies. Those who still call themselves Keynesians either try to reinterpret the *General Theory* models or focus on different problems; others claim that the Keynesian era is over.[4]

Disillusion with the power of government to effect beneficial social change is a widespread phenomenon; it is only partially reflected in the factional disputes which have racked the British Labour party. While many attribute the declining faith in government to the apparent failure of the welfare state and 'great society' programmes to end the class system or to eradicate poverty, the economic success of affluent western democracies combined with the network of social services has effectively wiped out the most obvious cruelties of the unregulated market system. In the 1930s the conditions of the poor were truly terrible, and for those who believed them to be unnecessary and curable a moral outrage was inflamed against the evils of that system. Affluence has undermined this sense of political passion. Where there is social injustice, it is diffused; it results from a wide range of problems, the care of the elderly, the alienation of youth in decaying city slums, the struggles of female-headed families and the pollution of the environment. Thus, the political consensus in favour of social reform has become fragmented in many countries. The success of the mixed economy has cured capitalism's most blatant injustices, while revealing the social problems most difficult to remove and creating others not easily foreseen.

Although it is easy to criticize particular arguments and difficult to recapture the faith in the power of rational scientific progress, there is nevertheless much of value to be relearnt from this study of democratic socialist thinking in the 1930s. First, it demonstrates why economic policy cannot be formulated in a social and political vacuum. Practical policies require careful analysis of the complex interactions between political goals and strategy, between economic theories and their application to relevant issues, as well as informed knowledge of the institutions, motivations and behaviour of the important actors in the process. Second, it emphasizes why those who believe that government action is essential for social progress must define their goals and strategy explicitly. Without prior appraisal of realistic alternatives, it is impossible to establish the critical targets for change in the existing system, and, therefore, to outline an appropriate economic policy to meet the chosen ends.

Social reformers are on the defensive these days; too often they acquiesce to reactionary claims that postwar social legislation has been a failure. Particularly in Great Britain and the United States, the resurgent forces in favour of reducing the powers of the state meet ineffective political opposition and little intellectual resistance. While specific programmes were not as successful as anticipated, and some-times had unforeseen budgetary effects, the reasons are not always clear. Certainly, many advocates were naively optimistic about the possibility of solving complex social problems legislatively. Economists have also shown theoretically that the government can fail to guarantee efficient allocation of resources, as well as the market. Yet, in practice, market economies have grown more monopolistic, not less, and the distinction between public and private activities has become murky in such industries as defence, communications and transport. In this situation, it is equally naive to suppose that simply removing controls will improve efficiency; in fact, the abrogation of governmental respon-sibilities is more likely to lower standards of public accountability than to increase private enterprise.

In short, active government intervention is still essential to stimulate economic growth, to allocate resources in the public interest and to ensure social justice and a better life for all. The ability to improve government's effectiveness depends upon the skills and the commit-ment of social scientists to define problems and to suggest solutions. Thus, economists who believe in the progressive role of public policy should resist popular demands to cut back social programmes indiscri-minately and to renege on public commitments to provide opportuni-ties for the disadvantaged, to tackle the polluters and exploiters of dwindling natural resources, and to help the underdeveloped nations of the world. They must reassert forcefully the lessons of the 1930s: that the benefits of laissez-faire are an illusion in highly organized interdependent economies; that only government intervention can instigate the necessary policies to increase the collective good of all; that only state authority can prevent the unfettered licence of sectional interests from riding roughshod over the public interest. In the 1930s the New Fabian economists expanded the criteria for government intervention and helped to design practical economic policies to improve efficiency. Once again economists are needed to redesign a coherent policy for progressive intervention. They will have to rethink the unsolved problems of growth and stability, to redefine the appropriate allocative criteria for the far broader range of activities which are demanded from modern governments, and to reanimate the search for economic policies which can also bring more social justice.

Leaders who care about reducing economic insecurity and injustice must devise effective programmes to address specific problems and feasible ways to establish public control of vital economic functions, which private market forces cannot perform unaided. Now, as in the 1930s, the central question is to find a strategy which can secure economic growth and egalitarian policies through the practice of the democratic method. To rediscover the way forward will require knowledge, discipline, foresight and imagination. British democratic socialist thought has a rich tradition of designing realistic programmes, which are in tune with their age and which can inspire the necessary vision of a 'New Jerusalem' for the next generation.

NOTES

Full publication details for books and articles are given at their first mention within each chapter.

The author consulted the papers of the following organizations:

The Fabian Society in Nuffield College, Oxford
The Labour party in Transport House, London

She also had access to the private papers of the following:

Colin G. Clark in Brasenose College, Oxford
G. D. H. Cole in Nuffield College, Oxford
Hugh Dalton in the British Library of Political and Economic Science, London School of Economics
Evan Durbin, privately held by Mrs A. M. Durbin
Hugh Gaitskell, now in University College, London
John Maynard Keynes in the Marshall Library, Cambridge
F. W. Pethick-Lawrence in Trinity College, Cambridge
James Meade in the British Library of Political and Economic Science, London School of Economics

The sources of other private papers and special copies are described in the relevant footnote.

All journals and newspapers are cited without abbreviation. Only the following abbreviations have been used:

CCP   Colin Clark papers
EDP   Evan Durbin papers
FAB   Fabian Society papers
FTC   Finance and trade committee of the policy subcommittee of the Labour party's national executive committee
GCP   G. D. H. Cole papers

HDP	Hugh Dalton papers
HGP	Hugh Gaitskell papers
JKP	John Maynard Keynes papers
JMP	James Meade papers
LPCR	Labour party conference report (annual)
LPNEC	Labour party national executive committee
NFRB	New Fabian Research Bureau
PLP	Pethick-Lawrence papers
PPE	Philosophy, politics, and economics honours school at Oxford University
SSIP	Society for Socialist Inquiry and Propaganda

Introduction

1 E. F. M. Durbin, *What Have We To Defend?*, London, Labour Book Service, 1942

2 Philip M. Williams, *Hugh Gaitskell*, London, Jonathan Cape, 1979, Chapter 1, for full details; also for evaluation of the importance of Durbin's friendship.

3 Roy Jenkins, 'Leader of the Opposition', in W. T. Rodgers (ed.), *Hugh Gaitskell: 1906–1963*, London, Thames & Hudson, 1964, p. 131.

4 In a letter to J. A. L. Hammond dated 27 March, 1940 and quoted by Peter Clarke, *Liberals and Social Democrats*, Cambridge, Cambridge University Press, 1978, p. 269.

5 Evan to Henry Phelps Brown, 13 April, 1927; letter kindly made available by the recipient.

6 Williams, op. cit., p. 15. Many of Durbin's friends made the same kind of comments about him.

7 See also Professor R. H. Tawney's address at the memorial service for Durbin in St Margaret's, Westminster, 16 September 1948. The Earl of Longford (Frank Pakenham at the time) was a strong Tory, who worked at Conservative party headquarters until he converted to socialism in the mid-1930s under the influence of his wife and Durbin. Always an intimate friend, Longford credits Durbin with many lucky breaks in his life; see his autobiography *Born to Believe*, London, Hutchinson, 1953.

8 Evan Durbin to Hugh Gaitskell, 14 April 1945, in HGP, folder F-8.

9 The Countess of Longford (née Elizabeth Harman) was at Lady Margaret Hall, Oxford, and a close friend of Hugh's; she later married Frank Pakenham, who also shared digs with Hugh in their last year at Oxford.

10 See Ben Pimlott, *Labour and the Left in the 1930s*, Cambridge, Cambridge University Press, 1977, chapter 4.

Chapter 1 Economics, policy making and the Labour party

1 See, for example, Robert Skidelsky on Oswald Mosley in *Politicians and the Slump*, London, Macmillan, 1967.
2 Sidney Pollard, 'Trade Union Reactions to the Economic Crisis', *Journal of Contemporary History*, vol. 4, 1969, reprinted in Sidney Pollard (ed.), *The Gold Standard and Employment Policy Between the Wars*, London, Methuen, 1970.
3 For early Labour party history see Roger Eatwell, *The 1945–1951 Labour Governments*, London, Batsford Academic, 1979, and Henry Pelling, *A Short History of the Labour Party*, London, Macmillan, 5th edn, 1976.
4 For late nineteenth-century and Liberal party history see R. C. K. Ensor, *England: 1870–1914*, London, Oxford University Press, 1936, and George Dangerfield, *The Strange Death of Liberal England*, London, Paladin, 1970 edn (first published by Granada Publishing in 1935). For a full discussion of the intellectual roots of new liberalism see Peter Clarke, *Liberals and Social Democrats*, Cambridge, Cambridge University Press, 1978.
5 Margaret Cole, *The Story of Fabian Socialism*, New York, John Wiley, 1964, Appendix 1.
6 Clarke, op. cit., pp. 34–6 passim.
7 Cole, op. cit., p. 18.
8 Ibid., p. 32.

Chapter 2 Market theory and socialist economics

1 T. W. Hutchison, *A Review of Economic Doctrines 1870–1929*, Oxford, Oxford University Press, 1953, p. 10.
2 For a fuller discussion, see T. W. Hutchison, *On Revolutions and Progress in Economic Knowledge*, Cambridge, Cambridge University Press, 1978, p. 65. For fuller discussion of the history of economic thought, see Mark Blaug, *Economic Theory in Retrospect*, Homewood, Illinois, Irwin, 1968, revised edn, Eric Roll, *History of Economic Thought*, London, Faber & Faber, 1938, and J. A. Schumpeter, *History of Economic Analysis*, New York, Oxford University Press, 1954.
3 John Maynard Keynes, *Essays in Biography*, New York, Norton, 1951, edn, pp. 182–92.

4 See Peter Clarke, *Liberals and Social Democrats*, Cambridge, Cambridge University Press, 1978, chapter 1, and M. Cranston, 'Keynes: His Political Ideas and Their Influence', in A. P. Thirlwall (ed.), *Keynes and Laissez-Faire*, London, Macmillan, 1978, pp. 101–15.

5 For an interesting discussion of economic theorizing about unemployment policies in the 1920s, see Keith Hancock, 'Unemployment and the Economists in the 1920s', *Economica*, vol. 27, 1960, pp. 305–21.

6 Sir Austin Robinson, 'Discussion', in Thirlwall, op. cit., p. 60.

7 Donald Winch, *Economics and Policy*, London, Hodder & Stoughton, 1969, pp. 169–70.

8 D. E. Moggridge, *Keynes*, London, Macmillan, 1976, chapter 3, and Hutchison, 1953, chapter 23, for a fuller discussion.

9 James Meade, 'The Keynesian Revolution', in Milo Keynes (ed.), *Essays on John Maynard Keynes*, Cambridge, Cambridge University Press, 1975, p. 82.

10 The following discussion is taken from Winch, op. cit., pp. 167–9, and Moggridge, op. cit., chapter 4. The policy implications of *A Treatise* are discussed in considerable detail in Susan Howson and Donald Winch, *The Economic Advisory Council 1930–1939*, Cambridge, Cambridge University Press, 1977, pp. 55–7.

11 Winch, op. cit., p. 170.

12 Hancock, op. cit., p. 310.

13 Winch, op. cit., p. 77.

14 Clarke, op. cit., p. 32.

15 Dan H. Laurence (ed.), *Bernard Shaw, Collected Letters*, vol. 2, New York, Dodd, 1972, p. 558.

16 Hugh Gaitskell, 'The Ideological Development of Democratic Socialism in Great Britain', *Socialist International Information*, vol. 5, no. 52–3, 1955, p. 926.

17 Margaret Cole, *The Story of Fabian Socialism*, New York, John Wiley, 1964 edn, p. 328.

18 Winch, op. cit., pp. 40–1 passim.

19 Hugh Dalton, *Call Back Yesterday: Memoirs 1887–1931*, London, Frederick Muller, vol. 1, 1953, p. 58 and p. 60.

20 Hugh Dalton, *Some Aspects of the Inequality of Incomes in Modern Communities*, London, Routledge, 1920, p. 352.

21 Dalton, 1953, pp. 104–7, passim.

22 Dalton, 1920, p. 353.

23 Gaitskell, op. cit., p. 936.

24 J. A. Hobson, *Confessions of an Economic Heretic*, London, Allen & Unwin, 1938, p. 126.

25 Quoted in Hutchison, 1953, pp. 119–20.

26 J. M. Keynes, *The General Theory of Employment, Interest and Money*, London, Macmillan, 1936, pp. 364–8.
27 J. M. Keynes, *The Collected Writings of John Maynard Keynes*, London, Macmillan, 1973, vol. 13, p. 634.
28 Hobson, op. cit., p. 30.
29 Clarke, op. cit., p. 269.
30 Hobson, op. cit., pp. 46–8 passim.
31 Clarke, op. cit., p. 126 and pp. 48–9.
32 Hobson, op. cit., pp. 164–8 passim.
33 Winch, op. cit., p. 130.
34 José Harris, *Unemployment and Politics*, Oxford, Oxford University Press, 1972, p. 23, and Clarke, op. cit., p. 125.
35 Harris, op. cit., p. 5.
36 Robert Skidelsky, *Politicians and the Slump*, London, Macmillan, 1967, pp. 34–5.
37 Winch, op. cit., pp. 60–1.
38 Harris, op. cit., p. 6 footnote, and pp. 42–3.
39 Clarke, op. cit., pp. 124–5, 152 and 163.
40 See Hutchison, 1953, chapter 18, and Blaug, op. cit., pp. 604–5, for further details.
41 Clarke, op. cit., p. 234.
42 Hobson, op. cit., pp. 164–8 passim.
43 Dalton, 1920, p. 72 footnote 3.

Chapter 3 Economic policy and the Labour party 1918–31

1 Henry Pelling, *A Short History of the Labour Party*, London, Macmillan, 5th edn, 1975, p. 44.
2 Labour Party, *Seventeenth Annual Report*, London, 1918, p. 140. It was only in 1929 that 'distribution and exchange' were added, after 'the common ownership of the means of production'.
3 Donald Winch, *Economics and Policy*, London, Hodder & Stoughton, 1969, pp. 73–5.
4 Sidney Pollard, *The Gold Standard and Employment Policy Between the Wars*, London, Methuen, 1970, p. 103.
5 Donald Moggridge, *British Monetary Policy, 1924–31*, Cambridge, Cambridge University Press, 1972, p. 97.
6 Winch, op. cit., p. 111.
7 Keith Hancock, 'The Reduction of Unemployment as a Problem of Public Policy, 1920–1929', *Economic History Review*, vol. 15, 1962, reprinted in Pollard, op. cit., pp. 108–9.
8 Quoted by Winch, op. cit., p. 118, from *House of Commons Debates*, 15 April, 1929.
9 Ibid., p. 86. This account follows Winch, pp. 85–92.

10 Ibid., p. 158.
11 Ibid., pp. 121–2 passim.
12 G. D. H. Cole, *A History of the Labour Party from 1914*, London, Routledge & Kegan Paul, 1948, pp. 53–5; the book includes a summary of the twenty-six resolutions in Appendix 1 to chapter II and a comparison of the 1914 and 1918 constitutions as Appendix 2, pp. 63–81. Quotations are taken from this source.
13 Hugh Dalton, *Memoirs: Call Back Yesterday*, London, Frederick Muller, vol. 1, 1953, p. 128.
14 LPCR, 1927, pp. 262–4.
15 Colin Cross, *Philip Snowden*, London, Barrie and Rockliff, 1966, p. 83.
16 Ibid., p. 84.
17 Ibid., p. 207.
18 Hancock, op. cit., in Pollard, op. cit., p. 106.
19 Cross, op. cit., p. 205.
20 Alan Bullock, *The Life and Times of Ernest Bevin*, London, Heinemann, 1960, vol. 1, p. 267.
21 W. Adams Brown, 'The Conflict of Opinion and Economic Interest in England', chapter 10, in *England and the New Gold Standard, 1919–1926*, New Haven, Yale University Press, 1929; reprinted in Pollard, op. cit., p. 60.
22 Dalton, op. cit., p. 159.
23 Ibid., p. 129.
24 David Marquand, *Ramsay MacDonald*, London, Jonathan Cape, 1977, p. 478.
25 Labour Party, *Labour and the Nation*, London, Transport House, 1928, passim.
26 See LPCR, 1928, for full details of the debate and all quotations.
27 Dalton, op. cit., p. 183.
28 Ibid., p. 172.
29 Susan Howson and Donald Winch, *The Economic Advisory Council 1930–1939*, Cambridge, Cambridge University Press, 1977, p. 2 and p. 55.
30 Dalton, op. cit., 1953, p. 261.
31 Howson and Winch, op. cit., pp. 46–81 for full discussion of the committee of economists and the economists' report and its effects. The report and its appendices are reproduced on pp. 180–243.
32 Robert Skidelsky, *Politicians and the Slump*, London, Macmillan, 1969, pp. 340ff., and Ross McKibbin, 'The Economic Policy of the Second Labour Government', *Past and Present*, vol. 68, 1975.
33 Marquand, op. cit., p. 610, and J. M. Keynes, 'Some Consequences of the Economy Report', *New Statesman and Nation*, 15 August, 1931.

34 Bullock, op. cit., p. 484.

35 Skidelsky, op. cit., p. xii.

36 McKibbin, op. cit., p. 114.

37 Marquand, op. cit., p. 521.

38 Dalton, op. cit., p. 303.

39 See Reginald Bassett, *Nineteen Thirty-One: Political Crisis*, London, Macmillan, 1958; this was the first study to trace the daily events leading up to the formation of the National government and to absolve MacDonald of this charge in an impassioned defence of his actions. Marquand has confirmed Bassett's account and drawn similar conclusions from a less partisan position (see Marquand, op. cit., p. 614).

40 J. M. Keynes, 'Proposals for a Revenue Tariff', *New Statesman and Nation*, 7 March 1931, pp. 53–4 and subsequent weeks for letters to the editor, including one from E. F. M. Durbin.

41 Howson and Winch, op. cit., pp. 89–90 for full text of Keynes's letters.

42 Winch, op. cit., p. 143.

Chapter 4 New brooms, new policies: the Labour party 1931–5

1 For full details of Labour party history see G. D. H. Cole, *A History of the Labour Party from 1914*, London, Routledge & Kegan Paul, 1948; G. D. H. Cole, *Plans for Democratic Britain*, London, Odhams Press, 1939; Ben Pimlott, *Labour and the Left*, Cambridge, Cambridge University Press, 1977. Other details were taken from Labour party, national executive committee, *Minutes*, London, Transport House (LPNEC) and the annual Labour party conference reports (LPCR).

2 Major Attlee, 'Memorandum: Industrial Policy', Appendix C, typescript, undated, in CCP.

3 See Bernard Donoughue and G. W. Jones, *Herbert Morrison: Portrait of a Politician*, London, Weidenfeld & Nicolson, 1973, pp. 171–9, for a full assessment of Morrison.

4 Alan Bullock, *The Life and Times of Ernest Bevin*, London, Heinemann, vol. 1, 1960, p. 509.

5 Ibid., p. 512.

6 Ross M. Martin, *TUC: The Growth of a Pressure Group, 1868–1976*, Oxford, Clarendon Press, 1980, p. 219.

7 Margaret Cole, 'The Society for Socialist Inquiry and Propaganda', chapter 7 in Asa Briggs and John Saville, *Essays in Labour History: 1918–1939*, London, Croom Helm, 1977; Margaret Cole, *The Story of Fabian Socialism*, London, Heinemann, 1961; John Parker, 'The

New Fabian Research Bureau, 1931–1939', unpublished manuscript, 1976.

8 Donoughue and Jones, op. cit., p. 71.

9 A. W. Wright, *G. D. H. Cole and Socialist Democracy*, Oxford, Clarendon Press, 1979, p. 6.

10 Hugh Dalton, *Call Back Yesterday: Memoirs 1887–1931*, London, Frederick Muller, 1953, vol. 1, p. 285.

11 Vaughan Berry, 'XYZ: The Early Days', unpublished typescript, February 1962. A copy made available by Sir Vaughan Berry.

12 Francis Williams, *Nothing So Strange*, London, Cassell, 1970, p. 112.

13 Pimlott, op. cit., pp. 21–35, for further details.

14 Ibid., p. 24.

15 Evan Durbin, 'C. R. Attlee', unpublished typescript, undated in EDP.

16 Pimlott, op. cit., p. 33.

17 Bullock, op. cit., pp. 515–16.

18 Hugh Dalton, *The Fateful Years: Memoirs 1931–1945*, London, Frederick Muller, 1957, vol. 2, pp. 59–60.

19 See Dalton, 1957, for fullest details; also G. D. H. Cole, 1948, and Pimlott, op. cit.

20 Bullock, op. cit., p. 572, and Donoughue and Jones, op. cit., p. 242.

21 Hugh Dalton, 'Draft for Policy Sub-Committee on Finance and Trade', unpublished, 15 March 1933, in HDP IIA, Folder 2/1.

22 C. R. Attlee and Stafford Cripps, 'The Joint Stock Banks', FTC, Policy no. 102, mimeograph, January 1933, in HDP IIA, Folder 2/1.

23 This phrase first appeared in the 1931 election manifesto and was formally adopted as part of the party's resolutions on 'Currency, Banking and Finance' at the 1932 conference; see LPCR, 1932, pp. 182–94 for entire debate.

24 See Cole, 1948, pp. 287–97; Roger Eatwell, *The 1945–1951 Labour Governments*, London, Batsford, 1979, pp. 23–31; David Howell, *British Social Democracy*, London, Croom Helm, 1976, pp. 65–72.

25 Pimlott, op. cit., p. 198.

26 Howell, op. cit., p. 71.

27 Cole, 1948, pp. 308–12.

28 See Pimlott, op. cit., pp. 194–203; Eatwell, op. cit., pp. 23–31; John Stevenson and Chris Cook, *The Slump: Society and Politics During the Depression*, London, Jonathan Cape, 1977, pp. 245–60.

29 Howell, op. cit., p. 72.

Chapter 5 The new generation

1 Margaret Cole, *The Story of Fabian Socialism*, London, Heinemann, 1961, pp. 211–12.

2 M. P. Ashley and C. T. Saunders, *Red Oxford*, Oxford, Holywell Press, 1930, p. 41.

3 Hugh Gaitskell, 'At Oxford in the Twenties', in Asa Briggs and John Saville, *Essays in Labour History*, London, Macmillan, 1960, pp. 6–19.

4 Evan Durbin, 'The General Strike', unpublished manuscript, August 1926, in EDP.

5 John Parker, 'Oxford Politics in the Late Twenties', *Political Quarterly*, vol. 45, 1974, p. 226.

6 Douglas Jay, *Change and Fortune*, London, Hutchinson, 1980, p. 47.

7 Margaret Cole, *The Life of G. D. H. Cole*, London, Macmillan, 1971, pp. 158–60; the manuscript is in the Cole papers at Nuffield College, Oxford.

8 E. F. M. Durbin, *What Have We to Defend?*, London, Routledge, 1942.

9 Gaitskell in Briggs and Saville, op. cit., p. 15.

10 Gaitskell went straight into PPE; Meade took Honour Moderations in Literae Humaniores (classics) and then switched to PPE; Durbin took one degree in zoology, and then a second in PPE; Clark took his degree in chemistry, but had some tutorials in economics with Robbins.

11 Lord Robbins, *Autobiography of an Economist*, London, Macmillan, 1971, pp. 108–10.

12 Evan Durbin to Colin Clark, 21 February (1930), in CCP.

13 Robbins, op. cit., p. 70.

14 A. W. Coats, 'The Distinctive LSE Ethos in the Inter-war Years', *Atlantic Economic Journal*, vol. 10, March 1982, pp. 18–30 and José Harris, *William Beveridge*, Oxford, Clarendon Press, 1977.

15 Lord Beveridge, *The London School of Economics and Its Problems 1919–1937*, London, Allen and Unwin, 1960, p. 83, quoted in Coats, op. cit., p. 22.

16 Coats, op. cit., pp. 18–30, and Robbins, op. cit., pp. 106–8.

17 Lionel Robbins, 'The Present Position of Economic Science', *Economica*, vol. 10, March 1930, pp. 23–4, quoted in Coats, op. cit., p. 23.

18 Ronald Coase, 'Economics at LSE in the 1930's: A Personal View', *Atlantic Economic Journal*, vol. 10, March 1982, pp. 31–4, and letter to author 11 December 1981.

19 Interviews with Mrs A. M. Durbin, Lord Kaldor, Professor Henry Phelps Brown and Professor Brinley Thomas.

20 Robbins, 1971, pp. 129 and 136.

21 Hugh Dalton, *Diary*, 6–8 January 1932 (London School of Economics).

22 Professor Sir Austin Robinson, 'Keynes and his Cambridge Colleagues', in Don Patinkin and J. Clarke Leith (eds.), *Keynes, Cambridge and the General Theory*, Toronto, University of Toronto Press, 1978.

23 See A. F. W. Plumptre, 'Maynard Keynes as a Teacher', in Milo Keynes (ed.), *Essays on John Maynard Keynes*, Cambridge, Cambridge University Press, 1975, pp. 247–53; Robinson, op. cit.; and Robert Bryce, Walter Salant and Lorie Tarshis, 'Keynes as Seen by His Students in the 1930's', in Patinkin and Leith, op. cit.

24 Richard Stone, 'Keynes, Political Arithmetic and Econometrics', *Proceedings of the British Academy*, Seventh Keynes Lecture in Economics, 3 May, 1978, p. 14.

25 See also Keynes's letter to George Bernard Shaw in J. M. Keynes, *The Collected Works of John Maynard Keynes*, London, Macmillan, 1973, vol. 13, pp. 492–3.

26 Robbins, 1971, p. 193.

27 Robinson, in Patinkin and Leith, op. cit., p. 31.

28 For full detail see Professor Sir Henry Phelps Brown, 'Sir Roy Harrod: A Biographical Memoir', *Economic Journal*, vol. 90, March 1980, pp. 1–33.

29 Professor James Meade to author, 11 August 1982. See also Donald Winch, *Economics and Policy*, London, Hodder and Stoughton, 1969, p. 384, fn. 27 and p. 386, fn. 4.

30 Robbins, 1971, pp. 150–6, for full details.

31 Colin Clark, 'Memoir: the "Golden" Age of the Great Economists', *Encounter*, vol. 48, no. 6, June 1977.

32 F. A. von Hayek, 'Reflections on the Pure Theory of Money of Mr. Keynes, Part I', *Economica*, vol. 11, August 1931, pp. 270–95.

33 J. M. Keynes, 'The Pure Theory of Money', *Economica*, vol. 11, November 1931, p. 394.

34 Winch, op. cit., pp. 199–207, for full details of his views.

35 F. A. Hayek, *New Studies in Philosophy, Politics, Economics and the History of Ideas*, Chicago, University of Chicago Press, 1978, p. 284.

36 It is not clear if this is the same conference referred to by Donald Moggridge in a footnote to a letter from Joan Robinson to Keynes in Keynes, *The Collected Works*, vol. 14, p. 148, (See Select Bibliography).

37 Philip Williams, *Hugh Gaitskell*, London, Jonathan Cape, 1979, pp. 44–8, 61–72.

38 Unsigned, 'Labour Party Policy', mimeograph, February 1935, in HGP, File U3(1).

39 Michael Postan, 'Political and Intellectual Progress', in W. T. Rodgers

(ed.), *Hugh Gaitskell: 1906–1963*, London, Thames and Hudson, 1964, p. 52.

40 Williams, op. cit., pp. 42–3.

41 Ibid., pp. 53–60.

42 Nicholas Davenport, *Memoirs of a City Radical*, London, Weidenfeld and Nicolson, 1974.

43 Sir Vaughan Berry was quite distressed by the inaccuracies in Davenport's memoirs about the foundation of the XYZ club, for which Davenport claimed most of the credit. Since there were other discrepancies between documentary evidence and Davenport's account, this book has relied on Berry's version.

44 Douglas Jay, *Change and Fortune*, London, Hutchinson, 1980, p. 57.

45 Ben Pimlott, *Labour and the Left in the 1930s*, Cambridge, Cambridge University Press, p. 39; Roy Jenkins, *The Pursuit of Progress*, London, Heinemann, 1953, p. 68.

46 Hugh Gaitskell, 'The Ideological Development of Democratic Socialism in Great Britain', *Socialist International Information*, vol. 5, no. 52–53, 24 December 1955, p. 949.

47 Margaret Cole, 1971, p. 170.

48 Hugh Dalton, *The Fateful Years: Memoirs 1931–1945*, London, Frederick Muller, 1957, vol. 2, p. 76.

49 Douglas Jay, 'Civil Servant and Minister', in Rodgers, op. cit., p. 83.

Chapter 6 Cole and the New Fabians attack traditional policy

1 NFRB, *Minutes*, 30 March 1931.

2 Evan (Durbin) to Colin (Clark), 5 March 1931, in CCP.

3 New Fabian Research Bureau, *Memorandum on a Plan of Research into Economic Policy*, London, May 1931, p. 3.

4 Cole to Beatrice Webb, 9 December 1930, Passfield Papers, quoted in A. W. Wright, *G. D. H. Cole and Socialist Democracy*, Oxford, Clarendon Press, 1979, p. 163.

5 Undated list of eight proposed committees and conveners with handwritten notes by Gaitskell in GCP.

6 G. D. H. Cole, 'Memorandum on a Plan of Research into Economic Policy: Revision', mimeograph, undated, FAB, box J10/1.

7 G. D. H. Cole, 'Notes on the Preparation of a Plan for the Socialisation of Particular Industries', NFRB, mimeograph, GCP, file E, undated.

8 Margaret Cole, *The Story of Fabian Socialism*, London, Heinemann, 1961, p. 236.

9 Ben Pimlott, *Labour and the Left in the 1930s*, Cambridge, Cambridge University Press, 1977, p. 37.

10 G. D. H. Cole, *The Essentials of Socialisation*, NFRB pamphlet no. 1, 1931, p. 7.
11 Ibid, pp. 13–14.
12 G. D. H. Cole, 'Memorandum on the Disposal of Profits and the Control of the Expenditure of Socialised Undertakings', mimeograph, 14 December 1931, GCP, file F-2; C. R. Attlee, 'Observations on Cole's Memorandum on the Disposal of Profits and Control of Expenditure of Socialised Undertakings', socialisation committee, mimeograph, 6 January 1932, GCP, file G.
13 Cole, *Essentials of Socialisation*, p. 13.
14 Cole, 'Memorandum on a Plan of Research: Revision', op. cit., pp. 10–11.
15 NFRB, *Minutes*, economic committee, 5 June 1931; wages subcommittee, 19 June 1931 and 17 July 1931.
16 H. T. N. Gaitskell, 'Socialism and Wage Policy' and E. F. M. Durbin, 'Wage Policies and the Capitalist System', mimeographs, undated, FAB, box J24/2.
17 Evan Durbin to Hugh Gaitskell, 15 April 1933, HGP, folder F42.
18 Geoffrey Faber to Hugh Gaitskell, Esq., 28 November 1932; G. D. H. Cole to Durbin, 6 November 1933, in HGP, folder F42.
19 NFRB, *Minutes*, economic committee, 14 November 1932.
20 NFRB taxation committee, *Taxation under capitalism: Effects on Social Services*, NFRB pamphlet no. 12, 1933, p. 15.
21 Ibid., p. 23.
22 Ibid., p. 27.
23 Ibid.

Chapter 7 The New Fabians attack unemployment

1 For early research see Donald Winch, *Economics and Policy*, London, Hodder & Stoughton, 1969. Winch revised these views in Susan Howson and Donald Winch, *The Economic Advisory Council 1930–1939*, Cambridge, Cambridge University Press, 1977. See also D. E. Moggridge and Susan Howson, 'Keynes on Monetary Policy, 1910–1946', *Oxford Economic Papers*, vol. 26, June 1974; D. E. Moggridge, *John Maynard Keynes*, New York, Penguin, 1976; Don Patinkin, *Keynes' Monetary Thought: A Study of Its Development*, Raleigh, North Carolina, Duke University Press, 1976; Don Patinkin and J. Clark Leith (eds.), *Keynes, Cambridge, and the 'General Theory'*, London, Macmillan, 1977; T. W. Hutchison, *On Revolutions and Progress in Economic Knowledge*, Cambridge, Cambridge University Press, 1978; Don Patinkin, *Anticipations of the General Theory?*, Chicago, University of Chicago Press, 1982.
2 Patinkin, 1982, p. 22.

3 See Gottfried Haberler, *Prosperity and Depression*, New York, Atheneum, 1963, for a useful survey of the state of business cycle theory in the mid-1930s. The study was originally commissioned by Alan Loveday, director of economic intelligence for the League of Nations, to discover once and for all whether Keynesian expansion or Hayekian deflation would solve the unemployment problem; he also hired Jan Tinbergen to analyse the statistical evidence. Meade worked on the study in the early days; he recollects that Loveday sought to resolve the 'squabble' between Keynes and Hayek by hiring a theorist to analyse the models and a statistician to test which was right.

4 Haberler, op. cit., p. 33; Norman P. Barry, *Hayek's Social and Economic Philosophy*, London, Macmillan, 1979, chapter 8, especially pp. 160–74.

5 Ronald H. Coase, 'How Should Economists Choose?', Third G. Warren Nutter Memorial Lecture, delivered at the American Enterprise Institute, Washington, D. C., 18 November 1981 and in a letter to the author, 11 December 1981.

6 E. F. M. Durbin, 'Memorandum on the Inquiry into the Price Level and Industrial Fluctuation', NFRB, committee 8, mimeograph, 12 June 1931, in FAB, box J24/3.

7 E. F. M. Durbin, 'Wage Policies and the Capitalist System', mimeograph, undated, in FAB, box J24/2, p. 2.

8 Hugh Gaitskell, 'Four Monetary Heretics,' in G. D. H. Cole (ed.), *What Everybody Wants to Know about Money*, London, Gollancz, 1933.

9 E. F. M. Durbin, *Purchasing Power and Trade Depression*, London, Jonathan Cape, 1933, p. 190.

10 Hobson, who was apparently hurt to have been lumped together with crude money cranks, wrote a reply to Durbin's attack on his view that unemployment was caused by excessive saving, which generated a controversy between the two. See J. A. Hobson, 'Underconsumption: An Exposition and a Reply', and 'A Rejoinder', and E. F. M. Durbin, 'A Reply to Mr. Hobson', *Economica*, no. 42, November 1932, pp. 402–27; for discussion of Hobson's reactions see Peter Clarke, *Liberals and Social Democrats*, Cambridge, Cambridge University Press, 1978, pp. 269–70.

11 Professor Sir Austin Robinson, 'Keynes and His Cambridge Colleagues', in Patinkin and Leith, op. cit., p. 36.

12 Ibid., and interviews. See also Patinkin, 1982, pp. 3–35, and 189–214.

13 E. F. M. Durbin, 'Memorandum on Future Conclusions', mimeograph, undated in JMP, folder 125.

14 NFRB, 'Conference Report on Socialisation of Banking', mimeograph, January 1932, in FAB, box J14/1.

15 Evan F. M. Durbin to Meade, 6 February (1932), in JMP, folder 125.

16 Richard F. Kahn to Meade, 18 April 1932, in JMP, folder 125.

17 Draft of Meade and Harrod letter and all other correspondence in JMP, folder 124. Gaitskell letter is dated 20 June 1932.

18 J. E. Meade, *The Rate of Interest in a Progressive State*, London, Macmillan, 1933. In the preface he acknowledged his debt to Keynes, Robertson, Kahn and W. M. Allen; in addition, he noted that 'Dr Hayek's book *Prices and Production* has also suggested many very important ideas and problems to my mind, though I believe that there is still no argument in that book which I can both understand and accept'.

19 Joan Robinson, '*The Rate of Interest in a Progressive State*, by J. E. Meade: A Review', *Economic Journal*, vol. 44, June 1934, pp. 282–5.

20 Evan F. M. Durbin to Meade, 15 November (1933), in JMP, folder 125.

21 James Meade to Evan Durbin, 18 November 1933, located inside Durbin's copy of J. E. Meade, *The Rate of Interest*, in the Special Collection of the Library of Political and Economic Science at the London School of Economics.

22 J. E. Meade, *Public Works in Their International Aspect*, NFRB pamphlet no. 4, January 1933, pp. 11–13, with an introduction by H. B. Butler, director of the International Labour Office.

23 Colin Clark, *The Control of Investment*, NFRB pamphlet no. 8, 1933, p. 15.

24 Winch, op. cit., p. 355.

25 E. F. M. Durbin, *Purchasing Power and Trade Depression*, London, Jonathan Cape, 1933, p. 180.

26 Gaitskell, op. cit., pp. 346–413. See also Haberler, op. cit., p. 118n and Lawrence R. Klein, *The Keynesian Revolution*, London, Macmillan, 1968, p. 142.

27 E. F. M. Durbin, *Socialist Credit Policy*, NFRB pamphlet no. 15, December 1933, pp. 30–6.

28 John Parker, 'Conference on Some Aspects of Socialist Planning: A report', NFRB, mimeograph, 16 January, 1934, in FAB, box J14/2.

29 Margaret Cole, *The Life of G. D. H. Cole*, London, Macmillan, 1971, p. 199.

30 G. D. H. Cole, *The Next Ten Years in British Social and Economic Policy*, London, Macmillan, 1930, p. 246.

31 Ibid., p. 45.

32 G. D. H. Cole, 'A Socialist View', *The Economist*, 17 October 1931.

33 Colin Clark, 'Investment, Savings and Public Finance', in Cole, *What Everybody Wants to Know*, pp. 434–5.

34 H. T. N. Gaitskell, 'Notes on the Period of Production', *Zeitschrift für National Ökonomie*, vol. 7, no. 5, 1936, and vol. 9, no. 2, 1938. See also Mark Blaug, *Economic Theory in Retrospect*, Homewood, Illinois, Irwin, 1968, p. 569; he noted that Gaitskell was particularly 'illuminating' on the problem of valuation in the average period.

35 E. F. M. Durbin, *The Problem of Credit Policy*, London, Chapman & Hall, 1935, p. 223.

36 R. F. Harrod, '*The Problem of Credit Policy*, by E. F. M. Durbin: A Review', *Economic Journal*, vol. 45, December 1935, pp. 725–9.

37 J. M. Keynes, *The General Theory of Employment, Interest and Money*, London, Macmillan, 1936, p. xxiii.

38 J. M. Keynes, 'The General Theory of Employment', *Quarterly Journal of Economics*, February 1937; reprinted in *The Collected Writings of John Maynard Keynes*, London, Macmillan, 1973, vol. 14, pp. 122–3.

39 F. A. Hayek, *New Studies in Philosophy, Politics, Economics and the History of Ideas*, Chicago, Chicago University Press, 1978, p. 284.

40 Lionel Robbins, *The Autobiography of an Economist*, London, Macmillan, 1971, pp. 145–62.

41 James E. Meade, 'A Simplified Model of Mr. Keynes' System', *Review of Economic Studies*, vol. 4, 1936/37.

42 J. M. Keynes, '*Consumers' Credits and Unemployment* by J. E. Meade: A Review', *Economic Journal*, vol. 48, March 1938, p. 70.

43 Douglas Jay, *Change and Fortune*, London, Hutchinson, 1980, pp. 62–3.

44 Ben Pimlott, *Labour and the Left in the 1930s*, Cambridge, Cambridge University Press, 1977, pp. 38–9.

45 *New Statesman*, 20 November 1937.

46 *New Statesman*, 15 February 1936.

47 G. D. H. Cole, *Socialist Economics*, London, Victor Gollancz, 1950, chapter 2, 'The Socialists and the Keynesians', pp. 49–54.

48 John Hicks, 'Recollections and Documents', *Economica*, vol. 40, p. 9. For further details see William Fellner, 'The Robertsonian Evolution', *American Economic Review*, vol. 42, June 1952; Paul A. Samuelson, 'D. H. Robertson (1890–1963)', *Quarterly Journal of Economics*, vol. 77, November 1963; John R. Presley, *Robertsonian Economics*, London, Macmillan, 1978; Thomas Wilson, 'Robertson, Money and Monetarism', *Journal of Economic Literature*, vol. 18, December 1980.

49 D. H. Robertson, 'Alternative Theories of the Rate of Interest', *Economic Journal*, vol. 47, September 1937, pp. 428–36.

50 Interview with Michael Danes, 3 July 1979; Sir John Hicks, 'A

Memoir', in Sir Dennis Robertson, *Essays in Money and Interest*, London, Fontana edn, 1966. Hicks concluded that Robertson was both a critic and a forerunner of the next generation's theory of economic growth.

51 E. F. M. Durbin to Mr Robertson, 4 February (1936), in EDP.

52 E. F. M. Durbin to J. M. Keynes, 21 April (1936), in JKP. Most of the following correspondence can be found in Keynes, *Collected Writings*, vol. 29, 1979.

53 Conversations with Professor Laurence Moss, Babson College, Wellesley, Massachusetts, February 1983.

54 Dennis Robertson to Durbin, 29 July 1935, in EDP.

55 Harrod, December 1935, op. cit.; Dennis Robertson to Durbin, 23 February 1936, in EDP.

56 Durbin to Robertson, 4 February 1936, in EDP.

57 Durbin, *Problem of Credit Policy*, p. 226; letter to Dalton in December 1936, quoted in Hugh Dalton, *The Fateful Years: Memoirs, 1931–1945*, London, Frederick Muller, 1957, vol. 2, p. 124, footnote.

58 Hugh Gaitskell, 'The Banking System and Monetary Policy', in Margaret Cole and Charles Smith (eds.), *Democratic Sweden*, London, Routledge, 1938, pp. 96–107; Winch, 1966, op. cit., p. 67.

59 See chapter 10 for details.

60 J. M. Keynes, *The General Theory of Employment, Interest and Money*, 1936, p. 374, London, Macmillan.

61 E. F. M. Durbin to Mr Keynes, 29 April 1936, in Keynes, *Collected Works*, vol. 29, p. 234.

Chapter 8 The New Fabians plan for socialism

1 For example, David Howell, *British Social Democracy*, London, Croom Helm, 1976, p. 72.

2 Colin Clark, *National Planning*, London, SSIP pamphlet no. 5, December 1931; see also Colin Clark, 'National Planning in the Modern State', *Political Quarterly*, vol. 2, no. 4, 1931, pp. 531–47.

3 R. F. Harrod, 'Central Banking', NFRB Conference on the Socialisation of Banking, mimeograph, 27 January 1932, in FAB, box J14/1.

4 NFRB, 'Week-end Conference on the Socialisation of Banking', mimeograph, 30 January 1932, in FAB, box J14/1, pp. 1–2.

5 Ibid., p. 6. This position was rather different in tone from Davenport's later reminiscences in *Memoirs of a City Radical*, London, Weidenfeld and Nicolson, 1974, where he left the impression that he had always agreed with and advocated Keynesian views, calling him 'my guru' (p. 113).

6 J. E. Meade, 'Financial Policy of a Socialist Government during the

Transition to Socialism', Labour party, constitutional committee, policy no. 189, mimeograph, December 1933, p. 4, in HDP IIA, folder 2/1, and JMP, folder 1 (first two pages missing).

7 G. F. Shove, 'The Supply and Direction of Capital', mimeograph, undated, in GCP, series E, and NFRB, *Minutes*, economic committee, 12 June 1931, in FAB, box J7.

8 Colin Clark, *The Control of Investment*, NFRB pamphlet no. 8, 1933, p. 18.

9 John Parker, 'Conference on Some Aspects of Socialist Planning: A Report', NFRB, mimeograph, 16 January 1934, in FAB, box J14/2. All quotations are taken from this report.

10 E. A. Radice, 'The State and Investment', in G. D. H. Cole (ed.), *Studies in Capital and Investment*, London, Gollancz, 1935, p. 194.

11 Francis Williams, 'Insurance Companies and Investment Trusts', in Cole, op. cit., p. 294.

12 E. S. Watkins, 'Building Societies', in Cole, op. cit., p. 212; NFRB, *Minutes*, executive committee, 30 January 1933, in FAB, box J7.

13 Interviews with Professor Harold Barger, Sir Vaughan Berry, Dame Margaret Cole, Douglas Jay and James Lawrie. Forty years later Margaret Cole still remembered Evan Durbin riding a duck on the roundabout at the fair.

14 NFRB, 'Report of a Weekend Conference on Banking and Financial Policy', Royal Star Hotel, Maidstone, 18–19 May 1935, mimeograph in FAB, box J15/2.

15 Hugh Gaitskell, 'The Theory of Socialist Policy', undated, in FAB, box J19/1; identifiable from NFRB, *Minutes*, economic committee, 12 June 1931, in FAB, box J7.

16 H. D. Dickinson, 'The Economic Basis of Socialism', *Political Quarterly*, vol. 1, no. 4, Sept./Dec. 1930.

17 H. D. Dickinson, 'Price Formation in a Socialist Community', *Economic Journal*, vol. 43, 1933, and 'Failure of Economic Individualism', in Cole, op. cit., pp. 11–50.

18 Nancy Ruggles, 'The Welfare Basis of the Marginal Cost Pricing Principle', *Review of Economic Studies*, vol. 17, no. 42, 1949–50, p. 43.

19 Maurice Dobb, 'Economic Theory and the Problems of a Socialist Economy', *Economic Journal*, vol. 43, December 1933, pp. 588–98; Abba Lerner, 'Economic Theory and Socialist Economy', *Review of Economic Statistics*, vol. 2, March 1934, pp. 51–61.

20 Maurice Dobb, 'Economic Theory and Socialist Economy: A Reply', *Review of Economic Statistics*, vol. 2, June 1934, pp. 144–51.

21 Abba Lerner, 'A Rejoinder', *Review of Economic Statistics*, vol. 2, June 1934, pp. 152–4.

22 G. D. H. Cole, *Economic Tracts for the Times*, London, Macmillan, 1932.
23 Margaret Cole, *The Story of Fabian Socialism*, London, Heinemann, 1961, pp. 227–9.
24 NFRB, *Twelve Studies in Soviet Russia*, London, Gollancz, 1933, p. 31.
25 See Hugh Dalton, *The Fateful Years: Memoirs 1931–1945*, London, Frederick Muller, 1957, vol. 2, p. 57.
26 Hugh Dalton, *Practical Socialism for Britain*, London, Routledge, 1935, p. 247.
27 E. F. M. Durbin, 'Memorandum on the Principles of Socialist Planning', Labour party subcommittee, policy no. 197, January 1934, in FAB, box J24/3. In Gaitskell's absence it fell to Durbin to summarize what might well have become another of their joint productions on the economics of socialism.
28 Philip M. Williams, *Hugh Gaitskell*, London, Jonathan Cape, 1979, p. 53, for account. Gaitskell's reaction is quoted from a letter to Harold Barger dated December 1933.
29 E. F. M. Durbin, 'The Importance of Planning', chapter 9 in G. E. G. Catlin (ed.), *New Trends in Socialism*, London, Lovat Dickson & Thompson, 1935. Reprinted in E. F. M. Durbin, *Problems of Economic Planning*, London, Routledge & Kegan Paul, 1949.
30 Barbara Wootton, *Plan or No Plan*, London, Gollancz, 1934.
31 Ibid., pp. 310–11.
32 Trevor Smith, *The Politics of the Corporate Economy*, London, Martin Robinson, 1979, p. 43.
33 A. W. Wright, *G. D. H. Cole and Socialist Democracy*, Oxford, Clarendon Press, 1979, chapter 8.
34 G. D. H. Cole, *Principles of Economic Planning*, London, Macmillan, 1935, pp. 224–5.
35 Ibid., p. 304.
36 Ibid., p. 339.
37 NFRB, 'Report on Weekend Conference on Socialist Planning', mimeograph, July 1935, p. 1. in FAB, box J15/3.
38 See Smith, op. cit., pp. 41–4, and Jacques Leruez, *Economic Planning and Politics in Britain*, New York, Barnes & Noble, 1976, pp. 9–10 and p. 31.

Chapter 9 The new generation rethinks economic strategy

1 Reginald Bassett, *Nineteen Thirty-One: A Political Crisis*, London, Macmillan, 1958. Lord Robbins has confirmed that Bassett's political views were a handicap to his professional advancement at LSE (interview, 24 March 1977).

2 E. F. M. Durbin, 'Democracy and Socialism in Great Britain', *Political Quarterly*, vol. 6, 1935, pp. 378–85; reprinted in E. F. M. Durbin, *Problems of Economic Planning*, London, Routledge & Kegan Paul, 1949.

3 E. F. M. Durbin, 'Memorandum on the Principles of Socialist Planning', Labour party subcommittee, policy no. 197, January 1934, in FAB, box J24/3.

4 E. F. M. Durbin et al., 'Labour Party Policy', typescript, 1935, p. 1, in HGP, folder U3(1).

5 Ibid., and E. F. M. Durbin et al., 'Purpose of Group', typescript, 1934, in HGP, folder U3(1) and FAB, box J19/2, for earlier notes. Except as noted, these documents are the source of all quotations in the remainder of this section. The resolutions which were not accepted unanimously concerned the circumstances under which force was necessary. The economic resolutions quoted here were all accepted unanimously; there were only two resolutions which received two negative votes each.

6 Hugh Gaitskell, 'The Ideological Development of Democratic Socialism in Britain', *Socialist International Information*, vol. 5, no. 52–53, 24 December 1955, p. 938.

7 Hugh Dalton, *The Fateful Years: Memoirs 1931–1945*, London, Frederick Muller, 1957, vol. 2, p. 127.

8 H. V. Berry and E. F. M. Durbin, 'Memorandum on the Nationalization of the English Banking System: Policy', no. 301, mimeograph, June 1935, p. 6, in HDP IIA, folder 2/2. See also E. F. M. Durbin, *The Problem of Credit Policy*, London, Chapman & Hall, 1935, pp. 203–5 and pp. 227–37.

9 J. E. Meade, 'Financial Policy of a Socialist Government during the Transition to Socialism', Labour party, constitutional committee, policy no. 189, mimeograph, December 1933, in HDP IIA, folder 2/1, and JMP, folder 1.

10 J. E. Meade, 'Outline of Economic Policy for a Labour Government', 1935, typescript, in JMP, folder 53. All quotations from this manuscript.

11 Roy Harrod to James Meade, 22 April 1935, in JMP, folder 53.

12 NFRB, *Minutes*, economic section, 14 October 1935, in FAB, box J8.

13 Philip Williams, *Hugh Gaitskell*, London, Jonathan Cape, 1979, p. 69.

14 G. E. G. Catlin (ed.), *New Trends in Socialism*, London, Lovat Dickson & Thompson, 1935, pp. ix-x.

15 Douglas Jay, 'The Economic Strength and Weakness of Marxism', in Catlin, op. cit., chapter 7, p. 122.

16 Hugh Gaitskell, 'Financial Policy in the Transition Period', chapter 10 in Catlin, op. cit., p. 197.
17 Durbin, 'Democracy and Socialism', 1935, p. 382.

Chapter 10 Dalton organizes his experts and Labour's financial policy

 1 LPNEC, 26 February 1932. All committee meeting notes and dates are taken from the minutes of the Labour party's national executive.
 2 (H. V. Berry), 'London Money Market', FTC, policy no. 29, April 1932, in HDP IIA, folder 2/1. Author identified by Dalton on his copy.
 3 This entire correspondence can be found in Pethick-Lawrence's papers (PLP), folders P-L1–160, 161, 162, 166, 167 and 181.
 4 Labour Party, policy committee, 'Second Draft of Policy Resolutions for Annual Conference, 1932', policy no. 66, June 1932; 'Currency, Banking and Finance', policy no. 67, June 1932; 'Third Draft of Policy Resolutions for Annual Conference, 1932', policy no. 69, June 1932. All papers in HDP IIA, folder 2/1. Also Labour Party, *Currency, Banking and Finance*, London, Transport House, July 1932.
 5 J. M. Keynes, 'The Monetary Policy of the Labour Party', *New Statesman and Nation*, 17 and 24 September 1932, p. 306 and p. 338.
 6 LPCR, 1932, pp. 182–94 for entire debate.
 7 Hugh Dalton, *The Fateful Years: Memoirs 1931–1945*, London, Frederick Muller, 1957, vol. 2, pp. 30–1.
 8 See LPCR, 1932, p. 201 for final vote; the initial vote recorded as 2,241,000 for and 984,000 against (p. 194) gives a completely inaccurate view of the strength of the support for the Socialist League on this amendment.
 9 H. Dalton, 'Memorandum for Policy Subcommittee on Finance and Trade', typescript, March 1933, in HDP IIA, folder 2/1.
10 For correspondence with Professor James Meade, see his papers, JMP, folder 1.
11 Dalton, 1957, p. 26; Hugh Dalton and others, *Unbalanced Budgets: A Study of the Financial Crisis in Fifteen Countries*, London, Routledge, 1934, preface, pp. vii-xi.
12 Brinley Thomas, *Monetary Policy and Crises: A Study of Swedish Experience*, London, Routledge, 1937, preface by Hugh Dalton, pp. ix-xi.
13 LPCR, 1933, p. 159.
14 Alan Bullock, *The Life and Times of Ernest Bevin: 1881–1940*, London, Heinemann, 1960, p. 530.
15 'Proposals on the Control of a Financial Panic', FTC, policy no. 113, mimeograph, March 1933, p. 1, prepared by a 'group of Oxford

economists who are members of the Party', in HDP IIA, folder 2/1, FAB, box J25/3 and JMP, folder 1; 'Notes on Financial Policy', FTC, policy no. 119, mimeograph, March 1933, in HDP IIA, folder 2/1.

16 G. D. H. Cole, 'Industrial Compensation', FTC, policy no. 194, December 1933, in GCP, CZ1587A-C; William Mellor to G. D. H. Cole, 29 November 1933, in GCP, CZ1587C.

17 J. E. Meade, 'Compensation', FTC, policy no. 196, mimeograph, December 1933, and correspondence in JMP, folder 1.

18 E. F. M. Durbin to G. D. H. Cole 27 November 1933, in GCP, CZ1587B.

19 LPCR, 1934, pp. 191–9, for full debate.

20 (Subcommittee of FTC), 'Financial Panic and How to Meet It', FTC, policy no. 309, mimeograph, September 1935, in HDP IIA, folder 2/2. See also 'Measures to Combat Foreign Exchange Panic', FTC, policy no. 296, mimeograph, May 1935, and 'Notes on Internal Panic', FTC, policy no. 296x, mimeograph, May 1935, in the same source; these two were probably written by Meade, because he referred to them in his manuscript, 'Outline of Economic Policy for a Labour Government', which he submitted to the NFRB in April 1935 (see JMP, folder 53).

21 See FTC, policy no. 296 and 296x, and previous footnote. Gaitskell was identified by Christopher Mayhew as the author of an update of FTC, policy no. 309, in 1938 (See chapter 12). He also wrote a chapter on this subject for a book, which has been identified as one of the products of the Durbin/Gaitskell discussion groups: Hugh Gaitskell, 'Financial Policy in the Transition Period', in G. E. G. Catlin (ed.), *New Trends in Socialism*, London, Lovat Dickson & Thompson, 1935.

22 Christopher Mayhew briefly described 'Memorandum No. 111 by E. F. Wise' in his own 'Memorandum on the Official and Unofficial Material Dealing with the Labour Party's Official Financial Policy', NFRB, financial policy committee, November 1938, p. 18, in FAB, box J26/7.

23 'Further Notes on Financial Policy: Banks', FTC, policy no. 149, mimeograph, May 1933; author identified by internal reference to previous memoranda, policy no. 119, March 1933, and policy no. 29, April 1932. However, it should be noted that these memoranda were drawn up in close collaboration with other XYZ club members after extensive discussions at their monthly meetings; authors are identified only where the first person singular is used in the text.

24 'The National Control of Investment', FTC, policy no. 145, mimeograph, May 1933, in HDP IIA, folder 2/1; author identified as E. V. Davenport by reference to article in *New Statesman*, 10

October 1931 (see p. 10 of memorandum). For debate at the NFRB conference on banking in January 1932, see chapter 8.

25 J. E. Meade, 'Financial Policy of a Socialist Government during the Transition to Socialism', Labour party, constitutional committee, policy no. 189, mimeograph, December 1933, in HDP IIA, folder 2/1, and JMP, folder 1.

26 H. V. B. and E. F. M. D., 'Memorandum on the Nationalization of the English Banking System', FTC, policy no. 297, mimeograph, June 1935, and 'Memorandum on the Nationalization of the English Banking System', policy no. 301, mimeograph, June 1935, in HDP IIA, folder 2/2.

27 H. D. (Dalton), 'Heads of a Bill of Finance', FTC, policy no. 306, mimeograph, July 1935, p. 1, in HDP IIA, folder 2/2, and items 2, 4, 5 and 6 in folder 2/4.

28 Ben Pimlott, *Labour and the Left in the 1930s*, Cambridge, Cambridge University Press, 1977, p. 81; see also John Stevenson and Chris Cook, *The Slump*, London, Jonathan Cape, 1977.

29 Bullock, op. cit., pp. 516–18.

30 Hugh Dalton to Colin Clark, 18 May 1933, in CCP.

31 LPCR, 1935, pp. 146–53, and Appendix X and XI, pp. 298–301.

32 Labour Party, *Socialism and 'Social Credit'*, London, Transport House, 1935, pp. 30–4.

33 Meade, December 1933, op. cit., (see footnote 25); E. F. M. Durbin, 'Memorandum on the Principles of Socialist Planning', Labour party, policy subcommittee, policy no. 197, January 1934, in FAB, box J24/3.

34 J. E. Meade, 'The Exchange Policy of a Socialist Government', NFRB, mimeograph, 19 June 1934, in JMP, folder 1; Roy Harrod to James Meade, 7 June 1934, and R. Opie to James Meade, 10 July 1934, in JMP, folder 1. Harrod and Opie asked Meade to modify his language about the degree of control of foreign lending necessary before they would be willing to sign; the version in Meade's papers contains their recommended wording but does not include their names as authors.

35 E. V. Davenport, 'Supplement to Report No. 145 May 1933 on the National Control of Investment', FTC, policy no. 204, mimeograph, January 1934, in HDP IIA, folder 2/2; City Group, 'Further Notes on the Stock Exchange', FTC, policy no. 220, February 1934, in HDP IIA, folder 2/2; Francis Williams, 'The Organisation of the Stock Exchange', FTC, policy no. 245, May 1934, in HDP IIA, folder 2/2. Author identification provided by Christopher Mayhew in 'Memorandum on the Official and Unofficial Material Dealing with the Labour Party's Financial Policy', NFRB, financial policy committee, November 1938, in FAB, box J26/7.

36 Hugh Dalton to Colin Clark, 24 November 1934, in CCP.
37 Colin Clark, 'Memorandum on Budgeting Considerations', FTC, policy no. 276, February 1935, in JMP, folder 1; and *A Socialist Budget*, NFRB pamphlet no. 22, May 1935. The second source acknowledges the help of Clark's 'Cambridge' group including R. B. Braithwaite, H. L. Elvin, C. H. P. Gifford, Joan Robinson and G. F. Shove.
38 Dalton, *Unbalanced Budgets*, p. 458.
39 Dalton, 1957, pp. 58–9.
40 Roy Jenkins, *Pursuit of Progress*, London, Heinemann, 1953, p. 60.
41 E. F. M. Durbin, 'Democracy and Socialism in Great Britain', *Political Quarterly*, vol. 6, 1935; reprinted in Durbin's *Problems of Economic Planning*, London, Routledge & Kegan Paul, 1949.

Chapter 11 The new socialist economics

1 Austin Robinson, 'Keynes and His Cambridge Colleagues', in Don Patinkin and J. Clark Leith (eds.), *Keynes, Cambridge and the 'General Theory'*, Toronto, University of Toronto Press, 1978, pp. 26–7.
2 F. A. Hayek (ed.), *Collectivist Economic Planning*, London, Routledge, 1935.
3 For a full discussion see in particular Abram Bergson, 'Socialist Economics', in Howard Ellis (ed.), *Survey of Contemporary Economics*, Philadelphia, Blakiston, 1948; T. J. B. Hoff, *Economic Calculation in Socialist Society*, London, Hodge, 1949; Henry Smith, *The Economics of Socialism Reconsidered*, London, Oxford University Press, 1962; Benjamin N. Ward, *The Socialist Economy*, New York, Random House, 1967.
4 See Mark Blaug, *Economic Theory in Retrospect*, Homewood, Illinois, Irwin, 1968, chapter 13, and any intermediate-level microeconomic textbook.
5 Enrico Barone, 'The Ministry of Production in the Collectivist State', in Hayek, op. cit., pp. 245–90.
6 Ludwig von Mises, 'Economic Calculation in the Socialist Commonwealth', in Hayek, op. cit., p. 89.
7 Hayek, op. cit., pp. 207–26.
8 Ibid., pp. 232–41.
9 E. F. M. Durbin *Problems of Economic Planning*, London, Routledge & Kegan Paul, 1949, p. 127. In this posthumous book, the two articles from the *Economic Journal* are reprinted and Durbin's review of Hayek's *Road to Serfdom* for the 1945 *Economic Journal*.
10 Oskar Lange, *On the Economic Theory of Socialism*, Minneapolis,

University of Minnesota Press, 1938, reprinted from *Review of Economic Studies*, vol. 4, October 1936 and February 1937.

11 A. P. Lerner, 'Statics and Dynamics in Socialist Economics', *Economic Journal*, vol. 47, June 1937, pp. 253–70.

12 Bergson in Ellis, op. cit., pp. 428–34.

13 Abba Lerner, *The Economics of Control*, New York, Macmillan, 1944, chapters 5, 9, 10, 11; J. E. Meade, *An Introduction to Economic Analysis and Policy*, London, Oxford University Press, 1937, part II, chapter VIII.

14 Bergson, op. cit., pp. 433–4.

15 I. M. D. Little, *A Critique of Welfare Economics*, Oxford, Oxford University Press, 1950, p. 261. See also Donald Lavoie, 'Rivalry and Central Planning: A Re-Examination of the Debate over Economic Calculation under Socialism', unpublished Ph.D. dissertation, New York University, 1981, for an excellent modern review from the Austrian perspective. Lavoie concludes that the participants had diverging notions of competition and 'never properly came to grips with their adversaries' perspective'.

16 For a full discussion of decreasing-cost industries and marginal-cost pricing, see Nancy Ruggles, 'The Welfare Basis of the Marginal Cost Pricing Principle', *Review of Economic Studies*, vol. 17, no. 42, 1949/50, pp. 41–6.

17 H. D. Dickinson, 'Price Formation in a Socialist Community', *Economic Journal*, vol. 43, 1933.

18 Durbin, op. cit., pp. 149–50.

19 Lerner, 'Statics and Dynamics'. Lerner also criticized Lange for the same reasons; see A. P. Lerner, 'A Note on Socialist Economics', *Review of Economic Studies*, 1936/37, vol. 4, pp. 74–6.

20 Lerner, 'Statics and Dynamics', pp. 269–70.

21 Durbin, op. cit., p. 140.

22 Ibid., pp. 86–7.

23 E. F. M. Durbin, 'A Note on Mr Lerner's "Dynamical Propositions"', *Economic Journal*, vol. 47, September 1937, p. 579, footnote 2.

24 J. E. Meade, 'Price and Output Policy of State Enterprise', *Economic Journal*, vol. 54, 1944. See Ruggles, op. cit., pp. 110–17 for full details.

25 Little, op. cit., p. 194.

26 Y. K. Ng, 'Towards a Theory of Third Best', *Public Finance*, vol. 32, 1977, p. 10.

27 Trevor Smith, *The Politics of the Corporate Economy*, London, Martin Robertson, 1979, p. 40.

Chapter 12 Labour's new programme

1 Hugh Dalton, *The Fateful Years: Memoirs 1931–1945*, London, Frederick Muller, 1957, vol. 2, p. 124.

2 Labour Party, *Labour's Immediate Programme*, London, Transport House, November 1937.

3 Durbin, Gaitskell and Jay were asked to participate in the following: (1) Labour party NEC, advisory committee on imperial questions and advisory committee on international questions, joint special committee on demand for colonial territories and equality of economic opportunity (see LPNEC, *Minutes*, 19 September 1935, vol. 69, p. 628 and p. 727, and 17 June 1936, vol. 71, p. 545); (2) Labour party NEC, policy subcommittee, advisory committee no. 4 on Ottawa agreements (see LPNEC, *Minutes*, 14 January 1936, vol. 70, pp. 18–23); (3) Labour party NEC, policy subcommittee, food policy subcommittee (see LPNEC, *Minutes*, vol. 78, 21 March 1938, and 24 November 1938); (4) Labour party NEC, policy subcommittee, finance and trade subcommittee (FTC) (see LPNEC, *Minutes*, 13 July 1936, vol. 71. Clark and Durbin are listed as attending a meeting of the FTC; an earlier list of subcommittee members in January 1936 does not include their names among the co-opted, LPNEC, *Minutes*, vol. 69, 14 January 1936).

4 Margaret Cole, *The Story of Fabian Socialism*, London, Heinemann, 1961, p. 239.

5 LPNEC, *Minutes*, 15 November 1937, vol. 74; see 'Appendix to Minutes of the Policy Committee', pp. 664–9.

6 Ben Pimlott, *Labour and the Left in the 1930s*, Cambridge, Cambridge University Press, 1977, chapter 14.

7 Hugh Dalton, 'Note on Short Programme', Labour party, policy committee, research no. 324, mimeograph, January 1937, in HDP IIA, folder 3/1.

8 Dalton, 1957, p. 124, footnote.

9 Hugh Dalton, 'Revised Draft of Short Programme', Labour party policy committee, research no. 334, February 1937 and attached 'Further Note on Short Programme', in HDP IIA, folder 3/1; Dalton referred to '*Mr Attlee's Memorandum on the Labour Programme No. 331*' in the further note. David Howell has suggested that Dalton's version of events in his *Memoirs* exaggerates his own importance and minimizes Attlee's (see David Howell, *British Social Democracy*, London, Croom Helm, 1976, p. 95). But his account does not mention Dalton's role as the conference organizer, nor his influential membership of the policy subcommittee for many years.

10 Labour Party, *Immediate Programme*, for all final wording.

11 LPCR, 1937, pp. 181–83 for full speech.

12 G. D. H. Cole, *Plan for Democratic Britain*, London, Odhams Press, 1939, pp. 210–14.

13 Dalton, 1957, p. 120.

14 C. G. C., E. F. M. D., H. T. N. G., D. P. T. J., 'Memorandum by the Economic Group', FTC, research no. 311, mimeograph, June 1936, in CCP (with page 9 missing) and in two drafts in HGP, folder U3(1).

15 The first report that Ernest Bevin wrote for the Economic Advisory Council had been one on rationalization of the steel industry; Alan Bullock, *The Life and Times of Ernest Bevin*, London, Heinemann, 1960, vol. 1, p. 438.

16 Ross Martin, *TUC: The Growth of a Pressure Group 1868–1976*, Oxford, Clarendon Press, 1980, p. 213.

17 LPCR, 1934, p. 165.

18 Harold Barger, *Foreign Trade*, NFRB, pamphlet no. 30, July 1936.

19 NFRB, 'Report of a Conference on International Commercial Policy', mimeograph, October 1936, in FAB, box J15/10.

20 Ottawa and trade agreements subcommittee, 'The Ottawa Agreements and Commercial Policy', Labour party, research no. 356, November 1937, p. 21, in HGP, folder U3(1).

21 LPNEC, *Minutes*, FTC, 12 January 1938; Labour party subsidies advisory committee, 'Subsidies', November 1937, in HGP, folder U3(1).

22 FTC, 'Memorandum of Labour's Trade Policy', Labour party, policy no. 4, February 1938, in HGP, folder U3(1).

23 LPNEC, *Minutes*, 13 December 1938, vol. 78.

24 Stephen Bird, the archivist for the Labour party, has suggested that this may be one reason why the hundreds of policy memoranda written during the 1930s are not in the archives.

25 C. P. Mayhew, 'Memorandum on the Official and Unofficial Material Dealing with the Labour Party's Fiancial Policy', NFRB, financial policy committee, (November 1938), in FAB, box J26/7.

26 (Gaitskell), 'Labour Policy and the Foreign Exchange Market', Labour party, finance policy no. 1, 11 November 1938, p. 1, in HDP IIA, folder 2/3.

27 FTC, 'Labour's Financial Policy', Labour party, finance policy no. 2, 22 November 1938, p. 1, in HDP IIA, folder 2/3.

28 'A Citizen', *The City Today*, NFRB, pamphlet no. 38, February 1938, p. 13.

29 FTC, 'Heads of a Bill on Finance', Labour party, finance policy no. 3, December 1938; see also FTC, 'Legal Position of the Bank of England', Labour party, finance policy no. 4, December 1938; H. V. B. and E. F. M. D., 'Memorandum on the Nationalization of the English Banking System', Labour party, finance policy no. 5, January 1938. All these can be found in HDP IIA, folder 2/3.

30 Howell, op. cit., pp. 95–7. Also Samuel H. Beer, *Modern British Politics*, London, Faber & Faber, 1965, pp. 189–200.
31 G. D. H. Cole, *The Machinery of Socialist Planning*, London, Hogarth, 1938, p. 64.
32 Herbert Morrison to John Parker, 24 August 1937, and Clement R. Attlee to John (Parker), 2 August 1937, in GCP, folder F.
33 Dalton, 1957, pp. 422–3, and his diary for 14 January 1943.
34 Fabian Society, *Minutes*, economics committee, 6 April 1943, in FAB, box K18/2.
35 Dalton, 1957, p. 423.
36 Hugh Thomas, *John Strachey*, New York, Harper & Row, 1973, p. 273.

Chapter 13 The new economic revisionism

1 The folder containing Durbin's notes and the materials he had gathered together has kindly been returned to Mrs A. M. Durbin by Baroness Gaitskell. A typed manuscript on 'The Economics of Democratic Socialism' was found in the file. Internal evidence suggests it was written after Durbin's death, although it resembles much of Durbin's own handwritten introduction. A press release dated 12 April 1949, from the ministry of fuel and power, gives an outline for a speech Gaitskell was to deliver to the conference of Labour student organizatons the next day; this outline summarizes the typed manuscript. Philip Williams, Gaitskell's biographer, provided the press release and made the connection to the speech.
2 Arthur Marwick, 'Middle Opinion in the Thirties: Planning, Progress and Political Agreement', *English Historical Review*, vol. 79, April 1964, pp. 285–98.
3 Donald Winch, *Economics and Policy*, London, Fontana, 1972, pp. 223–8. Trevor Smith identifies Sir Arthur Salter's 1932 book, *Recovery*, as an important turning-point in the planning discussions; see Smith, *The Politics of the Corporate Economy*, Oxford, Martin Robinson, 1979, p. 32.
4 F. A. Hayek, *The Road to Serfdom*, London, Routledge, 1944, p. 30.
5 Barbara Wootton, *Freedom under Planning*, London, Allen & Unwin, 1945, p. 30 and p. 62.
6 Ibid., p. 92 and p. 117.
7 E. F. M. Durbin, *The Politics of Democratic Socialism*, London, Routledge & Kegan Paul, 1954 edn, Appendix II, p. 361.
8 E. F. M. Durbin, 'Professor Hayek on Economic Planning', *Economic Journal*, vol. 55, 1945, reprinted in his *Problems of Economic Planning*, London, Routledge & Kegan Paul, 1949, pp. 91–106.

9 Durbin, 1949, p. 181.

10 G. D. H. Cole, *The Machinery of Socialist Planning*, London, Hogarth Press, 1938, pp. 23–4, and chapters IV to X for full details.

11 Henri de Man, *Planned Socialism*, NFRB, pamphlet no. 25, December 1935.

12 G. D. H. Cole, *Socialist Economics*, London, Gollancz, 1950, p. 9.

13 Ibid, pp. 38–9.

14 Durbin, 1940 edn, p. 72.

15 J. E. Meade, 'Outline of Economic Policy for a Labour Government', 1935, unpublished typescript in JMP, folder 53.

16 See, for example, B. Corry, 'Keynes in the History of Economic Thought: Some Reflections', in A. P. Thirlwall (ed.), *Keynes and Laissez-Faire*, London, Macmillan, 1978.

17 See I. M. D. Little, *A Critique of Welfare Economics*, Oxford, Oxford University Press, 1950, for an early attack on the microeconomic aspects.

18 Cole, 1950, op. cit., p. 7.

19 G. D. H. Cole, 'The Dream and the Business', *Political Quarterly*, vol. 20, July-September 1949.

20 Durbin, 1949, op. cit., p. 82.

21 Cole, 1950, p. 9.

22 E. F. M. Durbin, 'The Nature of Economics', in *Economics: Man and His Material Resources*, London, Odhams, 1949; reprinted in Durbin, 1949, op. cit., pp. 159–80.

Chapter 14 Conclusions

1 Typescript in Durbin's folder 'The Economics of Democratic Socialism' in EDP, and Ministry of Fuel and Power, press release, 12 April 1949, in HGP.

2 E. F. M. Durbin, *Problems of Economic Planning*, London, Routledge & Kegan Paul, 1949, p. 23.

3 *New York Times*, 24 January 1983.

4 See Robert Skidelsky (ed.), *The End of the Keynesian Era*, London, Macmillan, 1977.

SELECT BIBLIOGRAPHY

Specific sources are quoted with full bibliographic citations in the notes for each chapter. This bibliography is intended to provide a more accessible list of the main *published* sources used in the course of the research. The locations of the *unpublished* materials are described at the beginning of the chapter notes; a list of people interviewed is given above. The authors in this bibliography are listed alphabetically, with their publications arranged chronologically, under three headings: contemporary sources; economic sources; historical sources. The first lists those publications which contributed to the process of discussion and debate about the Labour party's economic policy and socialist economics during the 1930s, with a few additional sources from the 1940s. The second contains the main sources analysing the 1930s debates, which can be found in the economics and planning literature, including the later recollections of those participants who were professional economists. The third group includes only the most important of the wide range of historical materials available on British history and on the history of the Labour party.

A Contemporary sources

The following abbreviations are used:
  NFRB = New Fabian Research Bureau
  SSIP = Society for Socialist Inquiry and Propaganda

Albu, A., *Management in Transition*, London, Fabian Society, 1942,
Barger, H., *Foreign Trade*, London, NFRB, pamphlet no. 30, 1936.
Berry, H. V., *The City Today*, London, NFRB, pamphlet no. 38, 1938
  (author identified in NFRB minutes).
Catlin, G. E. G. (ed.), *New Trends in Socialism*, London, Lovat,
  Dickson & Thompson, 1935.

Clark, C. G., *National Planning*, London, SSIP, pamphlet no. 5, 1931.

Clark, C. G., *The National Income*, London, Macmillan, 1932.

Clark, C. G., *The Control of Investment*, London, NFRB, pamphlet no. 8, 1933.

Clark, C. G., *A Socialist Budget*, London, NFRB, pamphlet no. 22, 1935.

Cole, G. D. H., *The Next Ten Years in British Social and Economic Policy*, London, Macmillan, 1929.

Cole, G. D. H., *Gold, Credit and Employment*, London, Allen & Unwin, 1930.

Cole, G. D. H., *The Essentials of Socialisation*, London, NFRB, pamphlet no. 1, 1931.

Cole, G. D. H., *Economic Tracts for the Times*, London, Macmillan, 1932.

Cole, G. D. H., *SSIP Study Guides*, London, SSIP, 1932.
  No. 1, The Gold Standard.
  No. 2, The Bank of England.
  No. 3, Banks and Credit.
  No. 4, The Socialisation of Banking.

Cole, G. D. H. (ed.), *What Everybody Wants to Know about Money*, London, Gollancz, 1933.

Cole, G. D. H., *Principles of Economic Planning*, London, Macmillan, 1935.

Cole, G. D. H. (ed.), *Studies in Capital and Investment*, London, Gollancz, 1935.

Cole, G. D. H., *The Machinery of Socialist Planning*, London, Hogarth Press, 1938.

Cole, G. D. H., *Plan for Democratic Britain*, London, Labour Book Service, 1938.

Cole, G. D. H., *Socialist Economics*, London, Gollancz, 1950.

Dalton, H., *Some Aspects of the Inequality of Incomes in Modern Communities*, London, Routledge, 1920.

Dalton, H., *Principles of Public Finance*, London, Routledge, 1923.

Dalton, H., Thomas, B., Reedman, J. N., Hughes, T. J. and Leaning, W. J., *Unbalanced Budgets: A Study of the Financial Crisis in Fifteen Countries*, London, Routledge, 1934.

Dalton, H., *Practical Socialism for Britain*, London, Routledge, 1935.

Dickinson, H. D., 'The Economic Basis of Socialism', *Political Quarterly*, vol. 1, 1930.

Dickinson, H. D., 'Freedom and Planning: A Reply to Dr. Gregory', *Manchester School*, vol. 4, 1933.

Dickinson, H. D., 'Price Formation in a Socialist Community', *Economic Journal*, vol. 43, 1933.

Dickinson, H. D., *Economics of Socialism*, London, Oxford University Press, 1939.

Dobb, M., 'The Problems of a Socialist Economy', *Economic Journal*, vol. 43, 1933.

Dobb, M., 'Economic Theory and Socialist Economy: A Reply', *Review of Economic Studies*, vol. 2, 1934–5.

Durbin, E. F. M., *Purchasing Power and Trade Depression*, London, Chapman & Hall, 1933.

Durbin, E. F. M., *Socialist Credit Policy*, London, NFRB, pamphlet no. 15, 1933, and new and revised, pamphlet no. 26, 1935.

Durbin, E. F. M., *The Problem of Credit Policy*, London, Chapman & Hall, 1935.

Durbin, E. F. M., *How to Pay for the War*, London, Routledge, 1939.

Durbin, E. F. M., *The Politics of Democratic Socialism*, London, Routledge, 1940.

Durbin, E. F. M., *Problems of Economic Planning*, London, Routledge & Kegan Paul, 1949. (Contains Durbin's important articles from the 1930s).

Fraser, R., *What's What in Politics*, London, Labour Book Service, 1939.

Gaitskell, H. T. N., 'Notes on the Period of Production', *Zeitschrift für National Ökonomie*, vol. 7, no. 5, 1936 and vol. 9, no. 2, 1938.

Gregory, T. E., 'An Economist Looks at Planning', *Manchester School*, vol. 4, 1933.

Haberler, G., *Prosperity and Unemployment*, Geneva, League of Nations, 1937.

Hall, R. L., *Economic System in a Socialist State*, London, Macmillan, 1937.

Hayek, F. A., *Prices and Production*, London, Routledge, 1931.

Hayek, F. A., *Monetary Theory and the Trade Cycle*, London, Jonathan Cape, 1933 (English version translated from the German edition of 1929).

Hayek, F. A., 'The Trend in Economic Thinking', *Economica*, vol. 1, 1933.

Hayek, F. A., (ed.), *Collectivist Economic Planning*, London, Routledge, 1935.

Hayek, F. A., *The Road to Serfdom*, London, Routledge, 1944.

Hicks, J. R., 'Mr Keynes and the Classics', *Economica*, vol. 5, 1937.

Hobson, J. A., *From Capitalism to Socialism*, London, Hogarth Press, Day to Day Pamphlets, no. 8, 1932.

Hobson, J. A., 'Underconsumption: An Exposition and Reply', *Economica*, vol. 1, 1933.

Hobson, J. A., *Confessions of an Economic Heretic*, London, Allen & Unwin, 1938.

Jay, D., *The Socialist Case*, London, Gollancz, 1937.

Jay, D., *The Nation's Wealth at the Nation's Service*, London, Labour Party, 1938.

Keynes, J. M., *The Collected Writings of John Maynard Keynes*, London, Macmillan, edited by Elizabeth Johnson and Donald Moggridge for the Royal Economic Society. See especially the following volumes:
Vols. 5 and 6, *A Treatise on Money* (1930).
Vol. 7, *The General Theory of Employment, Interest and Money*, (1936).
Vol. 9, *Essays in Persuasion* (1931).
Vol. 13, *The General Theory and After: Part I, Preparation*.
Vol. 14, *The General Theory and After: Part II, Defence and Development*.
Vol. 29, *The General Theory and After: Supplement*.
Labour Party, *Conference Reports*, London, Transport House, annual.
Labour Party, *Labour and the Nation*, London, Transport House, 1928.
Labour Party, *Currency, Banking and Finance*, London, Transport House, 1932.
Labour Party, *Socialism and the Condition of the People*, London, Transport House, 1933.
Labour Party, *For Socialism and Peace*, London, Transport House, 1934.
Labour Party, *Socialism and 'Social Credit'*, London, Transport House, 1935.
Labour Party, *Labour's Financial Policy*, London, Transport House, 1935.
Labour Party, *Why Banks Should be Nationalised*, London, Transport House, 1936.
Labour Party, *Labour's Immediate Programme*, London, Transport House, 1937.
Labour Party, *The Distressed Areas*, London, Transport House, 1937.
Labour Party, *Full Employment and Financial Policy*, London, Transport House, 1944.
Lange, O., 'Marxian Economics and Modern Economic Theory', *Review of Economic Studies*, vol. 2, 1934–5.
Lange, O., *On the Economic Theory of Socialism*, Minneapolis, University of Minnesota Press, 1938.
Lerner, A. P., 'Economic Theory and Socialist Economy', *Review of Economic Studies*, vol. 2, 1934–5.
Lerner, A. P., 'A Reply to Mr Dobb', *Review of Economic Studies*, vol. 2, 1934–5.
Lerner, A. P., 'Mr Keynes' *General Theory of Employment, Interest and Money*', *International Labour Review*, vol. 34, 1936.
Lerner, A. P., 'Statics and Dynamics in Socialist Economics', *Economic Journal*, vol. 47, 1937.
Lerner, A. P., *The Economics of Control*, New York, Macmillan, 1944.
Lewis, W. A., *The Principles of Economic Planning*, London, D. Dobson, 1949.

Mayhew, C. P., *Planned Investment*, London, Fabian Society, 1939.

Mayhew, C. P., *Socialist Economic Planning*, London, Fabian Society, 1946.

Meade, J. E., *Public Works in Their International Aspect*, London, NFRB, pamphlet no. 4, 1933.

Meade, J. E., *The Rate of Interest*, London, Oxford University Press, 1933.

Meade, J. E., *An Introduction to Economic Analysis and Policy*, London, Oxford University Press, 1936.

Meade, J. E., 'A Simplified Model of Mr Keynes' System', *Review of Economic Studies*, vol. 4, 1936–7.

Meade, J. E., *Consumer Credit and Unemployment*, London, Oxford University Press, 1938.

Meade, J. E., *Planning and the Price Mechanism*, London, Allen & Unwin, 1948.

Mitchison, G. R., *Industrial Compensation*, London, NFRB, pamphlet no. 2, 1932.

Munro, D. (ed.), *Socialism: The British Way*, London, Essential Books, 1948.

Pethick-Lawrence, F. W., *National Finance*, London, Fabian Society, tract no. 229, 1929.

Pethick-Lawrence, F. W., *The Money Muddle and the Way Out*, London, Allen & Unwin, 1933.

Planning for Employment: A Preliminary Study, by some Members of Parliament, London, Macmillan, 1935.

Robbins, L. A., 'Consumption and the Trade Cycle', *Economica*, no. 38, 1932.

Robbins, L. A., *An Essay on the Nature and Significance of Economic Science*, London, Macmillan, 1932.

Robertson, D. H., *A Study of Industrial Fluctuation*, London, P. S. King, 1915.

Robertson, D. H., *Banking Policy and the Price Level*, London, P. S. King, 1926.

Rowse, A. L., *Mr Keynes and the Labour Movement*, London, Macmillan, 1936.

Tawney, R. H., *The Acquisitive Society*, London, G. Bell, 1921.

Tawney, R. H., *Religion and the Rise of Capitalism*, London, John Murray, 1926.

Tawney, R. H., *Equality*, London, Allen & Unwin, 1931.

Thomas, B., *Monetary Policy and Crises: A Study of Swedish Experience*, London, Routledge, 1937.

Wootton, B., *Plan or No Plan*, London, Gollancz, 1934.

Wootton, B., *Full Employment*, London, Fabian Society, research series, no. 74, 1943.

Wootton, B., *Freedom under Planning*, London, Allen & Unwin, 1945.
Wootton, B., Barger, H., Radice, E. A., and Drake, B., *Taxation under Capitalism*, NFRB, pamphlet no. 38, 1938.

B Economics literature

Barry, N., *Hayek's Social and Economic Philosophy*, London, Macmillan, 1979.
Bergson, A., 'Socialist Economics', in Ellis, H. S. (ed.), *A Survey of Contemporary Economics*, Homewood, Illinois, Irwin, vol. 1, 1949.
Clark, C. G., 'Memoir: The "Golden" Age of the Great Economists', *Encounter*, June 1977.
Devons, E., *Papers on Planning and Economic Management*, Manchester, Manchester University Press, 1970.
Dow, J. C. R., *The Management of the British Economy: 1945–60*, Cambridge, Cambridge University Press, 1964.
Hancock, K., 'Unemployment and the Economists in the 1920s', *Economica*, vol. 27, 1960.
Harris, J., *Unemployment and Politics*, Oxford, Oxford University Press, 1972.
Hicks, J., *Critical Essays in Monetary Theory*, Oxford, Oxford University Press, 1967.
Hicks, J., 'Recollections and Documents', *Economica*, vol. 40, 1973.
Hicks, J., *The Crisis in Keynesian Economics*, Oxford, Basil Blackwell, 1974.
Hoff, T. J. B., *Economic Calculation in Socialist Society*, London, W. Hodge, 1949.
Howson, S., *Domestic Monetary Management in Britain 1919–38*, Cambridge, Cambridge University Press, 1975.
Howson, S., and Winch, D., *The Economic Advisory Council: 1930–1939*, Cambridge, Cambridge University Press, 1977.
Hutchison, T. W., *Economics and Economic Policy in Britain 1946–66*, London, Allen & Unwin, 1968.
Hutchison, T. W., *Keynes versus the 'Keynesians'. . . ?* London, Institute of Economic Affairs, 1977.
Hutchison, T. W., *On Revolutions and Progress in Economic Knowledge*, Cambridge, Cambridge University Press, 1978.
Johnson, E. S., and Johnson, H. G., *The Shadow of Keynes*, Chicago, University of Chicago Press, 1978.
Kahn, R., 'On Re-Reading Keynes', *Proceedings of the British Academy*, Keynes Lecture in Economics, 6 November 1974.
Kahn, R., 'Some Aspects of the Development of Keynes' Thought', *Journal of Economic Literature*, vol. 16, no. 2, 1978.

Kaldor, N., 'Conflicts on National Economic Objectives', *Economic Journal*, vol. 81, 1971.

Kaldor, N., 'An Introduction to "A Note on the General Theory"', *Journal of Post Keynesian Economics*, vol. 1, no. 3, 1979.

Keynes, M. (ed.), *Essays on John Maynard Keynes*, Cambridge, Cambridge University Press, 1975.

Klein, L., *The Keynesian Revolution*, London, Macmillan, 2nd edn, 1966.

Lavoie, D. C., 'Rivalry and Central Planning: A Re-Examination of the Debate over Economic Calculation under Socialism', unpublished dissertation, New York University, New York, 1981.

Lekachman, R. (ed.), *Keynes and the Classics*, Lexington, Heath, 1964.

Lekachman, R. (ed.), *Keynes' General Theory: Reports of Three Decades*, New York, St Martins Press, 1964.

Lekachman, R., *The Age of Keynes*, New York, Random House, 1966.

Lerner, A. P., 'On Keynes', *Journal of Economic Literature*, vol. 12, no. 1, 1974.

Lerner, A. P., 'From Pre-Keynes to Post-Keynes', *Social Research*, vol. 44, no. 3, 1977.

Leruez, J., *Economic Planning and Politics in Britain*, New York, Barnes & Noble, 1976.

Little, I. M. D., *A Critique of Welfare Economics*, London, Oxford University Press, 1950.

Machlup, F. (ed.), *Essays on Hayek*, New York, New York University Press, 1976.

McKibbin, R., 'The Economic Policy of the Second Labour Government 1929–1931', *Past and Present*, vol. 68, 1975.

Meltzer, A. H., 'On Keynes's *General Theory*', *Journal of Economic Literature*, vol. 19, no. 1, 1981.

Miller, F. M., 'The Unemployment Policy of the National Government, 1931–36', *Historical Journal*, vol. 19, 1976.

Minsky, H., *John Maynard Keynes*, New York, Columbia University Press, 1975.

Moggridge, D. E., *British Monetary Policy 1924–31*, Cambridge, Cambridge University Press, 1972.

Moggridge, D. E., *Keynes*, London, Fontana and Macmillan, 1976.

Patinkin, D., *Keynes' Monetary Thought: A Study of Its Development*, Raleigh, North Carolina, Duke University Press, 1976.

Patinkin, D., and Leith, J. C. (eds.), *Keynes, Cambridge and the General Theory*, Toronto, University of Toronto Press, 1978.

Phelps Brown, E. H., 'Evan Durbin, 1906–1948', *Economica*, vol. 18, 1951.

Phelps Brown, E. H., 'Sir Roy Harrod: A Biographical Memoir', *Economic Journal*, vol. 90, no. 1, 1980.

Pollard, S. (ed.), *The Gold Standard and Employment Policies between the Wars*, London, Methuen, 1970.

Presley, J. R., *Robertsonian Economics*, London, Macmillan, 1978.

Robbins, L., *Autobiography of an Economist*, London, Macmillan, 1971.

Ruggles, N., 'The Welfare Basis of the Marginal Cost Pricing Principle', *Review of Economic Studies*, vol. 17, 1949–50.

Samuelson, P., 'Sir D. H. Robertson', *Quarterly Journal of Economics*, vol. 77, 1963.

Shackle, G. L. S., *The Years of High Theory: Invention and Tradition in Economic Thought 1926–39*, Cambridge, Cambridge University Press, 1967.

Skidelsky, R., *End of the Keynesian Era*, London, Macmillan, 1977.

Smith, H., *The Economics of Socialism Reconsidered*, Oxford, Oxford University Press, 1962.

Smith, T., *The Politics of the Corporate Economy*, Oxford, Martin Robertson, 1979.

Stone, R., 'Keynes, Political Arithmetic and Econometrics', *Proceedings of British Academy*, Seventh Keynes Lecture in Economics, May 1978.

Thirlwall, A. P. (ed.), *Keynes and Laissez-Faire*, London, Macmillan, 1978.

Vaughn, K. I., 'Economic Calculation under Socialism: The Austrian Contribution', *Economic Inquiry*, vol. 18, no. 4, 1980.

Vicary, S., 'The Monetary Doctrines of Evan Durbin', unpublished M. A. thesis, no. 3200, Sheffield University, Division of Economic Studies, 1972.

Ward, B., *The Socialist Economy*, New York, Random House, 1967.

Wilson, T., 'Robertson, Money and Monetarism', *Journal of Economic Literature*, vol. 18, no. 4, 1980.

Winch, D., *Economics and Policy*, London, Hodder & Stoughton, Twentieth Century Studies, 1969.

C Historical literature

Addison, P., *The Road to 1945*, London, Jonathan Cape, 1975.

Barker, R., 'Political Myth: Ramsay MacDonald and the Labour Party', *History*, vol. 61, no. 201, 1976.

Beer, S. H., *Modern British Politics*, London, Faber & Faber, 1965.

Briggs, A., and Saville, J., (eds.), *Essays in Labour History*, London, Macmillan, vol. 1, 1967, and vol. 2, 1971; also *Essays in Labour History: 1918–1939*, London, Croom Helm, 1977.

Bullock, A., *The Life and Times of Ernest Bevin*, London, Heinemann, vol. 1, 1960.

Carpenter, L. P., *G. D. H. Cole: An Intellectual Biography*, Cambridge, Cambridge University Press, 1973.

Clarke, P., *Liberals and Social Democrats*, Cambridge, Cambridge University Press, 1978.

Cole, G. D. H., *History of the Labour Party from 1914*, London, Routledge & Kegan Paul, 1948.

Cole, M. I., *The Story of Fabian Socialism*, London, Heinemann, 1961 and New York, John Wiley, 1964.

Cole, M. I., *The Life of G. D. H. Cole*, London, Macmillan, 1971.

Cross, C., *Philip Snowden*, London, Barrie & Rockliff, 1966.

Crouch, C. J., *State and Economy in Contemporary Capitalism*, London, Croom Helm, 1979.

Dalton, H., *Call Back Yesterday: Memoirs 1887–1931*, London, Frederick Muller, vol. 1, 1953, and *The Fateful Years: Memoirs 1931–1945*, vol. 2, 1957.

Davenport, N., *Memoirs of a City Radical*, London, Weidenfeld & Nicolson, 1974.

Donoughue, B., and Jones, G. W., *Herbert Morrison: Portrait of a Politician*, London, Weidenfeld & Nicolson, 1973.

Eatwell, R., *The 1945–1951 Labour Government*, London, Batsford Academic, 1979.

Eatwell, R., and Wright, A., 'Labour and the Lessons of 1931', *History*, vol. 63, no. 207, 1978.

Francis-Williams, Lord, *Nothing So Strange*, London, Cassell, 1970.

Gaitskell, H., 'The Ideological Development of Democratic Socialism in Great Britain', *Socialist International Information*, vol. 5, no. 52–3, 1955.

Harris, J., *William Beveridge*, Oxford, Oxford University Press, 1977.

Haseler, S., *The Gaitskellites: Revisionism 1951–64*, London, Macmillan, 1969.

Howell, D., *British Social Democracy*, London, Croom Helm, 1976.

Jay, D., *Change and Fortune*, London, Hutchinson, 1980.

Macmillan, H., *The Winds of Change: 1914–1939*, New York, Harper & Row, 1966.

Marquand, D., *Ramsay MacDonald*, London, Jonathan Cape, 1977.

Marshall, T. H., *The Right to Welfare*, London, Heinemann, 1981.

Martin, D. E., and Rubinstein, D., (eds.), *Ideology and the Labour Movement*, London, Croom Helm, 1979.

Martin, R. M., *The TUC: The Growth of a Pressure Group, 1868–1976*, Oxford, Clarendon Press, 1980.

Marwick, A., 'Middle Opinion in the Thirties: Planning, Progress and Political Agreement', *English Historical Review*, vol. 79, 1964.

Mowat, C., *Great Britain Between the Wars*, London, Methuen, 1955.

Pakenham, F., *Born to Believe*, London, Hutchinson, 1953.

Parker, J., 'Oxford Politics in the Late 20s', *Political Quarterly*, vol. 45, 1974.

Pelling, H., *A Short History of the Labour Party*, London, Macmillan, 1976.

Pimlott, B., *Labour and the Left in the 1930s*, Cambridge, Cambridge University Press, 1977.

Rodgers, W. T. (ed.), *Hugh Gaitskell, 1906–1963*, London, Thames & Hudson, 1964.

Skidelsky, R., *Politicians and the Slump: The Labour Government of 1929–31*, London, Macmillan, 1967.

Stevenson, J., and Cook, C., *The Slump: Society and Politics during the Depression*, London, Jonathan Cape, 1977.

Taylor, A. J. P., *English History: 1914–1945*, Oxford, Clarendon Press, 1965.

Terrill, R., *R. H. Tawney and His Times: Socialism as Fellowship*, Cambridge, Mass., Harvard University Press, 1973.

Thomas, H., *John Strachey*, New York, Harper & Row, 1973.

Williams, P., *Hugh Gaitskell*, London, Jonathan Cape, 1979.

Woolf, L., *Downhill All the Way: An Autobiography of the Years 1919–1939*, London, Hogarth Press, 1967.

Wootton, B., *In a World I Never Made*, London, Allen & Unwin, 1967.

Wright, A. W., *G. D. H. Cole and Socialist Democracy*, Oxford, Oxford University Press, 1978.

INTERVIEWS

The author interviewed many of the participants who contributed to the formation of economic policy for the Labour party in the 1930s, as well as friends and colleagues of her father, Evan Durbin. The interviews ranged from social conversations to extended discussions and repeated visits; in some cases tape recordings were made. These recollections, comments and criticisms of earlier drafts were a crucial part of this study. In grateful recognition of their time, care and attention, all the people who were consulted are listed below.

The list is in alphabetical order with current titles, with subsequent positions *in italics* and with a brief note on their connections to the institutions and the people discussed in the book. In the main text people are given their contemporary titles only, except when reference is made to information or opinions expressed in these interviews. For example, Margaret Cole is only called Dame Margaret Cole when referring to things she said directly to the author in an interview. To avoid weighing down the text, information learned from the interviews has not generally been footnoted; thus, this list provides the only full source reference to the person quoted. There are a few exceptions where some additional comment was in order, or more than one person had corroborated the evidence.

The following abbreviations are used:

LPFTC	Labour party, Finance and Trade Committee
LSE	London School of Economics
NFRB	New Fabian Research Bureau
SSIP	Society for Socialist Inquiry and Propaganda
UC	University College, University of London
XYZ	XYZ Club

The 'Cole group' refers to the Oxford undergraduate group first formed by G. D. H. Cole following the general strike of 1926. The 'Durbin group' refers to the series of informal discussion groups organized by Evan Durbin, in conjunction with Hugh Gaitskell, in London throughout the 1930s. An asterisk (*) indicates that the author has a tape recording of conversations with the person.

Austin Albu, *Minister of State, Department of Economic Affairs; MP for Edmonton, 1948–74.* Works manager for Electrolux, 1930–46; member of NFRB and Durbin group.

Sir Roy Allen, *Professor of Statistics, London University.* Lecturer in statistics at LSE, 1928–39.

*Harold Barger, *Professor of Economics, Columbia University.* Graduate student at LSE; lecturer in statistics at UC, 1931–6; member of NFRB.

H. L. Beales, *University Reader in Economic History at LSE, 1931–56.* Served on NFRB executive committee.

Sir Vaughan Berry, *Member of Iron and Steel Corporation.* Member of Union Discount Company of London, 1925–45; co-founder of XYZ; member of NFRB.

Sir Anthony Bowlby, *Executive Director, Guest, Keen and Nettlefold.* Manager at GKN; member of Cole group, Durbin group and NFRB.

*Dr John Bowlby, *Chairman, Department for Children and Parents, Tavistock Clinic, London.* Medical student at UC hospital, 1930–2; Psychoanalytic Institute; staff psychologist at London Child Guidance Clinic, 1937–40; member of NFRB and Durbin group.

Ivor Bulmer-Thomas, *Chairman, Ancient Monuments Society; MP for Keighley 1942–50.* Editorial staff of *The Times* 1930–7; chief leader writer, *News Chronicle*, 1937–9.

Joan Bulmer-Thomas. Research assistant at NFRB, 1937–9.

Sir Norman Chester, *Fellow and Warden, Nuffield College, Oxford.* Lecturer in Public Administration, Manchester University, 1936–40.

Dr Colin Clark, *Monash University, Australia.* Lecturer in statistics, Cambridge University, 1931–7; member of Cole group; served on NFRB executive committee, convenor of capital supply committee.

*E. G. Cole, *Industrial Adviser, Industrial and Commercial Finance Corporation.* Labour party agent for Durbin in Edmonton.

Dame Margaret Cole, *President of Fabian Society 1963–80.* Lecturer for University Tutorial Classes, London, 1925–49; Honorary Secretary of NFRB, 1935–9.

Nicholas Davenport, *financial writer.* 'Toreador' for *New Statesman and Nation*, 1925–40; co-founder of XYZ.

*Ruth Davies. Sister of Evan Durbin.

*Lord Diamond, *Chief Secretary to the Treasury; MP for Blackley 1945–51 and Gloucester 1957–70.* Chartered accountant in Leeds;

parliamentary private secretary to Ministry of Works, when Durbin was junior minister.

Lionel Elvin, *Professor of Education, University of London.* Fellow of Trinity Hall, Cambridge, 1930–44; member of NFRB.

Lord Fletcher, *Deputy Speaker; Minister Without Portfolio; MP for East Islington 1945–70.* Solicitor in Gray's Inn; member of Fabian Society.

Sir Robert Fraser, *Director, Independent Television News.* Leader writer for *Daily Herald,* 1930–9; served on NFRB executive committee; member of Durbin group.

Baroness Gaitskell (Dora Frost). Wife of Hugh Gaitskell.

A. T. K. Grant, *Under Secretary at the Treasury.* Royal Institute of International Affairs and Leverhulme Research Fellow, 1932–8; lecturer in economics at UC, 1938–9; member of the Cole group and NFRB.

Dr Frank Hardie, *historian.* Student at Christ Church College, Oxford; President of the Union Society, 1933; member of NFRB.

Sir John Hicks, *Drummond Professor of Political Economy, Fellow of All Souls College, Oxford.* Lecturer in economics at LSE, 1926–35; Fellow of Gonville and Caius College, Cambridge, 1935–8.

H. D. Hughes, *Fellow and Principal, Ruskin College, Oxford.* Assistant Secretary, NFRB, 1937–9.

*Graham Hutton, *economic consultant.* Assistant editor for *The Economist,* 1933–8; co-opted onto LPFTC, 1937; member of NFRB.

*Rt Hon. Douglas Jay, *President of Board of Trade; MP for Battersea, 1946–83.* Staff writer for *The Times,* 1929–33 and for *The Economist,* 1933–7; City editor for *Daily Herald,* 1937–41; co-opted onto LPFTC, 1936–9; member of NFRB and XYZ.

Carol Johnson, *MP for Lewisham, 1959–74.* Practising solicitor in London; on Lambeth Borough Council; student at LSE; Secretary of Parliamentary Labour Party, 1943–59.

*Lord Kaldor, *Professor of Economics, Cambridge University.* Assistant lecturer in economics at LSE, 1932–47.

Ludwig Lachmann, *Professor of Economics, University of the Witwatersand, Johannesburg, South Africa.* Graduate student at LSE from 1933.

*James Lawrie, *Chairman, Air Transport Licensing Board; Managing Director, Gleneagles Productions.* Member of Lloyds Bank, 1930–7; Secretary and Manager, National Bank of New Zealand, 1937–45; member of NFRB and XYZ.

Abba Lerner, *Professor of Economics, Florida State University.* Student and lecturer in economics at LSE.

Sir W. Arthur Lewis, *Professor of Political Economy, Princeton*

University. Graduate student and lecturer in economics at LSE, 1938–47; member of Fabian Society.

*Earl of Longford (Frank Pakenham), *Lord Privy Seal, Leader of the House of Lords.* Student and lecture in politics Christ Church College, Oxford, 1932–46; funded NFRB research, 1938–9; Oxford friend of Durbin and Gaitskell.

*Countess of Longford (Elizabeth Pakenham), *author.* Member of SSIP and NFRB; Oxford friend of Durbin and Gaitskell.

Professor T. H. Marshall, *Professor of Sociology, London University.* Lecturer in social administration at LSE, 1925–30; University Reader in sociology, 1930–44.

Lord Mayhew, *Minister of Defence (RN), MP for Norfolk 1945–50 and for Woolwich East 1951–74.* Student at Christ Church College, Oxford; President of Union Society, 1937; research assistant at NFRB, 1938–9.

*James E. Meade, *Professor of Economics, Fellow of Christs College, Cambridge.* Fellow and lecturer in economics at Hertford College, Oxford, 1930–7; Economic section of League of Nations, 1938–40; member of Cole group and NFRB.

Lucy Middleton. Wife of James Middleton, Assistant Secretary of Labour Party (1903–35), Secretary of Labour Party (1935–44).

John Parker, *President of Fabian Society; MP for Dagenham 1945–74 and for Barking 1974–83.* General Secretary of NFRB, 1933–9; Labour MP for Romford, 1935–45; co-opted onto LPFTC, 1936–9; member of Cole group and Durbin group.

Rev. Ernest Payne, *President, World Council of Churches 1968–75.* Staff member of Baptist Missionary Society, 1932–40; member of John Bunyan Society at Oxford with Durbin.

*Sir E. Henry Phelps Brown, *Professor of Labour Economics, London University.* Fellow of New College, Oxford, 1930–47; public school and Oxford friend of Durbin.

Sir Michael Postan, *Professor of Economic History, Cambridge University.* Lecturer in history at UC, 1927–31; lecturer in economic history at LSE, 1931–5; lecturer in economic history at Cambridge, 1935–8.

Dr E. A. Radice, *Director of Economic Intelligence, Ministry of Defence.* General Secretary of NFRB and SSIP, 1931–3; member of Cole group.

*Lord Robbins, *Chairman, Financial Times.* Fellow of New College, Oxford, 1927–9; Professor of Economics at LSE, 1929–61.

Sir Austin Robinson, *Professor of Economics, Cambridge University.* Fellow of Sidney Sussex College, Cambridge, and lecturer in economics from 1931.

W. A. Robson, *Professor of Public Administration, London University.*

Reader in administrative law at LSE, 1933–46; chairman Political section of NFRB.

*Paul Rosenstein-Rodan, *Professor of Economics, Boston University.* Lecturer in economics at UC from 1931.

Celia Strachey. Wife of John Strachey.

Brinley Thomas, *Professor of Economics, University of Cardiff.* Student and lecturer in economics at LSE, 1931–9.

Thomas Wilson, *Professor of Economics, Glasgow University.* Doctoral student of Durbin and Kaldor at LSE.

Baroness Wootton, *Deputy Speaker, House of Lords; Professor of Social Studies, London University.* Director of Studies for Tutorial Classes, University of London, 1927–44; convenor of NFRB taxation committee; member of Durbin group.

INDEX